Programming Microsoft® Dynamics™ NAV

Create, modify, and maintain applications in
NAV 5.0, the latest version of the ERP application
formerly known as Navision

David Studebaker

PUBLISHING

BIRMINGHAM - MUMBAI

Programming Microsoft® Dynamics™ NAV

First published: October 2007

Production Reference: 2121007

Published by Packt Publishing Ltd.
32 Lincoln Road
Olton
Birmingham, B27 6PA, UK.

ISBN 978-1-904811-74-9

www.packtpub.com

Cover Image by David Studebaker (navbook@libertyforever.com)

Credits

Author

David Studebaker

Reviewers

Luc Van Dyck

Mark Brummel

Senior Acquisition Editor

Douglas Paterson

Development Editor

Mithil Kulkarni

Technical Editors

Nilesh Kapoor

Divya Menon

Kushal Sharma

Editorial Manager

Dipali Chittar

Project Manager

Patricia Weir

Project Coordinator

Abhijeet Deobhakta

Indexer

Bhushan Pangaonkar

Proofreader

Chris Smith

Production Coordinators

Shantanu Zagade

Manjiri Nadkarni

Cover Designer

Shantanu Zagade

Foreword

In 1986 the Navision founders Jesper Balser, Torben Wind, and Peter Bang were looking back on the successful release of their first product "PC-Plus". It was the first easy-to-use accounting package for the IBM PC on the Danish market. It immediately picked up a huge market share and the founders started thinking about how to expand the business. They decided to try to sell a vertical solution for auto-repair shop spare-part management—but they were immediately flooded with requests from potential customers who wanted to have the product tailored exactly to meet their needs. Because of this they decided to get out of the customization business, thus enabling partners to do the customization while providing them with the right tools. PC-Plus used a database, which was based on the ISAM database, which Anders Hejlsberg wrote as a sample program for his Pascal compiler. However the database was not multiuser and if the power went, data could easily get corrupted. Other database alternatives were either too expensive or of poor quality, so they decided to write their own database. The result of this was the Navision product, which had a rich set of tools for modifying the business application and a robust multiuser version-based database. The product became a huge success with a rapidly growing number of partners, who recognized a big business opportunity, and customers, who could have the product tailor-made to fulfill the specific needs of their businesses.

The Windows version of Navision was released in 1995 and became part of the Windows revolution. The rest is history: the company went international, went public, and in 2002 was acquired by Microsoft. I joined Navision in 1987 and have been a part of this amazing journey. Today as part of Microsoft, the team and I have started a new journey with the product now called Microsoft Dynamics NAV and will bring the product to the .net platform. Next, we will introduce a new role-tailored client, enabling us to reach even more partners and customers moving forward.

Michael Nielsen, Director of Engineering, Microsoft Dynamics NAV

About the Author

David Studebaker is currently a Principal of Liberty Grove Software, Inc., with his partner Karen Studebaker. Liberty Grove Software provides development, consulting, training, and upgrade services for Microsoft Dynamics NAV resellers and firms using NAV internally. Liberty Grove Software is a Microsoft Certified Partner. David has been recognized by Microsoft three times as a Certified Professional for NAV—in Development, in Applications, and in Installation & Configuration. He is also a Certified Microsoft Trainer for NAV. He began developing with C/AL in 1996.

David Studebaker has been programming since taking his first Fortran II course in 1962. In the fall of 1963 he took the first COBOL course taught at Purdue University, where the first U.S. computer science department was later created. The next spring, undergraduate student David was assigned to teach the graduate-level class. Since that time, David has been an active participant in each step of computing technology—from the early mainframes to today's technology, from binary assembly coding to C/AL. He has worked with over 40 different models and brands of computers, over a dozen operating systems, and over two dozen different programming languages.

Special projects include the development of first production SPOOL system in 1967. In the decades following, David was project manager and lead developer for several commercially distributed business application systems. Application areas in which David has worked range from engineering to manufacturing to freight carriage to general accounting to public mass transit to banking to not-for-profit and association management to legal billing to distribution/inventory management to shop floor data collection and production management.

David has a BS in Mechanical Engineering from Purdue University and an MBA from the University of Chicago, both with concentrations in Computer Science. David has been a computer operator, system programmer, application programmer, business analyst, consultant, service bureau operations manager, bureaucrat, teacher, project manager, trainer, documenter, software designer, mentor, writer, and entrepreneur. He has been partner or owner and manager of several computer systems businesses, while always maintaining a significant role as a business application developer. David's work with relational databases and 4th-generation languages with integrated development environments began in 1984.

David assisted in script-writing for a series of audio training courses for early PC operating systems and wrote for a newsletter *Computers in Education*. A series of articles by David concerning the use of computer systems to track and help manage manufacturing shop floor operations were published in several trade and professional magazines. He was lead author of the Product Identification and Tracking section of the SME Tool and Manufacturing Handbook. For over ten years, David was a reviewer of business applications-related publications for *Computing Reviews* of the Association for Computing Machinery (ACM). David has been a member of the ACM since 1963 and was a founding officer of two local chapters of the ACM.

About the Reviewers

Luc Van Dyck is active as a software consultant and works for a Belgian Microsoft partner. He started working with Dynamics NAV in 1997 (at that time it was called Navision Financials 1.10).

In the year 1999, he started the website http://myNavision.net to provide a forum and downloads for users of the Dynamics NAV ERP system. When Microsoft bought Navision Software A/S in 2002, the site was renamed to http://mibuso.com; mibuso.com is one of the largest on-line communities of Microsoft Dynamics professionals.

This on-line community gives users and developers of products from the Microsoft Dynamics family (Navision, Axapta, CRM, Great Plains, ...) a place to exchange ideas and tools, and to find business partners and products. The website provides you with a forum where you can ask questions about the different Dynamics products. It also contains a large selection of downloads, in different categories (code examples, demo versions, webcasts, factsheets, tools, etc.). Microsoft partners can submit their company details to the Business Directory and publish their add-ons or factsheets in the Product Directory.

In October 2004, he was awarded with the MVP status (Most Valuable Professional) by Microsoft, for his active participation in the Dynamics community.

Mark Brummel is an all-round NAV expert. He started 10 years ago in 1997 as an end user, being an early adopter of the system. Two years later he started working for a local reseller and used his end-user perspective to develop add-ons for NAV.

In the following years he has developed five major add-ons for three NAV partners and was involved in over a hundred implementations. Next to the development projects he has guided and trained both experienced consultants and young talent in becoming NAV experts.

Because of his experience in all aspects of NAV implementations Mark started to specialize in escalation engineering. In the year 2006, he started his own company specialized in this field, helping both end-users and partners with problems.

To share knowledge he writes articles and gives workshops. He also assists Microsoft at events like Tech Ed and Convergence and participates in product development.

One of his special skills is performance-tuning of NAV systems, combining both technical and functional knowledge to establish better-running systems and happier end users.

In the year 2006, Mark Brummel was rewarded with the MVP award by Microsoft.

Table of Contents

Preface

There are two mistakes one can make along the road to truth...
not going all the way, and not starting. – The Buddha

By choosing to study C/AL and C/SIDE, you have started down another road. The knowledge you gain here and subsequently about these tools can be applied to benefit yourself and others. The information in this book will shorten your learning curve on how to program for the NAV ERP system using the C/AL language and the C/SIDE integrated development environment.

By embarking on the study of NAV and C/AL, you are joining a high-quality, worldwide group of experienced developers. There is a collegial community of C/AL developers on the Web who readily and frequently share their knowledge. There are formal and informal organizations of NAV-focused users, developers, and vendor firms both on the Web and in various geographic locations. The NAV product is one of the best on the market and it continues to grow and prosper. Welcome aboard and enjoy the journey.

A Business History Timeline

The current version of Microsoft Dynamics NAV is the result of much inspiration and hard work along with some good fortune and excellent management decision-making over the last quarter century or so.

The Beginning

Three college friends, Jesper Balser, Torben Wind, and Peter Bang, from Denmark Technical University (DTU) founded their computer software business in 1984 when they were in their early twenties. That business was Personal Computing & Consulting (PC & C) and its first product was called PC Plus.

Single User PC Plus

PC Plus was released in 1985 with a primary goal of ease of use. An early employee said its functional design was inspired by the combination of a manual ledger journal, an Epson FX 80 printer, and a Canon calculator. Incidentally, Peter Bang is the grandson of one of the founders of Bang & Olufsen, the manufacturer of home entertainment systems par excellence.

PC Plus was PC DOS-based, a single user system. PC Plus' design features included:

- An interface resembling the use of documents and calculators
- Online help
- Good exception handling
- Minimal computer resources required

The PC Plus product was marketed through dealers in Denmark and Norway.

Multi-User Navigator

In 1987, PC & C released a new product, the multi-user Navigator and a new corporate name, Navision. Navigator was quite a technological leap forward. It included:

- Client/Server technology
- Relational database
- Transaction-based processing
- Version management
- High-speed OLAP capabilities (SIFT technology)
- A screen painter tool
- A programmable report writer

In 1990, Navision was expanding its marketing and dealer recruitment efforts into Germany, Spain, and the United Kingdom. Also in 1990, V3 of Navigator was released. Navigator V3 was still a character-based system, albeit a very sophisticated one. If you had an opportunity to study Navigator V3.x, you would instantly recognize the roots of today's NAV product. By this time, the product included:

- A design based on object-oriented concepts
- Integrated 4GL Table, Form, and Report Design tools (the IDE)
- Structured exception handling
- Built-in resource management

- The original programming language that became C/AL
- Function libraries
- The concept of regional or country-based localization

When Navigator V3.5 was released, it also included support for multiple platforms and multiple databases. Navigator V3.5 would run on both Unix and Windows NT networks. It supported Oracle and Informix databases as well as the one developed in-house.

At about this time, several major strategic efforts were initiated. On the technical side, the decision was make to develop a GUI-based product. The first prototype of Navision Financials (for Windows) was shown in 1992. At about the same time, a relationship was established that would take Navision into distribution in the United States. The initial release in the US in 1995 was V3.5 of the character-based product, rechristened Avista for US distribution.

Navision Financials for Windows

In 1995, Navision Financials V1.0 for Microsoft Windows was released. This product had many (but not all) of the features of Navigator V3.5. It was designed for complete look-and-feel compatibility with Windows 95. There was an effort to provide the ease of use and flexibility of development of Microsoft Access. The new Navision Financials was very compatible with Microsoft Office and was thus sold as "being familiar to any Office user". Like any V1.0 product, it was fairly quickly followed by a V1.1 that worked much better.

In the next few years, Navision continued to be improved and enhanced. Major new functionalities were added:

- Contact Relation Management (CRM)
- Manufacturing (ERP)
- Advanced Distribution (including Warehouse Management)

Various Microsoft certifications were obtained, providing muscle to the marketing efforts. Geographic and dealer base expansion continued apace. By 2000, according to the Navision Annual Report of that year, the product was represented by nearly 1,000 dealers (Navision Solution Centers) in 24 countries and used by 41,000 customers located in 108 countries.

Growth and Mergers

In 2000, Navision Software A/S and its primary Danish competitor, Damgaard A/S, merged. Product development and new releases continued for the primary products of both original firms (Navision and Axapta). In 2002, the now much larger Navision Software, with all its products (Navision, Axapta, and the smaller, older C5 and XAL) was purchased by Microsoft, becoming part of the Microsoft Business Systems division along with the previously purchased Great Plains Software business and its several product lines. Since that time, one of the major challenges for Microsoft has been to meld these previously competitive business into a coherent whole. One aspect of that effort was to rename all the products as Dynamics software, with Navision being renamed to Dynamics NAV.

Fortunately for those who have been working with Navision, Microsoft has not only continued to invest in the product, but has increased the investment. This promises to be the case for the foreseeable future.

C/AL's Roots

One of the first questions often asked by developers and development managers new to C/AL is "what other language is it like?" The proper response is "Pascal". If the questioner is not familiar with Pascal, the next best response would be "C" or "C#".

At the time the three founders of Navision were attending classes at Denmark Technical University (DTU), Pascal was in wide use as a preferred language not only in computer courses, but in other courses where computers were tools and software had to be written for data analyses. Some of the strengths of Pascal as a tool in an educational environment also served to make it a good model for Navision's business applications development.

Perhaps coincidentally (perhaps not) at DTU in this same time period, a Pascal compiler called Blue Label Pascal was developed by Anders Hejlsberg. That compiler became the basis for what was Borland's Turbo Pascal, which was the "everyman's compiler" of the 1980s because of its low price. Anders went with his Pascal compiler to Borland. While he was there Turbo Pascal morphed into the Delphi language and IDE tool set under his guidance. Anders later left Borland and joined Microsoft, where he led the C# design team. Much of the NAV-related development at Microsoft is now being done in C#. So the Pascal-C/AL-DTU connection has come full circle, only now it appears to be C#-C/AL. Keeping it in the family, Anders' brother, Thomas Hejlsberg is also now working at Microsoft on NAV and AX at the campus in Copenhagen.

In a discussion about C/AL and C/SIDE, Michael Nielsen of Navision and Microsoft, who developed the original C/AL compiler, runtime, and IDE, said that the design criteria were to provide an environment that could be used without:

- Dealing with memory and other resource handling
- Thinking about exception handling and state
- Thinking about database transactions and rollbacks
- Knowing about set operations (SQL)
- Knowing about OLAP (SIFT)

Paraphrasing some of Michael's additional comments, the language and IDE design was to:

- Allow the developer to focus on design, not coding, but still allow flexibility
- Provide a syntax based on Pascal stripped of complexities, especially relating to memory management
- Provide a limited set of predefined object types, reducing the complexity and learning curve
- Implement database versioning for a consistent and reliable view of the database
- Make the developer and end user more at home by borrowing a large number of concepts from Office, Windows, Access, and other Microsoft products

Michael is still working as part of the Microsoft team in Denmark on new capabilities for NAV. Another example of how, once part of the NAV community, most of us want to stay part of that community.

The Road Ahead

This book will not teach you programming from scratch, nor will it tutor you in business principles. To get the maximum out of this book, you should come prepared with some significant experience and knowledge. You will benefit most if you already have the following attributes:

- Experienced developer
- More than one programming language
- IDE experience
- Knowledgeable about business applications
- Good at self-directed study

If you have those attributes, then by careful reading and performance of the suggested exercises in this book, you should significantly reduce the time it will take you to become productive with C/AL and NAV.

This book's illustrations are from the W1 Cronus database V5.0.

Hopefully this book will smooth the road ahead and shine a little light on some of the potholes and the truths alike. Your task is to take advantage of this opportunity to learn and then use your new skills productively.

What This Book Covers

Chapter 1 covers basic definitions as they pertain to NAV and C/SIDE. Also, an introduction to seven types of NAV objects, Form and Report Creation Wizards, and tools that we use to integrate NAV with external entities is provided. There is a brief discussion of how different types of backups and documentation are handled in C/SIDE at the end.

Chapter 2 focuses on the top level of NAV data structure: tables and their structures. You will work your way through hands-on creation of a number of tables in support of an example application. We will review most types of tables found in the out-of-the-box NAV application.

In *Chapter 3*, you will learn about the basic building blocks of NAV data structure, fields and their attributes, data fields that are available, and field structure elements (properties, triggers) for each type of field. This chapter covers the broad range of Data Type options as well as Field Classes. You will see one of the date calculation tools that gives C/AL an edge in business. We will also discuss the concept of filtering and how it can be considered as you design your database structure.

In *Chapter 4*, we will review different types of forms and work with some of these, and review all the controls that can be used in forms. You will learn to use the Form Wizard and have a good introduction to the Form Designer. You will expand your example system, creating a number of forms for data maintenance and inquiry.

In *Chapter 5*, we will learn about on the structural and layout aspects of NAV Report objects. Also, you will be experimenting with some of the tools and continue to expand your example application.

Chapter 6 will help you learn about the general Object Designer Navigation as well as more specific Navision individual (Table, Form, Report) Designers. This chapter also covers variables of various types created and controlled by the developer or by the system, basic C/AL syntax and some essential C/AL functions.

Chapter 7 covers a number of practical tools and topics regarding C/AL coding and development. You will learn about the C/AL Symbol Menu and how it assists in development. This chapter also discusses various Computation, Validation and Data Conversion functions, Dates, Flowfields and SIFT, Processing Flow Control, Input—Output, and Filtering functions.

In *Chapter 8*, we will review a number of tools and techniques aimed at making the life of a NAV developer easier and more efficient. There is also a section on Code Analysis and Debugging is provided.

Chapter 9 will help you deal with the software design for NAV. This chapter covers designing NAV modifications, creating a new function area or enhancing an existing functional area. The chapter also provides you the information needed for designing a new NAV application.

Chapter 10 focuses on interfaces with NAV. Overall, you will learn about MenuSuites, Dataports, XMLports, and advanced Interfaces in this chapter.

Chapter 11 will help you become even more productive in C/AL development. It will provide you with some tips for design efficiency; it will help you learn about updating and upgrading the system and more about enjoying working with NAV.

What You Need for This Book

You will need some basic tools including at least the following:

1. A copy of the Application Designer's Guide manual for C/AL

2. A license and database that you can use for development experimentation. An ideal license is a full Developer's license. If the license only contains the Form, Report, and Table Designer capabilities, you will still be able to do many of the exercises, but you will not have access to the in inner workings of Forms and Tables.

3. The best database for your development testing and study would probably be a copy of the NAV Cronus demo/test database, but you may want to have a copy of a production database at hand for examination as well. This book's illustrations are from the W1 Cronus database for V5.0.

If you have access to other NAV manuals, training materials, websites and experienced associates, those will obviously be of benefit as well. But they are not required for your time with this book to be a worthwhile investment.

Who is This Book For?

- The business applications software designer/developer who:
    - ◦ Wants to become productive in NAV C/SIDE – C/AL development as quickly as possible
    - ◦ Understands business applications and the associated software
    - ◦ Has significant programming experience
    - ◦ Has access to NAV including at least the Designer granules, preferably a full development license and a standard Cronus demo database
    - ◦ Is willing to do the exercises to get hands-on experience
- The Reseller manager or executive who wants a concise, in depth view of NAV's development environment and tool set
- The technically knowledgeable manager or executive of a firm using NAV that is about to embark on a significant NAV enhancement project
- The technically knowledgeable manager or executive of a firm considering purchase of NAV as a highly customizable business applications platform
- The reader of this book:
    - ◦ Does not need to be expert in object-oriented programming
    - ◦ Does not need to have previous experience with NAV

Conventions

In this book, you will find a number of styles of text that distinguish between different kinds of information. Here are some examples of these styles, and an explanation of their meaning.

There are three styles for code. Code words in text are shown as follows: "We can include other contexts through the use of the `include` directive."

A block of code will be set as follows:

```
GLEntry."Posting Date" IN [0D,WORKDATE]
Description[I+2] IN ['0'..'9']
"Gen. Posting Type" IN ["Gen. Posting Type"::Purchase,
"Gen. Posting Type"::Sale]
SearchString IN ['','=><']
No[i] IN ['0'..'9']
"FA Posting Date" IN [01010001D..12319998D]
```

When we wish to draw your attention to a particular part of a code block, the relevant lines or items will be made bold:

```
GLEntry."Posting Date" IN [0D,WORKDATE]
Description[I+2] IN ['0'..'9']
"Gen. Posting Type" IN ["Gen. Posting Type"::Purchase,
"Gen. Posting Type"::Sale]
SearchString IN ['','=><']
No[i] IN ['0'..'9']
"FA Posting Date" IN [01010001D..12319998D]
```

New terms and **important words** are introduced in a bold-type font. Words that you see on the screen, in menus or dialog boxes for example, appear in our text like this: "clicking the **Next** button moves you to the next screen".

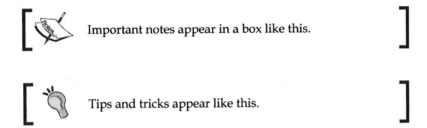

Important notes appear in a box like this.

Tips and tricks appear like this.

Reader Feedback

Feedback from our readers is always welcome. Let us know what you think about this book, what you liked or may have disliked. Reader feedback is important for us to develop titles that you really get the most out of.

To send us general feedback, simply drop an email to feedback@packtpub.com, making sure to mention the book title in the subject of your message.

If there is a book that you need and would like to see us publish, please send us a note in the **SUGGEST A TITLE** form on www.packtpub.com or email suggest@packtpub.com.

If there is a topic that you have expertise in and you are interested in either writing or contributing to a book, see our author guide on www.packtpub.com/authors.

Customer Support

Now that you are the proud owner of a Packt book, we have a number of things to help you to get the most from your purchase.

Errata

Although we have taken every care to ensure the accuracy of our contents, mistakes do happen. If you find a mistake in one of our books—maybe a mistake in text or code—we would be grateful if you would report this to us. By doing this you can save other readers from frustration, and help to improve subsequent versions of this book. If you find any errata, report them by visiting http://www.packtpub.com/support, selecting your book, clicking on the **Submit Errata** link, and entering the details of your errata. Once your errata are verified, your submission will be accepted,and the errata added to the list of existing errata. The existing errata can be viewed by selecting your title from http://www.packtpub.com/support.

Questions

You can contact us at questions@packtpub.com if you are having a problem with some aspect of the book, and we will do our best to address it.

1
The Basic Ingredients

*He who has not first laid his foundations may be able with great ability
to lay them afterwards, but they will be laid with trouble to the architect and
danger to the building – Niccolo Machiavelli*

*To me programming is more than an important practical art. It is also a gigantic
undertaking in the foundations of knowledge – Grace Murray Hopper*

In Chapter 1, we will deal with the basic foundations of Microsoft Dynamics NAV
(pronounced as N-A-V, spelling it out), the objects that make up an NAV application,
and their essential capabilities and limitations. While NAV has many structural and
syntactical similarities to other programming languages, particularly Object Pascal;
NAV has many unique features and facilities as well.

Once you are through with Chapter 1, you will feel more comfortable with the NAV
development environment, will get acquainted with the tools, and will look forward
to getting more detail. Also, you will develop knowledge that will allow you to begin
thinking about application development within the NAV environment, using the
NAV programming language.

While learning the NAV development environment, we will develop a simple
application as a functional enhancement to the base product. Our application will be
designed for the management of a fictitious association for those who work with
C/SIDE and **C/AL**. We'll call it the worldwide Charter/Association of NAV
Developers Ltd, or **C/ANDL** for short. The goal of C/ANDL is to shed a little light
into NAV Development. We will deal with member records, skills and education
information, hold meetings, and offer some training publications for sale. Our
application will be designed as a new application function, but with the plan of using
base functionality for various accounting functions.

Some Unique NAV Terms Defined

The following are some unique definitions in NAV:

- **C/AL**: Client/Application Language is the programming language meant for customization of NAV. It was built by the NAV development team using C++, though we never see any C++ code directly in the NAV product. C/AL is the tool used to define the processes by which data is manipulated, to define the business rules that will control the various applications, and to control the flow of all the logical processing sequences. C/AL is also used to manipulate objects, to control the execution flow of objects, to create new functions complementing the functions that are built in, and to manipulate data in many different ways.

- **C/SIDE**: Client/Server Integrated Development Environment is the development tool specified for using C/AL. It includes the language editor, compiler, debugger, reports and form generators and code management tools. Almost all the C/AL development is done within C/SIDE without the use of external tools. For most application development, NAV is entirely self sufficient except for those services provided by the Windows operating systems. It is possible, though generally not recommended, to write code using a text editor and then import it into C/SIDE.

- **Filtering**: The application of range constraints is to control what data is processed or made visible. For example, a filter for payment data for Customer No. 20134 would show the payments for that customer only. Although not really unique to NAV, filters combined with other NAV features are uniquely powerful in NAV. The extreme flexibility of filtering in NAV allows you to easily create very focused views into the data. Filters can be defined as ranges, boolean expressions, specific selections, etc. that delimit the data to be selected into a subset to be utilized in a process (display, calculation, report, etc.). Thus, NAV filters are a very powerful tool for both the developer and the user.

- **SIFT**: Sum Index Field Technology is a very clever method of providing instantaneous response to user inquiries. Most application systems provide fast response to requests for summary information by maintaining pre-calculated totals ("bucketed data"). NAV retains all data in detail and, through the use of SIFT and applied data filters, it provides the activity totals or subsets of information subject to a wide range of selection constraints instantly. Your data structure design will determine whether SIFT results are available and if available, how fast the response will be. Even though the designers of NAV were very clever in giving you special tools to use, you are still responsible for how well those tools will work for your users.

- **C/FRONT**: This is an application programming interface that allows you to develop applications in other programming languages to access a Microsoft NAV database, either the C/SIDE Database Server or the Microsoft SQL Server. The primary component of C/FRONT is a library of callable C functions, which provide access to every aspect of data storage and maintenance. This allows creation of custom components written in C, C++, VB, Delphi, and the Visual Studio.NET languages as well as other languages that support compatible calling conventions. C/FRONT is only tested by Microsoft for use with code built using either the Watcom C or Microsoft C++ compilers. C/AL triggers cannot be invoked via C/FRONT code. C/FRONT comes as a set of files to be installed guided by the instructions given in the C/FRONT manual.

- **C/OCX**: This is an application interface to allow integration between C/AL and a properly defined OCX routine. This allows access to many ActiveX controls available from third-party vendors. Such controls must be non-visual as far as NAV is concerned (but they may open their own windows for user interaction).

The C/SIDE Integrated Development Environment

The C/SIDE Integrated Development Environment is referred to as the **Object Designer** within NAV. It is accessed through the **Tools | Object Designer** menu option as shown in the following screenshot:

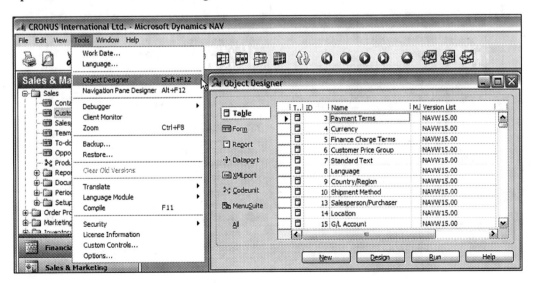

Object Designer Tool Icons

The following screenshot shows an **Object Designer** form, containing a list of several tool icons. These Object Designer tool **Icons** are shown isolated in the screenshot and then described briefly in the following table. Some of the terminologies in these descriptions will be explained later in this book. Additional information is available in the C/SIDE **Help** files and the Microsoft NAV documentation.

Icon	Name	Keys	Description
	Links	Ctrl+L	Links a NAV record to a document, a folder, a web site or another NAV record.
	New	F3	Open up a new record entry
	Delete	F4	Delete a record
	Find	Ctrl+F	Invoke the search capability
	Field Filter	F7	Enter a filter on the highlighted field
	Table Filter	Ctrl+F7	Enter (or edit) one or more filters on a table
	Flow Filter	Shift+F7	Enter, edit or remove a flow filter
	Show All	Shift+Ctrl+F7	Clear all filters, except flow filters
	Sort	Shift+F8	Display the active keys so that a new sort order may be chosen
	First	Ctrl+Home	Jump to the beginning of the table
	Previous	Down Arrow	Move to the Previous record
	Next	Up Arrow	Move to the Next record
	Last	Ctrl+End	Jump to the end of the table
	List	F5	Displays the defined List form
	Send to Microsoft Office Word	Ctrl+W	Export current record data to a Word document using the last previously used Style Sheet for this form
	Send to Microsoft Office Excel	Ctrl+E	Export the data in the current record to an Excel document using the last previously used Style Sheet for this form
	Send Options		Display the defined XML export targets and Style Sheets for the current record.

Seven Kinds of NAV Objects

NAV C/AL is not considered an object-oriented language even though C/AL uses seven kinds of objects. These seven object types are listed on the left side of the **Object Designer** window as shown in the following screenshot:

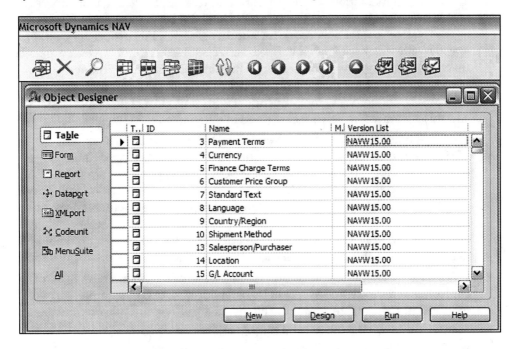

NAV is not an object-oriented language because you can only use the predefined object types. The seven types of objects in C/AL are as follows:

- **Table**: These are the definers and containers of data.
- **Form**: These are this screen display constructs for the user interface.
- **Report**: These allow the display of data to the user in "hardcopy" format, either onscreen (preview mode) or via a printer device. Report objects can also update data in processes with or without accompanying data display output to the user.
- **Dataport**: These allow the importing and exporting of data from/to external files.
- **XMLport**: These are similar to **Dataport** but specific to only XML files and XML formatted data.
- **Codeunit**: These are containers for code.
- **MenuSuite**: These contain menus and are structured differently from other objects.

More Definitions (Related to NAV)

The following are a few more definitions related to NAV:

- **Database**: This consists of two database definitions (physical and logical). There are two implementations of the physical database (C/SIDE Database Server and Microsoft SQL Server). The C/SIDE Database Server was formerly known as the "Native" database because for number of years, this proprietary server was the only database for NAV. In earlier versions, it did not have a name other than "the NAV (or Navision) Server". The logical database definition relates to the sum total of the relationships between data, the indexes that control data access, and in NAV, the **SumIndexFields** and **FlowFields** (special data summing features, which are explained in detail in a later chapter).

  NAV is a relational database system. The Development Environment (C/SIDE) and tools (C/AL), makes the choice of underlying database (C/SIDE Database Server or Microsoft SQL Server) platform almost transparent to the developer. In this book we will not concern ourselves with the physical database definition because, except in rare circumstances, our development work will not be guided by physical database factors. When you become involved in more complex design activities, you will likely need to be concerned about the differences between the two database options.

- **Properties**: These are the attributes of the element (e.g. object, data field, or control) that define some aspect of its behavior or use. For example, display length, font type or size, and if the elements are either editable or viewable.

- **Fields**: These are the individual data items.

- **Records**: These are group of fields (data items) that are handled as a unit in most Input/Output operations. The table data consists of rows of records and columns consisting of fields.

- **Controls**: These are containers for constants and data. The visible displays in reports and forms consist primarily of controls.

- **Triggers**: The generic definition is a mechanism that initiates (fires) an action when an event occurs such as reaching a certain time or date or upon receiving some type of input. A trigger generally causes a program routine to be executed. NAV triggers have some similarities to those in SQL, but they are not the same. NAV triggers are locations within the various objects where a developer can place comments or C/AL code. The following are the NAV triggers:

  - **Documentation Triggers** consist of comments only. Every object type except MenuSuite has a single Documentation trigger.

  - **Event Triggers** are "fired" when the specified event occurs. Each object type has its own set of predefined triggers. The event trigger name begins with the word "On" such as OnInsert, OnOpenForm, and OnNextRecord.

- ○ **Function Triggers** are "functions" that can be defined by the developer. They represent callable routines that can be accessed from other C/AL code either within or outside the object where the called function resides. Many function triggers are provided as part of the standard product. As a developer, you may add your own custom function triggers as needed.

- **License**: A data file supplied by Microsoft that allows a specific level of access to specific object number ranges. NAV licenses are very clever constructs, which allow distribution of a complete system, all objects, modules, and features while constraining exactly what is accessible and how it can be accessed. Of course, each license feature allowing access to various objects and system functions, including the ability to do development, has its price. Microsoft Partners have access to licenses to provide support and customization services for their clients. The broadly featured Partner licenses are often referred to as a developer's license, but end-user firms can also purchase licenses allowing them developer access to NAV.

- **Object numbers and field numbers**: The object numbers from 1 (one) to 50,000 and in the 99,000,000 (i.e. 99 million) range are reserved for use by NAV as part of the base product. Objects in this number range can be modified or deleted, but not created with a developer's license. Field numbers are often assigned in ranges matching the related object numbers (i.e. starting with 1 fields relating to objects numbered 1 to 50,000, starting with 99,000,000 for fields in objects in the 99,000,000 and up number range).

  Object and field numbers from 50,001 to 99,999 are generally available to the rest of us for assignment as part of an ad hoc customization developed in the field using a normal development license. But object numbers from 90,000 to 99,999 should not be used for permanent objects as those numbers are often used in training materials. Microsoft allocates other ranges of object and field numbers to ISV (Independent Software Vendor) developers for their add-on enhancements. Some of these (in the 14,000,000 range in North America, other ranges for other geographic regions) can be accessed, modified, or deleted but not created, using a normal development license. Others (such as in the 37,000,000 range) can be executed but not viewed or modified with a typical development license. The following table summarizes the content as:

Object Number Range	Usage
1 – 9,999	Base application objects
10,000 – 49,999	Country-specific objects
50,000 – 99,999	Customer-specific objects
100,000 – 99,999,999	Partner-created objects

- **Work Date**: This is a date controlled by the operator that is used as the default date for many transaction entries. The System Date is the date recognized by Windows. The work date can be adjusted at any time by the user, is specific to the workstation, and can be set to any point in the future or the past. This is very convenient for procedures such as closing off Sales Order entry for one calendar day at the end of the first shift, then having the Sales Orders entered by the second shift dated to the next calendar day. You can set the work date by selecting **Tools | Work Date**, and then entering a date.

NAV Functional Terminology

For various application functions, NAV uses terminology that is more akin to accounting terms than to traditional data processing terminology. Some examples are as follows:

- **Journal**: A table of transaction entries, each of which represents an event, an entity, or an action to be processed. There are General Journals for general accounting entries, Item Journals for changes in inventory, etc.

- **Ledger**: A detailed history of transaction entries that have been processed. For example, General Ledger, a Customer Ledger, a Vendor Ledger, an Item Ledger, etc. Some Ledgers have subordinate detail ledgers, typically providing a greater level of date plus quantity and/or value detail.

- **Posting**: The process by which entries in a Journal are validated, and then entered into one or more Ledgers.

- **Batch**: A group of one or more Journal entries that were Posted in one group.

- **Register**: An audit trail showing a history by Entry No. ranges of the Journal Batches that have been Posted.

- **Document**: A formatted report such as an Invoice, a Purchase Order or a Check, typically one page for each primary transaction.

Getting Started with Application Design

Our design for the C/ANDL application will start with the beginning of a Member Table, a Member Card, a Member List Form, and a Member List Report. Along the way we will review the basics of each of the NAV object types.

Tables

Table objects are the foundation of every NAV application. Every project should be started by designing the tables. Tables contain the definitions of the data structures, the data relationships within and between the tables, as well as many of the data constraints and validations. The coded logic in table triggers not only provides the basic control on the insertion, modification, and deletion of records, but also embodies many of the business rules of an application. As we see when we dig into tables further, such logic isn't just at the record level but also at the field level. Putting as much of an application design as possible within the tables makes the application easier to develop, debug, support, modify, and upgrade.

Example: Table Design

Let us try a simple introduction to creation of a table for our NAV Developer Association application. We will create a basic Member table. The first thing we will do is inspect the existing definitions for tables containing name and address information, such as the Customer table (table object 18) and the Vendor table (table object 23). From the common definitions in these tables, we see some patterns as to field names and definitions that we decide to copy. The Member table will contain the following data fields:

Field names	Definitions
Member ID	10 character text (code)
Title/Prefix	10 character text
First Name	20 character text
Middle Initial	3 character text
Last Name	20 character text
Suffix	10 character text
Address	30 character text
Address 2	30 character text
City	30 character text
State/Province	10 character text
Post code	20 character text (code)
Country/Region code	10 character text (code)

This is a good illustration of how the design must begin with the tables. As you can see, in the preceding data field list, three of the fields have special text formats. That is because these are going to be referenced by or will reference to other data tables, so these are data codes rather than descriptive data.

The **Member ID** will be a unique identifier for our Member record as it will also be referenced by other subordinate tables. The **Post code** and **Country/Region code** will reference other existing tables for validation. We choose the name, size, and data definition of these last two fields based on inspecting the equivalent field definitions in the Customer and Vendor tables.

We will have to design and define any referenced validation tables before we can eventually complete the definition of the Member Table. But our goal at the moment is just to get started.

Example: Table Creation

Open the **Object Designer**, click on **Table** (on the left column of buttons) and click on **New** (on the bottom row of buttons). Enter the first field name (**Member ID**) in the **Field Name** column and then enter the data type in the **Data Type** column. For those data types where length is appropriate, enter the maximum length in the **Length** column. Enter **Description** data as desired; these are only for display here as internal documentation.

As you can see in the following screenshot (and will have noticed already if you are following along in your system), when you enter a Text data type, the field length will default to 30 characters. This is simply an 'ease-of-use' default, which you should override as appropriate for your design. The 30 character **Text** default and 10 character **Code** default are used because this matches many standard application data fields of those data types.

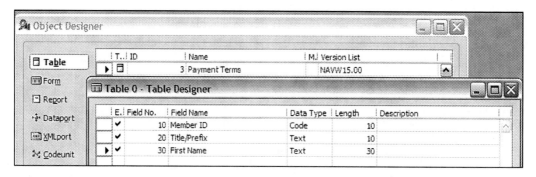

The question often arises as to what field numbering scheme to use. Various systems follow a variety of standard practices. In one system you might increment the field by twos, in another by fives, and in another by thousands but in NAV, when you are creating a new table from scratch, it is a good idea to increment the **Field No.** by 10 as you have seen in the above screenshot. The default increment for **Field No.** is 1. For a group of fields (such as an address block) where you are certain you will never add any intervening fields, you could leave the increment at 1. But there is no penalty or cost for using the larger increment, so it's not a bad thing to do all the time.

The numeric sequence of fields determines the default sequence in which data fields will display in a wide variety of situations. An example would be the order of the fields in any list presented to the user for setting up data filters. This default sequence can only be changed by renumbering the fields. The compiler references each field by its **Field No.** not by its **Field Name**, so the renumbering of fields can be a challenge once you have created other routines that reference back to these fields. At that point, it is generally better to simply add new fields where you can fit them without any renumbering.

In fact, it can be irritatingly painful to renumber fields at any point after a table has been defined and saved. In addition to the field numbers controlling the sequence of presentation of fields, the field numbers control bulk data transfer (those transfers that operate at the record level rather than explicitly field to field transfer—e.g. the TRANSFERFIELD instruction). In a record-level transfer, data is transferred from each field in the source record to the field of the same number in the target record.

So you can see that it is a good idea to define an overall standard for field numbering as you start. Doing so makes it easier to plan your field numbering scheme for each table. Before you begin, enter the definition into C/SIDE. Your design will be clearer for you and your user if you are methodical about your design planning before you begin writing code (i.e. try to avoid the Ready-Fire-Aim school of system development). The increment of **Field No.** by 10 allows you to insert new fields in their logical sequence as the design matures. While it is not required to have the data fields appear in any particular order, it is frequently convenient for testing and often clarifies some of the user interactions.

When you have completed this first table, your definition should be like the following screenshot:

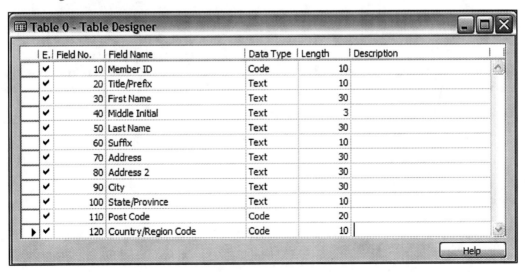

At this point, you can exit and save your Member Table. The easiest way to do this is to simply press *Esc* until you are asked to save your changes. When you respond by clicking **Yes**, you will be asked for the Object Number and Name you wish to assign. In a normal development situation, you will want to plan ahead what Object Number and descriptive Object Name you want to use. We will discuss Object Numbering in more detail later. In this case, we will use table Object No. 50000 and name it as Member. We are using 50000 as our Table Number just because it is the first (lowest) number available to us for a custom table through our Table Designer granule license.

Note that NAV likes to compile any object as it is saved, so the **Compiled** option is automatically checkmarked. A compiled object is one that can be executed. If the object we were working on was not ready to compile without error, we could unselect the **Compiled** option in the **Save As** window as shown in the following screenshot.

Be careful, as uncompiled objects will not be considered by C/SIDE when changes are made to other objects. Until you have compiled an object, it is a "work in progress", not an operable routine. As a matter of good work habits, make sure that all the objects get compiled before you end work for the day.

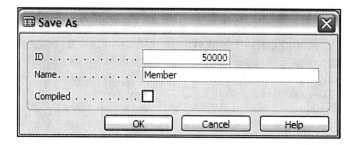

Forms

Forms fulfill two basic purposes. Firstly, they provide views of data or processes designed for on-screen display only. Secondly, they provide key points of user data entry into the system. In standard NAV, there are two basic types of forms:

- **Card forms**
- **Tabular forms**

From a practical point of view, there are also special versions of Card forms that use a Matrix Control and are therefore often referred to as **Matrix forms**. Beyond that, there is a variation of the Matrix form, which is called a **Trendscape form**. There are also combination forms consisting of a Card form plus a Tabular form, called a **Main/Sub Form**. These are user interfaces that appear as forms but are not Form objects. These user interfaces use various dialog functions.

Card Forms

Card forms display one record at a time. These are generally used for the entry or display of Master table records. For example, Customer Card for customer data, Item Card for Inventory items, and G/L Account Card for General Ledger accounts. Card forms often have multiple pages (tabs) with each tab on the **Customer Card** (for example) focusing on a different set of related customer data. Card forms for Master records display all the fields into which data must be entered by users. Typically, they also display summary data about related activity so that the Card form can be used as the primary inquiry form for its Master records. The following screenshot is a sample of a standard Customer Card:

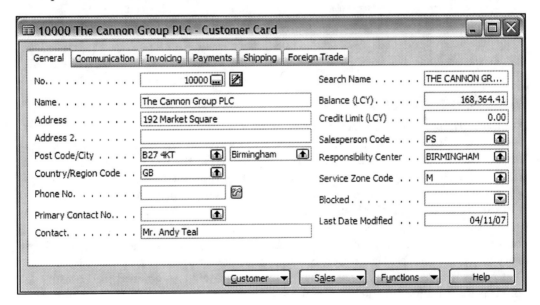

Tabular Forms

Tabular forms display a simple list of any number of records in a single table. The **Customer List** form in the following screenshot shows a subset of the data for each customer displayed. The Master record list show fields intended to make it easy to find a specific entry. Tabular forms for lists often do not allow entry or editing of the data. Tabular forms such as those for Journals are inherently intended for data entry.

Main/Sub Forms

Another form style within NAV consists of a Card form plus a List form. These are called Main/Sub forms and are also referred to more casually as Header/Detail forms. An example is the **Sales Order** form as shown in the following screenshot. In this example, the upper portion of the form (the Main form) is a Card form with several tabs showing Sales Order data fields that have one occurrence. The lower portion of the form (the Subform) is a Tabular form showing a list of all the line items on the Sales Order. Line items may include product to be shipped, special charges, comments and other pertinent order details. The information to the right of the data entry is related data and computations that have been retrieved and formatted. On top of the form, the information is for the Ordering customer and the bottom contains information for the item on the selected line.

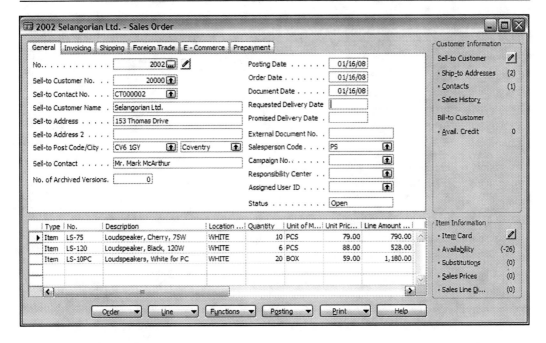

Matrix Forms

Matrix forms display multiple records at one time, and are also used to display the "intersect" of two related tables. For example: a spreadsheet-style matrix form showing the "intersect" (stock on hand) for each item at each location. The **Items** (**No.** and **Description**) are shown on the Y axis (vertically) in the leftmost column and the **Locations** on the X axis (horizontally) across the top, and each intersect point contains the count of inventory for an item at a location.

In the following screenshot, the **AMSTERDAM Lamp,** item number **1928-S**, has **149** lamps in stock in the **BLUE** warehouse and **55** in the **GREEN** warehouse. At the same time, we show a negative inventory in the **RED** warehouse, indicating that we have probably processed shipments for product for which the receipts have not yet been posted.

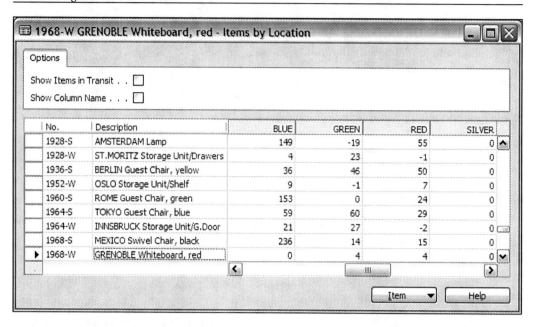

Trendscape Forms

Trendscape forms have similar format to Matrix forms but, with the addition of **Trendscape Option Buttons** and their underlying logic, the Trendscape forms are used to display time dependent data. The X-axis of a Trendscape matrix form is always date based, generally using the system Virtual Date table. The Trendscape option buttons allow the filtering and calculation of displayed information based on various accounting periods selected by the user. A Trendscape form is generally used for data that needs to be reviewed in summary form by various accounting periods (weeks, months, quarters, etc.).

The sample Trendscape form in the following screenshot shows **Budget** data by date. This image is summarized on a monthly basis (i.e. the **31** button is selected). The top of this form allows the entry of frequently used filter data, the left column (Y axis) shows the budget accounts, the X axis heading shows the date ranges for each column, and the individual cells display the budgeted total for each row-column intersect (i.e. for each budget account by period). Specifically, the budget for **Total Sales of Retail** for the month period starting **09/01/07** is **-100,610**.

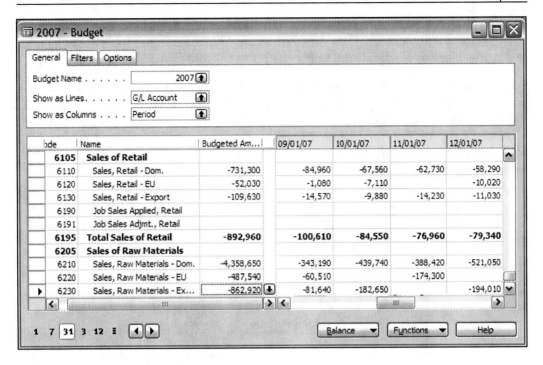

The image shows a Microsoft Dynamics NAV budget window titled "2007 - Budget" with tabs General, Filters, Options. Budget Name: 2007, Show as Lines: G/L Account, Show as Columns: Period.

Code	Name	Budgeted Am...	09/01/07	10/01/07	11/01/07	12/01/07
6105	**Sales of Retail**					
6110	Sales, Retail - Dom.	-731,300	-84,960	-67,560	-62,730	-58,290
6120	Sales, Retail - EU	-52,030	-1,080	-7,110		-10,020
6130	Sales, Retail - Export	-109,630	-14,570	-9,880	-14,230	-11,030
6190	Job Sales Applied, Retail					
6191	Job Sales Adjmt., Retail					
6195	**Total Sales of Retail**	**-892,960**	**-100,610**	**-84,550**	**-76,960**	**-79,340**
6205	**Sales of Raw Materials**					
6210	Sales, Raw Materials - Dom.	-4,358,650	-343,190	-439,740	-388,420	-521,050
6220	Sales, Raw Materials - EU	-487,540	-60,510		-174,300	
6230	Sales, Raw Materials - Ex...	-862,920	-81,640	-182,650		-194,010

All Forms

A Form consists of Form properties and Triggers, Controls, and Control properties and Triggers. Data controls generally are either labels displaying constant text or graphics, or containers that display data or other controls. Controls can also be elements such as buttons, menu items, and subforms. While there are a few instances where you must include C/AL code within form or form control triggers, in general it is a good practice to minimize the amount of code embedded within forms. Most of the time, any data-related C/AL code can (and should) be located within the table object rather than the form object.

Creating a Card Form

Let us try creating a Card form and a Tabular List form for the table we created a little while ago. The NAV IDE consists of some object generation tools (i.e. the Wizards) to create basic forms and reports. These tools are useful either to create simple objects or as a starting place for more complicated objects. One of the (many) nice features of C/SIDE is that you can generate an object, then climb into the generated object and modify it as though you had done all the coding from scratch by hand. This generation process is a one way process; once the generated object has been accepted and turned into an object under development, it cannot be manipulated within the form wizard again. For this reason, all of your wizard design work for a particular form needs to be done at one time, before any manual object manipulation occurs. The Form Wizard and Form Designer tools are available to anyone who has a license containing the Form Designer granule.

We will be using the Form Wizard to create both of our forms. Later we will do more with these forms, but for now we will just see how the Form Wizard works. Open the **Object Designer**, click on **Form** and then click on **New**. The Form Wizard's first screen will appear. Enter the name (**Member**) or number (50000) of the **Table** with which you want the form to be associated (bound). Choose the option **Create a form using a wizard**. This time choose a **Card-Type Form**. Then click on **OK** as shown in the following screenshot:

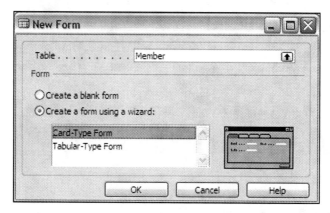

The next screenshot provides the option of creating a plain form (no tabs) or a tabbed form with one or more tabs. We can also name the tabs on this screen. This time, even though it is overkill at the moment to have a tabbed Card form, let us generate a form with one tab and use the default tab label of **General**. Now click on **Next**.

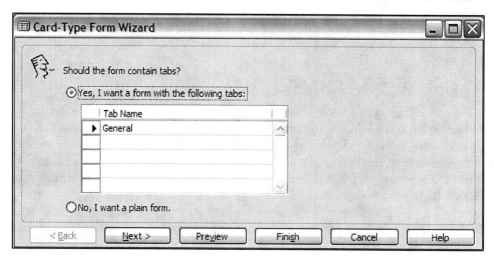

The next step is to choose what fields are to appear on our new form and how they will be placed. In this case, we are going to use all the fields and simply put them into two columns. First, let us take a quick walk through the controls on the Wizard form so we know what our basic toolkit is. There are six buttons associated with the design of the Card form on which we are working as shown in the following screenshot:

Button	Description
>	Choose one of the available fields
>>	Choose all the available fields
<	Remove one field from the object
<<	Remove all fields from the object
Separator	Insert a visual Separator (i.e. a horizontal line)
Column Break	Insert a Column Break (i.e. create a column split by ending one column and beginning another)
Preview	Display a Preview (screen display) of the object being created in the Wizard

The left column shown in the following screenshot, having the heading **Available Fields**, lists all the fields from the source table that have not yet been chosen for the Form object. The right column, headed **Field Order**, lists all the fields that have been chosen in the order in which they will appear on the form.

In the following screenshot, you can see that we have split the **Field Order** column into name information and address information. It is not a very elegant design but right now we are still in first grade, i.e. just learning basics. We will deal with appearance issues later. Put all the fields on the form that are in your table.

At any point during your work, you can take a sneak peek at what you are creating (i.e. click on the **Preview** button). When you are done with all the fields on your new form and you are satisfied with the layout, click on **Finish**. You will get the generated form object in the **Form Designer** as shown in the following screenshot:

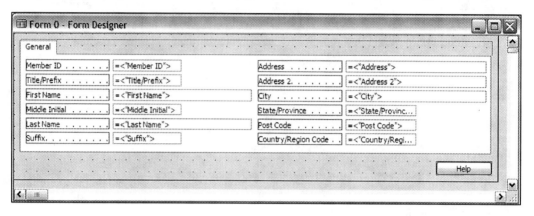

We are now through with the Form Wizard and have transitioned into the Form Designer. The Graphical User Interface Guidelines for NAV Card forms tell us that we should have all the long fields on the left side of the form and only short fields in the right column. Doing that with this form would have most, if not all, of the fields for this form in the left column. Obviously, there is an opportunity here for some subjective form design discussion or debate (which we are going to leave unaddressed). At the moment, we are going to leave our form as it is. If you want to experiment with different layouts later, that would be a good way to practice using some of the C/SIDE tools.

If we want to modify the form manually, we could do that now. If so, it would be a good idea to first save what we have done so far. We will do that the same way as we did when we saved our table earlier. Press *Esc* and respond **Yes** to the **Do you want to save the changes to the Form** query.

Now enter the Form number (ID), you want to assign (50000) and name (Member Card). We are using the number 50000 just because that is the first custom form object number available to us with our Form Designer granule license. After you have the form saved so you don't lose what you've done so far, you could start making manual changes. But we're not ready for that level of difficulty yet. We will get into that in the Chapter covering Forms.

Creating a List Form

Our next task is to use the Form Wizard to create a tabular Member List form. Open the **Object Designer**, click on **Form**, and then click on **New**. Once again the Form Wizard's first screen will appear. Enter the name (Member) or number (50000) of the table with which you want the form to be associated. Choose the option **Create a form using a wizard**. This time choose the option to create a **Tabular-Type Form**. Then click on **OK** as shown in the following screenshot:

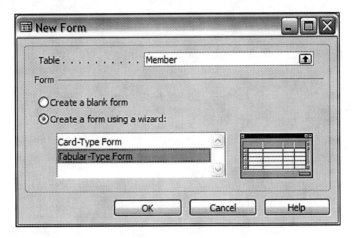

Now you will have the opportunity to choose which data fields will appear on each line of the tabular display. When List forms are designed for some type of referential lookup, generally they don't contain 100% of the data fields available, especially when working with a larger table. So let's choose a subset of the data fields to be displayed, just enough to make the display meaningful and easy to use.

Remember we can always return to the created form and easily add fields we left off or remove something we decide is not needed. In addition, NAV forms include a feature that allows you to have some field columns identified as Not Visible by default. This property is field specific and controls whether the column for a data field displays on screen or not.

On a Tabular form, even the non-programmer user can change the Visible property of each column to create a customized version. This user customization is tied to the individual user login and recorded in their ZUP file. ZUP files record user-specific system state information so it can be retrieved when appropriate. In addition to user screen changes, the ZUP file records the identity of the most recent record in focus for each screen, the most recent contents of report selection criteria and request form field contents, and a variety of other information. When the user returns to a screen or report, whether in the same session or after logout and return, data in the ZUP file helps restore the state of various user settings. This feature is very user friendly.

Let us choose just basic Name and Address fields for our initial List form as shown in the following screenshot.

 The Form Wizard functions essentially the same for Tabular forms as it does for Card forms.

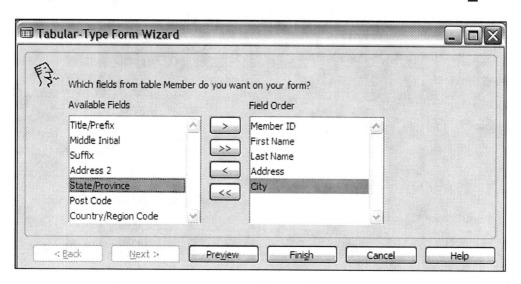

As with the Card form, at any point during your work you can take a sneak peek at what you are creating (i.e. click on the **Preview** button). If you feel like experimenting, you could move fields on and off the form or put fields in different orders. If you do experiment, use **Preview** to check the effects of your various actions. If your form gets hopelessly confused, which happens to all of us sometimes, just click on *Esc*, but be careful *not* to save the results and then start over. When you are done with all the fields on your new form and you are satisfied with the layout, click on **Finish**.

We are now done with the Form Wizard for our new List form and have transitioned into the Form Designer. If we want to modify the form manually, we could do that now. As before, just press *Esc* and respond **Yes** to the **Do you want to save the changes to the Form** query. Enter the Form number (ID), you want to assign (50001) and name (Member List). If you reused the Form object number 50000, you would have overwritten the Card form, you created earlier.

At this point, we have a data structure (Table 50000 – Member), a form to enter and maintain data (Form 50000 – Member Card) and a form to display or inquire into a list of data (Form 50001 – Member List). Let us use our Member Card to enter some data into our table. In a full application, we would be accessing our form from a Menu.

But for now, we will just run our form directly from the Object Designer.

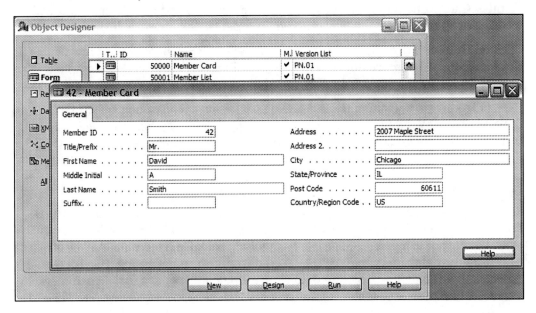

Choose **Object Designer | Form**, highlight the line for form 50000 (as shown in the background of the preceding screenshot), and then click the **Run** button at the bottom of the Object Designer form. You should now see your Member Card on the screen similar to the preceding screenshot, but with all fields empty (blank). Enter data into the fields. Put in your name and address for the first entry (just for fun).

When you have finished making the entry, press *F3* (the NAV **New Record** key) to file away the data just entered and prepare it for the entry of a new record. Do that. Enter at least a couple more Member records as shown in the following screenshot both for your experience of doing the data entry and to generate several Member records to use for later testing.

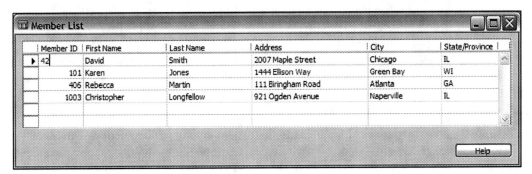

Now we are going to look at the data through the List form you created. Exit the Member Card form, highlight Form 50001, Member List, and then **Run** it. You will see a list of all the entries you just entered, in order by the Member ID number.

Click on **Help** on the main menu above the main toolbar. Choose **Overview of F Keys** and study the information shown by pressing *Shift, Control*, and *Shift* plus *Control*. These are the standard F Key functions throughout NAV.

Hopefully you are beginning to get a feeling for the ease of use and power of C/SIDE and NAV. Now that you have taken a quick look at where the data is defined and where it is entered, we will look at where it is extracted and reported.

Reports

Report objects can be used for several purposes, sometimes more than one purpose at a time. One type is for the display of data. This can be on-screen (called Preview mode) or output to a printer device (Print mode). The displayed data may be as read from the database or may be the result of significant processing. As you would expect, a report may be extracting data from a single table (e.g. a list of customers) or a combination of several tables (e.g. a Sales analysis report).

Another type of report object processes data, without any display formatted output of the processed results. Typically, such reports are referred to as batch processing reports. Reports can also be used as containers for program logic to be called from other objects or executed as an intermediate step in some sequence of processes. Normally this task would be handled by codeunit objects, but you could also use report objects if you want to do so.

Report formats are limited to a combination of your imagination, your budget, and the capabilities of NAV reporting. On one hand, NAV reporting is very powerful and flexible in terms of what data can be reported, plus the various types of filtering and combining can be done. On the other hand, NAV reporting is relatively limited in terms of formatting.

You can do most of what is normal and needed in terms of textual formatting, but have very limited graphical capability and almost no color capability. For these reasons, there are a number of good products, both from Microsoft and from third-party vendors, to provide additional reporting capabilities complementary to those within NAV. New to V5.0 is a built-in functionality to use XML Style Sheets to support exporting data to programs outside of NAV, especially those that are part of Microsoft Office such as Word and Excel.

Common report formats in NAV include document style (e.g. Invoices or Purchase Orders) also called Form-Type, list style (e.g. Customer List, Inventory Item List, Aged Accounts Receivable) also called Tabular-Type, and label format style (e.g. a page of name and address labels) called Label-Type.

A significant aspect of the NAV report object is the built-in read-then-process looping structure, which automates the sequence of read a record, then process it, and then read the next record. When manually creating or enhancing reports, you can define one data structure as subordinate to another, thus creating nested read-then-process loops. This type of predefined structure has its own good points and bad points. The good points usually relate to how easy it is to do the kind of things it is designed for and the bad points relate to how hard it is to do something that the structure doesn't anticipate. We will cover both sides of discussion when we cover Reports in more detail.

Creating a List Format Report

Let us create a simple list format report based on our Member table. We will use the Report Wizard this time. Just like the Form Wizard, the Report Wizard is quite useful for simple reports. The Report Wizard and Report Designer tools are available to anyone who has a license containing the Report Designer granule.

When you are doing more complex reports, it is often only modestly helpful to start with the Report Wizard. For one thing, the Report Wizard only deals with a single input table. However, even with complex reports, sometimes it is a good idea to create a little test version of some aspect of a larger report. Then you may create your full report without use of the Wizard, but letting the Report Wizard generate code to be your tutor in some aspect of layout or group totaling.

Open the **Object Designer**, click on **Report**, and then click on **New**. The Report Wizard's first screen will appear. Enter the name (Member) or number (50000) of the table with which you want the report to be associated. Choose the option **Create a report using a wizard**. This time choose a **Tabular-Type Report Wizard** to create a Member List. Then click on **OK** as shown in the following screenshot:

Next, you will be presented with the window show in the following screenshot for choosing what data fields you want on your report. The order in which you place the fields in the **Field Order** column, top to bottom, will be the order in which they appear in your report, left to right.

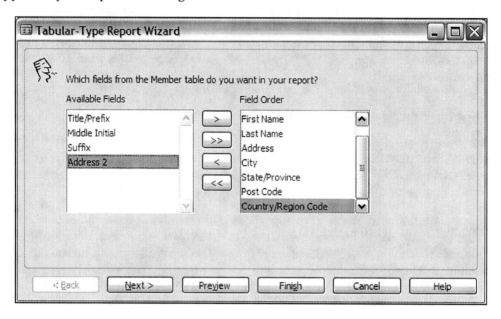

Just as with the Form Wizard, you can **Preview** your report in the process of its creation, to see if you are getting the layout you want. More often with reports than with forms, you will perform quite a bit of manual formatting, after you finish with the Wizard. Because the report preview function utilizes the driver for the current default printer for formatting, make sure you have a default printer active and available before you attempt to preview an NAV report.

After you have chosen the fields you want on your report (some are suggested in the preceding screenshot), click on **Next**. This will bring up a screen allowing you to predefine a processing/printing sequence for this report. You can select from any of the defined keys. At the moment our Member table only has one key so let's choose the **No, I don't want a special sorting of my data** option. As you will see later, that will generate a report where you can choose the sort sequence for each run. Click on **Next**.

Now you can choose a List Style or a Document Style layout. Click on each one of them to get an idea of the difference. If you like, **Preview** the report in process for each of these options chosen. Note that when you **Run** a report (and previewing it, is running it), the first thing you see is called the Report request screen. A Report request screen from the **Member List** report would look like the following screenshot:

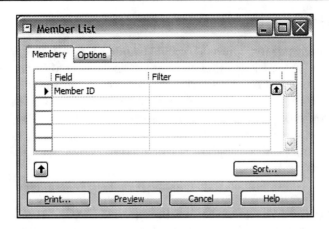

The Report request screen is where the user enters any variable information, data filters, page, printer setups, and desired sort order to control each report run. At the bottom right of the screen is the **Sort...** button, which allows the user to choose which predefined data key will apply to a particular report run. The user can also choose to **Print** the report (output to a physical device) or **Preview** it (output to the screen). To start with, just click on **Preview** to see your currently chosen layout.

Once you are satisfied with the layout, click on **Finish**. Again, just as with the Form Wizard, you will now be in the Report Designer, ready to make manual changes (isn't consistency great?). Exit the Report Designer by pressing the close-window icon, saying **Yes**, you do want to save the changes, and then saving your new report as ID 50000 and Name "Member List". If you then run your new report, using the **Run** button, it should look much like the following screenshot:

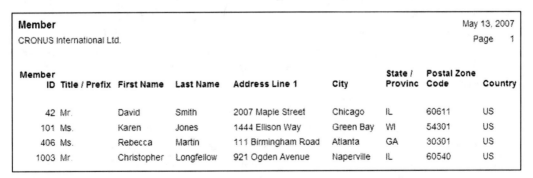

There is a lot more to learn about the design, creation, modification, and control of Reports.

For the moment, we are done with our introduction to development, but will continue with our introductory review of NAV's object types.

Codeunits

A codeunit is a container for "chunks" of C/AL code to be run "inline" or called from other objects. These "chunks" of code are properly called Functions. Since we said earlier that you could use a Report object as a container for code segments (i.e. functions), why do we need codeunits? One reason is that early in the life of C/SIDE, only codeunits could be used in this way. Somewhere along the line, the C/SIDE developers decided to relax that particular constraint, but from a system-design point of view, there are still very good reasons to use codeunits rather than other objects for function containers.

One important reason is that the license specifically limits access to the C/AL code within codeunits differently than that within reports. The C/AL code within a report can be accessed with a "lower level" license than is required to access the C/AL code in a codeunit. If your customer has license rights to the Report Designer, they can access C/AL code within Report objects. A large percentage of installations have Report Designer license privileges. But they cannot access C/AL code within codeunit objects unless they have access to a more expensive license with Developer privileges (i.e. Application Builder or Solution Developer).

Another reason is that the codeunits are better suited structurally to contain only functions. Even though functions could be placed in other object types, the other objects types have superstructures that relate to their designed primary use for forms, reports, etc. Use of such an object primarily as a repository for functions, designed to be called from other objects creates code that is often more difficult to interpret, use, and maintain.

Codeunits act only as a container for C/AL coded functions. They have no auxiliary functions, no method of user interaction, no predefined processing or predefined anything. If you are creating one or two functions that are closely related to the primary activity of a particular report, but are needed both from within and outside of the report, then, by all means, include the functions in the report. But otherwise, use a Codeunit.

There are several codeunits, delivered as part of the standard NAV product, which are really function libraries. These codeunits consist totally of utility routines, generally organized on some functional basis (e.g. associated with Dimensions or with some aspect of Manufacturing or some aspect of Warehouse management). Some developers create their own libraries of favorite special functions and include such a "function library" codeunit in systems on which they work.

MenuSuites

What is a MenuSuite? MenuSuites are the objects that are displayed as User Menus. They differ considerably from the other object types we have discussed earlier. MenuSuites have a completely different structure; they are also maintained differently. In older versions of NAV, menus were constructed as versions of Form objects. With the release of Version 4.0, MenuSuites were offered as a way of providing a User Interface essentially similar to that found in the Outlook Navigation panel. MenuSuites are also maintainable in a limited way by the end user without any special license requirements. In addition, MenuSuites have the advantage of only showing the menu items that the user has permissions to access.

MenuSuite entries do not have maintainable properties or contain triggers. With the advent of MenuSuites, NAV developers lost the ability to embed C/AL code within the menus. The only customizations that can be done with MenuSuites is to add, delete, or edit menu entries. In a later Chapter, we will discuss more about how to work with (and around) MenuSuite constraints.

Dataports

Dataports are specialized objects designed to export and import data between the NAV database (either implementation) and external text files. Dataports allow for a limited set of external data formats, generally focused around what are commonly referred to as "comma-delimited" files. Not that they literally have to be delimited only with commas, but that is the category of file structure.

Dataports can contain C/AL logic that applies to either the importing or the exporting process (or both). The internal structure of a dataport object is somewhat similar to that of a report object combined with a table object. Dataports are driven by an internal read-then-process loop similar to that in reports. Dataports contain field definitions that relate to the specific data being processed.

Dataports are relatively simple and quite flexible tools for importing and exporting data. The data format structure can be designed into the dataport as well as logic for accommodating editing, validating, combining, filtering, etc. of the data as it is passed through the dataport. Dataports can be accessed directly from a menu entry, in the same fashion as forms and reports.

XMLports

At first glance, XMLports are for importing and exporting data, similar to the Dataports. But XMLports differ considerably in their operation, setup, and intended usage. XMLport objects can only be used for XML-formatted data. They must be "fired off" by some other routine (i.e. cannot be run directly through a menu entry). XML stands for eXtensible Markup Language. XML is a markup language much like HTML. XML was designed to describe data so that it would be easier to exchange data between dissimilar systems, for example, between your NAV ERP system and your accounting firm's financial analysis and tax preparation system.

XML is designed to be extensible, which means that you can create or extend the definition so long as you communicate the revised XML format to your correspondents. There is a standard set of syntax rules to which XML formats must conform. XML is becoming more and more important because most software uses XML. For example, the new versions of Microsoft Office are quite XML "friendly".

Integration Tools

These integration tools are designed to allow direct input and output between NAV databases and external, non-NAV routines. But they do not allow access to C/AL-based logic. The internal business rules or data validation rules that would normally be enforced by C/AL code or trigger actions or various properties do not come into play when the data access is by means of one of the following integration tools. Therefore, you must be very careful in their use.

- N/ODBC: NAV provides the standard ODBC interface between external applications (such as Word, Excel, Delphi, Access, etc.) and the NAV database. This is a separately licensed granule.
- C/OCX: This provides the ability to use OCXes to interface with the NAV database. This is also a separately licensed granule.
- C/FRONT: This provides the ability to access the NAV database directly from code written in languages other than C/AL. Earlier, this type of interface was primarily coded in C, but with V4.0 SP1, we now have the ability to interface from various .NET languages. In future versions, this capability is likely to expand considerably. This too is a separately licensed granule.
- Automation: This allows access to registered automation controller libraries within Windows from in-line C/AL code (e.g. can directly push data into a Word document template or an Excel spreadsheet template from C/AL). Automation controllers cannot be used to add graphical elements to NAV but they can contain graphical user interfaces that operate outside of NAV. When it is feasible to use an automation controller for interfacing externally, it is a simple and flexible way to expand the capabilities of your NAV system.

Backups and Documentation

As with any system where you can do development work, careful attention to documentation and backing up your work is very important. C/SIDE provides a variety of techniques for handling each of these tasks.

When you are working within the Object Designer, you can back up individual objects of any type or groups of objects by exporting them. These exported object files can be imported in bulk or one object at a time to recover the original version of one or more objects. When objects are exported to text files, you can use a standard text editor to read or even change them. If, for example, you wanted to change all the instances of the field name **Customer** to **Patient**, you might export all the objects to text and make a mass "Find and Replace". You won't be surprised to find out that making such code changes in a text copy of an object is subject to a high probability of error, as you won't have all the safety features of the C/SIDE editor keeping you from hurting yourself.

You can also use the NAV Backup function to create backup files containing just system objects or including data (i.e. a typical full system backup). A developer would typically use backup only as an easy way to get a complete snapshot of all the objects in a system. Backup files cannot be interrogated as to the detail of their contents, nor can selective restoration can be done. So, for incremental development backups, object exporting is the tool of choice.

Internal documentation (i.e. inside C/SIDE, not in external documents) of object changes can be done in three areas. First is the Object Version List, a field attached to every object, visible in the Object Designer screen. Whenever a change is made in an object, a notation should be added to the Version List.

In every object type except *MenuSuites*, there is a Documentation trigger at the top of the object. That is the recommended location for noting a relatively complete description of any changes that have been made to the object. Then, depending on the type of object and the nature of the specific changes, you should also consider annotating each change in the code, so it can be easily identified as a change by the next developer looking at this object.

In short, everything you have learned earlier about good backup practices and good documentation practices applies, when doing development in NAV C/SIDE. This is true whether the development is new work or modifications of existing logic.

Summary

In this chapter, we have covered the basic definitions of terms related to NAV and C/SIDE. Then, we followed with the introduction of seven types of NAV objects (Tables, Forms, Reports, Codeunits, MenuSuites, Dataports and XMLports). We also had an introduction to Form and Report Creation Wizards through review and hands-on use with the beginning of an NAV Developer Association application. Finally, we looked briefly at the tools that we use to integrate with external entities and also discussed how different types of backups and documentation are handled in C/SIDE. Now that we have covered the basics in general terms, let's dive into the detail of the primary object types. In the next chapter, we will focus on Tables.

2
Tables

Design is a plan for arranging elements in such a way as to best accomplish a particular purpose – Charles Eames

The basic building blocks of any system are the data definitions. When you consider the full range of capabilities and features built into the table structure for Microsoft Dynamics NAV, that principle is even more applicable. In NAV, the data definitions are made up of tables and, within the tables, the individual data fields exist. Whether you are working on a new application or a tightly integrated modification, the first level of detailed design and development for a NAV application must be the data structure.

In NAV, the table definition can include considerably more than the traditional data fields and keys. The table definition can also include a considerable portion of the data validation rules, processing rules, business rules, and logic to ensure referential integrity. In this chapter, we will learn how to design and construct tables for data. We will review the various choices available and how these choices can affect the subsequent phases of design and development.

Overview of Tables

A table provides the basic definition for data in NAV. It is important to understand the distinction between the table (definition and container) and the data (the contents). The table definition describes the data structure, validation rules, storage, and retrieval of the data that is stored in the table. The data is the raw material that originates (directly or indirectly) from the user activities and subsequently resides in the table. The table is not the data, but the definition of data, though we commonly refer to data and table as if they were one and the same thing (internally in NAV, in the Permissions setup, for example, the data is logically referred to as **Table Data**). We will take the more relaxed approach here.

Tables are the critical foundation blocks of NAV applications. You can't have any permanent data that is not stored in a table. When you define temporary data variables within an object for use within the object only, you don't have the full range of data definition tools available. They are only available when the data is defined in a table.

In general, it is easy to design, develop and maintain, and embed much of the system design in the tables. You will find that this approach has a number of advantages as follows:

- Centralization of rules for data constraints
- Clarity of design
- More efficient development of logic
- Increased ease of debugging
- Improved compatibility with new versions of NAV

What does it mean to embed system design in the tables in NAV? How does this provide the mentioned advantages? In a nutshell, embedding the system design in the tables means fully utilizing the capability of NAV table objects to contain code, properties, etc. that define their content and processing parameters. This will include the code that controls the factors like what happens when new records are added, changed or deleted, and how data is validated. All these should be a part of the table. The table object should also include the common functions used in various processes to manipulate the table and its data. We will explore these capabilities more completely through examples and analysis of the structure of table objects.

What Makes Up a Table?

A table is made up of Fields, Properties, Triggers (some of which may contain C/AL Code), Keys, and SumIndexes. The table definition takes full advantage of these tools and reduces the effort required to construct the other parts of the application. It will have a considerable impact on the processing speed, efficiency, and flexibility of the application. These components combine to implement many of the business rules of the application as well as the rules for data validation.

A table can have:

- Up to 500 fields
- A defined record size of up to 4KB (up to 8KB for SQL Server)
- Up to 40 different keys

Table Naming

There are standardized naming conventions defined for NAV. Your modification will fit better within the structure of NAV, if you follow these conventions. In all the cases, the names for tables and other objects should be as descriptive as possible, while keeping them to a reasonable length. This is the one way to make your work self-documenting (which of course reduces the required amount of auxiliary documentation).

Table names should always be singular. The table containing customers should not be named "Customers", but rather "Customer". The table we created for our Developer Association NAV enhancement was named "Member", even though it contains data on many members.

In general, you should always name any table so that it is easy to identify the relationship between the table and the data it contains. Consistent with the principle of being as descriptive as possible, the two tables containing the transactions on which a main/subform combination form is based should normally be referred to as a Header table (for the main portion of the form) and a Line table (for the subform portion of the form). As an example, the tables underlying a Sales Order form are the `Sales Header` and the `Sales Line` tables. The `Sales Header` table contains all the data that occurs only once for a Sales Order and the `Sales Line` table contains the multiple lines from the order. Additional information on table naming can be found in the *Terminology Handbook for C/SIDE* from Microsoft.

Table Numbering

There are no hard and fast rules for table numbering, except that you must only use the table object numbers that you are licensed to use. If all you have is the rights to the Table Designer, then you are only allowed to create tables numbered from 50000 to 50009. In general, you should let your common sense be your guide.

If you are creating several related tables, you should ideally assign them related numbers, probably sequentially. But otherwise, there are no particular limitations or consequences for assigning table numbers in whatever way makes sense to you in the context of your design.

Table Properties

You can access the properties of a table while viewing the table in **Design mode**, highlighting the first blank field line (the one below all the fields) and clicking on the **Properties** icon or pressing *Shift + F4* as shown in the following screenshot.

You can also perform a similar operation via **Edit | Select Object**, and then pressing *Shift + F4*.

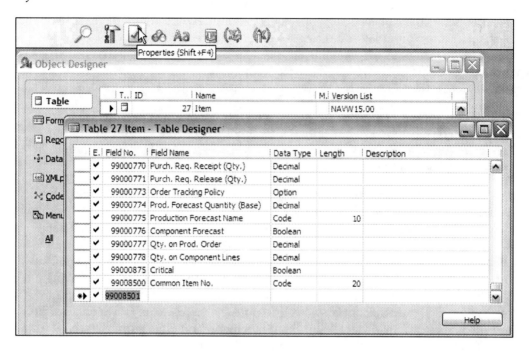

This will take you to the **Table - Properties** display. The following screenshot is the **Table - Properties** display for the Cronus Item table.

The contents of the screenshot are described as follows:

- **ID**: This is the Object Number of the table.
- **Name**: This is used as the default caption when data from this table is displayed.
- **Caption**: This contains the defined caption for the currently selected language. The default language for NAV is US English.
- **CaptionML**: This defines the MultiLanguage caption for the table. For an extended discussion on the language capabilities of NAV refer to the section on *MultiLanguage Functionality* in the NAV Application Designer's Guide manual.
- **Description**: This is optional for your documentation use.
- **DataPerCompany**: This lets you define whether or not the data in this table is segregated by company (the default) or is common (shared) across all the companies in the database.
- **Permissions**: This allows you to instruct the system to allow a user of this table to have certain levels of access (r=read, i=insert, m=modify, d=delete) to the table data in other table objects. For example, users of the Customer table are allowed to read (i.e. view, see) the data in the Cust.Ledger Entry table.
- **LookupFormID**: This allows you to define what Form is the default for looking up data in this table.
- **DrillDownFormID**: This allows you to define what Form is the default for drilling down into data that is summarized from this table.
- **DataCaptionFields**: This allows you to define specific fields whose contents will be displayed as part of the caption. For the Customer table, the No. and the Name will be displayed in the caption banner at the top of a form showing a customer record.
- **PasteIsValid**: This determines if the users are allowed to paste data into this table.
- **LinkedObject**: This lets you link this table to a SQL Server object.

As a developer, you will be most likely to deal with the two Form ID properties and occasionally with the **Caption, CaptionML, DataCaption,** and **Permissions** properties. You will rarely deal with the others.

Table Triggers

The first table trigger is the Documentation trigger. This trigger serves only the purpose of being a location for whatever documentation you require. No C/AL code is executed in a documentation trigger. There are no syntax or format rules here.

It is good, and should be a common practice, to briefly document every change to an object in the documentation trigger. Use of a standard format for such entries makes it easier to create them and understand them two years later.

There are four other Table Triggers, shown in the following screenshot, each of which can contain C/AL code:

The code contained in a trigger is executed prior to the event represented by the trigger. In other words, the code in the OnInsert() trigger is executed before the record is inserted into the table. This allows you, as the developer, a final opportunity to perform validations and to enforce data structure such as referential integrity. You can even abort the intended action at this point if data inconsistencies or conflicts are found. The contents of the screenshot are as follows:

- OnInsert(): This is executed when a new record is to be inserted in (added to) the table. New records are added when the last field of the primary key is completed and focus leaves that field.

- OnModify(): This is executed when any field (other than a primary key field) in a record is changed, determined by the "before" record image (**xRec**) being different from the "current" record image (**Rec**). During your development work, if you need to see what the "before" value of a record or field is, you can always reference the contents of xRec and, if you wish, compare that to the equivalent portion of Rec, the current value in memory.

- OnDelete(): This is executed when a record is to be deleted from the table.

- OnRename(): This is executed when some portion of the primary key of the record is about to be changed. Changing any portion (i.e. the contents of any field) of the primary key is considered as a Rename action to maintain referential integrity. Unlike most other systems, NAV allows the primary key of any master record to be changed and automatically maintains all the affected references that point back from other records.

It is interesting to note that there is an apparent inconsistency in the handling of data integrity by NAV. On one hand, the Rename trigger automatically maintains referential integrity by changing all the references back to a record whose primary key is changed (renamed). However, if you have deleted that record, NAV doesn't do anything to maintain referential integrity. In other words, child records could be orphaned by a deletion, left without any parent record. As the developer, you are responsible for ensuring this aspect of referential integrity.

When you write C/AL code that updates a table within some other object (e.g. a Codeunit, a Report, etc.), you can control whether or not the applicable table update trigger fires (executes). For example, if you were adding a record to our Member table and used the following C/AL code, the OnInsert() trigger would fire.

```
Member.INSERT(TRUE);
```

However, if you use either of the following C/AL code options instead, the OnInsert trigger would not fire and none of the attendant logic would be executed.

```
Member.INSERT(FALSE);
```

or

```
Member.INSERT;
```

Default logic such as enforcing primary key uniqueness will still happen whether or not the OnInsert trigger is fired.

Keys

Every NAV table must have at least one key, the primary key. The primary key is always the first key in the key list. By default, the primary key is made up of the first field defined in the table. In many of the reference tables that is the only field in the primary key and the only key is the primary key, such as in the **Payment Terms** table as shown in the following screenshot:

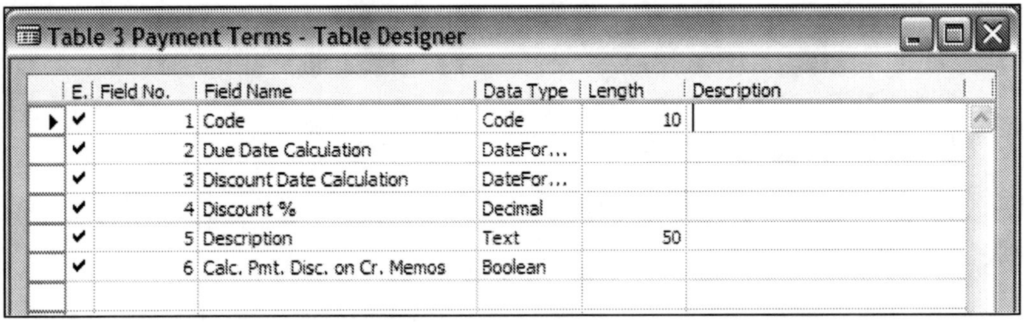

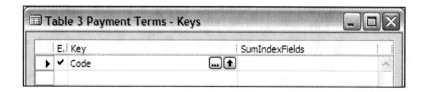

The primary key must have a unique value in each table record. You can change the primary key to be any field or combination of fields that serve the functional design up to 20 fields, but the uniqueness requirement must be met. It will automatically be enforced by NAV, i.e. NAV will not allow you to add a second record in a table with a duplicate primary key.

If you look at the primary keys in the supplied tables, you will note that many of them consist of or terminate in a Line No., an Entry No., or some data field whose contents serve to make the key unique. For example, the `Ledger Entry` table in the following screenshot uses the **Entry No.** only as the primary key. It is a NAV standard that **Entry No.** fields contain a value that is unique for each record.

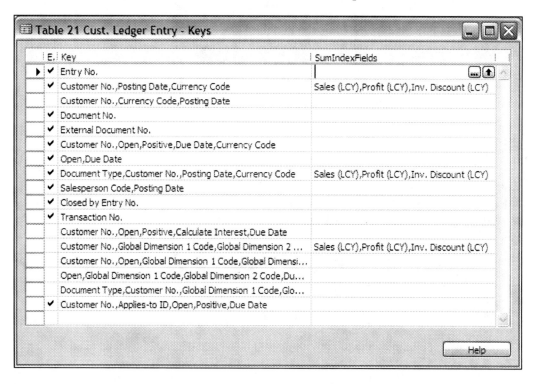

The primary key of the Sales Line table shown in the following screenshot is made up of multiple fields, with the **Line No.** of each entry as the terminating key field. In NAV, **Line No.** fields are assigned a unique number within the associated document. The **Line No.** combined with the preceding fields in the primary key (usually including fields such as **Document Type** and **Document No.**) makes each primary key entry unique.

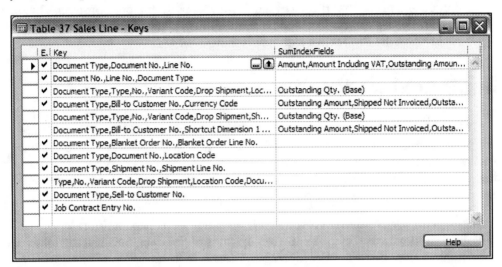

All keys except the primary key are secondary keys. There are no uniqueness constraints on secondary keys. There is no requirement to have any secondary keys. If you want a particular secondary key not to have any duplicate values, you must code that logic by checking for duplication before completing addition of a new entry.

The maximum number of fields that can be used in any one key is 20. The total number of different fields that can be used in all the keys cannot exceed 20. If the primary key includes three fields (as in the preceding screenshot), then the secondary keys can utilize up to seventeen other fields (20 minus 3) in various combinations plus any or all of the fields in the primary key. If the primary key has 20 fields, then the secondary keys can only consist of different groupings and sequences of these 20 fields.

Some other significant key attributes include:

- Keys can be enabled or disabled. Disabled keys are not automatically updated until they are enabled again. Since you can only enable or disable keys manually from the Table Designer key viewing screen (i.e. not through program control), there is very limited utility to this capability. There is a **Key Group** property that can be set up by the developer to allow users to enable and disable groups of keys at one time (i.e. by Key Group).

- SQL Server-specific key properties: As Microsoft strongly encourages more and more of the NAV installations to be based on SQL Server, as opposed to the native C/SIDE database, more such SQL Server-specific parameters are added to NAV. If you are developing modifications for a single installation and they are using SQL Server, then you would be wise to tailor what you do to SQL Server. Otherwise, in the near future, you should still design your enhancements so that they will work well on both database options. The key properties can be accessed by highlighting a key in the **Keys** form, then clicking on the **Properties** icon or pressing *Shift+F4*.

SumIndexFields

Since the origination of NAV as Navision, one of its unique capabilities has been the **SIFT** feature. SIFT stands for SumIndexField Technology. SumIndexFields are decimal fields attached to a table key definition. These fields serve as the basis for FlowFields (automatically accumulating totals) and are unique to NAV. This feature allows NAV to provide almost instant responses to user inquiries for summed data related to the SumIndexFields.

SumIndexFields are accumulated sums of individual fields (e.g. columns) maintained automatically by NAV during updates of the data. Because the totals are pre-calculated, they provide very high speed access to inquiries.

For example, users might want to know the total of the **Amount** values in a `Ledger` table. The **Amount** field could be attached to any (or all) keys. Then, FlowFields can be defined in another table as display fields that take the advantage of the SumIndexFields to give the users almost instantaneous response to Ledger Amount inquires relating to those keys.

In a typical system, hundreds or thousands of records might have to be processed to give such results. Obviously, this could be very time consuming. In NAV, using the C/SIDE database, as few as two records need to be accessed to provide the requested results.

Because the SIFT functionality is not natively built into SQL Server as it is in the C/SIDE database, FlowField inquiries require more processing by the system when using the SQL Server. However, they still provide the same logical advantages and are very fast when calculating the values.

In the C/SIDE database, SumIndexFields (SIFT fields) are stored as part of the key structure. This makes them very quick to access for the calculation task, and relatively quick when they need to be updated. In SQL Server, the SIFT data is stored in a separate table, one for each primary table having SIFT fields.

In the SQL Server environment, updating data that has a heavy component of SIFT fields can become painfully slow, if not properly and regularly maintained. In a nutshell, you should be more conservative about using SIFT fields in the SQL Server environment and more careful about maintenance of the database. We will discuss FlowFields more a bit later.

Expanding Our Sample Application

Before moving on, we need to expand the design of our C/ANDL application. Our base Member table design has to be enhanced, both by adding and changing some fields. We also need to add some reference tables.

Some of our design decisions here will be somewhat arbitrary. While we want a design that is relatively real, our primary goal is to create a design that we can use as a learning tool. We want to set up the data structures that can serve as a logical base for several different form types. If you see some missing capabilities and you want to add them, you should feel free to do so. You can also adjust these examples to make them more meaningful to you.

Table Creation and Modification

In Chapter 1, we created a Member table for our Developer Association application. When we did that, we just included the minimum fields to give us something to start with. Now let us add a few more data fields to the Member table and then create an additional table, which will contain reference data for our application. Then, we will revise our Member table to refer to this new table.

Our new data fields are shown in the following table:

Field No.	Field Name	Description
1000	Member Type	Choose only one out of **Student, Professional, Retired**. This will be an Option data type, with the choices being the options. In order to allow for the possibility of a partial entry without the Member Type, we will make the first option a blank (one space followed by a comma).
1010	NAV Involvement Since	Choice of entries from a list of years.
1020	Business Class	Choose one entry from a maintainable list, which will initially include **Government, Education, Manufacturing, Service, Distribution, Microsoft**.
1050	Executive	From **1050** to **1100**; A list of mutually exclusive choices of business roles.

Field No.	Field Name	Description
1050	Executive	
1060	Technical Management	
1070	Development	
1080	Sales	
1090	Consulting	
1100	Training	
2000	Status	Inactive or Active—another Option field. We will use an Option field here rather than the Boolean (Active—Yes or No) because it allows us to add another status option later relatively easily if we need to do so.

Because the first few of these are a new type of data describing the Member, we will assign field numbers in a new range (1000 and up). Before **Status** and any other fields, we will leave space for additional Member descriptive fields to be added later. That's why we have numbered **Status** at 2000, to leave space in the lower number range.

Your task at this point is to open up your NAV, get to the **Object Designer | Tables** and find your Member table (number **50000**, remember?). Highlight the Member table and click the **Design** button. When you are done, the bottom part of your Member table should look similar to the following screenshot:

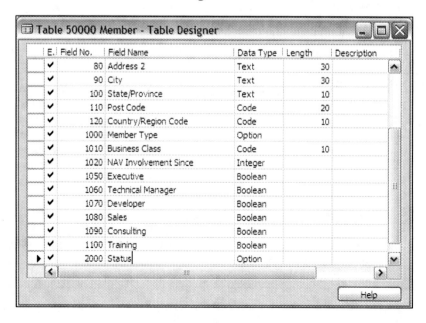

Next, we need to fill in the **OptionString** and **Caption** for the two option fields. Highlight the **Member Type** field, click on the **Properties** icon or press *Shift+F4*. Enter the **OptionString** as shown in the next screenshot; don't forget the leading space followed by a comma to get a blank option. Then, copy and paste the same information into the **Caption** property. The **CaptionML** property should fill in automatically with your default language choice. Your resulting properties should look similar to the following screenshot:

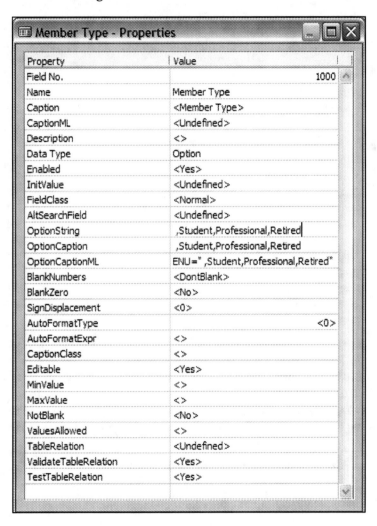

Property	Value
Field No.	1000
Name	Member Type
Caption	<Member Type>
CaptionML	<Undefined>
Description	<>
Data Type	Option
Enabled	<Yes>
InitValue	<Undefined>
FieldClass	<Normal>
AltSearchField	<Undefined>
OptionString	,Student,Professional,Retired
OptionCaption	,Student,Professional,Retired
OptionCaptionML	ENU=",Student,Professional,Retired"
BlankNumbers	<DontBlank>
BlankZero	<No>
SignDisplacement	<0>
AutoFormatType	<0>
AutoFormatExpr	<>
CaptionClass	<>
Editable	<Yes>
MinValue	<>
MaxValue	<>
NotBlank	<No>
ValuesAllowed	<>
TableRelation	<Undefined>
ValidateTableRelation	<Yes>
TestTableRelation	<Yes>

Now, similarly enter the **OptionString** of **Inactive,Active** for the **Status** field. We are not going to have a blank option here as we will let the default **Status** be **Inactive** (a design decision). Your resulting **Status** field Option properties should look like the following screenshot:

Next, we want to define the reference table we are going to tie to the **Business Class** field. We will keep this table very simple, just containing a **Code** as the unique key field and a text **Description**. You should create a **New** table, define the two fields, and save this as **Table 50001 Business Class**, as in the following screenshot:

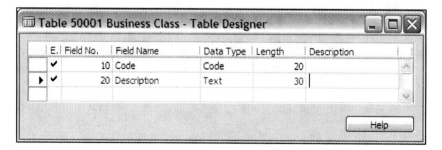

The next step is to use the **Form Designer** to create a List form for this table (Form 50002—Business Classes). You should be able to zoom through this process pretty quickly. Go to **Forms,** click on **New,** enter **50001** in the **Table** field, choose the **Create a form using a wizard** option, and finally choose **Tabular-Type Form**. Then, populate the form with all (both) the fields from your Business Class table and exit, saving the form as number 50002, named Business Classes.

Now, go back to the Business Class table, set the **Table - Properties** of **LookupFormID** and **DrillDownFormID** to the new form we have just created. As a reminder, you will use **Design** to open the table definition, focus on the empty line below the **Description** field, and either click on the **Properties** icon or press *Shift+F4*. In the values for the two FormID Properties, you can enter either your Form name (**Business Classes**) or the Form Object Number (50002). Either one will work and gives the result shown in the following screenshot. Then, exit and save the table as compiled.

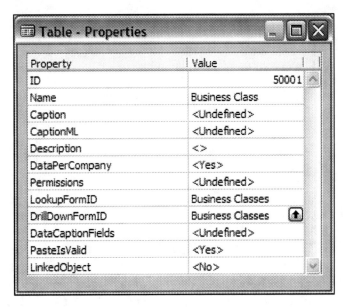

Finally, again open the Member table. This time highlight the **Business Class** field and access its properties screen. Fill in the **Property** value for **TableRelation** as 50001 (the table number) or Business Class (the table name) as shown in the following screenshot:

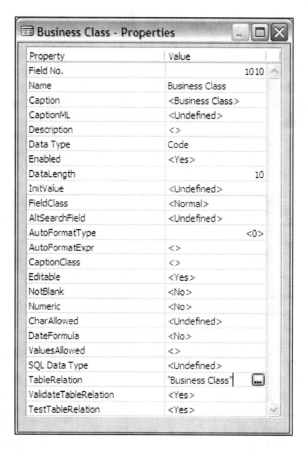

Exit and save the table. To check that the last couple of changes are working properly, run the Member table (i.e. highlight the table name and click on the **Run** button) and scroll to the right until you have the cursor in the Business Class field.

If all has gone according to plan, the Business Class field will display a **Lookup Button** (the upward pointing arrow button). If you click on that button or press *F6*, you should invoke Form 50002 — **Business Classes,** which you have just created. While you are in that form, go ahead and make some entries such as the examples shown in the following screenshot (feel free to add more choices if you feel creative at the moment):

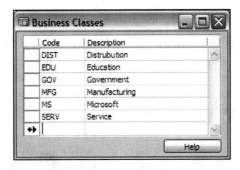

The other `Member` table field that we can further define at this point is NAV Involvement, which will contain the year in which the member began their work with NAV (Navision). We could possibly refer to the virtual table Date but it would get a little tricky to just focus on years as that table contains individual month and day and year. We could use the **MinValue** and **MaxValue** properties, and constrain the entries between **1990** and **2010**, but that would not allow a 0 (zero) to be entered when the correct answer is not known. So, let us choose to use the **ValuesAllowed** property and enter a list of the specific years we want to allow. There certainly are more sophisticated ways to accomplish this through C/AL code, but this approach works for now and uses knowledge we already have. The result looks like the following screenshot:

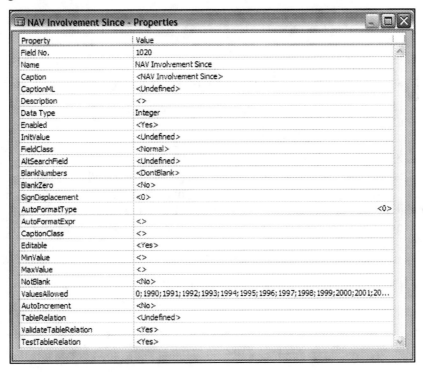

Keys

Let us add a couple of additional keys to our Member table. Our original Member table has a primary key consisting of just the Member ID. You might find it useful to be able to view the Member list geographically or alphabetically. To make that change you will have to access the window for maintenance of a table's key by selecting **View**, then **Keys** from the **Menu** bar at the top of the screen as shown in the following screenshot:

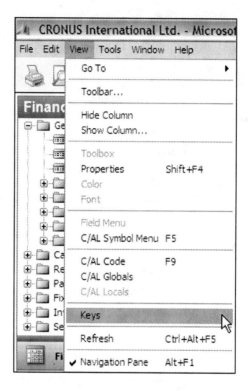

Once you have displayed the **Keys**, you can then change the existing keys or add new ones. To add a new key, highlight the first blank line (or press *F3* to create a additional blank line above an existing key) and then click the ellipsis button (the one with three dots) to access the screen that will allow you to select a series of fields for your key.

You can also use the lookup arrow if you want to enter only a single key field or want to enter several key fields one at a time for some reason. However, the end result will be the same. You should choose the tool option (ellipsis or arrow) that is easier for you to use. The fields will control the sort order of the table in the order they are listed on this screen, for example the top field is the most important, the next field is the second most important, etc. When you exit this screen, make sure that you click **OK**, otherwise your changes will be discarded.

For a good geographical **Key**, you might choose **Country/Region Code, State/Province, City** and for an alphabetical key, you might choose **Last Name, First Name, Middle Initial**. Since these are secondary keys you do not have to worry about there being a duplicate entry. And remember, the primary key is automatically and invisibly appended to each secondary key.

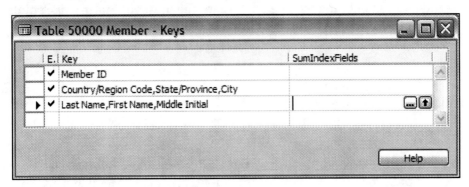

In the Chapter on Forms, we will create a new version of the Member form, which will show the new fields we have just added. For the time being, you can experiment with updating the Member table by using the **Run** button from the Object Designer. Enter some data into the table and don't forget to experiment with the sort feature by clicking on the **Sort** icon or pressing *Shift+F8*. In the later chapters, we will add C/AL code to both table and field triggers, explore SumIndexFields and other features, and will also build a more fully featured application.

Adding Some Activity-Tracking Tables

Our Association (C/ANDL) is a busy group. We need to keep track of information about our members that will allow C/ANDL to facilitate networking between members with similar attributes. That means, we have to record certain important member attributes such as their employer type, job category, and the certifications they have obtained.

In addition, C/ANDL is sponsoring some educational activities at which our members may be either instructors or students. For example, C/ANDL may put on a course relating to NAV Development with one member acting as an instructor and several other members attending as students. We need to keep track of each member's involvement in the education program and keep track of whether the participation was as a student or teacher. If they attended as a student, then we want to track the credits earned.

Finally (at least for now), C/ANDL is encouraging the members to volunteer at a local school that has financial problems and can really use their help. We have a large corporation, BigC Inc., to sponsor us for this project. Different activities will be worth so many points per hour of volunteer work. BigC has agreed to donate $5 for each earned volunteer point. We are going to use this money to buy computers for the schools and also to honor the members who earn the most volunteer work points. So we also want to track the volunteer efforts of our members and the work points earned by each.

Based on these requirements, we need to expand our application design. Up to now, we have defined a minimal Member table, one reference table (Business Class) and also created the forms for each of them. Ideally, you have also entered some test data and then added a few additional fields to the Member table (which we will not add to our forms).

Now we will further expand the Member table, add some more reference tables, plus add a couple of Ledger (i.e. activity history) tables relating to Member activities. Following that we will also create some forms to utilize our new data structures.

Our C/ANDL application will now include the following tables:

- Member: A master list of all members
- Business Class: A reference list of possible business class values
- Certification: A reference list of available certifications
- Volunteer Activity: A reference list of defined volunteer activities
- Course: A reference list of available courses
- Member Certification: A list of the certifications that have been achieved by our members
- Volunteer Activity Ledger: A detailed history of all the volunteer activity by our members
- Education Activity Ledger: A detailed history of all the courses taken by our members

Remember, the purpose of this example system is to follow along on a hands-on basis in our system. You might like to try different data structures and other object features. It will also be good if you make some mistakes and see some new error messages. This is meant to be a learning experience and a test system is the right place to learn from mistakes. To put it simply, you should create each of these objects in your development system and learn by experimenting.

New Tables

We will be adding a reference table, which will contain the possible Certifications of our members, as shown in the following screenshot:

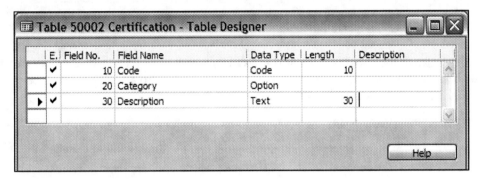

Then, we will add a reference table as shown in the following screenshot, which will contain the information on various Volunteer Activities that our system will be tracking.

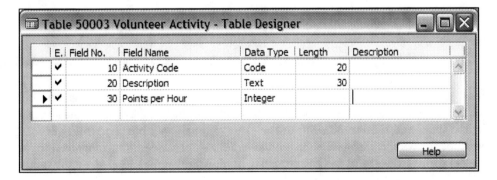

Next, we will add a reference table that will contain information on the Courses and Seminars that C/ANDL will hold as shown in the following screenshot.

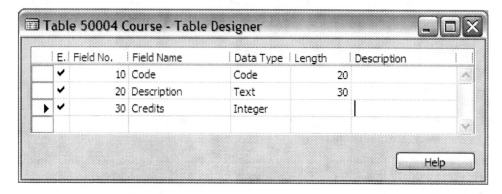

In order to track the certifications and activities, we need to have tables to assemble data about members. For certifications, we need to maintain a list of all Member Certifications, as shown in the following screenshot:

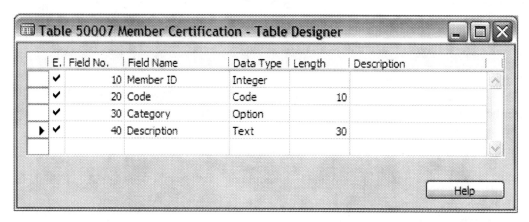

In order to operate the table in a relational fashion, the references to other related tables must be defined. In this case, the **Member ID** field must refer to the Member table and the **Code** field must refer to the Certification table. The following screenshot shows the **Code** field reference example. You need to add a similar **TableRelation** property to the **Member ID** field, pointing to the Member table.

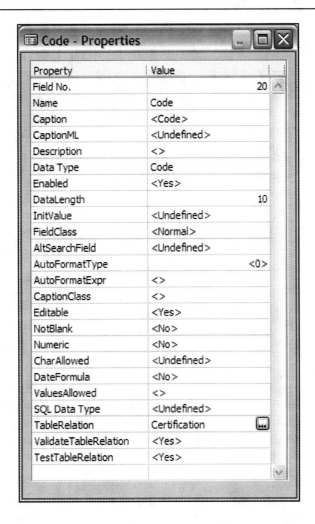

For the activities that we are tracking, we need to have Ledger (history) tables. Since we have not yet discussed how we would get data into such tables, we will simply define them and then define the associated forms that will allow us to enter enough test data to take us through our next testing steps. This, by the way, is a normal way to tiptoe into a full system development effort. It allows us to validate our base table/data design (our foundation), before we spend too much effort on building system functions.

First we will create the `Volunteer Activity Ledger` table as shown in the following screenshot, designed to track the volunteer effort of each Member by **Date** with the number of **Hours** and the extended number of **Points** earned (for those BigC donations tied to the points).

The fields that need to reference other tables are **Member ID** to the Member table and **Activity Code** to the Volunteer Activity table.

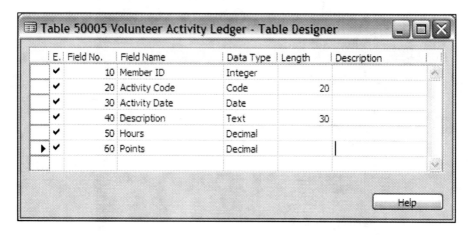

In addition to the information that is required to uniquely identify each entry (**Member ID, Activity Code**, and **Activity Date**) and the information we are tracking (**Hours** and **Points**), we will also include the **Description** field.

It would be a fair suggestion, based on the principles of relational database normalization, to suggest that the **Description** field should not be duplicated into this ledger record. This particular table is not the strongest possible illustration of the reasoning. You might look at the Sales Order Header and Sales Order Line tables, where there are a lot more fields that were duplicated from the source tables. There are a considerable number of instances in NAV (and other similar systems), where the better design decision is to duplicate data into related files.

There are two primary reasons for this. Firstly, this approach allows the user to tailor the data each time it is used. In this case, it might mean that the description of the volunteer activity could be edited occasionally or even frequently to provide more specific detail of what was done. Secondly, it allows easier and faster processing of the table data in question. In this case, if you want to sort the data on the **Description** field for reporting purposes, you should have the **Description** in the table or, if you want to filter out and review only entries with certain key words in the **Description**, you want to have the **Description** in the table.

The following screenshot is of our `Education Activity Ledger`. The fields that need to reference other tables here are the **Member ID** to the `Member` table and **Course Code** to the `Course` table.

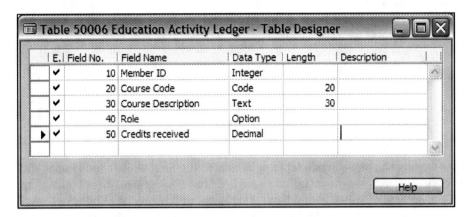

The **Role** field allows us to define whether the participation in a particular course is as a student or instructor. The following screenshot is for the **Properties** of the **Role** field:

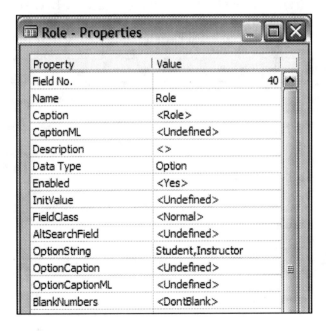

Keys and SumIndexFields in Our Examples

The following screenshot is displaying the **Keys** (we initially defined one) for our
`Volunteer Activity Ledger`:

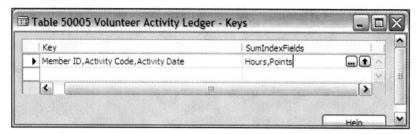

Since we want to have a quick and easy access to the total volunteer **Hours** and
Points accumulated, we must define these fields as being **SumIndexFields**. This
activates NAV's SIFT (Sum Index Flow Technology) feature, as shown in the
preceding screenshot. The fields in question are associated with one or more keys.
If we want to access similar totals when we are processing the table sequenced by
the **Description** field, the first thing we should have is a key that includes that field,
and the second is to have these fields identified as **SumIndexFields** for that key. The
following screenshot shows how the keys will look after we have defined a second
key, containing the **Description** field (it may not be the first field in the key). It also
illustrates the fact that it does not matter what sequence the **SumIndexFields** are in.

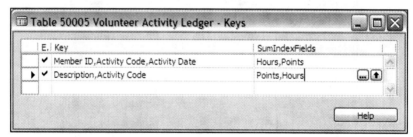

The following screenshot is of **Keys** structure we defined for our
`Education Ledger` table:

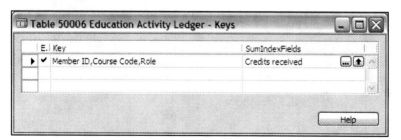

Now that we have put together the support tables, we can update the Member table to integrate with these and begin to take advantage of the structure we are building.

In the preceding screenshot, the **Description** field for the objects entered is a Version tracking code. A **Description** of **PN.01**, **PN.02**, and **PN.03** indicates that a field was added in modification 1 and then changed in both modifications 2 and 3 The goal is to keep track of the circumstances under which the object is modified and to identify what is the current level of updating for each object. In this case, we have chosen a version code consisting of **PN** (for Programming NAV) and a two digit number referring to a modification instance where the object is created or changed.

You can make up your own version identification codes, but you should be consistent and faithful in their use. These codes should be tied to comments inside the objects and should allow you to maintain external documentation describing the purpose of various modifications and enhancements.

Three of our new fields in the preceding screenshot are FlowFields. Let us take a quick look at each of them. The following image shows the **Properties** for the **Volunteer Hours** FlowField.

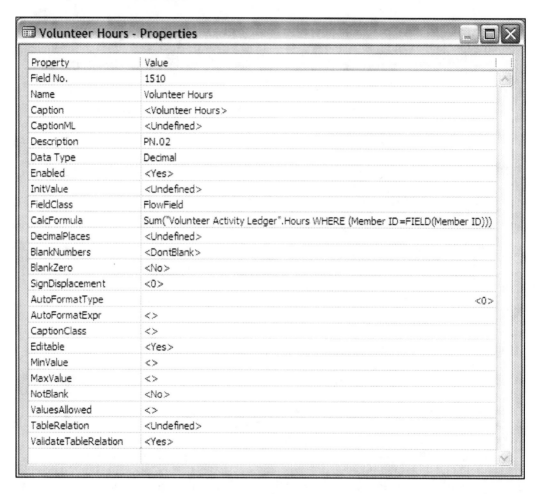

The following screenshot illustrates how a FlowField is defined. When you click on the **CalcFormula** property, an ellipsis icon will appear and clicking it will give you the **Calculation Formula** screen. In the following screenshot, the values filled in are the same as in the preceding screenshot (**CalcFormula** property).

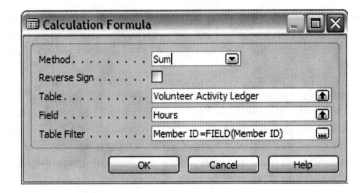

In the following two screenshots, the other two FlowFields are shown. A bit more is shown, so that the **FieldClass** and **CalcFormula** properties can be illustrated effectively.

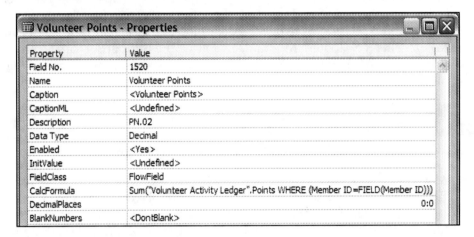

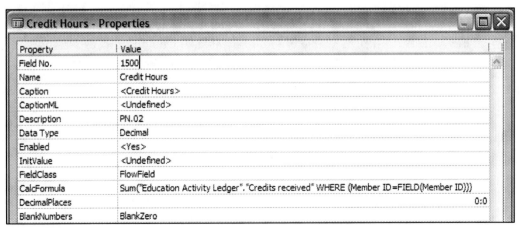

Each of these FlowFields is a **Sum** and each of them is the sum of the data **WHERE (Member ID = FIELD(Member ID))**. In other words, this is a summation of all the applicable data belonging to this member (whatever member's record is being processed).

The other properties that you should note are the **DecimalPlaces** and **BlankNumbers** properties. They have been set to control the display of the data, to appear in a format other than that which would result from the default values. You should adjust them to whatever values your subjective sense of visual design dictates. But remember, consistency with other parts of the system should be an overriding criterion for the design of an enhancement.

Types of Tables

For our discussion, we will break the table types into three groups. As a developer, you can change the definition and the contents of the first group (i.e. Totally Modifiable Tables). You cannot change the definition of the second group, but can change the contents (i.e. Content Modifiable Tables). The third group can be accessed for information, but data within is not modifiable (i.e. these table are intended to be Read-Only Tables).

Totally Modifiable Tables

The following are the tables in the Totally Modifiable Tables group:

- **Master**: This contains primary data (such as Customers, Vendors, Items, Employees, etc.). These are the tables that should be designed first. If you consider the data definition as the foundation of the system, the Master tables are the footings providing a stable base for that foundation. When working on a modification, any necessary changes to Master tables should be defined first. Master tables always use card forms as their primary user input method. The Customer table is a Master table. A Customer record is shown in the following screenshot:

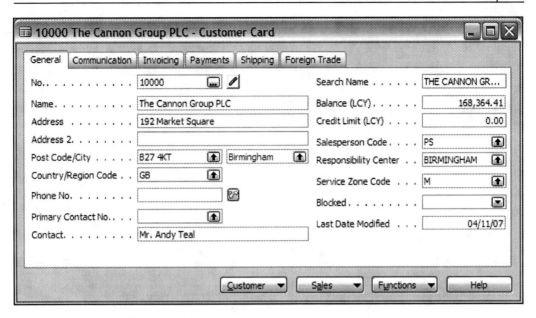

The preceding screenshot shows how the Card form segregates the data into categories on different tabs (e.g. **General, Communications, Invoicing,** etc.) and includes primary data fields (e.g. **No., Name, Address**), reference fields (e.g. **Salesperson Code, Responsibility Center**), and a FlowField (e.g. **Balance (LCY)**).

- **Journal**: This contains unposted activity detail, the data that other systems refer to as "transactions". Journals are where most repetitive data entry occurs. The standard system design has all Journal tables matched with corresponding Template tables (i.e. a Template table for each Journal table). The standard system includes journals for Sales, Cash Receipts, General Journal entries, Physical Inventory, Purchases, Fixed Assets, and Warehouse Activity among others.

  The transactions of a journal can be segregated into batches for entry, edit review, and processing purposes. Journal tables always use tabular forms as their primary user input method. The following screenshot shows two Journal Entry screens. They both use the General Journal table, but with different forms and different templates (templates are explained in the following section).

The two journals appear quite different from each other, even though they are based on the same table.

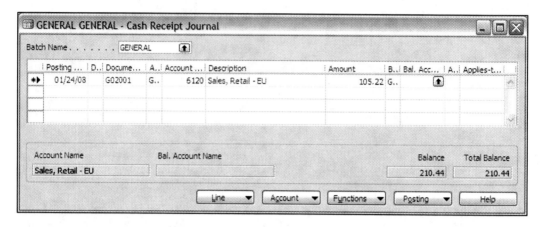

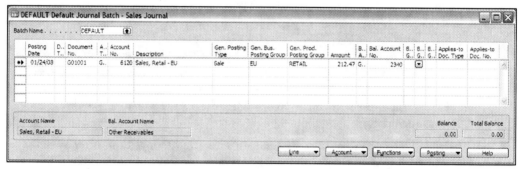

- **Template**: This table type operates from behind the scenes, providing control information for a Journal, which operates in the foreground. By use of a template, multiple instances of a Journal can be tailored for different purposes. Control information contained by a template includes the following:

  ° The default type of accounts to be affected (e.g. Customer, Vendor, Bank , General Ledger)

  ° The specific account numbers to be used as defaults including balancing accounts

  ° What transaction numbering series will be used

  ° Default encoding to be applied to transactions for this journal (e.g. Source Code, Reason Code)

  ° Specific Forms and Reports to be used for data entry and processing of both edits and posting runs

As an example, **General Journal Templates** allow the General Journal table
to be tailored to display fields and perform validations that are specific to
the entry of particular transaction categories, for example, Cash Receipts,
Payments, Purchases, Sales, and other transaction entry types. Template
tables always use tabular forms for user input. The following screenshot
shows a listing of the various **General Journal Templates** defined in the
Cronus International Ltd. demonstration database. Not all of the fields
available in these particular templates are displayed in this illustration.

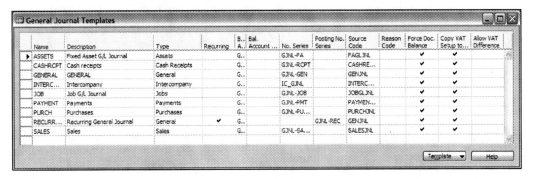

- **Ledger**: This table type contains posted activity detail, the data that other
  systems call "history". The basic data flow is from a Journal through a
  Posting routine into a Ledger. A distinct advantage of the way NAV
  Ledgers are designed is the fact that NAV Ledgers allow the retention of all
  detail indefinitely.

  While there are protocols and supporting routines to allow compression of
  the ledger data (i.e. summarization), as long as your system has sufficient
  disk space, you can (and should) always keep the full historical detail of all
  activity. This allows users to have total flexibility for historical data analysis.

  Most other systems require some type of periodic summarization of data (e.g.
  by accounting period, by month, by year). That summarization definition
  (also called "bucketing") constrains the ways in which historical data analysis can be done. By allowing the retention of historical data in full detail, the
  NAV system designer is allowed to be less visionary because future
  analytical functionality can still take advantage of this detail. User views of
  Ledger data are generally through use of tabular forms. In the end, the NAV
  approach of long-term data retention in complete detail lets users obtain the
  most possible value out of their data.

Ledger data is considered as accounting data in NAV. That means you are not allowed to directly enter the data into a ledger, but must "Post" to a ledger. (Although you can physically force data into a ledger with your Developer tools, you should not do so.) Because it is accounting data, it also means that you are not allowed to delete data from a `Ledger` table; you can compress or summarize data using the provided compression routines, thus eliminating a level of detail, but you cannot eliminate anything that would affect accounting totals for money or quantities.

The following screenshot shows a **Customer Ledger Entries** list (financially oriented data) and an **Item Ledger Entries** list (quantity-oriented data). In both the cases the data represents historical activity detail with accounting significance, and there are other data fields in addition to those shown in the following screenshot. The fields shown are typical and representative. The users can utilize some of the tabular form tools (which we will discuss in the chapter on Forms) to change the data columns that are displayed.

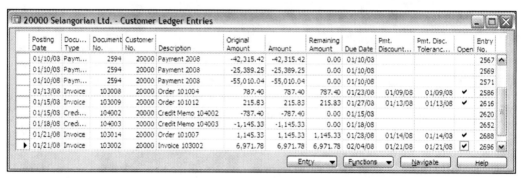

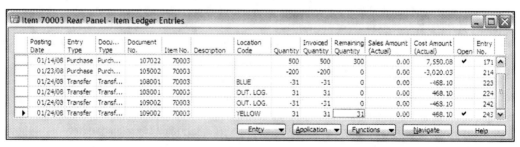

In the Customer Ledger Entries form, you can see critical information such as the **Posting Date** (the effective accounting date), the **Document Type** (the type of transaction), the **Customer No.**, the **Original** and **Remaining Amount** of the transaction, and **Entry No.**, which uniquely identifies each record. **Open** entries are those where the transaction amount has not been fully applied, such as an Invoice amount not fully paid or a Payment amount not fully consumed by Invoices.

In the Item Ledger Entries form, you can see similar information pertinent to inventory transactions. As previously described, **Posting Date**, **Entry Type**, and **Item No.**, along with the assigned **Location** for the Item, control the meaning of each transaction. Item Ledger Entries are expressed both in **Quantity** and **Amount** (Value), as you can see. **Open** entries here are tied to the **Remaining Quantity**, for example, material that has been received but not yet fully shipped out. In other words, the **Open** entries represent current inventory.

- **Reference**: This table type contains lists of codes as well as other validation and interpretation reference data that is used (referred to) by many other table types. Reference table examples are postal zone codes, country codes, currency codes, exchange rates, etc. Reference tables are often accessed under **Setup** menu options as they must be set up prior to being used for reference purposes by other tables.

The following screenshots show some sample reference tables; i.e. for (warehouse) **Locations**, for **Countries**, and for **Payment Terms**. Each table contains data elements that are appropriate to its use as a reference table, plus, in some cases, fields that control the effect of referencing a particular entry. These data elements are usually entered as a part of a setup process, then updated on occasion as appropriate, i.e. they generally do not contain data originating from system activity.

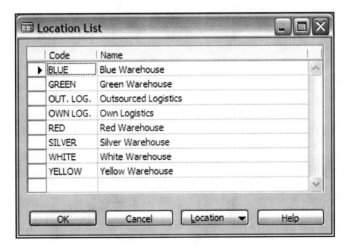

The **Location List** in the preceding screenshot is a simple validation list of the Locations for this implementation. Usually, they represent physical sites, but depending on the implementation they can also be used simply to segregate types of inventory.

For example, locations could be Refrigerated versus Un-refrigerated or there could be a location for "Failed Inspection".

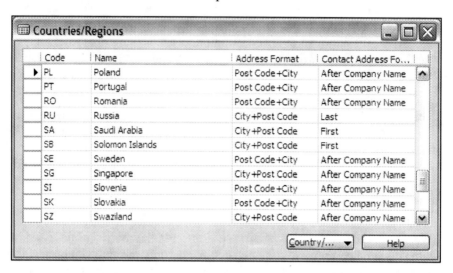

The **Countries/Regions** list in the preceding screenshot acts as validation data, controlling what **County Code** is acceptable, but it also provides control information for the mailing **Address Format** (general organization address) and the **Contact Address Format** (for the individual).

The **Payment Terms** table shown in the following screenshot provides a list of payment terms codes along with a set of parameters that allows the system to calculate specific terms. In this set of data, for example, the code **1M(8D)** will yield payment terms of **1 month** with a discount of **2%** applied for payments processed within 8 dats of the invoice date. In another instance, **14DAYS** payment terms will calculate the payment as due in **14 days** from the date of invoice with no discount available.

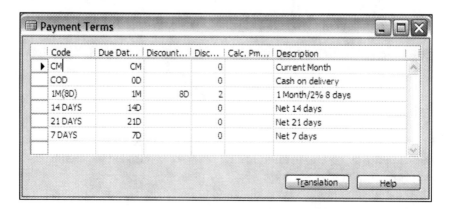

- **Register**: This table type contains a record of the range of transaction ID numbers for each batch of posted ledger entries. Register data provides an audit of the physical timing and sequence of postings. This combined with the full detail retained in the ledger makes NAV a very auditable system, i.e. you can see exactly what activity was done and when it was done.

  Another NAV feature, the Navigate function, which we will discuss in detail later, provides a very useful auditing tool. The Navigate function allows the user (who may be a developer doing testing) to highlight a single ledger entry and find all the other ledger entries and related records that resulted from the posting that created the highlighted entry. User views the Register through a tabular form as shown in the following screenshot. You can see that each Register entry has the **Creation Date**, **Source Code**, **Journal Batch Name**, and the identifying **Entry No.** range for all the entries in that batch.

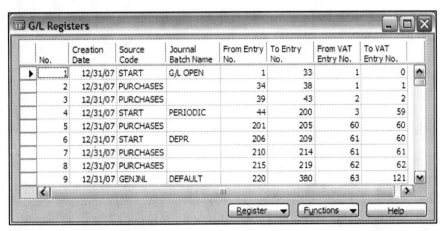

- **Posted Document**: This table type contains the posted copies of the original documents for a variety of data types such as Sales Invoices, Purchase Invoices, Sales Shipments, and Purchase Receipts. Posted documents are designed to provide an easy reference to the historical data in a format similar to what one would normally store in paper files.

  It is important to note that posted documents are not considered accounting data in NAV, therefore are allowed to be deleted. There are times when it is useful to create critical management reports based on the information contained in a posted document table. In that case, it is important through code modification or procedures to ensure that valuable data is not allowed to be deleted or otherwise manipulated to give misleading results to the system users. A posted document will look very similar to the original source document, i.e. a posted invoice will look very similar to the original Sales Order or Sales Invoice. The posted documents are included in the Navigate function.

The following screenshots show a **Sales Order** before Posting and the resulting **Posted Sales Invoice** document. Both documents are in a Header/Detail format, where the information in the Header applies to the whole order and the information in the detail is specific to the individual Order Line. As part of the Sales Order form, there is information displayed to the right of the actual order, designed to make life easier for the user, by giving clues to related data available without a separate lookup action.

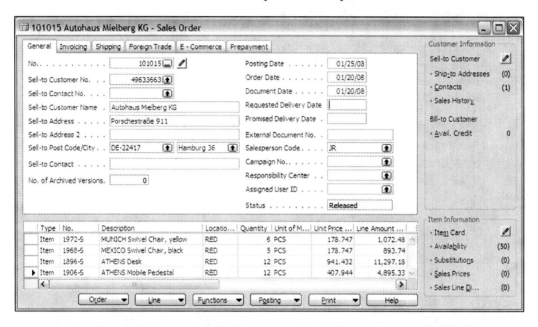

- **Setup**: This table type contains system or functional application control information. There is one setup table per functional application area, e.g. one for **Sales & Receivables**, one for **Purchases & Payables**, one for **General Ledger**, one for **Inventory**, etc. Setup tables contain only a single record. Since a setup table only has a single record, it can have a null value primary key field.

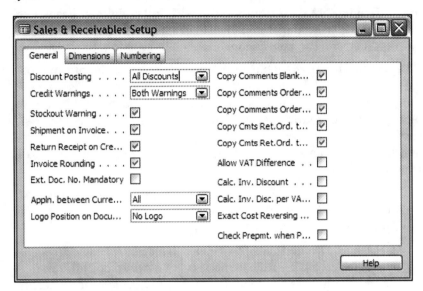

- **Temporary**: This table type is used within objects to hold temporary copies of data. A temporary table is defined within an object as a variable using a permanent table as the template. That means a temporary table will have exactly the same data structure as the permanent table after which it is modeled, but with a limited subset of various other attributes.

  Temporary tables are created and are empty when the parent object execution initiates and they disappear along with their data when the parent object execution terminates (i.e. when the temporary table variable goes out of scope). The data in a temporary table resides in the client system and not in the system database. This provides an advantage for faster processing because all the processing is local.

  Temporary tables are not directly visible or accessible to users. They cannot directly be the target of a form or report object. Temporary tables are intended to be work areas and as such, temporary containers of data. The definition of a temporary table can only be changed by changing the definition of the permanent table after which it has been modeled.

Content-Modifiable Tables

The only table type included in the Content-Modifiable Table group is as follows:

- **System**: This table type contains user-maintainable information that pertains to the management or administration of the NAV application system. System tables are created by NAV. You cannot create system tables as they affect the underlying NAV executables. But with full developer license rights, you can modify these system tables to extend their usage. With full system permissions, you can also change the data in system tables.

  An example is the User table, which contains user login information. This particular system table is often modified to define special user access routing or processing limitations. Other system tables contain data on report-to-printer routing assignments, transaction numbers to be assigned, batch job scheduling, etc. The following are examples of system tables in which definition and content can be modified. The first six relate to system security functions.

  - ○ User: The table of identified users and their login password for the Database Server access method.
  - ○ Member Of: This contains User Security Role information.
  - ○ User Role: This contains the defined User Security Roles available. Each User Role is made up of a group of individual object permissions i.e. Read, Insert, Modify, Delete, and Execute Permissions.
  - ○ Permission: The table of the individual object access permissions.
  - ○ Windows Access Control: The table of the security roles that are assigned to each Windows Login.
  - ○ Windows Login: The table for Windows Logins that have been created for this database.

The following two tables are used to define system data structure:

- Company: The companies in this database. Most NAV data is automatically segregated by Company.
- Database Key Groups: This defines all the key groups that have been set up to allow enabling and disabling table keys.

The following tables contain information about various system internals. Their explanation is outside the scope of this book.

- User Menu Level
- Send-to Program
- Style Sheet
- User Default Style Sheet
- Record Link

Read-Only Tables

The only table type included in the Read-Only Table group is as follows:

- **Virtual**: This table type is computed at run time by the system. A Virtual table contains data and is accessed like other tables, but you cannot modify either the definition or the contents of a virtual table. Some of these tables (such as the Database File, File, and Drive tables) provide access to information about the computing environment. Other virtual tables (such as Table Information, Field, and Monitor tables) provide information about the internal structure and operating activities of your database.

  Some virtual tables (such as Date and Integer) provide tools that can be used in your application routines. The Date table provides a list of calendar periods (days, weeks, months, quarters, and years) to make it much easier to manage various types of accounting and managerial data handling. The Integer table provides a list of integers from -1,000,000,000 to +1,000,000,000. As you explore standard NAV reports, you will frequently see the Integer table being used to supply a sequential count to facilitate a reporting sequence.

  You cannot see these tables presented in the list of table objects, but can only access them as targets for Forms or Reports or Variables in C/AL code. The knowledge of the existence, contents or usage of these virtual tables is not useful to an end user. However, as a developer, you will regularly use some of the virtual tables. You may find educational value in studying the structure and contents of these tables and also be able to create valuable tools through knowledge of and accessing one or more virtual tables.

The following screenshot shows a list of many virtual and system tables:

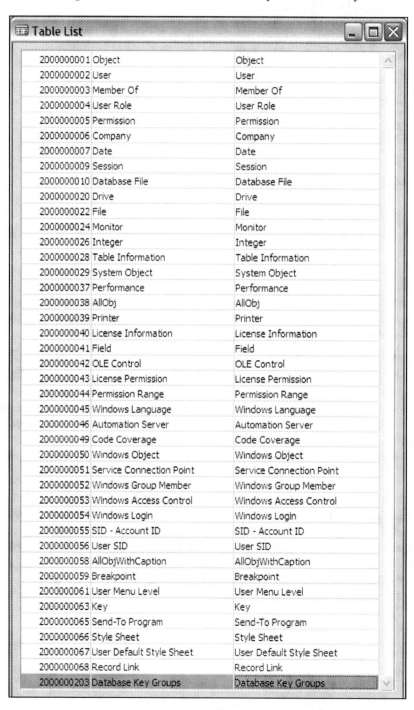

Summary

In this chapter, we have focused on the top level of NAV data structure, tables and their structures. We worked our way through hands-on creation of a number of tables and their data structures in support of our C/ANDL application. In the next chapter, we will focus on what more can be done in the Triggers. We also reviewed most of the types of tables found in the out-of-the-box NAV application. Finally, we identified the essential table structure elements including Properties, Object numbers, Triggers, Keys, and SumIndexFields.

In the next chapter, we will dig deeper into the NAV data structure to understand how fields and their attributes are assembled to make up the tables. Then, we will explore using tables in other object types, heading towards obtaining a full kit of tools to perform NAV development.

3
Fields

The secret of getting ahead is getting started. The secret of getting started is breaking your complex overwhelming tasks into small manageable tasks, and then starting on the first one — Mark Twain

As you know, design of an application starts with the data. The data design depends on the types of data that your development tool set allows you to use. Since NAV is designed specifically to develop financially oriented business applications, the NAV data types are financially and business oriented, and also have some special features that make it easier to design and develop typical business applications. Furthermore, these same special features can make your applications run faster.

In this chapter, we will cover the data types that you are most likely to use. We will also take an overview of the others. In addition, we will also cover field classes, which are where the special features are enabled.

Fields

A field is the basic element of data definition in NAV — the "atom" in the structure of a system. The mechanical definition of a field consists of its number, its description (name), and its data type (and, of course, any parameters required for its particular data type). From a logical point of view, a field is also defined by its Properties and the C/AL code contained in its Triggers.

Field Properties

The specific properties that can be defined for a field partially depend on the data type. First we will review the universal field properties. Then we will review the properties that are data-type dependent plus some other field properties. You can check out the remaining properties by using **Help** within the Table Designer.

You can access the properties of a field while viewing the table in Design mode, by highlighting the field line whose properties you wish to examine and clicking on the **Properties** icon or pressing *Shift + F4*. All the property screenshots in this section are obtained in this way for fields within the standard Customer table. As we review various field properties, you will learn more if, using the Object Designer, you follow along in your NAV system. Poke around and explore different properties and the values they can have. Use the **Field Help** function liberally and read the help for various properties.

The property value enclosed in **< >** (less than sign, greater than sign), is the default value for that property. When you set a property to any other value, **<** and **>** should not be present unless they are supposed to be the part of the property value (e.g. part of a Text string value).

All data types have the following properties:

Property	Property Description
Field No.	Identifier for the field within the table object.
Name	Label by which code references the field. The name can be changed at any time and NAV will automatically ripple that change throughout the code.
Caption and Caption ML	Work similarly to the Name table property.
Description	Used for internal documentation only.
Data Type	Identifies what kind of data format applies to this field (e.g. Integer, Date, Code, Text, etc.).
Enabled	Determines if the field is activated for data handling or not. This property defaults to yes and is rarely changed.

The following screenshot shows the BLOB properties for the **Picture Field** in the Customer table:

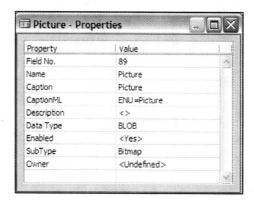

This set of properties, for fields of the BLOB data type, is the simplest set of field properties. After the properties that are shared by all data types, appear the BLOB-specific properties—SubType and Owner:

- **SubType**: This defines the type of data stored in the BLOB. The three sub-type choices are Bitmap (for bitmap graphics), Memo (for text data), and User-Defined (for anything else). User-Defined is the default value.

- **Owner**: The usage is not defined.

The available properties of Code and Text fields are quite similar to one another. The following are some common properties between the two as shown in the screenshot overleaf:

- **DataLength**: This specifies how many characters long the data field is.

- **InitValue**: This is the value that the system should supply as a default when the system actively initializes the field.

- **AltSearchField**: This allows definition of an alternative field in the same table to be searched for a match if no match is found on a lookup on this data item. For example, you might want to allow customers to be looked up either by their Customer No. or by their Phone No. In that case, in the **No. field** properties you would supply the Phone No. field name in the **AltSearchField** field. Then, when a user searches in the **No. field**, NAV will first look for a match in the **No. field** and, if it is not found there, it will then search the **Phone No.** field for a match. Use of this property can save you a lot of coding, but make sure both fields have high placement in a key so the lookup will be speedy.

- **Editable**: This is set to **No** when you don't want to allow a field to ever be edited for example, if this is a computed or assigned value field that the user should not change.

- **NotBlank**, **Numeric**, **CharAllowed**, **DateFormula**, and **ValuesAllowed**: All these support placing constraints on the specific data that can be entered into this field.

- **TableRelation** and **ValidateTableRelation**: These are used to control referencing and validation of entries against another table. (**TestTableRelation** is an infrequently used property, which controls whether or not this relationship should be tested during a database validation test.)

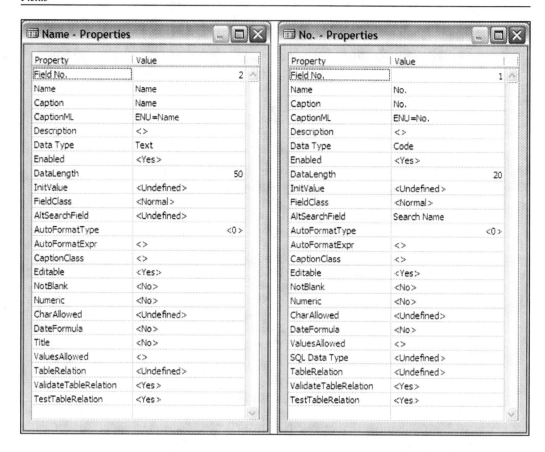

Let us take a look at the properties of couple more Data types, **Integer** and **Decimal**. You may find it useful to explore them on your own as well. Specific properties related to the basic numeric content of these data types are as follows and are also shown in the following screenshot:

- **DecimalPlaces**: This sets the number of decimal places in a Decimal data item.

- **BlankNumbers**, **BlankZero**, and **SignDisplacement**: All these can be used to influence the formatting and display of the data in the field.

- **MinValue** and **MaxValue**: These can constrain the range of data values allowed.

- **AutoIncrement**: This allows setting up of one field in a table to automatically increment for each record entered. This is almost always used to support automatic updating of a field used as the last field in a primary key, enabling creation of a unique key.

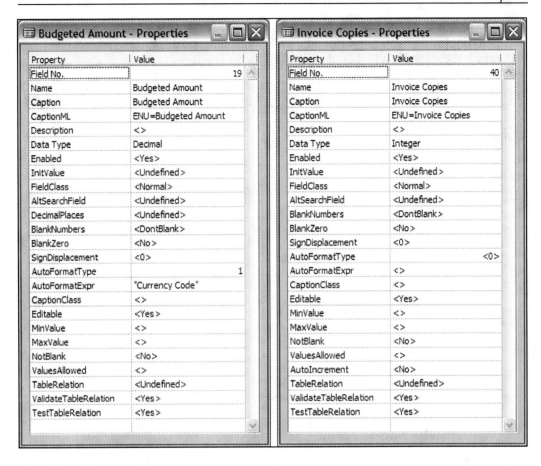

The field properties for an Integer field with a **FieldClass** property of FlowField are similar to those of a field with a **FieldClass** property of Normal. The differences relate to the fact that the field does not actually contain data but holds the formula by which the displayed value is calculated, as shown in the following screenshot overleaf.

Note the presence of the **CalcFormula** property and the absence of the **AltSearchField, AutoIncrement,** and **TestTableRelation** properties. Similar differences exist for FlowFields of other data types.

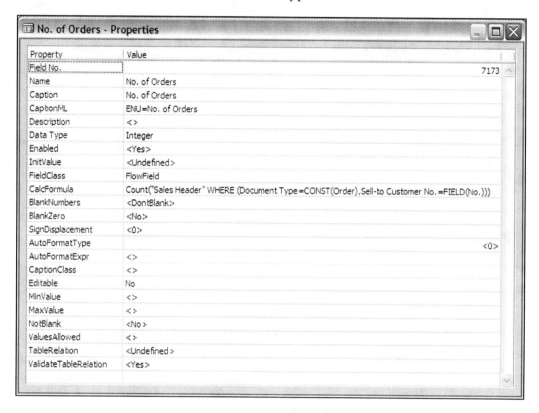

The properties for an Option data type, whose properties are shown in the following screenshot, are essentially like those of the other numeric data types, but with a data type-specific set of properties as described below:

- **OptionString**: This spells out the text interpretations for the stored integer values contained in Option data type fields.

- **OptionCaption** and **OptionCaptionML**: These serve the same captioning and multi-language purposes as other caption properties.

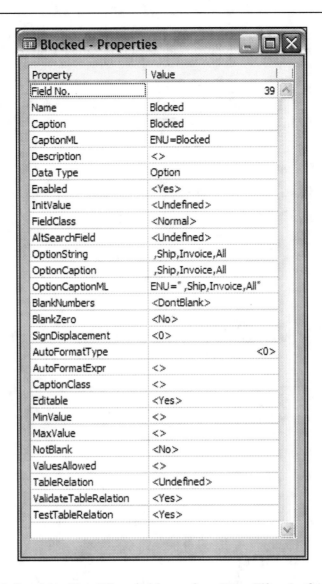

The properties defined for FlowFilter fields, such as **Date Filter** in the following screenshot overleaf, are similar to those of Normal data fields. Take a look at the **Date Filter** field (a **Date FlowFilter** field) and the **Global Dimension 1** Filter field (a **Code FlowFilter** field) in the Customer table. The **Date Filter** field property looks similar to a Normal **FieldClass** field.

The **Global Dimension 1** Filter field property values are different than those of the Date Filter because of the data type and its attributes rather than the fact that this is a FlowFilter field.

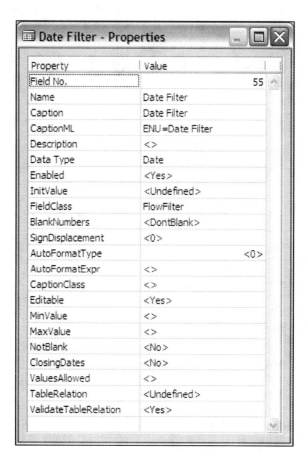

Field Numbering

The number of each field within its parent table object is the unique identifier that NAV uses internally to identify that field. You can easily change a field number when you are initially defining a table layout. But after you have a number of other objects (e.g. forms, reports, or codeunits) referencing the fields in a table, it becomes challenging (and therefore inefficient, sometimes to the point of almost impossible) to change the numbers of one or more fields. Therefore, you should plan ahead to minimize any need to renumber the fields. You should also be cautioned that, although you can physically delete a field and then reuse its field number for a different purpose, doing so is likely to cause you much grief.

You must take care about how the field numbers affect your users because the numeric sequence of fields within the table controls the sequence of the field names when they are displayed in field selection lists. These field selection lists are presented when a user or developer constructs a data Filter, does Form or Report Designer field selection, views a zoom display or creates a default form or report. If the fields in a table are not in relatively logical sequence, or fields with a similar purpose are not grouped, the system will be harder to understand and therefore harder to use.

Unfortunately, that criticism could be made about the field sequence structure of some of the standard system's principle Master tables (e.g. Customer, Vendor, and Item). This has happened over a decade of changes and functional expansion. During that time, the original field numbers have largely remained unchanged in support of backward compatibility. At the same time, new related fields have been added in less than ideally related field number sequences. The result is a list of fields presented to users in a sequence that follows very few logical rules.

For new fields that you add to tables which are part of the standard NAV product, the new field numbers must be in the 50000 to 99999 number range, unless you have been explicitly licensed for another number range. Field numbers for fields in new tables that you create may be anything from 1 to 999,999,999 (without the commas).

Renumbering a Field

What if, after considering the layout of the fields in the Member table, it looks like it would make more sense to have the **Business Class** field sequenced after the **NAV Involvement Since** field (admittedly a very subjective and arbitrary design decision). Since we have not yet tied these fields to other objects in a complicated way, maybe it's still easy to do the renumbering.

Before we try the next experiment, make sure that you have data in your Member table for at least one Member. For this test, make sure the **Business Class** field is filled in. Now, open the Member table with the Designer, then renumber field **1010** (**Business Class**) to **1025**. Exit, save, and compile the table. Since you have data in field **1010**, you will get a message similar to the following screenshot:

Microsoft Dynamics NAV

⚠ You cannot delete or change the type of the Business Class field (in the Member table) before the value in the field is reduced to 0 (zero) or " (blank) in all records. This message occurred because a nonzero value was found for the record Member ID='42' in company CRONUS International Ltd..

[OK]

In the screenshot, NAV is explaining that you cannot make this change. Why not? Because, C/SIDE is checking the consistency of the definition of the stored data of that field in the table definition and that checking is based on the field number, not the field name. You are not allowed to change the field numbers when data is present in the field.

This particular situation comes up regularly when we are enhancing existing routines. For example, we want to reduce the size of a text field for some reason. If the data already in the table has any values that would exceed the new smaller field size, NAV will not allow us to make the change until we resolve the inconsistency. We can expand the field, because that will not create any inconsistency.

NAV acts like the understanding parent of a teenager. It gives us enough freedom to do lots of creative things on our own, but every now and then it warns us and keeps us from hurting ourselves.

Changing the Data Type of a Field

The larger issue here is the question of how to change the Data Type of a field. This change may be the result of a field renumbering, as we just saw in our experiment or it could be the result of an enhancement. Of course, if the change is at our discretion, we might decide simply not to do it. But what if we have no choice? For example, perhaps we had originally designed the Postal Zone field as an Integer to only handle US ZIP Codes, which are numeric. Then later we decide to generalize and allow postal codes for all countries. In that case, we must change our data field from integer to code, which allows all numerals and upper case letters.

In this case, how do we solve the data definition — data content inconsistency caused by the change? We have a couple of choices. The first option, which could work in our C/ANDL database because we have very little data and it's just test data, is simply to delete the existing data, proceed with our change, then restore the data through keyboard entry.

When dealing with a significant volume of production data (more typical when changing a production system), you must take a more conservative approach. Of course, more conservative means more work.

Let us look at the steps required for a common example of changing the data type because of a design change. In this example, we will assume that the field **110 Post Code** was defined as Data Type of **Integer** and we need to change it to Data Type of **Code**, Length **20**. The steps are as follows:

1. Create a new, temporary field **111** named **Temp Post Code**, data type **Code**, and Length **20**. Any allowable field number and unique name would work.

2. Copy the data from the original field **110 Post Code** into the new temporary field **111**, deleting the data from field 110 as you go, using a Processing Only report object created just for this purpose.

3. Redefine field **110** to new Data Type.

4. Copy the data from the temporary field **111** back into the redefined field **110**, deleting the data from field 111, using a second Processing Only report object created just for this purpose.

5. Delete the temporary field **111**.

If we had to renumber the fields, we would essentially have to do the same thing as just described, for each field. Whenever you attempt a change and see the earlier message, you will have to utilize the procedure just described.

What a lot of work just to make a minor change in a table! Hopefully, this convinces you of the importance of carefully considering how you define fields and field numbers initially. By the way, this is exactly the sort of process that Upgrade Data Conversions go through to change the field structure of a table in the database to support added capabilities of the new version.

Field Triggers

To see what field triggers are, let us look at our **Table 50000 Member**. Open the table in **Design** mode, highlight the **Member ID** field and press *F9*. The window shown in the following screenshot will appear:

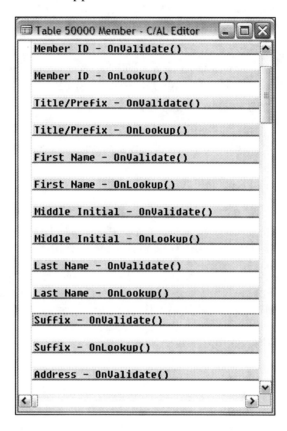

Each field has two triggers, the OnValidate() trigger and the OnLookup() trigger, which function as follows:

- OnValidate(): The C/AL code in this trigger is executed whenever an entry is made by the user. It can also be executed under program control through use of the VALIDATE function (which we will discuss later).

- OnLookup(): The C/AL code in this trigger is executed in place of the system's default Lookup behavior, even if the C/AL code is only a comment. Lookup behavior can be triggered by pressing *F6* or by clicking on the lookup arrow in a field as shown in following screenshot:

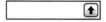

If the field's **TableRelation** property refers to a table and that table has a default **LookupFormID** defined, then the default behavior for that Lookup form is to display that form, to allow selection of an entry to be stored in this field. You may choose to override that behavior in a special case by coding different behavior.

 Be careful. Any entry whatsoever in the body of an OnLookup() trigger will eliminate the default behavior. This is true even if the entry is only a comment and there is no executable code present. A comment line could make an intended default lookup not occur

Some Data Structure Examples

Some good examples of tables in the standard product to review for particular features are:

- Table 18—Customer, for a variety of Data Types and Field Classes. This table contains some fairly complex examples of C/AL code in the table Triggers. A wide variety of field property variations can be seen in this table as well.
- Tables 21 and 32—Cust. Ledger Entry and Item Ledger Entry, for a variety of complex secondary key formats.
- Table 37—Sales Line, for the SumIndexFields attached to various keys.
- Table 50—Accounting Period, has a couple of very simple examples of Field OnValidate trigger C/AL code. For slightly more complex examples, take a look at Table 167—Job. For much more complex examples, you can look at almost all of the master tables such as Customer, Vendor, Item, etc.

You can find all the tables at **Tools | Object Designer**, by clicking on **Tables**.

More Definitions

Let's get some more basic definitions for NAV available, so we can make sure that our terminology is clear.

Data Type: This describes/defines what kind of data can be held in this storage element, whether it be numeric (e.g. integer, decimal), text, binary, time, date, Boolean, and so forth. The data type defines the constraints that are placed on what the contents of a data element can be, defines the functions in which that data element can be used, and defines what the results of certain functions will be.

Fundamental (Simple) data type: This has a simple structure consisting of a single value at one time, e.g. a number, string of text, character, etc.

Complex data type: This has a structure made up of or relating to simple data types, e.g. records, program objects such as Forms or Reports, BLOBs, DateFormulas, an external file, an indirect reference variable, etc.

Constant: This is a data element explicitly specified in the code by value, not modifiable 'on the fly', known in some circles as 'hard wired' data. All simple data types can be represented by constants.

Variable: This is a data element that can have a value assigned to it dynamically, as the program runs. Except for special cases, a variable will be of a single, unchanging, and specific data type.

Variable Naming

Variable names in NAV can either be global (defined across the breadth of an object) or local (defined only within a single function). Variable names must be unique within their sphere of definition. There must not be any duplication between global and local names. Even though the same local name can be used in more than one function within the same object, doing so can confuse the compiler. Therefore, you should make your working variable names unique within the object.

Variable names in NAV are not case sensitive. They are limited to 30 characters in length and can contain most of the standard ASCII character set.

Uniqueness includes not duplicating reserved words or system variables. That is an interesting challenge as there is no comprehensive published list of the reserved words available. A good guideline is to avoid using as a variable name any word that appears in either the C/SIDE Help or the Application Designer's Guide as an UPPER CASE word.

There is a 30-character length limit on variable names. Variable names can contain all ASCII characters except for control characters (ASCII values 0 to 31 and 255) and the asterisk (*, ASCII value 42). Note that the compiler won't tell you an asterisk cannot be used in a variable name. It is also a very good idea to avoid using the question mark (?, ASCII value 63).

The first character must be a letter A to Z (upper or lower case) or an underscore (_, ASCII value 95). It can be followed by any combination of the legal characters. If you use any characters other than the alphabet, numerals, and underscore, you must surround your variable name with double quotes (e.g. "cust list", which contains an embedded space, or "No." which contains a period). While the Application Designer's Guide doesn't tell you that you can't use a double quote character within a variable name, common sense and the compiler tell you not to do so.

Data Types

We are going to segregate the data types into relatively obvious groupings. Overall we will first look at Fundamental (aka simple) data types, and then Complex data types. Within fundamental data types, we will consider Numeric, String, and Time Types, while in complex data types we will look at Data Items, Data Structures, Objects, Automation, Input/Output, References, and others.

Fundamental Data Types

Fundamental data types are the basics from which the complex data types are formed. They are grouped into Numeric, String, and Time Data Types.

Numeric Data

Just like other systems, NAV allows several types of numeric data types. What numeric data types you may use and how you may use them will be dependent on whether you are designing your code to run only on the C/SIDE database, only on the SQL Server database, or to be database independent. If the C/SIDE database approach works on SQL Server, then that is the database-independent approach. For details on the SQL Server-specific representations of various data elements, you can refer to the Application Designer's Guide documentation. The various numeric data types are as follows:

- **Integer**: An integer number ranging from -2,147,483,648 to +2,147,483,647.

- **Decimal**: A decimal number ranging from -10^{63} to $+10^{63}$ stored in memory with 18 significant digits.

- **Option**: A special instance of an integer, stored as an integer number ranging from -2,147,483,548 to +2,147,483,547 (we have not identified any instances of the negative values being used for options). An option is normally represented in the body of your C/AL code as an option string. You can compare an option to an integer in C/AL rather than using the option string, but that is not a good practice because it eliminates the self-documenting aspect of an option field.

  An option string is a set of choices listed in a comma-separated string, one of which is chosen and stored as the current option. The currently selected choice within the set of options is stored as the ordinal position of that option within the set. For example, selection of an entry from the option string of red, yellow, blue would result in the storing of 0 (red), 1 (yellow), and 2 (blue). If red were selected, 0 would be stored in the variable; and if blue were selected, 2 would be stored.

- **Boolean**: These are stored as 1 or 0, programmatically referred to as True or False, but displayed as Yes or No.

- **Binary**: This is just what its name indicates, binary data. There are limited tools available to deal with binary data in NAV but, with persistent effort, it can be done.

- **BigInteger**: 8-byte Integer as opposed to the 4 bytes of Integer. BigIntegers are for very big numbers.

- **Char**: A numeric code between 0 and 256 representing an ASCII character. To some extent **Char** variables can operate either as text or as numeric. Numeric operations can be done on **Char** variables. **Char** variables can be defined with character values. **Char** variables cannot be defined as permanent variables in a table, but only as working variables within C/AL objects.

String Data

The following are the data types included in String Data:

- **Text**: This contains any string of alphanumeric characters from 1 to 250 characters long. The actual physical string in memory consists of a length byte plus the data. Thus an empty text field is only 1 byte long, providing the efficient use of space. When calculating the 'length' of a record for design purposes (relative to the maximum record length of 4096 characters), the full defined field length should be counted.

- **Code**: This contains any string of alphanumeric characters from 1 to 250 characters long. All letters are automatically converted to uppercase when entered. All numeric entry is automatically right justified on display, otherwise the entry display is left justified. SQL Server applies a somewhat different set of sorting rules for code fields than does the C/SIDE database.

Time Data

The following are the data types included in Time Data:

- **Date**: This contains an integer number, which is interpreted as a date ranging from January 1, 0 to December 31, 9999. A 0D (numeral zero, letter *dee*) represents an undefined date.

  A date constant can be written as a letter **D** preceded by either six digits in the format MMDDYY or eight digits as MMDDYYYY (where M = month, D = Day and Y = year). For example 011908D or 01192008D, both representing January 19, 2008. Later, in DateFormula, we will find D interpreted as Day, but here the trailing D is interpreted as date (data type) constant.

NAV also defines a special date called a "Closing" date, which represents the point in time between one day and the next. The purpose of a closing date is to provide a point at the end of a day, after all real date- and time-sensitive activity is recorded, when accounting "closing" entries can be recorded.

Closing entries are recorded, in effect, at the stroke of midnight between two dates i.e. this is the date of closing of accounting books, designed so that one can include or not include, at the user's option, closing entries in various reports. When sorted by date, the closing date entries will get sorted after all normal entries for a day. For example, the normal date entry for December 31, 2006 would display as 12/31/06 (depending on your date format masking), and the closing date entry would display as C12/31/06. All C12/31/06 ledger entries would appear after all normal 12/31/06 ledger entries. The following screenshot shows some **closing date entries** from **2003** and **2004**.

67350 Dues & Publications - General Ledger Entries

Posting ...	Docu...	Docume...	G/L Acco...	Description	Gen. P...	Gen. Bus...	G..	Amount
12/31/03	Payment	866	67350	12 mo subscription to Kiplinger's				1
C12/31/03		G00159	67350	Close Income Statement				-6
03/11/04	Invoice	PINV1492	67350	Kiplinger subscription thru 01/06	Purchase	STANDARD		1
04/30/04	Invoice	PINV1506	67350	Money Mag. 26 issues subscri...	Purchase	STANDARD		1
11/18/04	Invoice	PINV1601	67350	Business Week supbscription	Purchase	STANDARD		3
12/31/04	Invoice	PINV1633	67350	ACM 2005 membership dues	Purchase	STANDARD		9
C12/31/04		G00258	67350	Close Income Statement				-16
12/15/05	Invoice	PINV1860	67350	Chase: November 2005 purch...	Purchase	STANDARD		49
06/22/06	Invoice	PINV1985	67350	Chase MC June Statement	Purchase	STANDARD		11
▶ 10/08/06	Invoice	PINV2084	67350	APICS 2007 annual dues	Purchase	STAN.... ⬆		11

- **Time**: This contains an integer number, which is interpreted on a 24 hour clock, in milliseconds, from 00:00:00 to 23:59:59:999. A 0T (numeral zero, letter tee) represents an undefined time.

- **DateTime**: This represents a combined Date and Time, stored in Coordinated Universal Time (UTC) and always displays local time (i.e. the local time on your system). DateTime fields do not support NAV "Closing Date". DateTime values can range from January 1, 1754 00:00:00.000 to December 31, 9999 23:59:59.999. An undefined DateTime is 0DT.

- **Duration**: This represents the positive or negative difference between two DateTime values, in milliseconds.

Complex Data Types

Complex Data Types are constructed from the Fundamental Data Types. They are grouped into Data Item, Date Formula, Data Structure, Objects, Automation, Input/Output, References, and Other.

Data Item

The data types included in Data Item are as follows:

- **BLOB**: This can contain either a graphic in the form of a bitmap or specially formatted text or other developer-defined binary data, up to 2 GB in size. The term BLOB stands for Binary Large OBject. BLOBs can be included in tables.

- **BigText**: This can contain large chunks of text, up to 2GB in size. For working storage, BigText data are not included in tables for permanent storage, BigText data must be moved to BLOB variables. BigText variables cannot be directly displayed or seen in the debugger. There is a group of functions that can be used to handle BigText data (e.g. to move it to or from a BLOB, to read or write BigText data, to find a substring, to move data back and forth between BigText and normal Text variables, etc.).

 If you wish to handle text strings in a single data element greater than 250 characters in length, you can use a combination of BLOB and BigText variables.

- **GUID**: This is used to assign a unique identifying number to any database object. GUID stands for Globally Unique Identifier, a 16-byte binary data type that is used for the unique global identification of records, objects, etc. The GUID is generated by an algorithm created by Microsoft.

DateFormula

The only data type defined in DateFormula is as follows:

DateFormula, provides the storage of a simple, but clever set of constructs to support the calculation of run-time sensitive dates. A DateFormula is a combination of:

- Numeric multipliers (e.g. 1, 2, 3, 4…)
- Alpha time units (all must be upper case)
  - D for a day
  - W for a week

- WD for day of the week, i.e. day 1 through day 7 (either in the future or in the past, not today), Monday is day 1, Sunday is day 7
- M for calendar month
- CM for current month
- P for accounting period
- Y for year

- Math symbols
  - + (plus) as in CM + 10D means the Current Month end plus 10 Days or the 10th of next month
  - – (minus) as in –WD3 means the date of the previous Wednesday

- Positional notation (D15 means the 15th of the month and 15D means 15 days)

Payment Terms for Invoices make very productive use of DateFormula. All DateFormula results are expressed as a date based on a reference date. The default reference date is the system date, not the Work Date.

Here are some sample DateFormulas and their interpretations (displayed dates are based on the US calendar) with a reference date of March 9, 2007, a Friday:

- CM = the last day of Current Month, 03/31/07
- CM + 10D = the 10th of next month, 04/10/07
- WD6 = the next sixth day of week, 03/10/07
- WD5 = the next fifth day of week, 03/17/07
- CM – M + D = the end of the current month minus one month plus one day, 03/01/07
- CM – M = the end of the current month minus one month, 02/28/07

Let us do some experimenting with some hands-on evaluations of several DateFormula values. What we will do is create a table that will calculate the entered dates using DateFormula and Reference Dates.

First, create a table using the **Table Designer** as you did in earlier instances. Go to **Tools | Object Designer | Tables**. Click on the **New** button and define the fields as in the following screenshot. Save it as **Table 60000**, named **Date Formula Test**. After you are done with this test, we will save this table for some later testing.

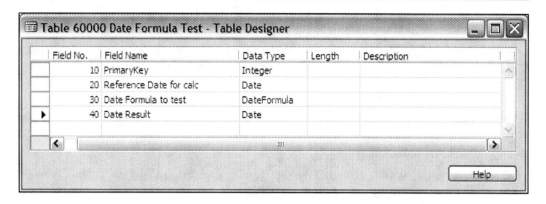

Now we will add some simple C/AL code to our table so that when we enter or change either the Reference Date or the DateFormula data, we can calculate a new result date.

First, access the new table via the **Design** button, then go to the global variables definition form through the **View** menu option, suboption **Globals,** and then choose the **Functions** tab. Type in our new Function's, name as CalculateNewDate on the first blank line as shown in the following screenshot and then exit from this form back to the list of data fields.

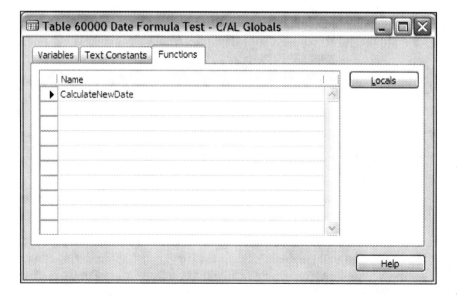

From the list of data fields, either press *F9* or click on the **C/AL Code** icon:

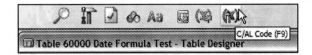

In the following screenshot, you will see all the field triggers plus the trigger for the new function you just defined, all ready for you to add some C/AL code. The table triggers are not visible unless we scroll up to show them.

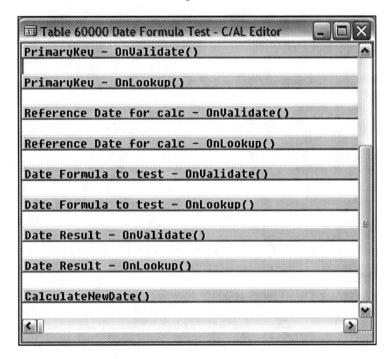

Since our goal this time is to focus on experimenting with the DateFormula, we are not going to go into much detail about the logic we are creating. Hopefully, your past experience will allow you to understand the essence of the code.

We are simply going to create the logic within our new function, `CalculateNewDate()`, to evaluate and store a result date based on the DateFormula and Reference Date that we enter into the table.

Just copy the C/AL code exactly as shown in the following screenshot, exit, compile, and save your table.

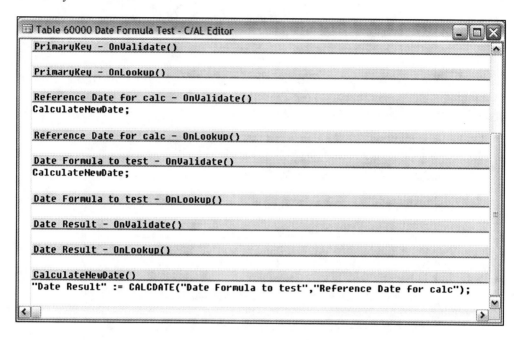

When you close and save the table, if you get an error message of any type, you probably have not copied the C/AL code exactly as it is shown in the screenshot.

This code will cause the function `CalculateNewDate()` to be called any time an entry is made in either the **Reference Date for calc** or the **Date Formula to test** fields. The result will be placed in the **Date Result** field. The use of an integer value in the redundantly named **PrimaryKey** field allows you to enter several records into the table (by numbering them 1, 2, 3, and so forth) and also allows you to compare the results of date calculations using several different formulae.

Let us try a few examples. We will access the table via the Run button. Enter a **Primary Key** value of 1 (i.e. one).

```
PrimaryKey = 1
```

For **Reference Date for calc** enter the letter **t** (*tee*), upper case or lower case, it doesn't matter. That will give you the date for Today, whatever the system date is while experimenting. The same date will appear in the **Date Result** field, because at this point there is no DateFormula entered. Now enter **1D** (numeral **1** followed by the letter *dee*, upper case or lower case, C/SIDE will take care of making it upper case) in the **Date Formula to test** field. You will see the **Date Result** field contents are changed to be one day beyond the date in the **Reference Date for calc** field.

Let us enter another line. Start with a numeral 2 in the **PrimaryKey** field. Again, enter the letter **t** (*tee*) in the **Reference Date for calc** field and just enter the letter **W** in the **Date Formula to test** field. You should get an error message telling you that your formulas should include a number. Make the system happy and enter **1W**. You should see a date in the **Date Result** field that is one week beyond your testing date.

Set the system's Work Date to a date about in the middle of a month. Start another line with the number 3 in the Primary Key, followed by a **W** (for Work Date) in the **Reference Date for calc** field. Enter **cm** (or CM or cM or Cm, it doesn't matter) in the **Date Formula to test** field. Your result date will be the last day of your work-date month. Now enter another line using the Work Date, but enter a formula of **–cm** (the same as before, but with a minus sign). This time your result date will be the first day of your work-date month.

Enter another line with a new Primary Key. Skip over the **Reference Date for calc** field and just enter **1D** in the **Date Formula to test** field. What happens? You get an error message. NAV cannot deal with making calculation without a Reference Date. If we put this function into production, we might enhance our code to check for a Reference Date before calculating. We could default an empty date to the System Date or the Work Date and avoid this particular error.

The following screenshot shows more sample calculations. Build on these and experiment on your own. You can create lots of different algebraic formulae and get some very interesting results. One NAV user has due dates on Invoices on 10th of the next month. The Invoices are dated at various times during the month they are actually printed. But by using the DateFormula of **CM + 10D**, the due date is always the 10th of the next month.

Date Formula Test - Table

PrimaryKey	Reference D...	Date Formula to test	Date Result
1	09/25/08	1D	09/26/08
2	09/18/08	1W	09/25/08
3	09/18/08	-1W	09/11/08
4	09/25/08	1M	10/25/08
5	09/25/08	-1M	08/25/08
6	09/25/08	CM	09/30/08
7	09/25/08	-CM	09/01/08
8	09/25/08	-CM-1D	08/31/08
9	09/25/08	CM+1D	10/01/08
10	02/15/08	CM	02/29/08
11	02/15/08	CM+1D	03/01/08
12	03/15/08	-CM	03/01/08
13	03/15/08	-CM-1D	02/29/08
14	03/15/07	-CM-1D	02/28/07

Help

Don't forget to test with WD (weekday), P (period), Q (quarter), and Y (year).

It may seem that we overemphasized this experiment. But you got to see a lot more here than just date calculations.

- You created a new table, just for the purpose of experimenting with a C/AL feature that you might use. This is a technique that comes in handy when you are learning a new feature, trying to decide how it works or how you might use it.

- We put some critical logic in the table. When data is entered in one area, the entry is validated and, if valid, the defined processing is done instantly.

- We created a common routine as a new function. That function is then called from multiple places to which it applies.

- We did our entire test with a table object and a default tabular form that is automatically generated when you **Run** a table. We didn't have to create much of a supporting structure to do our testing. Of course, when you are designing a change to a complicated existing structure, it is likely that you will have a more complicated testing scenario. But one of your goals will always be to simplify your testing scenarios to both minimize the setup effort and to keep your test narrowly focused on the specific issue.

- We saw how NAV tools make a variety of relative date calculations easy. These are very useful in business applications, many aspects of which are very date centered.

Data Structure

The following are the data types in Data Structure:

- **File**: This refers to any standard Windows file outside the NAV database. There is a reasonably complete set of functions to allow creating, deleting, opening, closing, reading, writing and copying (among other things) data files. For example, you could create your own NAV routines in C/AL to import or export data from a file that had been created by some other application.

- **Record**: This refers to a single line of data within a NAV table. Quite often multiple instances of a table are defined for access, to support some validation process. The working storage variable for the table will be of the data type Record.

Objects

Form, **Report**, **Dataport**, **Codeunit**, **XMLPort**, each represents an object of the type Form, Report, Dataport, Codeunit or XMLPort respectively. Object data types are used when there is a need for reference to an object or some portion of an object from within another object. Examples are cases where one object invokes another (e.g. calling a Report object from a Form object or from another Report object) or where one object is taking advantage of data validation logic that is coded as a function in a Table object or a Codeunit object.

Automation

The following are the data types in Automation:

- **OCX:** This allows the definition of a variable that represents and allows access to an ActiveX or OCX custom control. Such a control is typically another, external application object, small or large, which you can then invoke from your NAV object.

- **Automation:** This allows the definition of a variable that you may access similarly to an OCX but is more likely to be a complete independent application. The application must act as an Automation Server and must be registered with the NAV client calling it. For example, you can interface from NAV into the various Microsoft Office products (e.g. Word, Excel) by defining them in Automation variables.

Input/Output

The following are the data types in Input/Output:

- **Dialog:** This allows the definition of a simple user interface window without the use of a Form object. Typically, dialog windows are used to communicate processing progress or to allow a brief user response to a go/no-go question. There are other user communication tools as well, but they do not use a dialog data item.

- **InStream** and **Outstream:** These are variables that allow reading from and writing to external files, BLOBS, and objects of the Automation and OCX data types.

References and Other

The following data types are used for advanced functionality in NAV, typically supporting some type of interface with an external object.

- **RecordID**: This contains the object number and primary key of a table.

- **RecordRef**: This identifies a field in a table and thereby allows access to the contents of that field.

- **KeyRef**: This identifies a key in a table and the fields it contains.

- **Variant**: This defines variables typically used for interfacing with Automation and OCX objects. Variant variables can contain data of a number of other data types.

- **TableFilter**: This defines variables used only by the permissions table related to security functions.

Data Type Usage

Some data types can be used to define permanently stored data (i.e. in tables) or working storage data definitions (i.e. within a Global or Local data definition within an object). A couple of data types can only be used to define permanently stored data. A much larger set of data types can only be used for working storage data definitions.

The list in the following screenshot shows which data types can be used where:

Table Data Types	Working Storage Data Types
	Action
	Automation
	BigInteger
	BigText
Binary	Binary
Blob	
Boolean	Boolean
	Char
Code	Code
	Codeunit
	Dataport
Date	Date
DateFormula	DateFormula
DateTime	DateTime
Decimal	Decimal
	Dialog
	Duration
	FieldRef
	File
	Form
GUID	GUID
	Instream
Integer	Integer
	KeyRef
	OCX
Option	Option
	Outstream
	Record
RecordID	RecordID
	RecordRef
	Report
TableFilter	
Text	Text
Time	Time
	TransactionType
	Variant
	XMLport

FieldClasses

Each data field has a Field Class Property. We will cover most of the properties in the next chapter, but the FieldClass has as much affect on the content and usage of a data field as does the data type, maybe even more in some instances. For that reason, we will discuss FieldClasses as a follow-on to our discussion on Data Types.

The following are the three FieldClasses:

- **Normal**: The FieldClass containing all the 'normal' data. If the FieldClass is Normal, then the field contains just what you would expect, based on the Data Type and all the descriptions.

- **FlowField**: The FieldClass that connects a datafield to a previously defined SumIndexField in a table. The FlowField is an important and controlling property of a field. FlowFields do not contain data in any conventional sense. They are really virtual fields. A FlowField contains the definition of how to calculate the data that it represents at run time.

  A FlowField value is always 0, unless something happens to cause it to be calculated. If the FlowField is displayed directly on a form, then it is calculated automatically on initial display. FlowFields are also automatically calculated when they are the subject of predefined filters as part of the properties of a Data Item in an object (this will be explained in more detail in the chapters covering Reports and Dataports). In all other cases, a FlowField must be forced to calculate using the C/AL `<Record>.CALCFIELDS` function. This is also true if the underlying data is changed after the initial display of a form (i.e. the FlowField must be recalculated to take the change into account).

 Because a FlowField does not contain any actual data, it cannot be used as a field in a key.

When a data item has its FieldClass set to FlowField, another directly associated property becomes available: **CalcFormula**. The CalcFormula is the place where you can define the formula for calculating the FlowField. This formula consists of five components as follows:

- FlowField type (aka Method)
- Sign control (aka Reverse Sign)
- Table
- Field
- Table Filter

On the CalcFormula property line, there is an ellipsis button displayed. Clicking on that button will bring up the form similar to the following screenshot:

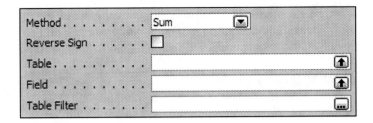

The following screenshot shows seven FlowField types:

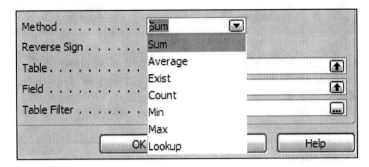

The explanation of the seven FlowFields is given in the following table:

FlowField Type	Field Data Type	Description (in all cases it applies to the specified set within a specific column in a table (i.e. field)
Sum	Decimal	The sum total
Average	Decimal	The average value (i.e. the sum divided by the count)
Exist	Boolean	Yes or No, does an entry exist?
Count	Integer	The number of entries that exist
Min	Any	The smallest value of any entry
Max	Any	The largest value of any entry
Lookup	Any	The value of the specified entry

The **Reverse Sign** control allows you to change the displayed sign of the result for FlowField types Sum and Average only; the underlying data is not changed.

Table and **Field** allow you to define to what Table and to what Field within that table your Calculation Formula will apply. When you make the entries in your Calculation Formula screen, there is no validation checking by the compiler that you have chosen an eligible table–field combination. That checking doesn't occur until run time. Therefore, when you are creating a new FlowField, you should test it as soon as you get it defined.

The last, but by no means least significant, component of the FlowField Calculation Formula is the **Table Filter**. When you click on the ellipsis in the table filter field, the window shown in the following screenshot will appear:

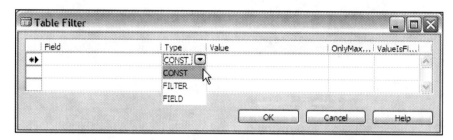

When you click on the **Field** column, you will be invited to select a field from the table that was entered into the **Table field** earlier. This field will have the filter rules you define on this line, which will also indicate which type of filter is this. The explanation is given in the following table:

Filter Type	Value Description	Filtering Action	OnlyMax-Limit	Valuels-Filter
Const	A constant which will be defined in the Value field	Uses the constant to filter for equally valued entries		
Filter	A filter which will be spelled out as a literal in the Value field	Applies the filter expression from the Value field		
Field	A field from the table within which this FlowField exists	Uses the contents of the specified field to filter for equally valued entries	False	False
		If the specified field is a FlowFilter and the OnlyMaxLimit parameter is True, then the FlowFilter range will be applied on the basis of only having a Max Limit, i.e. having no bottom limit. For example, this is useful for date filters for Balance Sheet data.	True	False
		If the specified field is a FlowFilter and the OnlyMaxLimit parameter is True, then the FlowFilter range will be applied on the basis of only having a Max Limit, i.e. having no bottom limit. For example, this is useful for date filters for Balance Sheet data.	False	True

- **FlowFilters**: These do not contain any information permanently. They are defined for the purpose of holding filters on a per user basis, with the information being stored at the local workstation. A FlowFilter field allows a filter to be entered at a parent record level by the user (e.g. G/L Account) and applied (through the use of FlowField formulas, for example) to constrain what child data (e.g. G/L Entry records) is selected.

A FlowFilter allows you to provide very flexible data selection functions to the users in a way that is very simple to understand. The user does not need to have a full understanding of the data structure to apply filtering in intuitive ways, not just to the primary data table but also to the subordinate data. Based on your C/AL code design, FlowFilters can be used to apply filtering on more than one subordinate table. Of course, it is your responsibility as the developer to make good use of this tool. As with many C/AL capabilities, a good way to learn more is by studying standard code.

A number of good examples on the use of FlowFilters can be found in the Customer (Table 18) and Item (Table 27) tables. In the Customer table, some of the FlowFields using FlowFilters are Balance, Balance (LCY), Net Change, Net Change (LCY), Sales (LCY), and Profit (LCY). There are others as well. The **Sales (LCY)** FlowField FlowFilter usage is shown in the following screenshot:

Similarly constructed FlowFields using FlowFilters in the Item table include Inventory, Net Invoiced Qty. Net Change, Purchases (Qty.), and a whole host of other fields.

Throughout the standard code there are a number of FlowFilters that appear in most of the Master table definitions. These are the Date Filter and Global Dimension Filters (Global Dimensions are user defined codes to facilitate the segregation of accounting data by meaningful business break-outs such as divisions, departments, projects, customer type, etc.). Other FlowFilters that are widely used in the standard code, for example, related to Inventory activity, are Location Filter, Lot No. Filter, Serial No. Filter, and Bin Filter.

Filtering

As mentioned earlier, filtering is one of the very powerful tools within NAV C/AL. Filtering is the application of defined limits on the data to be considered in a process. Filter structures can be applied in at least three different ways, depending on the design of the process. The first way is for the developer to fully define the filter structure and the value of the filter. This might be done in a report designed to show only information on a selected group of customers, for example those with an open Balance on Account. The Customer table would be filtered to report only customers who have an Outstanding Balance greater than zero.

The second way is for the developer to define the filter structure, but allow the user to fill in the specific value to be applied. This approach would be appropriate in an accounting report that was to be tied to specific accounting periods. The user would be allowed to define what period(s) were to be considered for each report run.

The third way is the ad hoc definition of a filter structure and value by the user. This approach is often used for general analysis of ledger data where the developer wants to give the user total flexibility in how they slice and dice the available data.

It is quite common within the standard NAV applications and in the course of enhancements to use a combination of the different filtering types. For example, the report just mentioned that lists only customers with an open Balance on Account (via a developer-defined filter) could also allow the user to define additional filter criteria. Perhaps, the user wants to see only Euro currency-based customers, so they would filter on the Customer Currency Code field.

Filters are an integral part of FlowFields and FlowFilters, two of the three Field Classes. These are very flexible and powerful tools, which allow the NAV designer to create forms, reports, and other processes that can be used by the user under a wide variety of circumstances for various purposes. In most systems, user inquiries (forms and reports) and processes need to be quite specific to different data types and ranges. The NAV C/AL toolset allows you to create relatively generic user inquiries and processes and then allow the user to apply filtering to fit their specific needs.

Defining Filter Syntax and Values

Let us go over some common ways in which we can define filter values and syntax. Remember, when you apply a filter, you will only view or process records where the filtered data field satisfies the limits defined by the filter.

- Equality and inequality
  - either an equal (=) sign or no sign filters for data "equal to" the filter value.

Data Type - description	Example Filters
Integer	=200
Integer	200
Text	Chicago
Text	" (two single quote marks)

  - a greater than (>) sign filters for data greater than the filter value

Data Type - description	Example Filters
Integer	>200
Date	>10/06/07
Decimal	>450.50

  - a less than (<) sign filters for data less than the filter value

Data Type - description	Example Filters
Integer	<150
Date	<10/07/07

  - the equal sign can be combined with the greater than (>=) or less than (<=) signs to filter for data "greater than or equal" OR "less than or equal" to the filter value

Data Type - description	Example Filters
Integer	<=100
Date	<=12/31/07
Date	>=1/1/08
Text	'>= Grade B

- Not Equal is represented by the combination of the "less than" symbol plus the "Greater than" symbol to filter for data not equal to the filter value

Data Type - description	Example Filters
Integer	<>1
Date	<>TODAY (TODAY is a system variable representing the current system date
Boolean	<>yes (an awkward way of stating "No"

- Ranges
  - Ranges are defined by an expression containing two dots in a row (in other words ..). Ranges are inclusive, that is the maximum and minimum values are included within the range. Ranges have three variations. The first is the from - to version which includes both a bottom end or minimum to the range and a top end or maximum.

Data Type - description	Example Filters
Integer	1..10
Date	5/1/07..5/31/07
Text	Jones..Smith
Decimal	100.01..199.99

  - The second range variation consists of the range operator (the two dots ..) plus a range maximum This means "give me all the values from the lowest possible value up to and including the range maximum. This is generally the same as using the less than or equal to (<=) format.

Data Type - description	Example Filters
Integer	..10 (Gives the same results as <=10)
Date	..12/31/07
Decimal	..99.99

○ The third range variation consists of a lower limit (minimum) value flowed by the range operator (..).

Data Type - description	Example Filters
Integer	100.. (Gives the same results as >=100)
Date	1/1/07..
Decimal	100000.00..

- Boolean operators

  ○ There are two Boolean operators. The operators are the ampersand sign (&) representing the logical AND operation and the pipe symbol (|) representing the logical OR operation.

  ○ The OR operator can be used to create a discontinuous set of allowed values.

Data Type - description	Example Filters
Integer	5|10|15|20 (This will give you matches on all four of the stated values and only on those values.)
Date	10/1/07|11/1/07|12/1/07 (This filter will pass through on records dated on the first date of the three months)

  ○ The AND operator can generally only be used in combination with other filtering operators.

Data Type - description	Example Filters
Integer	(>=100) & (<=1000) (Gives the same result as the range 100.1000)
Date	<>TODAY (TODAY is a system variable representing the current system date
Boolean	<>yes (an awkward way of stating "No"

- Wild cards
  - There are three wild card characters that can be used within filter constructs. Wild cards only apply to string data. You will not find the term wildcard defined or the usage of wildcards described in the Microsoft documentation or **Help**.
  - Asterisk (*) represents any character and any number of characters.

Data Type - description	Example Filters
Text	*st* (Includes all data containing the lowercase letters 'st')
Text	st* (Includes only the data starting with the lowercase letters 'st')
Text	*st (Includes only the data ending with the lowercase letters 'st')

  - Question mark (?) represents any character, but only one character.

Data Type - description	Example Filters
Text	?st? (Includes all data which is four characters long with the middle two characters being the lowercase letters 'st')
Text	????st (Includes all data which is exactly six characters long ending with the lowercase letters 'st')

  - "At" symbol (@) eliminates case sensitivity for the value following. The @ is often used in combination with the asterisk to make the filter value satisfy a wider range of data

Data Type - description	Example Filters
Text	*@st* (Includes all data containing any of the strings 'st', 'St', 'ST' or 'sT')
Text	@*st* (Gives the same results as the previous example)

- Combinations – Many of these filter constructs can be used in combination. Again, the caution applies about thoroughly testing your creations before inflicting them on unsuspecting users. It is relatively easy to create a filter which, on initial thought seems logical, but which won't work the way you thought it would. In addition, the C/AL compiler routine which interprets filters is not perfect. It can get confused or just fail.

Be very cautious about using combinations that contain wildcards, especially (but not limited to) those expressions containing both wildcards and Boolean operators. Be very cautious about constructing filters based on exclusions. Generally, the limited "inclusive" approach works better. For example, you might want to print a Customer list excluding all Customers for the Salespeople with codes of JR and MD.

You might try create a filter on Salesperson Code such as **(<>JR) AND (<>MD)**. The C/SIDE routine that checks filter will not accept that as a valid entry. The same goes for **<> (JR AND MD)**, as well as the attempt to put in two separate filter entries (only one filter string is allowed per data field.). What to do?

To simplify, let us assume all our Salesperson Code are just two characters long. You should create a filter on the Salesperson Code in the form **(..JQ) | (JP..MC) | (ME..)**. This translates to all the Customers having either a Salesperson Code less than or equal to JQ or (the pipe symbol: |) from JP to MC or greater than or equal to ME. In other words, all the two character codes except JR and MD.

Experimenting with Filters

Now it is the time for you to do some creative experimenting with filters. We want to accomplish several things through our experimentation. Our first purpose is to get more comfortable with how filters are entered. Secondly, we want to see the effects of different types of filter structures and combinations. If we had a database with a large volume of data in it, we could also experience the speed of effecting the filtering on fields in keys and fields not in keys. But the amount of data in the Cronus database is small and our computers are very fast, so any speed differences will be difficult to see.

We could experiment on any report that allows filtering. To give us some options for our experimentation, we will use the **Customer/Item List**. This will report which Customer purchased what Items. The **Customer/Item** List can be accessed on the NAV user menu via **Sales & Marketing | Reports | Customer | Customer/Item List**.

When you initially run the **Customer/Item** List, you will see just three data fields listed for entry of Filters on the Customer table as shown in the following screenshot:

There are also three data fields listed for entry of Filters on the Value Entry table as shown in the following screenshot:

In each case, these are the fields that the developer determined should be emphasized. If you run the report without any filters at all, using the standard Cronus data, the contents of the first page of the report will resemble the following screenshot:

Item No.	Description	Invoiced Quantity	Unit of Me	Amount	Discount Amount	Profit	Profit %
10000	The Cannon Group PLC						
	Phone No.						
70011	Glass Door	5	PCS	361.50	0.00	177.00	49.0
1920-S	ANTWERP Conference Table	0	PCS	0.00	0.00	0.00	0.0
1964-W	INNSBRUCK Storage Unit/G.Door	10	PCS	2,920.00	0.00	1,208.00	41.4
1968-S	MEXICO Swivel Chair, black	3	PCS	351.40	18.50	63.10	18.0
1996-S	ATLANTA Whiteboard, base	7	PCS	6,029.56	317.34	1,079.16	17.9
	The Cannon Group PLC			9,662.46	335.84	2,527.26	26.2
20000	Selangorian Ltd.						
	Phone No.						
1896-S	ATHENS Desk	0	PCS	0.00	0.00	0.00	0.0
1928-S	AMSTERDAM Lamp	5	PCS	172.66	5.34	33.66	19.5
766BC-C	CONTOSO Storage System	0	PCS	0.00	0.00	0.00	0.0
	Selangorian Ltd.			172.66	5.34	33.66	19.5
30000	John Haddock Insurance Co.						
	Phone No.						
1920-S	ANTWERP Conference Table	0	PCS	0.00	0.00	0.00	0.0
8908-W	Computer - Highline Package	3	PCS	342.60	0.00	342.60	100.0
8924-W	Server - Enterprise Package	1	PCS	346.30	0.00	346.30	100.0
	John Haddock Insurance Co.			688.90	0.00	688.90	100.0
40000	Deerfield Graphics Company						
	Phone No.						
8908-W	Computer - Highline Package	3	PCS	342.60	0.00	342.60	100.0
8916-W	Computer - TURBO Package	2	PCS	374.20	0.00	374.20	100.0
8924-W	Server - Enterprise Package	1	PCS	346.30	0.00	346.30	100.0
	Deerfield Graphics Company			1,063.10	0.00	1,063.10	100.0

If you want to print information only for customers whose names begin with a letter **A**, your filter will be very simple, similar to the following screenshot:

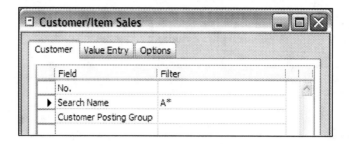

The resulting report will be similar to the following screenshot, showing only data for the two customers on file whose names begin with the letter A.

Customer: Search Name: A*

Item No.	Description	Invoiced Quantity	Unit of Me	Amount	Discount Amount	Profit	Profit %
32656565	Antarcticopy						
	Phone No.						
70011	Glass Door	1	PCS	61.45	10.84	24.55	40.0
1960-S	ROME Guest Chair, green	7	PCS	875.70	0.00	193.20	22.1
1968-S	MEXICO Swivel Chair, black	4	PCS	493.20	0.00	108.80	22.1
1976-W	INNSBRUCK Storage Unit/W.Door	5	PCS	1,152.46	128.05	399.46	34.7
	Antarcticopy			2,582.81	138.89	726.01	28.1
49633663	Autohaus Mielberg KG						
	Phone No.						
1896-S	ATHENS Desk	12	PCS	7,792.79	0.00	1,713.59	22.0
1906-S	ATHENS Mobile Pedestal	13	PCS	3,658.20	0.00	804.70	22.0
1968-S	MEXICO Swivel Chair, black	5	PCS	616.50	0.00	136.00	22.1
1972-S	MUNICH Swivel Chair, yellow	6	PCS	739.80	0.00	163.20	22.1
	Autohaus Mielberg KG			12,807.29	0.00	2,817.49	22.0
Total				15,390.10	138.89	3,543.50	23.0

If you want to expand the customer fields on which you can apply filters, click on the first empty field and you will see something similar to the following screenshot. The size of the pop-up window can be stretched as large as your display image allows and you can then scroll down to see rest of the fields.

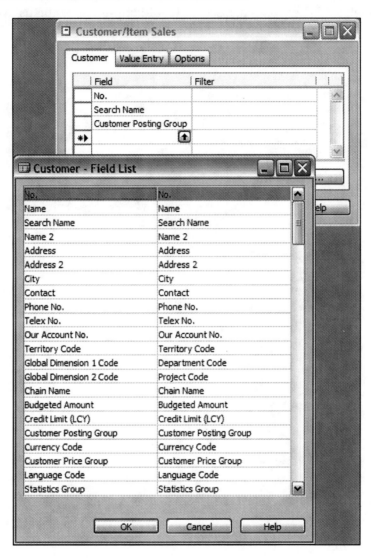

This provides us access to all the fields in the customer record, the table identified in the Tab heading. From this list we can choose one or more fields and then enter filters on those fields. If we chose **Territory Code**, for example, then the Request Form would look similar to the following screenshot. And if we clicked on the lookup arrow in the **Filter** column, a screen would pop-up allowing us to choose data items from the related table, in this case, `Territories`.

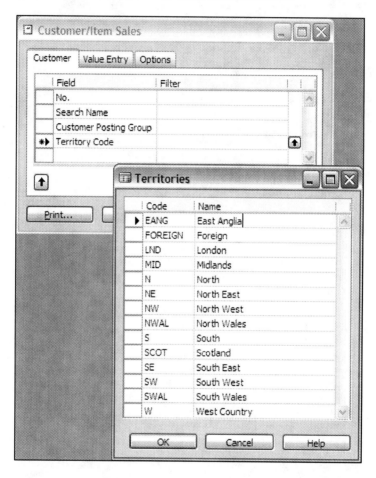

This particular Request Form has tabs for each of the two primary tables in the report. Click on the **Value Entry** tab to filter on the Item-related data. If we filter on the **Item No.** for Item No's that contain the letter **W**, the report will be similar to the following screenshot:

Value Entry: Item No.: *W*						
Item No.	Description	Invoiced Quantity	Unit of Me	Amount	Discount Amount	Profit
						Profit %
10000	The Cannon Group PLC					
	Phone No.					
1964-W	INNSBRUCK Storage Unit/G.Door	10	PCS	2,920.00	0.00	1,208.00 41.4
	The Cannon Group PLC			2,920.00	0.00	1,208.00 41.4
30000	John Haddock Insurance Co.					
	Phone No.					
8908-W	Computer - Highline Package	3	PCS	342.60	0.00	342.60 100.0
8924-W	Server - Enterprise Package	1	PCS	346.30	0.00	346.30 100.0
	John Haddock Insurance Co.			688.90	0.00	688.90 100.0
40000	Deerfield Graphics Company					
	Phone No.					
8908-W	Computer - Highline Package	3	PCS	342.60	0.00	342.60 100.0
8916-W	Computer - TURBO Package	2	PCS	374.20	0.00	374.20 100.0
8924-W	Server - Enterprise Package	1	PCS	346.30	0.00	346.30 100.0
	Deerfield Graphics Company			1,063.10	0.00	1,063.10 100.0
50000	Guildford Water Department					
	Phone No.					
1984-W	SARAJEVO Whiteboard, blue	10	PCS	0.00	0.00	-7,086.00 0.0
8916-W	Computer - TURBO Package	1	PCS	187.10	0.00	187.10 100.0
8924-W	Server - Enterprise Package	1	PCS	346.30	0.00	346.30 100.0
	Guildford Water Department			533.40	0.00	-6,552.60 -1,228.5

If we want to see all the items containing either the letter W or the letter S, our filter would be *W* | *S*. If you made the filter **W | S**, then you would get only entries equal exactly to W or to S because we didn't use any wild cards.

You should go back over the various types of filters we discussed and try them all. Then you should try some combinations. Get creative! Try some things that may or may not work and see what happens. Explore a variety of reports or list screens in the system and try applying filters to see what happens. A good screen to which to apply filters is the Customer List (**Sales & Marketing** menu | **Sales** | **Customers** | *F5*). This is supposed to be a non-threatening learning experience (you can't hurt anything or anyone).

This is also an opportunity to learn more about the NAV User Interface, because that is what you must use to do your filtering. There are four buttons at the top of the screen that relate to filtering, plus one for choosing the active key. In Windows XP, they look like the following screenshot:

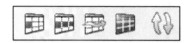

From left to right, they are as follows:

- **Field Filter** (*F7*) — Highlight a field, press *F7* (or select **View | Field Filter**), and the data in that field will appear in a display ready for you to define a filter on that data field. You can edit the filter in any way before you click **OK**.

- **Table Filter** (*Ctrl+F7*) — Press the *Ctrl* Key and *F7* simultaneously (or select **View | Table Filter**). You will be presented with a form that allows you to choose any number of fields in the left column and, in the right column, enter filters to apply to those fields. Each of these individual filters is a Field Filter, the same as would have been applied using the Field Filter option just described. The filters for the individual fields are "ANDed" together (i.e. they all apply simultaneously). If you invoke the Table Filter form when any Field Filters are already applied, they will be displayed.

- **Flow Filter** (*Shift+F7*) — Press the *Shift* Key and *F7* simultaneously (or select **View | Flow Filter**). You will be presented with a form that allows you to choose any number of fields in the left column and in the right column, enter filters to use with those fields. On initial display, it will show all the Flow Filter fields available. For any Flow Filter field, you can enter a filter, which will then be applied to the underlying data for FlowFields whose definition includes a constraint by that particular Flow Filter field.

  You can also use this form to enter Field Filters, but you will not be able to see the field filters that are already in effect via this form. To remove Flow Filters, you must call up this form and manually remove the filters, by deleting the filter lines or at least the filter values.

- **Show All** (*Shift+Ctrl+F7*) — This will remove all Field Filters, but will not remove any Flow Filters.
- **Sort** (*Shift+F7*) — allows you (or your user) to choose which key is active on a displayed data list (unless the underlying C/AL code overrules). By properly choosing a key that contains the field on which you wish to filter, you can significantly affect the speed of the filtering process. Of course this is true for filtering processes coded in C/AL as well.

When you are viewing a form and want to check if filters are in effect, check the bottom of the screen for the word FILTER as shown in the next image.

One of the most frequent support calls by new users seems to be "My data has disappeared." The proper response is "Does it say FILTER at the bottom of the screen?" Almost always the answer is "Yes", in which case the proper assistance is to use the Filter icons we just reviewed to inspect and/or clear unwanted filters (typically using the Table Filter and Flow Filter to inspect, possibly using the Show All and Flow Filter to clear filters.

Summary

In this chapter, we have focused on the basic building blocks of NAV data structure, fields and their attributes. We reviewed the types of data fields, properties, and trigger elements for each type of field. Then, we walked through a number of examples to illustrate most of these elements, though we have postponed exploring triggers until we have enough knowledge of C/AL coding techniques to make that worthwhile.

The Data Type and FieldClass determine what kind of data can be stored in a field. When you combine the table structure with properly designed fields, the essence of your application system design is defined. In this chapter, we have covered the broad range of Data Type options as well as the FieldClasses.

We also considered some examples of different types and classes, and discussed how they are used in an application. We dug into the date calculation tool that gives C/AL an edge in business applications. We also discussed Filtering in some detail, and how filtering is considered as we design our database structure, and how the users will access data. Finally, more of our NAV application was constructed with some features worth emulating in your own future designs.

In the next chapter, we will look at Forms in more detail and see how we can design Forms to take advantage of the data structures we have now put in place.

4
Forms

Form follows function — that has been misunderstood. Form and function should be one, joined in a spiritual union — Frank Lloyd Wright

While *Frank Lloyd Wright* may not have been referring to NAV Forms when he talked about form and function, what he said certainly applies to NAV systems. Forms are the window of the system through which the users can view the data in real time.

Forms and their functions must be one and the same to the users. If the forms bring attention to themselves rather than to the data that they expose or make harder for the users to see critical patterns and trends in the data, then the design has not been achieved as per Wright's goal of a "spiritual union".

In this chapter, we will explore the various types of forms that NAV offers you. We will review many of the options for formatting, for data access, and for tailoring your forms. We will also learn about the Form Designer tools and the inner structures of forms.

What Is a Form?

Forms serve the purpose of both input and output. Forms are views of data or process information designed for on-screen display only. Forms can also be a user data entry vehicle. Either type of form, card or tabular, can be used both for inquiry or data entry.

Controls

Controls are the containers on forms. They can display data, text, pictures, or the results of an expression in C/AL. Container controls, such as Frames and Tab pages, can contain other controls. Frames make it easy for the developer to treat a set of other controls as a group, and Tabs make it easy for the user to consider a set of controls as a group.

Bound and Unbound

Forms created can be "bound", tightly associated with a specific table, or "unbound", not associated with a table. Typically, a card or a list form would be bound. Instances of unbound forms are rare. An example in recent versions is Form 591 – Payment Tolerance Warning. In older versions, (before V4.0) menu forms were unbound. When a form is bound to a table, it is easy to tie the controls on the form to the fields in the table.

A bound form can have unbound controls, i.e. controls that display computational results or values entered into working storage variables. Generally controls on an unbound form are generally unbound. Either category, bound or unbound, can have controls that refer to tables to which the form is not bound. Unbound forms are generally used for displaying information or processing status.

NAV Form Look and Feel

Most of the time the particular form type will be relatively obvious. The specific layout and features of the form object available to you as a developer, will offer many choices. Thus, some forms require many design decisions. C/SIDE allows you to create forms with vastly different "look and feel" attributes. But the standard NAV application only uses a few of the possibilities, and closely follows a set of GUI (Graphical User Interface) guidelines, already published, that offer close compatibility with other Windows and Microsoft applications.

Good design practice dictates that enhancements should integrate seamlessly unless there is an overwhelming justification for being "different". The best advice you can follow for design of forms is to make your new forms have the same look and feel as the forms in the "out-of-the-box" product. When you add changes to forms, make changes look as similar to the original form look and feel as your new functionality allows.

There certainly will be instances where you will need to provide a significantly different form layout in order to address a need that the standard NAV system simply does not need to address. Perhaps, you need to provide two or more tabular displays in the same form. Maybe you need to use colors to warn of a critical situation or you need to create a screen layout for a display significantly different from a standard desktop video display. Each in such cases, remember that the basic NAV forms look and feel has withstood the test of time for usability and for (reasonably) good taste. Even when you are going to be different, continue to be guided by the environment and context in which you are planting your new work.

An example of such a non-standard form is shown in the following screenshot. In this case, the goal is to have the header information visible all the time, while making a variety of related detail information readily accessible. A basic Header/Detail format is used, but the Detail section is a tabbed form where some of the tabs are in card format and some are in a tabular format as shown overleaf.

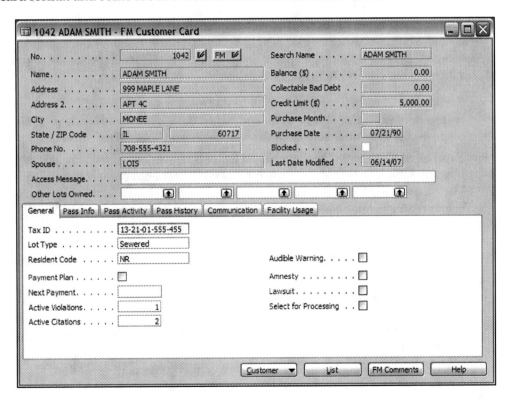

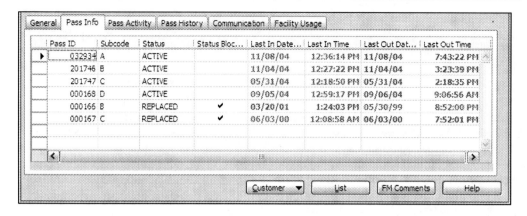

Types of Forms

Let us briefly review types of forms that we will use in an application. Then we will step to several examples using our C/ANDL system to illuminate our path. From an application design point of view, we need to consider which form type to use under what circumstances. The following are the different form types:

- **Card form**: These display and allow updating of a single record. A Card form is generally used for `Master` table and Setup data. Complex cards can contain a number of tabs, and may even display data from subordinate tables.

- **Tabular** or **List form**: These display a list of any number of records at one time, one line per record, with each displayed data field shown as a column. The Reference table maintenance and inquiry use Tabular forms. List forms use the same format as Tabular forms but (usually) are not editable. They can be used, for example, to show a list of master records to allow the user to compare records or to easily choose one master record on which to focus. Some specific List forms, such as Ledger Entries, allow editing of some fields (such as Invoice Due Dates).

Tabular/List forms are widely used as transaction entry forms. One of NAV's design features is to allow volume data entry activities to be done with little or no mouse usage. This provides higher data entry speed in situations where volume entry is feasible.

You can create a version of Tabular forms that is particularly suitable for high volume data entry into transaction journals. In the NAV documentation these are referred to as "Worksheet Forms". Worksheet forms use the **AutoSplitKey** property combined with an integer field as the last field in the table's primary key. This results in the entered data being automatically sequenced as it is entered. The C/AL code must handle the incrementing of the integer field as new records are appended.

The **AutoSplitKey** property will handle the creation of a new integer for a record being inserted between two other existing records. It does so by "splitting" the number range between the two original records to assign an integer value to the new, inserted record. For example, if the original records had keys ending in the values 50000 and 60000, then **AutoSplitKey** will assign the value 55000 to the new inserted record key.

A simple tabular form may show all the fields in a reference table to allow entering data or choosing one entry from among the available set. A complex tabular or list form might show data from several tables and some computed fields.

- **Main/Sub** or **Header/Detail form**: This consists of combination of two forms. The primary form is a card form that contains a subform control. This control references a secondary form, which is a tabular form. This form type is often appropriate whenever you have a parent record tied to a subordinate or child set of data in a one-to-many relationship.

  Header/Detail forms are used in Sales and Purchasing functions for Quotes, Orders, and Invoices, both before and after Posting. Header/Detail forms are also used in other areas such as Manufacturing Work Orders, Production Bills of Material, and Production Routings.

- **Matrix form**: This form type display results based on the intersections of two tables, called the source table and the matrix source table. The display is in a spreadsheet-style matrix format. The displayed data element of the source table is the leftmost column. The matrix source table principle data element is displayed across the top row, in the column header row position, with the results of the cell source data expression filling out the body of the matrix.

  The actual data displayed for each matrix cell may be computed from the intersection of these two tables. For it could be from some other table, but selected based on the results of the intersection of these two tables, for example, where values from the intersects are used in an algorithm with or to filter values in other tables.

- **Trendscape form**: This is equipped with Trendscape control buttons, which allows the displayed data to be filtered by a user selected date range. The following screenshot shows Trendscape buttons at the bottom of a form:

Trendscape forms may use different form types for the display of date-filtered data, and several variations occur in the standard NAV system. In Form 490, the **Acc. Schedule Overview**, the Trendscape date filter applies to all data appearing on the screen and the form is a Matrix form supplemented with a Tab control.

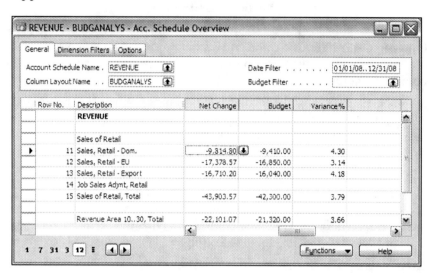

In Trendscape Form 492, **Item Availability by Location**, shown in the following screenshot, the date-filtered data is displayed using the subordinate Form 515, **Item Avail. by Location Lines**, which is a Tabular form placed in a subform control on the parent Form 492. All the data being displayed by Form 492 has the same date filter applied to it. The result is that the form is displaying the data "as of" the date filter range.

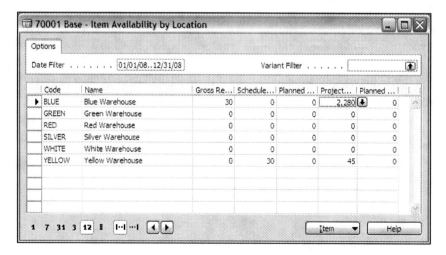

In Form 5983, **Service Item Trendscape**, shown in the following screenshot, the data is also displayed in a subform control, this time referring to form 5984. This form displays data for one date range on a line. The increment in the date range from line to line is controlled by the selected Trendscape button.

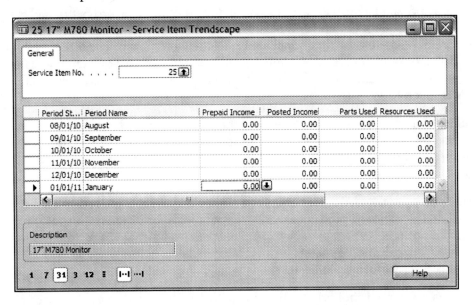

Take a look at these additional standard out-of-the-box forms for a representative sample of Trendscape forms: Forms 113, 157, 415, 490, 492, 5226, and 5983. You can access all of these forms via **Tools | Object Designer | Form**. Obviously, the data displayed must be time related (e.g. generally tied to a Posting Date).

- **Dialog form**: This is a simple display form embedded in a process, used to communicate with user/operator.

- **Request form**: This is a relatively simple form consisting of several tabs, allowing control information to be entered to control the execution of a report object.

All the form types above, except the last two, are Bound forms associated with Tables, displaying the data from those tables. Such forms, properly designed, are the key to easy and efficient use of a Navision application. Matrix and Trendscape forms are sometimes bound to virtual tables (e.g. Date, Integer). The Dialog and Request forms are generally associated with Reports and will be discussed further in that context.

Form Names

Card forms are named similarly to the table with which they are associated plus the word Card. For example, Customer table and Customer Card, Item table and Item Card, Vendor table and Vendor Card.

There is a special instance of Card forms used for the single record Setup tables that are used for unique setup and control information throughout NAV. The Setup tables are named after the functional area plus the word Setup. The associated form should also be (and generally is) named similarly to the table. For example, General Ledger Setup table and General Ledger Setup form, Manufacturing Setup table and Manufacturing Setup form.

Tabular forms are also named similarly to the table with which they are associated, but in the plural form as they display multiple entries at once. For example, Country table and Countries form, Shipment Method table and Shipment Methods form, Work Shift table and Work Shifts.

Journal entry (worksheet) forms are given names tied to their purpose plus the word Journal. In the standard product several Journal forms for different purposes may be associated with the same table. For example, the Sales Journal, Cash Receipts Journal, Purchases Journal, and Payments Journal all associated to the Gen. Journal Line table (i.e. different forms, same table).

List forms are named similarly to the table with which they are associated. The List forms, which are simple non-editable lists, have the word list associated with the table name. For example, Customer List, Item List, and Vendor List. The List forms associated with Ledger Entry tables are named after the tables, but in the plural format. For example, Customer Ledger Entry table and Customer Ledger Entries, Item Ledger Entry table and Item Ledger Entries, BOM Ledger Entry table and BOM Ledger Entries.

Ideally, if there is a Header and Line table associated with a data category, such as Sales Orders, the related main form and subform should be named to maintain the relationship between the tables and the forms. In some cases, it is better to tie the form names directly to the function they address rather than the underlying tables. An example of that approach is the two forms making up the form called by the Sales Order menu entry, Sales Order tied to the Sales Header table and the Sales Order Subform tied to the Sales Line table.

Sometimes, while naming forms you will have a conflict between naming based on the associated tables and naming based on the use of the data. For example, the menu entry Contacts invokes a Main form/Subform named Contact Card and Contact Card Subform. The respective tables are the Contact table and the Contact Profile Answer table. The context usage should take precedence in the form naming.

Accessing the Form Designer

The **Form Designer** is accessed via **Tools | Object Designer | Form**. The Form Designer can be opened either with a new form via the **New** button or on an existing form via the **Design** button (more detail on this process will follow shortly). Once the Form Designer is open, a row of control icons appear at the top of your screen. The following table explains the icons:

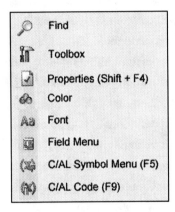

At various points during the creation and maintenance of a form, you can use these icons or their keystroke shortcuts or, in some cases, their right-click menu shortcuts, to access these various Form Designer functions.

What Makes Up a Form?

All forms are made up of certain common components. How are these components assembled to create the different form types? The basic elements of a form object are the Form Triggers and Properties, plus the Controls with their Control Triggers and Properties.

The following screenshot shows the Form Triggers. We will not spend much time on Form Triggers because it is generally a bad practice to insert any C/AL code in forms. You probably wonder "Why do triggers exist if we shouldn't use them?" The most likely answer is that they exist for historical reasons; as NAV has new capabilities added over the years, the need to use Form Triggers has become reduced almost to the point of non-existence.

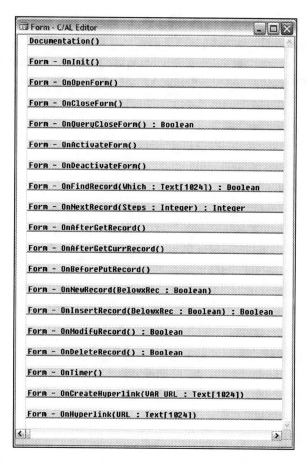

However, some of the standard objects have code in Form Triggers and there are still a few instances where the best way to accomplish a data form linkage requires insertion of C/AL code into a Form Trigger. Be forewarned that future versions of NAV will further constrain, or may even eliminate, our ability to insert C/AL code within a form. The correct approach is to put your logic within the tables or in well-organized functions defined in a Codeunit.

Form Properties

The following screenshot shows the **Forms - Properties** screen. We will step through the list briefly, but you should actually go to the **Form - Properties** screen and invoke **Help** for each field.

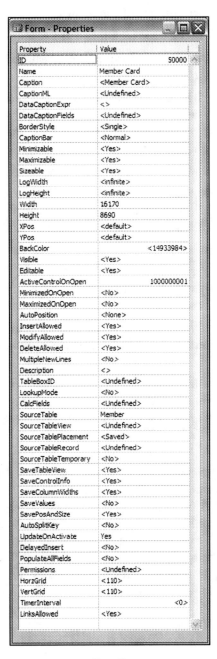

To illustrate Form properties, we chose to look at the properties of our Member Card that we have created earlier. Many of the properties are typically left in their default condition. The following are the properties with which we are most likely to be concerned:

- **ID**: The unique object number of the form.

- **Name**: The unique name by which this form is referenced in C/AL code.

- **Caption** and **CaptionML**: The form name displayed, depending on the language option in use.

- **Width** and **Height**: These define the operating size of the form when opened. These are generally used when the form is a subform. Then they must match the size of the subform control as it is defined on the main form.

- **Editable**: This determines whether the controls in the form can be edited (assuming the table and field **Editable** properties are **Yes**).

- **MultipleNewLines**: When set to **Yes**, allows the insertion of multiple new lines between existing records. By default, it is set to **No**, which prevents users from inserting new lines between records.

- **TableBoxID**: This must be filled in with the appropriate Table Box Control ID number for any List-style form, as the list appears in a Table Box control.

- **SourceTable**: The name of the table to which the form is bound. It must be filled in if this is a Bound form.

- **SourceTableView**: This can be utilized automatically and without exception to apply certain filters or open the form with a default key other than the Primary key.

- **AutoSplitKey**: This allows for the automatic assignment of a primary key, provided the last field in the primary key is an integer (there are exceptions to this, but we won't worry about them). This feature enables each new entry to be assigned a key that will cause it to remain sequenced in the table following the record appearing above it.

  On a new entry at the end of a list of entries, the trailing integer portion of the primary key is automatically incremented by 10000 (the increment value cannot be adjusted). When an entry is inserted between two previously existing entries, their current key-terminating integer values are summed and divided by two (hence the term **AutoSplitKey**) with the resultant key value being used for the new entry. Since 10000 can only be divided by two and rounded to a non-zero integer result 17 times, only 17 new entries can be inserted between two previously recorded entries.

- **DelayedInsert**: This delays the insertion of a new record until the user moves focus from the new line being entered. If this value is **No**, then a new record will automatically be inserted in the table as soon as the primary key fields have been completed. This property is generally set to **Yes** when **AutoSplitKey** is set to **Yes**. It makes it easier to have complex new data records entered with all necessary fields completed.

- **Permissions**: This allows you to instruct the system to allow a user of this form to have certain levels of access (**r**=read, **i**=insert, **m**=modify, **d**=delete) to the **TableData** in the specified table objects. For example, users of the Customer form are allowed to read (i.e. view) the data in the Cust. Ledger Entry table. Anytime you are defining special permissions, be careful to test with an end user license.

- **TimerInterval**: This defines a time interval in milliseconds for the firing of the active form's OnTimer trigger, thus executing the code in that trigger. This property is not used very often. When used, it requires thorough and careful testing.

We will discuss a number of the different types of controls that can appear on forms. In the course of that discussion, we will touch on a couple of controls where the use of trigger-based C/AL code is required in NAV versions up through V4.0 SP3.

Forms Controls

Controls on Forms serve a variety of purposes. Some controls are containers for constants and data (text and graphics). The following screenshot is from the **Form Designer** showing some of the constants (the left column) and data controls (the right column) on the Customer Card (Form 21):

A second group of controls (e.g. tabs, frames, and subforms) act as containers for other child controls.

The following two screenshots are developer's views of a tab control (from the **Customer Card**, Form 21) and of a frame (from Form 256, **Payment Journal**), each of which in turn contains basic controls for text and data:

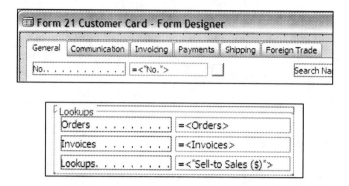

The third group of controls contain action instructions (e.g. command and menu buttons). The following screenshot is of the user's view of the command and menu buttons at the bottom of the Customer Card (Form 21) after the user has clicked on the **Customer** button showing some action options:

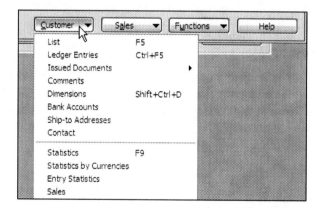

Explore

When you are using the **Form Designer**, the new Controls for your form can be accessed via the **Toolbox**:

The Controls Toolbox is shown in the center section in the following screenshot:

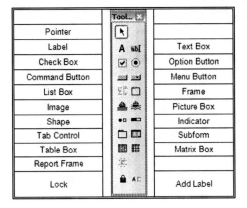

The description of the the control represented by each of the Toolbox icons follows:

- **Label**: This contains a literal, which must be defined prior to compilation.
- **Text Box**: This contains the value of a text, integer, or decimal variable bound to the control.
- **Check Box**: This contains the value of a Boolean, showing a check mark for Yes (True).
- **Option Button**: This shows a bullet for the current option value of the bound variable. There should be a count of option buttons equal to the number of possible options for the designated variable (e.g. three buttons for three options, etc.).
- **Command Button**: This contains C/AL code and/or properties that will invoke an action when the button is clicked/pushed.
- **Menu Button**: This provides access to a list of actions, each of which contains C/AL code and/or properties similar to a Command Button, in other words, a Menu Button is equivalent to a list of Command Buttons.
- **List Box**: A feature not implemented in the Designer, but accessible to a clever (and knowledgeable) developer editing the form in text mode (not recommended as a normal development technique).
- **Frame**: This has the purpose of containing other controls, which are either managed as a group by the developer or should be seen by the user as belonging together (such as the frame screenshot near the top of the page opposite).
- **Image**: This allows the display of a picture. The only data format supported for images is the bitmap format of up to 32KB in size. The image control is analogous to a text label in which the contents of the image control must be defined during development before compilation.

- **Picture Box**: This allows the display of a picture from bitmap formatted data. The contents of a picture box can be changed dynamically during program execution.

- **Shape**: This allows a very minimal graphical capability through the selection of one out of eight shape alternatives. The shape options provided are rectangle, rounded rectangle, oval, triangle, NW-Line (back leaning line), NE-Line (forward leaning line), HorizLine, and VertLine. The use of these shapes allows some very limited on-screen graphics. The properties support choosing at least the size, line width, and line color plus a couple of other attributes depending on the specified shape.

- **Indicator**: This provides a progress bar graphical display. Not often used because in most cases it requires the dedication of a form object for which there is a license fee, but more importantly, because a form cannot be used during some types of transaction processing. There is an equivalent code snippet available that you can use with a Dialog form (no object is consumed). **Indicators** are used on some statistics forms to show, for example, the percentage complete of a task.

- **Tab Control**: A container control that provides tabs as on card forms. Tabs make it easier to organize a large number of fields into related groupings. **Tab Controls** can also be used on a form that is not a card form (for example, Form 113 Budget).

 Although moving from one Tab to another on a form is usually done with a mouse click, it can also be done by the keyboard with *Ctrl+PageUp* and *Ctrl+PageDown*.

- **Subform**: A container control that allows you to nest one form within another form (but not within another subform). The typical use is a header/detail form where you have a one (header) to many (detail) data relationship, but subform controls certainly are not limited to that usage.

- **Table Box**: The essential base container control for any tabular form. A **Table Box** gives you rows and columns in a spreadsheet-style format. It is usually bound to a table. It contains label and text box controls bound to the fields in the table. The label controls become the column headers and the text box controls replicate down the columns and form the rows of records going across the table box.

- **Matrix Box**: This allows the placement of a matrix box control, which can then be set up and utilized as briefly described earlier in the description of form types.

- **Report Frame**: This has never been implemented.
- **Lock**: This allows you to select a control, then "lock" it to allow multiple insertions of the selected control. It is not often useful.
- **Add Label**: This allows you to add a label control to whatever controls you select until you close the toolbox.

Inheritance

One of the attributes of an object-oriented system is the attribute inheritance of properties. While NAV is more properly described as object based rather than object oriented, the properties that affect data validation are inherited. In addition, a property like decimal formating is also inherited. If the property is explicitly defined in the table, it cannot be less restrictively defined elsewhere. This basic concept applies on inheritance of data properties beginning from fields in tables to forms and reports, and from forms and reports to controls within forms and reports.

Experimenting with Controls

The best way to get familiar with the various controls is to create an empty form on which we can experiment arbitrarily. Pop up the Controls Toolbox and, one at a time, select each control type and place it on the form. Look at the control's properties, change a property and then **Run** the form, while remaining inside the **Form Designer**, by pressing *Ctrl+R*. By repeating the above steps, keep experimenting until you can identify the various controls fairly specifically.

 Running from within the Designer is a very quick and easy way to see the results of a form change without committing to the change (i.e. without saving and compiling the object). Because it does an instant compile first, it is a good basic error check. Then you can see the results of your change, adding a field, changing field location, or changing validation logic, without committing to overwriting the old version.

To get started, let us create a test form and bind it to the Customer table. The Customer table has a variety of data types and using an existing table will make the testing easier. Go to **Tools | Object Designer | Form** and click on the **New** button. Enter Customer in the **Table** field, select **Create a blank form**, and click **OK**. Now you should see a blank form in the **Form Designer** workspace.

Click on the Controls Toolbox icon. Select the textbox icon and place it on your test form. Your screen will look similar to the following screenshot:

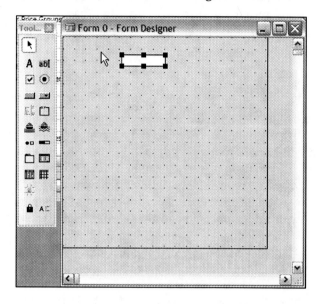

Press *Ctrl+R* to run the form. An error message will be displayed, as shown in the following screenshot:

When you click **OK**, C/SIDE will take you directly to the property field (**SourceExpr**) that must be filled in before the form is compiled and run. An easy choice is to assign the **Name** field to this control and then, click *Ctrl+R*. This time your test form will run and you should see at least a part of a **Customer Name** as shown in the following screenshot:

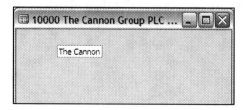

Make a note of the Customer Name, and then change it. To update the modified record, page down (*PgDn*) to the next Customer record, and then page up (*PgUp*) again. Note that the Customer Name has been changed. For the sake of consistency of test data, it would be a good idea to change the name back to what it was originally by editing it a second time.

Now, *Esc* from the running form back to the Form Designer worksheet. Either right click on the Text Box control or right-click + choose **Properties** or click on the Properties icon at the top of the screen. You will see the Properties list for a Text Box control. Find the **Editable** property and change it from the default **<Yes>** to **No**. Again, click *Ctrl+R* to run the test form. Now you will see that the text box is gray, rather than white, as shown in the following screenshot, indicating that you cannot change the contents (i.e. it is not editable). Try to change the displayed Customer Name; you cannot.

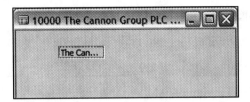

We have just touched the tip of the iceberg in terms of possible combinations of controls, properties, and settings. You should spend at least an hour or two experimenting with various combinations. Later, when you feel you have a better grasp for the combinations that you may want to use, then you can experiment with some more. The best two ways to understand the possibilities of C/AL are to study existing code and to experiment. Another good way is to study the available documentation. The better sources for additional information on controls are the **Help** files and the NAV Application Designer's Guide manual. In the manual, search for the control name and scan the manual text for all the matching hits.

Control Triggers

To illustrate all the Control triggers, we will take a look at the following two screenshots. The first screenshot consists of Control Triggers for a **Text Box** control and the second consists of Control Triggers for a **Command Button** control including the OnPush trigger, which is not present for a text box.

The guideline for the use of these triggers is the same as the one for Forms Triggers: if there is a choice, don't put C/AL code in a Control Trigger. It is always a good policy not to put code in Forms, even though NAV doesn't follow that advice. There may be occasions where you have to put code in a control trigger, but don't do it just because it is the easy way out. Remember that in future versions of NAV, it is very likely that our ability to put C/AL logic within a form will be very limited. Not only will this approach make your code easier to upgrade in the future, but it will also make it easier to debug and easier for the developer following you to decipher your changes.

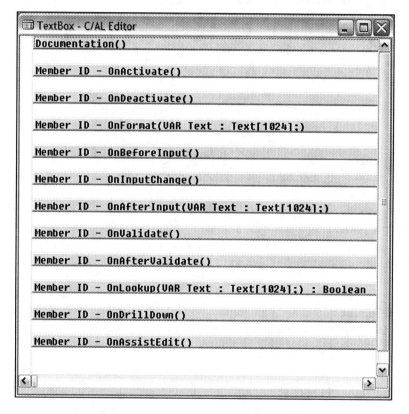

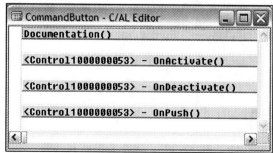

Control Properties

The following two screenshots show all the properties for form controls and also which controls have which properties. If you do not see a property listed here, it is not available. This matrix makes it obvious which properties have controls in common and which are unique to specific controls.

Property	Label	Text Box	Check Box	Option Button	Commd Button	Menu Button	Frame	Image	Picture Box	Shape	Indicatr	Tab Control	Subform	Table Box	Matrix Box
ID	X	X	X	X	X	X	X	X	X	X	X	X	X	X	X
Name	X	X	X	X	X	X	X	X	X	X	X	X	X	X	X
Xpos	X	X	X	X	X	X	X	X	X	X	X	X	X	X	X
Ypos	X	X	X	X	X	X	X	X	X	X	X	X	X	X	X
Width	X	X	X	X	X	X	X	X	X	X	X	X	X	X	X
Height	X	X	X	X	X	X	X	X	X	X	X	X	X	X	X
HorzGlue	X	X	X	X	X	X	X	X	X	X	X	X	X	X	X
VertGlue	X	X	X	X	X	X	X	X	X	X	X	X	X	X	X
Visible	X	X	X	X	X	X	X	X	X	X	X	X	X	X	X
Enabled		X	X	X	X		X		X			X	X	X	X
Editable		X	X	X			X					X	X	X	X
Focusable		X	X	X	X		X		X			X	X	X	X
FocusOnClick			X	X	X	X									
Default					X										
Cancel					X										
ParentControl	X	X	X	X	X	X	X	X	X	X	X	X	X	X	X
InFrame	X	X	X	X	X	X	X	X	X	X	X	X	X	X	X
InPage	X	X	X	X	X	X	X	X	X	X	X	X	X	X	X
InColumn		X	X	X					X			X			
InColumnHeading	X							X			X				
InMatrix		X	X	X					X			X			
InMatrixHeading		X	X	X					X			X			
Caption	X	X	X	X	X	X	X		X			X			
CaptionML	X	X	X	X	X	X	X		X			X			
ShowCaption			X	X	X	X	X								
HorzAlign	X	X	X	X	X	X									
VertAlign	X	X	X	X	X	X									
ForeColor	X	X	X	X	X	X	X					X	X		
BackColor	X	X	X	X	X	X	X	X	X	X	X	X		X	X
BackTransparent	X	X	X	X	X	X	X	X	X	X	X	X			
Border	X	X	X	X	X	X	X	X	X	X	X	X		X	X
BorderColor	X	X					X	X	X	X		X		X	X
BorderStyle	X	X					X	X	X	X		X		X	X
BorderWidth	X	X					X	X	X			X		X	X
Shape Style										X					
RowHeight														X	X
MatrixColumnWidth															X
HeadingHeight														X	X
FontName	X	X	X	X	X	X	X					X			
FontSize	X	X	X	X	X	X	X					X			
FontBold	X	X	X	X	X	X	X					X			
FontItalic	X	X	X	X	X	X	X					X			
FontStrikethru	X	X	X	X	X	X	X					X			
FontUnderline	X	X	X	X	X	X	X					X			
TopLineOnly							X								
MultiLine	X	X													
PadChar	X	X													
LeaderDots	X	X													
Orientation											X				
Percentage											X				
MaxLength		X													
PasswordText		X													
AutoEnter		X													
BitmapPos			X	X	X	X									
PushAction			X												

Property	Label	Text Box	Check Box	Option Button	Commd Button	Menu Button	Frame	Image	Picture Box	Shape	Indicatr	Tab Control	Subform	Table Box	Matrix Box
Bitmap			X			X		X							
BitmapList												X			
Ellipsis					X										
PageNames												X			
PageNamesML												X			
ToolTip	X	X	X	X	X	X	X	X	X	X	X	X	X	X	X
ToolTipML	X	X	X	X	X	X	X	X	X	X	X	X	X	X	X
Lookup		X													
DrillDown		X													
AssistEdit		X													
DropDown		X													
PermanentAssist		X													
InLineEditing														X	X
Description	X	X	X	X	X	X	X	X	X	X	X		X	X	X
OptionString		X													
OptionCaption		X													
OptionCaptionML		X													
DecimalPlaces		X													
Title		X													
MinValue		X	X	X							X				
MaxValue		X	X	X							X				
NotBlank		X													
Numeric		X													
CharAllowed		X													
DateFormula		X													
ClosingDates		X													
ValuesAllowed		X	X	X							X				
NextControl		X	X	X	X	X			X		X		X		
ClearOnLookup		X													
Format		X													
BlankNumbers		X													
BlankZero		X													
SignDisplacement		X													
AutoFormatType		X													
AutoFormatExpr		X													
CaptionClass	X	X	X		X	X	X		X		X				
Divisor		X													
SourceExpr		X	X	X					X		X				
AutoCalcField		X	X	X					X		X				
TableRelation		X													
ValidateTableRelation		X													
LookupFormID		X													
DrillDownFormID		X													
RunObject			X	X	X										
RunFormView			X	X	X										
RunFormLink			X	X	X										
RunFormLinkType			X	X	X										
RunCommand			X	X	X										
RunFormOnRec			X	X	X										
UpdateOnAction			X	X	X										
Timer Interval					X										
SubFormID													X		
SubFormView													X		
SubFormLink													X		
MatrixSourceTable															X

Generally you will choose a control based on the primary functionality of the controls but sometimes you may choose a control based on the particular properties a control has. Obviously, properties that controls size (e.g. **Width**, **Height**, etc.), position (e.g. **Xpos**, **Ypos**, **HorzGlue**, **VertGlue**, **Visible**, etc.), and appearance (e.g. **HorizAlign**, **VertAlign**, **ForeColor**, **BackColor**, **BackTransparent**, **Border**, **BorderColor**, **BorderStyle**, **BorderWidth**, **FontName**, **FontSize**, **FontBold**, **FontItalic**, etc.) are important and applied to most controls. Properties that control access, contents or actions are applied to fewer controls but have more impact on the application (e.g. **Enabled**, **Editable**, **Focusable**, **MinValue**, **MaxValue**, **NotBlank**, **Numeric**, **CharAllowed**, **DateFormula**, etc.).

You will find more detail on control properties in the C/SIDE **Help**. It would be a good idea at this point to review the contents of C/SIDE **Help** for a number of the controls shown in the preceding screenshots. Most of the properties have reasonable descriptions in the **Help** file.

Experimenting with Control Properties

Once you have reviewed the controls, you should then reinforce them by experimenting. You can explore the Control properties by doing the following:

1. Create an empty test form.
2. Call up the Controls Toolbox.
3. Select a control and place it on the form.
4. With the new control highlighted, call up the Properties list.
5. Change the property of interest and see what happens.

For most controls, this type of testing works best if you make just one change at a time. After you get comfortable with the effect of changing individual properties, you may want to change multiple properties at one time to see how they interact.

Some Control Property Tips

The following are a few tips about various properties that you might find useful:

- All the properties that represent measurements are in units of 1/100 of a millimeter. You cannot change the unit of measure to anything else. In the English system, there are 2540 1/100 mm in an inch. If a **YPos** property is equal to 5080 then that control is positioned two inches to the right of the left margin.

- **HorizGlue** (options are Left, Right, or Both) and **VertGlue** (options are Top, Bottom, or Both) are the properties that determine the control's anchoring on a form. When you set these properties to **Both**, the control will resize when the form resizes. In fact, you can just set one of these properties to **Both** and the control will resize on that axis.

  On a tabular form, at least one control should always have the **HorzGlue** property set to **Both**. The Form Wizard will do that automatically. To keep buttons positioned in their usual location at the bottom right of a form, you should set **HorzGlue** to **Right** and **VertGlue** to **Bottom**. When you create a Subform, which generally contains a TableBox for tabular data display, you should set these properties to **Both** for both the Subform and the **TableBox** so that they will resize in unison with each other and with the parent form.

- A number of the controls can be reset dynamically during run time. This allows you to change the look or the behavior of controls (and thereby the parent form) based on user actions or the data contents of the form. For example, you can dynamically set control properties **Height, Width, Decimal Places, ForeColor, FontBold, Editable, Indent, Visible, LogHeight, LogWidth, XPos** and **YPos** with the C/AL commands as shown in the following **Help** list:

```
ACTIVATE
DECIMALPLACESMAX
DECIMALPLACESMIN
EDITABLE
ENABLED
HEIGHT
INLINEEDITING
UPDATEEDITABLE
UPDATESELECTED
UPDATEFONTBOLD
UPDATEFORECOLOR
UPDATEINDENT
VISIBLE
WIDTH
XPOS
YPOS
```

- The graphical capabilities of NAV are very limited. You can set control border, foreground, and background colors of controls using a numerical value to define the setting (see the **Help** for "**RGB Color Model**")—no WYSIWYG tool here. You can set various font attributes, but again with a very limited set of choices. You can display a few graphical shapes and, with quite a bit of effort, use them to create some primitive graphics. You can even display pictures, but only in bitmap format. There are some third-party tools available to compensate for these limitations, but if you want to use graphics in any meaningful way with NAV, you should look to interface with a friendly tool with capabilities, such as one of the Microsoft Office Excel components.

- Some properties can be used in lieu of C/AL code. For example, the **PushAction** property can be used in some instances rather than embedding C/AL code in the **OnPush** trigger. Read **Help** to learn more about **PushAction**.

- Controls that are bound to a table field will inherit the settings of those properties that are common to both. Inherited property settings that involve data validation cannot be overridden, but all others can be changed. This is another instance where it is generally best to define the properties in the table for consistency and ease of maintenance, rather than defining them for each instance of use in a form or report.

More Illumination with C/ANDL

For each of our most recently defined tables, we need to create new forms. We have six new tables. So we need six new tabular forms because these tables are all simple in structure. At the moment, all we want to do is enter or look up data, therefore we can use the **Form Designer** to create all six of these. Assign names and object numbers to your new forms as follows:

Table No.	Table Name	Form No.	Form Name
50002	Certification	50003	Certifications
50003	Volunteer Activity	50004	Volunteer Activities
50004	Course	50005	Courses
50005	Volunteer Activity Ledger	50006	Volunteer Activity Ledger
50006	Education Activity Ledger	50007	Education Activity Ledger
50007	Member Certification	50008	Member Certifications

Let us step quickly through the creation of Form 50003 Certifications as follows:

1. Access the **Form Designer** and prepare to create a new form: **Tools | Object Designer | Form**, then the **New** button, enter the Table name **Certification**, choose the option **Create a form using a wizard:** and choose **Tabular-Type Form**.

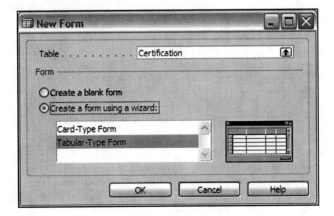

2. Since this table only has three fields, use the **>>** button to populate the form with all the fields in one click.

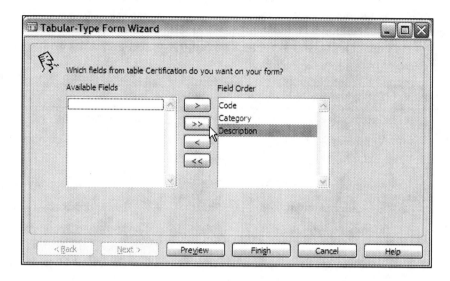

3. Click on **Finish**. Use the design tools to adjust the columns to be easier to read and better looking. Obviously, these terms are subject to your interpretation.

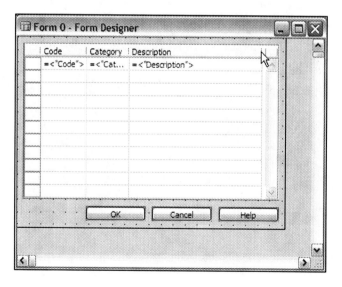

4. Finally, close the Form Designer and save the new Form object with the appropriate **ID** and **Name** (in this case, **50003** and **Certifications**).

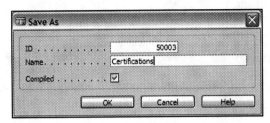

Obviously we would like each table to be readily accessible by both the lookup and drilldown functions that are created automatically when table references are defined in other tables. In order to do that, we must define the **LookupFormID** and **DrillDownFormID** for each of these tables. The following screenshot shows the properties defined for the `Certification` table. You should do the same in your database. Now follow the same sequence of form creation and table property update for the other five new tables.

Now that you have completed that, you should be able to go through the following test data entry task with the aid of the lookup function on those fields that reference other tables.

Run the Certifications form (Form Object No. 50002).

Create a couple of new entries as shown in the following table:

Code	Category	Description
DEVELOP	NAV	NAV Development
MCP	MS	Microsoft Certified Professional

Close this form and open the **Member Certifications** form (Form Object No. 50008). You should see a Lookup arrow on the **Member ID** field (although in the following screenshot it looks as if the Lookup arrow is at the left of the **Code** field, it is really hanging off the right end of the **Member ID** field).

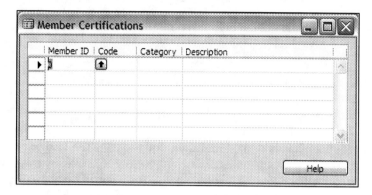

Click on the arrow and it will bring up your Member list, allowing you to select a member. Moving to the next member field will display the lookup arrow for the `Certifications` table. Click on that arrow and your display should look similar to the following screenshot:

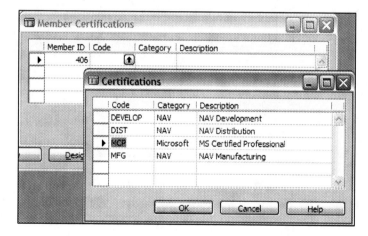

Once you have learned more about C/AL coding, we will create the logic to automatically fill in the **Description** field in this table and "copy from reference table" fields in the other tables. But for now we can either enter fields manually or just leave them blank.

Update the Member Forms

The Member Card and Member List, as originally created, are now out of date as we have added quite a few fields to the Member table. Since we created the original forms with the Form Wizard, we don't have a big time investment. So, rather than manually modifying forms through the Form Designer, let us start by creating new versions with the Form Wizard, and then making manual modifications as needed.

Create a New Member List

Let us start with the simpler form, the **Member List**. The first step is to use the Form Wizard and create a form based on the Member table that contains all the fields in that table. After creating a form, save it with the same object name and number as we used originally (**Form 50001 Member List**).

Now let us simplify our form a little. Some users may want to see only a minimal set of the data fields, whereas other users may want to view a larger set, maybe all the available fields. Since our new **Member List** form contains all the fields in the table, we have satisfied the latter need. Assuming the majority of users won't need to see many fields, we will make other fields default to **Invisible**, but still available if desired.

This can be done by simply changing one property on each desired field i.e. **Visible** to **No**. We will start with the **Title** field. Highlight that field on the form in the **Form Designer** and click on the **Properties** icon.

Set the **Visible** property to **No** as shown in the following screenshot:

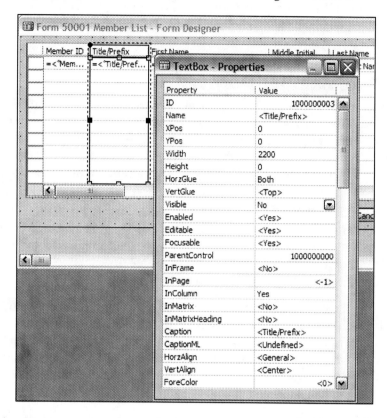

If we do the same thing for all the fields except **Member ID, First Name, Last Name**, the various **Address** fields, and the **Member Status** field, we will have a form similar to the following screenshot. You can make your form similar to the following screenshot by adjusting the column widths to better fit the data and by expanding the column heading row vertically (it is automatically set up to display in multi-line format).

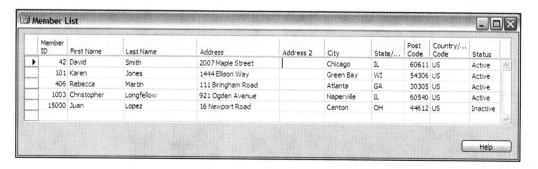

Whenever a user makes adjustments to a form such as column widths and heading row height, the adjustments will be "remembered" in the user-specific ZUP file, (ZUP referring to User Profile) while you can set some system and object properties to override the standard behavior. Normally, the ZUP file will record every form size and layout adjustment as well as the identity of the specific record highlighted the last time the form was opened.

 Whenever you change and recompile a form in C/SIDE, it resets all user modifiable parameters back to the default condition. Therefore, whenever you make a form change for your user, no matter how minor, you will be affecting all users who utilize that form.

If a user wishes to make a column **Visible** that you have defaulted to **Invisible**, they simply need to use the **Show Columns** function available from the **View** menu at the top of the screen as shown in the following screenshot.

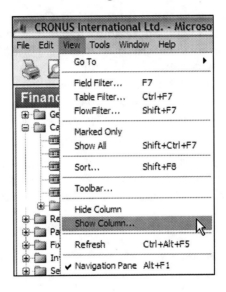

Show Column will list all the columns on the currently active form with a check mark beside all those that are currently visible. The check mark space on this list can be toggled to allow total user control of visibility of the listed columns. The user can also highlight a column on a form, and then select the **Hide Column** option and that column will become invisible immediately.

The user can also "grab and squeeze" one edge of a column to make it invisible. Just a caution: this feature can sometimes be invoked accidentally, allowing a user to lose a column inadvertently. Columns that have been made invisible through any of these methods can be made **Visible** again through the **Show Column** option.

A variety of other user-controlled layout changes can also be made. Column widths can be changed. Header or detail row heights can be changed. Columns can be moved left and right. All these capabilities apply only to tabular forms. All user changes disappear when a form is recompiled by a developer.

Create a New Member Card

Now let us take on the creation of a new **Member Card**. We are going to start with the Form Wizard and create a usable, but not fully featured, **Member Card**. Then we are going to use the Form Designer and enhance the Wizard generated Form.

First, start up the **Form Wizard** just as you did for the Member List form, but this time choose the Card format option. You will do this by accessing the **Form Designer** to create a new form via **Tools | Object Designer | Form**, then the **New** button, entering the table name **Member**, choosing the option **Create a form using a wizard**, and choose **Card-Type Form**.

We are going to have tabs for **General Information**, **Communications,** and **Education Activity**. This is a good opportunity to use tabs to organize our information and to present more information than can comfortably fit on one tab (i.e. page) or is more clearly organized by having more than one tab. Remember, don't use the tabs if there is no particular good reason to use them, the user's navigation task becomes easier, if a form doesn't have tabs. You will note that most (if not all) NAV card forms have at least one tab. Exceptions include many of the statistics forms.

Using the capabilities of the Form Wizard, create a **Member Card** similar to the following screenshot. The **Education Activity** Tab will be empty for the moment, but we will soon be using the Form Designer to add a subform control there.

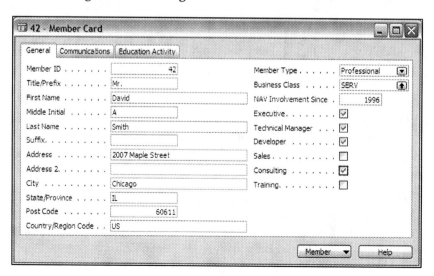

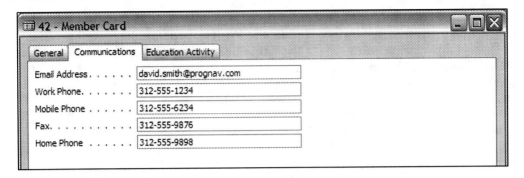

As you can see, a nice looking and relatively complete multi-tab card form can be created just using the Form Wizard. Now we will use the Form Designer to work on our generated Card form. What we want to do is add a display to the **Education Activity** Tab listing all the Education Activity entries for the Member. We obviously need to add one or more controls and associate them with the Education Activity table, linked by Member **ID**.

Our first task is just to add a **TableBox** control to the form on that tab. But look at the properties list of **TableBox**. There is no **Source Table** for any control; only the **SubFormView** and **SubFormLink** properties exist, giving us a hint of what we need to do. It turns out that what we need to do is set up a MainForm/SubForm structure similar to that used for Sales Orders or Purchase Orders. Typically a subform is a Tabular form, a form with a TableBox. So let's create one for ourselves.

Using the Controls Toolbox, add a Subform control to the **Education Activity** Tab. You should be working in a reduced screen size, not full screen. Size the subform box so it nicely fits to the form. Look at the subform control properties and note the size (**Width** and **Height** properties), so you can match the size when you create the form that is going to fit here. Set the **Border** control to **None** so that the subform control will be invisible (only the TableBox contained within will be visible). Now exit and save your changes.

Next, we are going to create a form that will fit in the subform control, named Form 50009, Education Activity Subform. Actually, if we wanted to attempt to be clever and very conserving of form objects (as they cost license fee), we can probably just rework on our Form 50007, Education Activity Ledger, to serve a dual purpose. Generally, experience says being too clever ends up causing more trouble than it's worth.

In this case, we can follow a relatively simple path. The data layout of the table, Education Activity Ledger, is simple and we will show all the fields. We will use the Form Wizard, create a tabular form including all the fields, remove the buttons from the form (select and delete), and then size the resulting **TableBox** to match

the size of the Subform control we created in the Member Card **Education Activity**
Tab (access the properties and set **Height** and **Width**). Squeeze the Form Designer
worksheet down to the same size as the **Table Box**. Set the **HorzGlue** and **VertGlue**
of this tabular form to **Both** so that it will be resized along with the parent control
and form. Now, save this new form as Form 50009, Education Activity Subform.

Return to the **Member Card** and open it in the Form Designer. Focus on the
Education Activity Tab, the subform control, and open the subform control's
properties. Edit the **SubformID** property to Education Activity Subform. Edit the
SubformLink property to have the `Member` table field Member ID linked to the
`Education Activity Ledger` table field Member ID (i.e. Member ID to Member
ID — seems logical enough, right?). Be sure to set **HorizGlue** and **VertGlue** to **Both** so
that your subform will resize in synch with the main form.

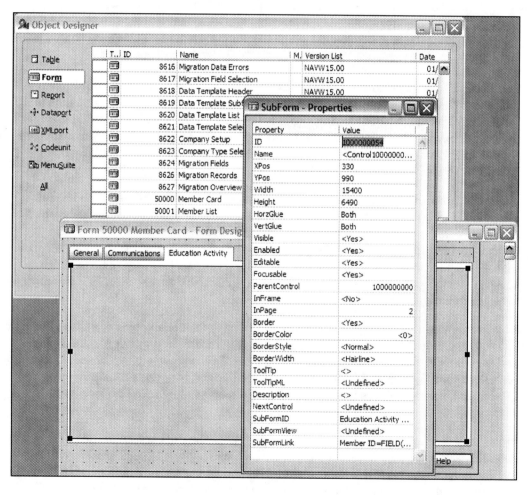

Testing Forms

We have just created a couple of forms using the Form Wizard. This was a one-way process (you can't take a generated form object back into the Wizard). Then we stepped gently into the forms we generated and made some minor modifications. Often, when you are creating totally new forms, the modifications you make to a generated form will be more significant. The modifications may involve C/AL code, moving a number of fields around, manually adding new controls, etc.

These are normal development activities. The point to remember is that you should test and retest thoroughly. Make backup copies of your work every time you get a new set of changes working relatively well. While it is exceedingly rare for the NAV native database to be corrupted, it is not all that unusual for something you are performing in a test mode to confuse C/SIDE to the point that it crashes. If that happens, any unsaved changes will be lost. Therefore, after each change, or controlled group of changes, you should save your object. In fact, if you are doing complicated things, it is not a bad idea to have a second backup copy of your object that you refresh every hour or two of development effort.

Your testing should include the everyday items such as field to field transition. Highlight the first field on the form, then use the *Tab* key to move from field to field. If you don't get the focus flow pattern that is going to be best for your user, the simplest solution is to use the **NextControl** property to adjust the field to field focus sequence. To use the **NextControl** property, do the following steps:

1. Identify the two controls you wish to have in sequence, i.e. first, then second.
2. Access the properties of the second control and copy the **ID** value into the clipboard.
3. Access the properties of the first control and paste that value into the **NextControl** property field value.

Creative Plagiarism

When you want to create new functionality that you haven't developed recently (or at all), start with a simple test example. Better yet, find another object that has that capability and study it. In many lines of work, the term "plagiarism" is a nasty term. But when it comes to modifying a system such as NAV, plagiarism is a very effective research and design tool.

Define what you want to do. Search through the Cronus demonstration system (or your system) to find one or more forms that have the feature you want to emulate (or a similar one). If there are both complex and simpler instances of forms that contain this feature, concentrate your research on the simpler one first. Make a test copy of the form and dig into it. Make liberal use of the **Help** information. Search the PDF copy of the Application Designer's Guide manual. The reality is that your best guide will be an existing object that does something much like what you want to do.

There is an old saying "Plagiarism is the sincerest form of flattery". When designing modifications for NAV, the more appropriate saying might be "Plagiarism is the quickest route to a solution that works". If you like to learn by exploring (a very good way to learn more about how NAV works), then you should allocate some study time to simply exploring the NAV Cronus demo system.

One of your goals could be to identify forms that represent good models to study further. At the extreme you might plagiarize these (a better phrase — "use them as models for your development work"); at the minimum you will learn more about how the expert developers at NAV design their forms.

Form Design Hints

Whenever possible, start a new form just as we have done in our work here. Use the Form Wizard to generate a basic structure, and then begin modifying it from there. Sometimes, the form you want to create is so different from what comes out of the Wizard that using the Wizard is an impediment, not assistance. But usually, you can get a jump start from the Wizard and, sometimes you can even do the whole job there. Automation can be a good idea, even for developers.

One aspect of NAV that is often overlooked is its ability to cater to the user doing high volume data entry. Whether you are making modifications to Order Entry or Journal Entry forms, or you are creating brand new forms, you need to keep the touch typist's needs in mind. NAV forms can be designed so that no mouse action is required, i.e. everything can be done from the keyboard. It's good to respect that feature.

Minimize the use of Tab controls except when they are needed. Use shortcut keys for frequently used functions. Group information on forms similarly to the way it will be entered from source material. It is a good idea to spend time with users reviewing the form layout before locking in a final form design. If necessary, you may want to develop two forms for a particular table, one laid out for ease of use for inquiry purposes and another laid out for ease of use for volume data entry.

Wherever it is rational to do so, make your new forms similar in layout and navigation to the forms delivered in the standard NAV product. These generally conform to Windows design standards and standards that are the result of considerable research. Since someone has spent a lot of money on that human interface research, it's usually safer to follow the Windows and NAV standards than to follow one's own intuition.

The exceptions come, of course, when your client says "this is the way I want it done". Even then you may want to work on changing the client's opinion. There is no doubt that training is easier and error rates are lower when the different parts of a system are consistent in their operation. Users are often challenged by the complications of a system with the sophistication of Dynamics NAV. It is not really fair to make their job any harder. In fact, your job is to make the user's job easier and more effective.

A Quick Tour of the Form Designer

Although we have created a number of forms using the Form Wizard and modified a couple of them with the Form Designer, there are a number of features of the Form Designer that we have not yet discussed.

Let us start with the **Font Tool**. First, highlight a control that contains text. The control can be any control that has properties affecting Font Tool. That can be font or horizontal alignment properties. The Font Tool can be accessed by clicking on the **Font** icon at the top of the Form Designer screen or via the menu bar **View | Font** option. In either case, the Font Tool will pop up as shown in the following screenshot.

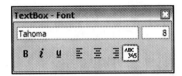

You can define a font in the box on the top left and a font size in the box on the top right. Font attributes of Bold, Italic, and Underline are represented by the obvious *b*, *i*, and *u* respectively. Horizontal alignment is selected by the left align, center align, right align and "left for alphanumeric, right for numeric" alignment options. The box is a visual shortcut to the properties. You can always go directly to the properties to make settings there.

Next is the **Color Tool**. To view the Color Tool, highlight a control that has **ForeColor**, **BackColor**, or **BorderColor** properties. The Color Tool can be accessed by clicking on the **Color** icon at the top of the Form Designer screen or via the menu bar **View | Color** option. In either case, the Color Tool will pop up.

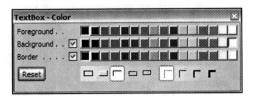

The tool provides a limited set of color choices. Clicking on a color button will choose that color for you. In the preceding screenshot, *Black* is chosen for the **ForeColor**, *White* for the **BackColor**, and *Black* for the **BorderColor**. At the bottom of the tool you can choose a **BorderStyle** and a **BorderWidth**. The two check boxes determine whether or not a color will be displayed at all for that property.

If you make these settings directly in the Properties screen, more choices will be available than in the Color Tool. If you are using colors, it is not a bad idea to start with the Color Tool and then adjust from there. Colors are defined by a number that represents a particular color. The best information on color setting on forms is found in **Help** by looking up **RGB Color Model**. You still have to experiment, but at least you'll have an idea where you are heading and how bumpy the path will be.

Finally, there is the **Field Menu**. For a Bound form, the Field Menu provides a list of all fields in the table. This lets you to use a click and drag approach for placing additional data field controls on a form. To view the Field Menu, click on the **Field Menu** icon at the top of the Form Designer screen or go via the menu bar **View | Field Menu** option. In either case, the Field Menu will pop up. The following screenshot shows the field menu for the Volunteer Activity table:

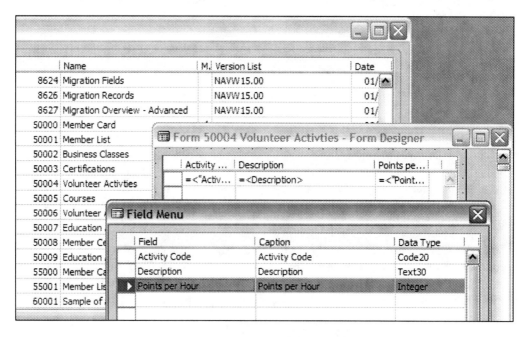

Two additional Form Designer features that are of interest at this point are the **Grid option** and the **Ruler option**. These control displays that are intended to assist you in placing controls on a form. The Grid option controls the display of a grid pattern of dots in the background. The Ruler option controls the display of X and Y axis rulers around the form. These are of modest use in helping you to visually align control placement. But if you want to place controls accurately, you should really use the properties for positioning.

The last Form Designer features we are going to review at this point are the **Format menu** options. They can be seen in the following screenshot.

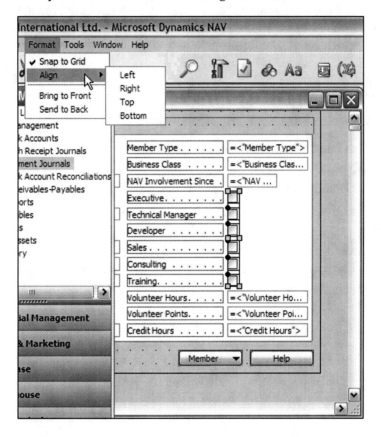

The **Snap to Grid** option will make any control placements snap to specific horizontal and vertical Grid lines. The Application Designer's Guide implies the "snap to" points are spaced at 1/100 millimeter increments. But when you use **Snap to Grid** and view the resulting **XPos** and **YPos** property changes, the increment appears to be 110/100 mm. If you want full flexibility in control positioning, you can turn this option off. For quick positioning and alignment, it is a very useful feature.

The **Align** option allows you to select a group of controls (see the preceding screenshot where a group of check boxes are selected to be aligned) and then choose a basis for alignment (one of **Left, Right, Top** or **Bottom**). Backup up your form work before you use this option and then make your choice very carefully. It is all too easy to end up with a group of controls in a stack. There is no undo! The only way to undo a bad choice with this tool is to exit the Form Designer without saving the changes to your form. On the positive side, this is a very useful tool to align a group of similar controls, if you are careful.

The **Bring to Front** and **Send to Back** option gives you a tool to use with overlapping controls. This can be useful when you are creating a complicated form. Usually this happens when you are using Frame, Image, Picture, or Shape controls. This allows you to control which set of overlapping controls is in front and which is at the back.

Keys to Learning NAV

Remember the keys to learn NAV are as follows:

- Read this book and do the exercises.
- Read the Application Designer's Guide; study the parts of it that seem most applicable and useful to you.
- Experiment with and explore the NAV Cronus demonstration system as a user.
- Study existing objects.
- Create new objects trying out ideas. The best time to fail is when a customer is not depending on you.

Summary

At this point you should be feeling relatively comfortable in the navigation of NAV and with your own use of the Object Designer. You should be able to use the Form Wizard readily and Form Designer in an "advanced beginner" mode. Hopefully, you have taken full advantage of the various opportunities to create tables and forms both to our recipes and experimentally on your own.

In this chapter, we have covered a lot of ground. Our focus has been the interactive windows into NAV Forms.

We have also reviewed different types of forms and worked with them. We have reviewed all the controls that can be used in forms and we worked with several. We have also lightly reviewed form and control triggers, learned to use the Form Wizard, and acquired a good introduction to the Form Designer.

With the knowledge gained, we have expanded our C/ANDL system, creating a number of forms for data maintenance and inquiry, as well as studied the full Form Designer environment and tools.

In the next chapter, we will learn our way around the NAV Report Wizard and Report Designer. We will dig into the various triggers and controls that make up reports. We will also create a number of reports to better understand what makes them tick and what we can do within the constraints of the Report Designer tool.

5
Reports

Simple things should be simple and complex things should be possible – AlanKay

The library of reports provided as part of the standard NAV product distribution from Microsoft are considered relatively simple in design and limited in their features. Some people feel that the provided reports should satisfy most needs because of their simple and basic structure, which is made much more powerful and flexible through the multiplier of NAV's filtering and SIFT capabilities. Others say that leaving the base product very simple creates more opportunities for creative NAV Partners and Developers to sell their services to customers who want reports that are fancier, either in complexity or appearance.

Whatever the reason, the fact remains that NAV's standard reports are basic and, to obtain more complex or more sophisticated reports, we must creatively utilize the Report Designer. Through creative use of the Report Designer, many different types of complex report logic may be implemented. You can also use the Report Designer to output processed data to other reporting tools such as Excel or to 'third-party' reporting products.

In this chapter, we will review different types of reports and the components that go to make up reports. Just as with forms, we'll look in detail at the triggers, properties, and controls. We'll create some reports with the Report Wizard and some manually through direct use of the Report Designer. We'll also modify a report or two using the Report Designer (the only way C/SIDE to modify a report object). We'll examine the data flow of a standard report and the concept of reports used for processing only (with no report output).

What is a Report?

A report is a vehicle for organizing, processing, and displaying data in a format suitable for outputting to a hardcopy device. Reports may be displayed on-screen in Preview mode rather than being printed, but with the same formatting as though they were printed. In fact, all the report screenshots in this book were taken of reports generated in Preview mode.

Once generated, a report is static, not interactive. All specification of the criteria for a report must be done at the beginning, before it is generated. Once generated, the contents of the report cannot be modified or drilled into. Drillable content would not be suitable for printing and therefore wouldn't be a report. It is possible that a future version will contain drillable on-screen reports (but then that might be just another version of forms).

In NAV, report objects can also be classified as **ProcessingOnly** by setting the correct report property (i.e. setting the **ProcessingOnly** property to **Yes**). A **ProcessingOnly** report will display no data to the user in the traditional reporting manner, but will simply process and update data in the tables. A report can add, change, or delete data in tables, whether the report is **ProcessingOnly** or it is a normal printing report.

In general, reports are associated with one or more tables. A report can be created without being externally associated with any table, but that is the exception, not the rule. Even if a report is associated with a particular table, it can freely access and display data from other referenced tables.

NAV Report Look and Feel

C/SIDE will allow you to create reports of many different kinds with vastly different "look and feel" attributes. Consistency of report look and feel does not have the same level of design importance as does consistency of form look and feel. The standard NAV application only uses a few of the possible report styles, most of which are in a relatively "plain-Jane" format. While good design practice dictates that enhancements should integrate seamlessly unless there is an overwhelming justification for being different, there are many opportunities for providing replacement or additional reporting capabilities. The tools that are available within NAV for accessing and manipulating data in textual format are very powerful. But in order to provide information in a graphical format, you really need to export the data to a tool such as Excel.

NAV Report Types

The following are the types of reports:

- **List**: This is a formatted list of data. A sample list report in the standard system is the **Customer – Order Detail** list shown in the following screenshot:

```
Customer - Order Detail                                                          June 28, 2008
Shipment Date:                                                                   Page      1
CRONUS International Ltd.

All amounts are in LCY

Customer: No.: 10000|40000
```

Shipment Date	Typ	No.	Description	Quantity	Outstandin Quantity	Quantity on Back Order	Unit Price Excl. VAT	Line Discount Amount	Inv. Discount Amount	Outstanding Orders
		10000	**The Cannon Group PLC**							
		Order No.	**2001 01/16/08**							
01/16/08	Item	LS-MAN-10	Manual for Loudspeakers	4	4	4	0.00	0.00	0.00	0.00
		Order No.	**2006 01/16/08**							
01/16/08	Item	LS-MAN-10	Manual for Loudspeakers	10	10	10	0.00	0.00	0.00	0.00
		Order No.	**2011 01/16/08**							
01/16/08	Item	LS-150	Loudspeaker, Cherry, 150W	10	10	10	129.00	0.00	0.00	1,290.00
			The Cannon Group PLC							**1,290.00**
		40000	**Deerfield Graphics Company**							
		Order No.	**2004 01/16/08**							
01/16/08	Item	LS-10PC	Loudspeakers, White for PC	30	30	30	59.00	0.00	0.00	1,770.00
		Order No.	**2009 01/16/08**							
01/16/08	Item	LS-10PC	Loudspeakers, White for PC	12	12	12	59.00	0.00	0.00	708.00
01/16/08	Item	LS-150	Loudspeaker, Cherry, 150W	8	8	8	129.00	0.00	0.00	1,032.00
		Order No.	**2014 01/16/08**							
01/16/08	Item	LS-75	Loudspeaker, Cherry, 75W	8	8	8	79.00	0.00	0.00	632.00
			Deerfield Graphics Company							**4,142.00**

- **Document**: This is formatted along the lines of a pre-printed form, where a page (or several pages) represents a complete, self-contained report. Examples are Customer Invoice, Packing List (even though it's called a list , it's a document report), Purchase Order, and Accounts Payable check.

The following screenshot is a **Customer Sales Invoice** document report:

Sales - Invoice
Page 1

The Cannon Group PLC
Mr. Andy Teal
192 Market Square
Birmingham, B27 4KT
Great Britain

CRONUS, Birmingham RC.
Aaron Nicholls
Main Street, 14
B27 4KT Birmingham

Phone No.	+44-161 818192
Fax No.	+44-161 818100
VAT Reg. No.	GB777777777
Giro No.	888-9999
Bank	World Wide Bank
Account No.	99-99-888

Bill-to Customer No.   10000

January 16, 2008

VAT Registration No.   789456278
Salesperson   Peter Saddow

Invoice No.	103023
Order No.	2001
Posting Date	01/16/08
Due Date	02/16/08
Prices Including VAT	No

No.	Description	Posted Shipment Date	Quantity	Unit of Measure	Unit Price	Disc. %	VAT Identifier	Amount
LS-MAN-10	Manual for Loudspeakers	01/16/08	4	Piece	3.15		VAT25	12.60
70100	Paint, black	01/16/08	2	Can	2.70		VAT25	5.40
70201	Doorknob	01/16/08	1	Piece	1.20		VAT25	1.20

Total GBP Excl. VAT	19.20
25% VAT	4.80
Total GBP Incl. VAT	24.00

VAT Amount Specification

VAT Identifier	VAT %	Line Amount	Inv. Disc. Base Amount	Invoice Discount Amount	VAT Base	VAT Amount
VAT25	25	19.20	19.20	0.00	19.20	4.80
Total		**19.20**	**19.20**	**0.00**	**19.20**	**4.80**

Payment Terms   1 Month/2% 8 days
Shipment Method   Ex Warehouse

The List and Document report types are defined based on their layout. The next three report types are defined based on their usage rather than their layout.

- **Transaction**: These reports provide a list of ledger entries for a particular `Master` table. For example, a Transaction list of Item Ledger entries for all items matching particular criteria or a list of General Ledger entries for some specific accounts as shown in the following screenshot:

Posting Date	D Ty	Document No.	G/L Account No.	Name	Description	VAT Amount	G P	Ge Bu	Ge Pro	Amount	Entry No.
Register No		**67**									
01/10/08	Cr	109001	7110	Purch., Retail - Dom.	Credit Memo 109001	-7,086.00	Pu	NA	RET	-28,344.00	2564
01/10/08	Cr	109001	5630	Purchase VAT 25 %	Credit Memo 109001	0.00				-7,086.00	2565
01/10/08	Cr	109001	5410	Vendors, Domestic	Credit Memo 109001	0.00				35,430.00	2566
Register No		**68**									
01/10/08	Pa	2594	2310	Customers Domestic	Payment 2008	0.00				-42,315.42	2567
01/10/08	Pa	2594	5310	Revolving Credit	Payment 2008	0.00				42,315.42	2568
01/10/08	Pa	2594	2310	Customers Domestic	Payment 2008	0.00				-25,389.25	2569
01/10/08	Pa	2594	5310	Revolving Credit	Payment 2008	0.00				25,389.25	2570
01/10/08	Pa	2594	2310	Customers Domestic	Payment 2008	0.00				-55,010.04	2571
01/10/08	Pa	2594	5310	Revolving Credit	Payment 2008	0.00				55,010.04	2572
Register No		**69**									
01/12/08	In	103006	6120	Sales, Retail - EU	Order 101010	0.00	Sa	EU	RET	-1,602.90	2573
01/12/08	In	103006	2320	Customers, Foreign	Order 101010	0.00				1,602.90	2574
Register No		**70**									
01/12/08	In	103007	6120	Sales, Retail - EU	Order 101011	0.00	Sa	EU	RET	-2,498.10	2575
01/12/08	In	103007	2320	Customers, Foreign	Order 101011	0.00				2,498.10	2576
Register No		**71**									
01/12/08		2595	8710	Wages	Salaries, Week 1-2 2008	0.00				769.44	2577
01/12/08		2595	8710	Wages	Salaries, Week 1-2 2008	0.00				230.83	2578
01/12/08		2595	5310	Revolving Credit	Salaries, Week 1-2 2008	0.00				-1,000.27	2579

G/L Register — CRONUS International Ltd. — February 28, 2008 — Page 58

- **Test**: These reports are printed from `Journal` tables prior to posting transactions. Test reports are used to pre-validate data before posting.

The following screenshot is a Test report for a **General Journal** batch:

```
General Journal - Test                                                    February 28, 2008
CRONUS International Ltd.                                                  Page    1

Journal Template Name      GENERAL
Journal Batch              CASH

Gen. Journal Line: Journal Template Name: GENERAL, Journal Batch Name: CASH, Posting Date: 02/25/08

Posting     D   Document   A                                  G  Ge  Ge           Bal.
Date        Ty  No.        Ty  Account No.  Name    Description   P  Bu  Pro  Amount  Account No.  Balance (LCY)

02/25/08        G00001     G/  2330    Accrued Inte  Accrued Interest        27.50    2910         0.00
02/25/08        G00002     G/  2340    Other Receiv  Other Receivables       55.10    2910         0.00
02/25/08        G00003     G/  2330    Accrued Inte  Accrued Interest        11.15    2910         0.00
02/25/08        G00004     G/  2340    Other Receiv  Product Sales Bonu     190.00    2910         0.00

                                                     Total (LCY)            283.75                 0.00


Reconciliation

                                      Net Change in  Balance after
No.         Name                            Jnl.        Posting

2910        Cash                         -283.75       -84.74
```

The following screenshot is for another **General Journal** batch, containing only one transaction but with multiple problems, as indicated by the warning messages displayed:

```
General Journal - Test                                                    February 28, 2008
CRONUS International Ltd.                                                  Page    1

Journal Template Name      CASHRCPT
Journal Batch              GENERAL

Gen. Journal Line: Journal Template Name: CASHRCPT, Journal Batch Name: GENERAL

Posting     D   Document   A                                  G  Ge  Ge           Bal.
Date        Ty  No.        Ty  Account No.  Name    Description   P  Bu  Pro  Amount  Account No.  Balance (LCY)

01/24/08        G02001     G/  6120    Sales, Retail  Sales, Retail - EU   Sa  EU  RET  105.22              105.22
Warning!        Document G02001 is out of balance by 105.22.
Warning!        As of 01/24/08, the lines are out of balance by 105.22.
Warning!        The total of the lines is out of balance by 105.22.

                                                     Total (LCY)           105.22              105.22
```

- **Posting**: This is a report printed as an audit trail as part of a "Post and Print" process. The printing of these reports is actually controlled by the user's choice of either a **Posting Only** option or a **Post and Print** option. The Post portions of both the options work similarly. The Post and Print option runs a user-definable report, which is similar to the report one would use as a transaction report. This means that such an audit trail report, which is often needed by accountants, can be re-generated completely and accurately at any time.

| G/L Register | | | | | | | | | | | February 28, 2008 | |
| CRONUS International Ltd. | | | | | | | | | | | Page 1 | |

G/L Register: No.: 106

Posting Date	D Ty	Document No.	G/L Account No.	Name	Description	VAT Amount	G P	Ge Bu	Ge Pro	Amount	Entry No.
Register No		106									
01/24/08		2605	8320	Consultant Services	Payment, Accounting Syst	11.05	Pu	NA	SER	110.52	2734
01/24/08		2605	5631	Purchase VAT 10 %	Payment, Accounting Syst	0.00				11.05	2735
01/24/08		2605	5310	Revolving Credit	Payment, Accounting Syst	0.00				-121.57	2736
01/24/08		2607	8910	Other Costs of Operations	Packing Tape 2008	4.92	Pu	NA	MIS	19.70	2737
01/24/08		2607	5630	Purchase VAT 25 %	Packing Tape 2008	0.00				4.92	2738
01/24/08		2607	2910	Cash	Packing Tape 2008	0.00				-24.62	2739
01/24/08		2608	2910	Cash	Repair and Upgrade of Spr	0.00				-277.00	2740
01/24/08		2608	1120	Increases during the Year	Repair and Upgrade of Spr	36.93	Pu	NA	MIS	147.73	2741
01/24/08		2608	5630	Purchase VAT 25 %	Repair and Upgrade of Spr	0.00				36.93	2742
01/24/08		2608	8910	Other Costs of Operations	Repair and Upgrade of Spr	18.47	Pu	NA	MIS	73.87	2743
01/24/08		2608	5630	Purchase VAT 25 %	Repair and Upgrade of Spr	0.00				18.47	2744
01/24/08	W4-01		8450	Delivery Expenses	Parking fee	4.98	Pu	NA	MIS	19.92	2745
01/24/08	W4-01		5630	Purchase VAT 25 %	Parking fee	0.00				4.98	2746
01/24/08	W4-01		2910	Cash	Parking fee	0.00				-24.90	2747
01/24/08	Cr	2810	6120	Sales, Retail - EU	Autohaus Mielberg KG 200	0.00	Sa	EU	RET	344.90	2748
01/24/08	Cr	2810	2320	Customers, Foreign	Autohaus Mielberg KG 200	0.00				-344.90	2749

Report Types Summarized

Type	Description
List	Used to list volumes of like data in a tabular format, such as Sales Order Lines, a list of Customers, or a list of General Ledger Entries.
Document	Used in "record-per-page" situations, such as a Sales Invoice, a Purchase Order, a Manufacturing Work Order, or a Customer Statement.
Transaction	Generally a list of transactions in List format, such as a list of General Ledger Entries, Physical Inventory Journal Entries, or Salesperson To-Do List.
Test	Printed in List format as a pre-validation test and data review prior to a Journal Posting run. A Test Report option can be found on any Journal form such as General Journal, Item Journal, or the Jobs Journal.
Posting	Printed in List format as a record of what data transactions were Posted into permanent status (i.e. moved from a Journal to a Ledger). A Posting report can be retained as an audit trail of posting activity.

Report Naming

Simple reports are often named the same as the table with which they are primarily associated plus a word or two describing the basic report purpose. The report type examples we've already looked at illustrate this: **General Journal–Test**, **G/L Register**, **Customer Order–Detail**.

Common key report purpose names include the words Journal, Register, List, Test, and Statistics.

The naming of reports can have a conflict between naming based on the associated tables and naming based on the use of the data. Just as with forms, the usage context should take precedence in naming reports.

Report Components Overview

What we generally refer to as the report or report object is technically referred to as a Report Description. The Report Description is the information describing the layout for the planned output and processing logic to be followed when processing the data. Report Descriptions are stored in the database in the same way as other table or form descriptions.

As with forms, we will just use the term reports, whether we mean the output, the description, or the object. Reports share many other attributes with forms including aspects of the Designer, features of various Controls, some Triggers, and even some of the Properties. Where those parallels exist, we should take notice of that. The consistency of any toolset, including NAV, makes it easier to learn and to use. This applies to developers as well as to the users.

The overall structure of an NAV Report consists of all the following elements. Any particular report may utilize only a small number of the possible elements, but many, many different combinations are feasible and logical.

- Report Properties
- Report Triggers
- Data Items
    - Data Item Properties
    - Data Item Triggers
    - Data Item Sections
        - Section Properties
        - Section Triggers
        - Controls
            - Control Properties

- Request Form
- Request Form Properties
  - ° Request Form Triggers
  - ° Request Form Controls
    - ° Request Form Control Properties
    - ° Request Form Control Triggers

The Components of a Report Description

A Report Description consists of a number of primary components, each of which in turn is made up of secondary components. The primary components **Report Properties and Triggers** and **Data Item Properties and Triggers** define the data flow and overall logic for processing the data. Another set of primary components, **Data Item Sections and Controls**, define the appearance of the information that is presented for printing (or equivalent) output. The component is constructed using a moderately primitive, yet useful, report layout "painter". The report painter allows us to create a report layout in a semi-graphical format, a limited WYSIWYG. Even though the primary parts of a report are separate and different, they are only semi-independent. Each interrelates with and is dependent on the others.

There is another primary functional component of a report description, the **Request Form**. It displays as a form when a report is invoked. The purpose of the Report Request Form is to allow users to enter information to control the report. Control information entered through a Request Form may include filters, control dates, other control parameters, and specifications as well as which available formatting or processing options to use for this instance of the report (i.e. for this run). The Request Form appears once at the beginning of a report at run time.

Report Data Flow

One of the principle advantages of the NAV report is its built-in data flow structure. At the beginning of any report, you must define the data item(s), i.e. tables, that the report will process. There are rare exceptions to this requirement, where you might create a report for the purposes of processing only. In such a case, you might have no data item, just a set of logic whose data flow is totally self-controlled. Normally though, NAV automatically creates a data flow process for each data item. This automatically created data flow provides specific triggers and processing events:

1. Preceding the data
2. For each record of the data
3. Following the end of the data

The underlying "black-box" report logic (the part we can't see or affect) loops through the named tables, reading and processing one record at a time. That flow is automatic, i.e. we don't have to program it. Therefore, any time we need a process that steps through a set of data one record at a time, it is quite likely we will use a report object.

If you've ever worked with some of the legacy report writers or the RPG programming language, you will likely recognize this behavior. That recognition may allow you to more quickly understand how to take advantage of NAV reports.

The reference to a table in a report is referred to as a **Data Item**. One of the capabilities of the report data flow structure is the ability to nest data items. If Data Item 2 is nested within Data Item 1 and related back to Data Item 1, then for each record in Data Item 1, all the related records in Data Item 2 will be processed. The following screenshot shows the data item screen.

This particular example uses tables from our C/ANDL system. The design is for a report to list all the Education Activities by **Course** for each Member. Thus Member is the primary table (i.e. **DataItem1**). For each Member, we want to list all the Courses that have had activity (i.e. **DataItem2**). And for each **Course**, we want to list its **Education Activity** (i.e. **DataItem3**).

On the Data Item screen, we initially enter the table name Member, as you see in the following screenshot. The Data Item Name, which is what the C/AL code will refer to, is **DataItem1** in our example here. When we enter the second table, Course, then we click on the right arrow at the bottom of the screen. That will cause the selected data item to be indented relative to the data item above (the "superior" data item). What that does to data flow is to nest the processing of the indented data item within the processing of the superior data item. In this instance, we have renamed the Data Items only for the purpose of our example illustrating data flow within a report. The normal default behavior would be for the **Name** in the right column to default to the table name shown in the left column (e.g. the Name for Member would display by default as <Member>). This default Data Item Name would only need to be changed if the same table appeared twice within the Data Item list. In that case, for the second instance of Member, for example, you would simply give it the Name Member2.

For each record in the superior data item, the indented data item will be fully processed. What records are actually processed in the indented table will depend on the filters, and the defined relationships between the superior and indented tables. In other words, the visible indentation is only part of the necessary definition. We'll review the rest of it shortly.

For our example, we enter a third table, `Education Activity Ledger`, and enter our example name of **DataItem3**.

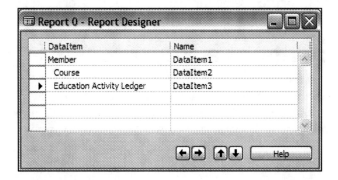

The following chart shows the data flow for this Data Item structure. The chart boxes are intended to show the nesting that results from the indenting of the Data Items in the preceding screenshot. The Course Data Item is indented under the Member Data Item. That means for every processed Member record, all selected Course records will be processed. That same logic applies to the Course records and Education Activity records (i.e. for each Course record processed, all selected Education Activity records are processed).

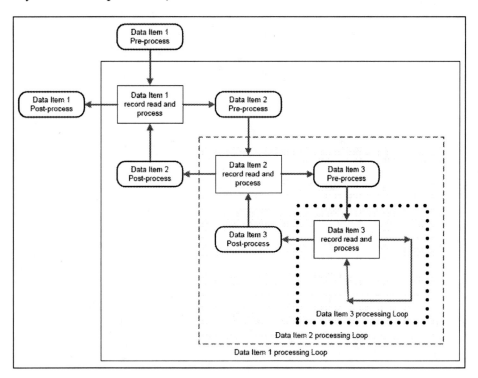

Again, the blocks illustrate how the data item nesting controls the data flow. As you can see, the full range of processing for **DataItem2** occurs for each **DataItem1** record. In turn, the full range of processing for **DataItem3** occurs for each **DataItem2** record.

The Elements of a Report

Earlier we reviewed a list of all the elements of a Report object. Now we're going to learn about each of those elements. Our goal here is to understand how the pieces of the report puzzle fit together to form a useful, coherent whole. Following that, we will do some development work for our C/ANDL system to apply some of what we've reviewed.

Report Properties

The Report Properties are shown in the following screenshot. A number of these properties have essentially the same purpose as those in forms (and other objects too). We won't spend much time on those.

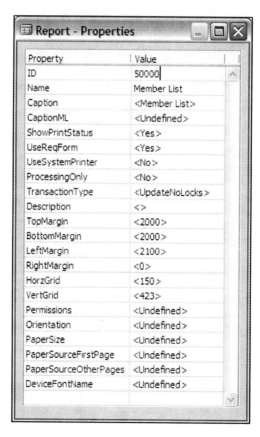

The description is as follows:

- **ID**: The unique report object number.
- **Name**: The name by which this report is referred to within C/AL code.
- **Caption**: The name that is displayed for this report; **Caption** defaults to **Name**.
- **CaptionML**: The **Caption** translation for a defined alternative language.
- **ShowPrintStatus**: Determines if the status of print processing is shown along with a user-accessible **Cancel** button.
- **UseReqForm**: Determines if a Request Form should be displayed to allow the user choice of Sort Sequence and entry of filters and other requested control information.
- **UseSystemPrinter**: Determines if the default printer for the report should be the defined system printer or if NAV should check for a setup-defined User/Report printer definition.
- **ProcessingOnly**: This should be set to **Yes** when the report object is being used only to process data and no report output is to be generated. If this property is set to **Yes**, then that overrides any other property selections that would apply in a report-generating situation.
- **TransactionType**: This can be in one of four basic options: **Browse**, **Snapshot**, **UpdateNoLocks**, and **Update**. These control the record locking behavior to be applied in this report. The default is **UpdateNoLocks**. This property is generally only used by advanced developers
- **Description**: This is for internal documentation; it is not often used.
- **TopMargin, BottomMargin, LeftMargin, RightMargin**: Define the default margins for the report document. The units are in 1/100 millimeters (just like placement of controls on forms and, as you will see later, in report layouts). These settings can be overridden by the user if the Request Form is active (in that case the user can access **File | Page Setup** from the menus at the top of the screen and change any of the margin values).
- **HorzGrid, VertGrid**: Define the values for the visible grid, which is intended to help you align controls in the report layout "painter" screen. (Not very useful.)
- **Permissions**: This provides report-specific setting of permissions, which are the rights to access data, subdivided into Read, Insert, Modify, and Delete. This allows the developer to define report and processing permissions that override the user-by-user permissions security setup.

The following printer-specific properties can be overridden by user selections made at run time.

- **Orientation**: Defines whether the default print orientation for printed output will be portrait or landscape.

- **PaperSize**: Defines the default paper size to be used. See **Help** for additional information.

- **PaperSourceFirstPage, PaperSourceOtherPages**: These allow defining the printer tray to be used for the first and subsequent report pages. Because the control codes for printers differ greatly from one to another, the various tray descriptions are not likely to be meaningful except for a particular printer. Choosing the desired control code will be a matter of trial and error testing.

- **DeviceFontName**: This allows defining a printer resident font to be used. Most useful for controlling impact printers to keep the printer from operating in a graphic (i.e. slow) mode.

Report Triggers

The following screenshot shows the Report Triggers available in a report:

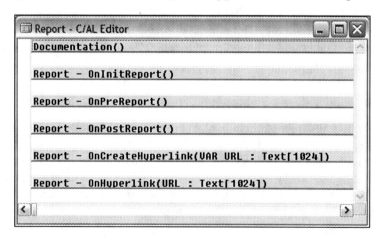

The description is as follows:

- `Documentation()` serves only the purpose of containing whatever documentation you care to put there. No C/AL code is executed in a `Documentation` trigger. You have no format restrictions, other than common sense and your defined practices.

- `OnInitReport()` executes once when the report is opened.

- `OnPreReport()` executes once after the Request Form completes. All the Data Item processing follows this trigger.

- `OnPostReport()` if the report is completed normally, this trigger executes once at the end of all other report processing. All the Data Item processing precedes this trigger.

- `OnCreateHyperlink()` contains code to be executed when a user creates a hyperlink, for example to send a report by email.

- `OnHyperlink()` executes a URL string.

There are general explanations of Report Triggers both in the Application Designer's Guide and the on-line **Help**; you should also review those explanations.

Data Items

The following screenshot is very similar to the example we looked at when we reviewed Data Item Flow. This time though, we allowed the **Name** assigned to the Data Items to default. That means the names will be assigned to be the same as the table names they reference.

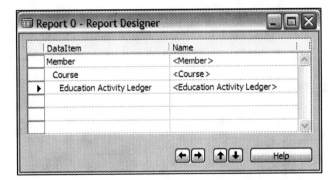

Reasons for changing the names assigned include making them shorter for ease of coding or making them unique, which is required when the same table is referred to multiple times in a report. For example, suppose you were creating a report that was to list first Open Sales Orders, then Open Sales Invoices, and then Open Sales Credit Memos. Since all three of these data sets are in the same tables (`Sales Header` and `Sales Line`), you might create a report with Data Item names of SalesHeader1, SalesHeader2, and SalesHeader3, all referencing Sales Header Data Items.

Data Item Properties

The following screenshots show the properties of the three Data Items in the previous screenshot. The first one shows the **Member-Properties**:

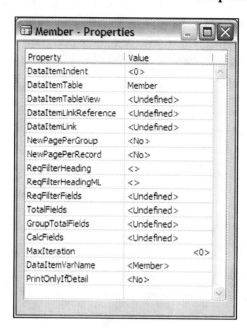

The following screenshot shows **Course-Properties**:

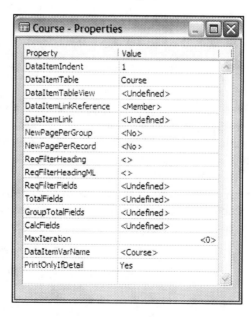

The following one shows the **Education Activity Ledger — properties**:

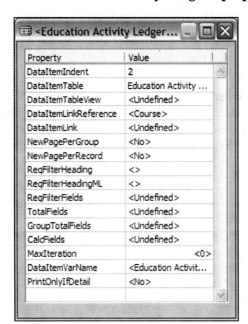

These are the descriptions of each of the properties mentioned:

- **DataItemIndent**: This shows the position of the referenced Data Item in the hierarchical structure of the report. A value of **0** (zero) indicates that this Data Item is at the top of the hierarchy. Any other value indicates the subject Data Item is subordinate to (i.e. nested within) the preceding Data Item with a lower valued **DataItemIndent** property (e.g. a **DataItemIndent** of 1 is subordinate to 0).

  Looking at the first property listed in each of the three preceding screenshots, we see Member with **DataItemIndent = 0**, Course with **DataItemIndent = 1**, and Education Activity Ledger with **DataItemIndent = 2**. Referring back to the earlier discussion about data flow, we can see that the specified Course table data will be processed through for each record processed in the Member table and the specified Education Activity Ledger table data will be processed through completely for each record processed in the Course table.

- **DataItemTable**: This names the table assigned to this Data Item.

- **DataItemTableView**: Definition of the fixed limits to be applied to the Data Item (what key, ascending or descending sequence, and what filters to apply). If you don't define a key, then the users can choose what key they wanted to control the data sort used during processing.

If you choose a key and, in the **ReqFilterFields** property, you do not specify any Filter Field names to be displayed, this Data Item will not have a tab displayed as part of the Request Form. That will keep the user from filtering this Data Item.

- **DataItemLinkReference**: This names the Data Item in the hierarchy above the Data Item to which this one is linked. The linked Data Item could also be referred to as the parent Data Item. As you can see, this property is **Undefined** for Member because Member is at the top of the Data Item hierarchy for this report.

- **DataItemLink**: This identifies the field-to-field linkage between this Data Item and its parent Data Item. That linkage acts as a filter because only those records in this table will be processed that have a value match with the linked field in the parent data item. In our sample, the Course Data Item does not have a **DataItemLink** specified. That means that no field linkage filter will be applied and all of the records in the Course table will be processed for each record processed in its parent table, the Member table.

- **NewPagePerGroup, NewPagePerRecord**: These define whether or not a page break should automatically be taken at the start of each new group or each new record. Groups of data provide the basis for generated breakouts and totalling functions.

- **ReqFilterHeader, ReqFilterHeadingML**: The heading that will appear at the top of the Request Form tab for this Data Item. That tab is where the user can enter filters for this Data Item.

- **ReqFilterFields**: This allows you to choose certain fields to be named on the appropriate Report Request Form tab to make it easier for the user to use them as filter fields. So long as the Report Request Form tab is activated for a Data Item, the user can choose any available field in the table for filtering, regardless of what is specified here. Note the earlier comments for the **DataItemTableView** property are relative to this property.

- **TotalFields, GroupTotalFields**: These define all the fields in the Data Item for which you want the system to automatically maintain totals for all the data processed. **GroupTotalFields** are subtotals by group. These totals can be printed in any of the appropriate footer sections.

- **CalcFields**: This names the FlowFields that are to be calculated for each record processed. Because FlowFields do not contain data, they have to be calculated to be used. When a FlowField is displayed in a form, NAV automatically does the calculation. When a FlowField is to be used in a report, you must instigate the calculation. That can either be done here in this property or explicitly within the C/AL code.

- **MaxIteration**: This can be used to limit the number of iterations (i.e. loops) the report will make through this Data Item to a predefined maximum. An example would be to set this to **7** for processing with the virtual Date table to process one week's worth of data.

- **DataItemVarName**: This contains the name shown in the right column of the Data Item screen, the name by which this table is referenced in this report's C/AL code.

- **PrintOnlyIfDetail**: This should only be used if this Data Item has a child Data Item, i.e. one indented/nested below it. If **PrintOnlyIfDetail** is **Yes**, then sections associated with this Data Item will only print when data is processed for the child Data Item.

  In the preceding screenshots, you have seen that this property is set to **Yes** only for the **Course** Data Item. That is done so that if there is no **Education Activity** for a particular **Course** for that **Member**, nothing will print for that **Course**. If we wanted to print only Members who have Education Activity, we could also set to **Yes** the **PrintOnlyIfDetail** property on the Member Data Item.

Data Item Triggers

Each Data Item has the following Triggers available:

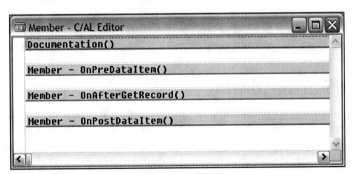

The description is as follows:

- Documentation() is actually the same instance of this trigger that showed when we looked at the report triggers. There is only one Documentation trigger in any object.

  The rest of the Data Item triggers are where the bulk of the flow logic is placed for any report. Additionally, developer defined functions may be freely and voluminously added, but, for the most part, they will be called from within these three triggers.

- `OnPreDataItem()` is the logical place for any pre-processing to take place that couldn't be handled in report or Data Item properties or in the two report pre-processing triggers.

- `OnAfterGetRecord()` is the data "read/process loop". Code placed here has full access to the data of each record, one record at a time. This trigger is repetitively processed until the logical end of table is reached for this table. This is where you would likely look at data in the related tables. This trigger is represented on our report Data Flow diagram as any one of the boxes labeled Data Item processing Loop.

- `OnPostDataItem()` executes after all the records in this Data Item are processed unless the report is terminated by means of a User **Cancel** or execution of a C/AL BREAK or QUIT function, or an error.

Data Item Sections

Earlier in our discussion of reports, we referred to the primary components of a report. The Triggers and Properties we have reviewed so far are the data flow components. Now we're going to review the elements of sections, which are the output layout and formatting components.

Each report layout can consist of a number of layout sections, each defining a portion of the printed report structure. Each section can appear not at all, one time, or several times. Each section can appear (or not) for each Data Item. Your work on sections occurs on the **Section Designer** screen. The Section Designer is accessed from the **Report Designer Data Item** screen via the top menu bar, selecting **View | Sections**.

Run-Time Formatting

When NAV prints a report (to screen, or to hardcopy, or to PDF, or whatever), NAV will use the printer driver for the currently assigned printer to control the formatting. If you change the target printer for a report, the output results may change depending on the attributes of the drivers of the first printer and the second printer.

In most cases, the display on screen in **Preview** mode will accurately represent how the report will appear when actually printed. In some cases though, NAV's output generation on screen differs considerably from the hardcopy version. This appears to be most likely to occur when the selected printer is either an impact printer (e.g. dot matrix) or a special purpose printer (e.g. a bar code label printer).

Report Wizard-Generated Sections

If you create a report using the Report Wizard, you will get some sections created by the Wizard. All the sections shown in the following screenshot of our **Report 50000 Member List**, which we created in an earlier chapter, were generated by the Report Wizard. The generated sections include the controls that display headings (**Member, Header (1)** and **Member, Header (2)**) and data (**Member, Body (3)**).

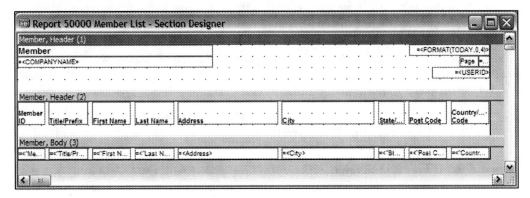

In one way, sections are similar to triggers. They are executed based on the occurrence of certain processing events. All the report sections are listed and described in the following section. Very few reports contain all of these in one report. You can have multiples of any of the sections and can have any combination of sections. Each section can display just one line or a whole page. In fact a section may display no lines, but simply be present as a container for some C/AL code to be executed at the right point in the report processing sequence. You cannot have more than one section on a report line. The sequence of sections is fixed and cannot be changed, but any section may be skipped in the course of processing.

Report Section Descriptions

The report sections are described in the following list:

- **Header**: This generally describes the beginning of the report. At least one header section for the primary Data Item is usually set to appear at the top of each page. The first header section in the preceding screenshot illustrates a header that we would likely print at the top of each page.

- **Group Header**: This is generated at the beginning of a defined group, a group usually being a sub-total level. For example, a report showing Sales by Customer, with Customers grouped by Territory, could have a group header for each Territory.

- **TransHeader**: This is generated at the point of a page transition, on the new page. This allows for report design features such as the carry forward of totals from a previous page to the next page, a common layout style.

- **Body**: This is typically the primary point to output data for the report. But a summary report, for example, might not have a body section at all, but only a footer section.

- **TransFooter**: This is generated at the point of a page transition (page overflow), at the bottom of a page. Often used in combination with a TransHeader section, showing the accumulative totals at the bottom on one page, these same totals then being printed by a TransHeader section at the top of the next page. Or, in a variation of that, you might show just the total for the page in the TransFooter and have no following TransHeader section.

- **Group Footer**: This is generated at the end of a group of data. This section typically contains subtotals. It may also contain fixed data such as contract terms on the bottom of an Invoice, etc.

- **Footer**: This is generated at the end of the processing for a Data Item. If the report contains nested data items, then the footer for the child data item would be invoked for every record in the parent data item. A Footer section usually contains higher-level totals. If it is the footer for the primary Data Item for the report, it will often contain grand totals. Obviously it can contain whatever information is appropriate for the end of the particular report.

When a report is created totally within the Report Designer using the Wizard only to access the **Create a blank report** option, only the body sections are generated automatically as you define Data Items. Any additional sections are added while working in the Section Designer screen. You can invoke the **Insert New Section** screen from the **Edit** menu **New** option, or by simply pressing *F3*. In either case, you will see the window shown in the following screenshot:

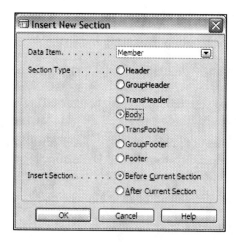

Using our Member Education Activity report as an example, if we added a new section for each of the possible choices, we would have the following. Note that the nesting (indentation) of the dependent (child) data items is shown by the **>** and **>>** symbols leading the individual section names where appropriate.

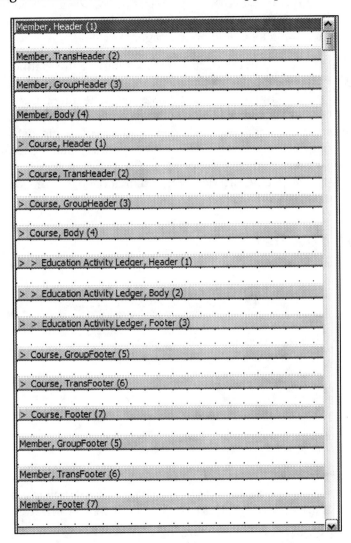

Also, note the sequential numbering in parentheses for the sections. Each sequence relates to the Data Item tied to that set of sections. In our example, there are seven sections tied to `Member`, seven tied to `Course`, and only three sections tied to `Education Activity Ledger`.

More Run-Time Formatting

NAV's report processing logic is not directly visible to us (it is one of those software "black boxes" that we aren't allowed to see into) and that makes understanding how it works more difficult. When NAV prepares to execute a section for printing, it evaluates how much print space this section will take and compares that to the calculated space remaining available on the page.

If NAV calculates that printing this section would overflow the defined physical page, then NAV will force a page break (with the associated TransFooter, Header, and TransHeader processing) and print this section on the new page. If you've defined any combination of footer sections (TransFooter, GroupFooter, Footer), you may have a circumstance where the NAV report processing logic just seems to go crazy. Your challenge is to figure out what it is projecting when it tries to print a section and then seems to haphazardly print several pages in order to get that section out. If you accidentally specify a section bigger than a page in size, your results can be even more unusual.

Section Properties

The properties for a **Header** section are shown in the following screenshot:

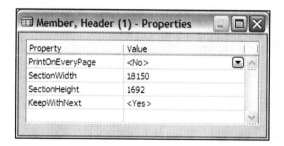

The description is as follows:

- **PrintOnEveryPage**: This is self-explanatory. Set it to **Yes** if you want this section to be printed at the top of every page. The default is **No** (obviously), but the Report Wizard sets this to **Yes** when it creates a header section.
- **SectionWidth**: This is the measure in 1/100 mm of the physical width of the print section.
- **SectionHeight**: This is the measure in 1/100 mm of the physical height of the print section. The default height for a single line is 423 mm/100. The value here will be used by NAV's print management routine to determine if this section can be printed on this page or if a page break should be forced first.

- **KeepWithNext**: If this is set to **Yes**, then NAV will attempt to keep this section's output on the same page with the output of the next section of the same type for the same Data Item. If you have several of these strung together, you may occasionally get some surprising results.

The properties for a **Body** section are a subset of what was just described for header.

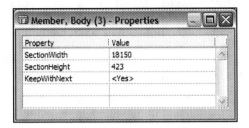

The properties for a **Footer** section are a superset of those for a header.

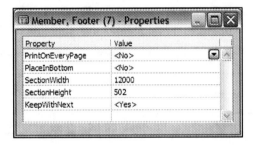

The following is the only additional property:

- **PlaceInBottom**: This allows you to control whether the footer will just follow whatever printed previously without any special positioning (the default) or if the footer should be forced to the bottom of the page. If you have two footer sections defined, this property must be the same in both.

Section Triggers

The following are the section triggers:

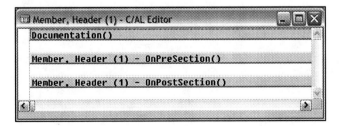

Their description is as follows:

- `OnPreSection()` contains code that is executed before NAV begins processing the section. Intended primarily as a place to decide "print or don't print" based on data or some status of the processing, when this trigger is processed, the NAV report processing has not yet done its report spacing calculations to determine page positioning. The Application Designer's Guide makes a strong point that data manipulation processing should not occur here.

- `OnPostSection()` contains code to be executed after the section is processed but before it is printed (i.e. the page number is correct). Again, data manipulation processing should not occur here.

Controls for Reports

Only the controls that are actually implemented for reports are listed. Even though the controls toolbox has all the same icons in the Report Designer as it does in the Form Designer, the inoperable ones are grayed out. Look at the following screenshot:

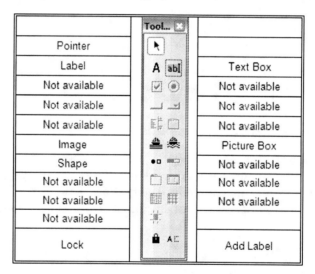

	Tool...	
Pointer		
Label		Text Box
Not available		Not available
Not available		Not available
Not available		Not available
Image		Picture Box
Shape		Not available
Not available		Not available
Not available		Not available
Not available		
Lock		Add Label

The following is the description of those controls that are mostly implemented for reports:

- **Label**: This contains a literal, which must be defined (i.e. to a fixed value) before compilation.

- **Text Box**: This contains the value of a variable, bound to the control, which can be displayed in one or more characters.

- **Image**: This allows the display of a picture. The only data format supported for images is the bitmap format with a maximum size of 32 Kb. The image control is analogous to a text label in that the contents of the image control must be defined during development, before compilation.

- **Picture Box**: This allows the display of a picture from bitmap-formatted data (maximum size of 32 Kb) or a BLOB (bitmaps with a maximum size of 2 GB). The contents of a picture box can be changed dynamically during program execution. In Chapter 7, we will discuss the C/AL function CALCFIELDS. That function must be applied to any BLOB data before it can be displayed.

- **Shape**: This allows a very minimal graphical capability through the selection of one of eight shape alternatives. The shape options provided are rectangle, rounded rectangle, oval, triangle, NW-Line (back leaning line), NE-Line (forward leaning line), HorizLine, and VertLine. The use of these shapes does allow some very limited on screen graphics. The properties support choosing at least the size, line width, and line color plus a couple of other attributes depending on the specified shape. But NAV won't print colors, only display them on-screen.

- **Lock**: A toolbox function, not a control, which allows you to select a control, then "lock" it in to allow multiple insertions of the selected control. Frankly, this is not often useful.

- **Add Label**: This is also a toolbox function, not a control, which adds a label control to whatever controls you select until you close the toolbox. Interesting, but also not all that useful.

 Report controls don't have any triggers.

Control Properties

The list of properties for individual report controls is the same as the list for those same controls in the forms context. But some of those properties either don't make sense in the report context (e.g. ToolTip) or just don't work in that context (e.g. those properties relating to color). The following screenshot lists the properties for report controls. Those with **X** serve a purpose similar to their defined purpose in a form control. Those properties with blank entries serve no purpose in a report.

Property	Label	Text Box	Image	Picture Box	Shape
ID	X	X	X	X	X
Name	X	X	X	X	X
Xpos	X	X	X	X	X
Ypos	X	X	X	X	X
Width	X	X	X	X	X
Height	X	X	X	X	X
HorzGlue					
VertGlue					
Visible	X	X	X	X	X
Enabled					
Editable					
Focusable					
ParentControl	X	X	X	X	X
InFrame					
InPage					
InColumn					
InColumnHeading					
InMatrix					
InMatrixHeading					
Caption	X	X		X	
CaptionML	X	X		X	
HorizAlign	X	X			
VertAlign	X	X			
ForeColor					
BackColor					
BackTransparent					
Border	X	X	X	X	X
BorderColor					
BorderStyle	X	X	X	X	
BorderWidth	X	X	X	X	
Shape Style					X
FontName	X	X			
FontSize	X	X			
FontBold	X	X			
FontItalic	X	X			
FontStrikethru	X	X			
FontUnderline	X	X			
MultiLine	X	X			
PadChar	X	X			
LeaderDots	X	X			
MaxLength		X			

Property	Label	Text Box	Image	Picture Box	Shape
PasswordText					
AutoEnter					
Bitmap			X		
BitmapList				X	
ToolTip					
ToolTipML					
Lookup					
DrillDown					
AssistEdit					
DropDown					
PermanentAssist					
Description	X	X	X	X	X
OptionString		X			
OptionCaption		X			
OptionCaptionML		X			
DecimalPlaces		X			
Title		X			
MinValue		X			
MaxValue		X			
NotBlank		X			
Numeric		X			
CharAllowed		X			
DateFormula		X			
ClosingDates		X			
ValuesAllowed		X			
NextControl					
ClearOnLookup					
Format		X			
BlankNumbers		X			
BlankZero		X			
SignDisplacement		X			
AutoFormatType		X			
AutoFormatExpr		X			
CaptionClass	X	X		X	
Divisor		X			
SourceExpr		X		X	
AutoCalcField		X		X	
TableRelation		X			
ValidateTableRelation		X			
LookupFormID					
DrillDownFormID					

Inheritance

Inheritance operates for data displayed through report controls just as it does for forms controls, but obviously limited to print-applicable properties. Properties, such as decimal formatting, are inherited. Remember, if the property is explicitly defined in the table, it cannot be less restrictively defined elsewhere. This is one reason why it's so important to focus on table design as the foundation of the system.

Request Form

The Request Form is a form that is executed at the beginning of a report. Its presence or absence is under developer control. A Request Form looks similar to the following screenshot based on one of our C/ANDL reports:

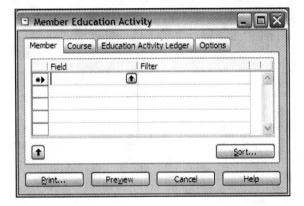

The tabs tied to the Data Items appear as a result of report and Data Item property settings. The **Options** tab appears when you, as the developer, create a form requesting user interaction with the report beyond the entry of filters. You should also note in the screenshot above that the Request Form is where the **Sort, Print,** and **Preview** buttons appear. If you create a report with no Request Form (i.e. **UseReqForm** property set to **False**), you won't have the **Print** and **Preview** options available.

A complicated **Options** tab is represented in the following screenshot of the **Options** tab for the Statement Report 116.

A Request Form **Options** tab can be created from the Report Designer's Data Item screen by accessing **View, Request Form**. When you do that for a new **Request Options Form,** you are presented with a blank slate similar to the following screenshot:

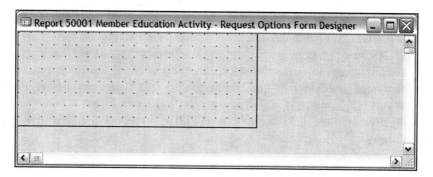

From that point, the layout design process is very much similar to the general-purpose Form Designer. There are some important differences though. First, this is an unbound form. It is not tied to any table. Second, at the point where the Request Form executes, not much has happened within the report. The OnInitReport() trigger has run and the **Data Item Table Views** have been set in accordance with what was defined in the Data Item properties. These differences significantly affect the logic flow and associated C/AL code that we create to support a Request Form.

Request Form Properties

While there is a full set of form properties available for viewing and setting any Request Form, they do not seem to be useful. Setting these does not appear to change the behavior of a Request Form.

Request Form Triggers

A considerable number of triggers show up when you look at the C/AL code (*F9*) display for a Request Form. Only six of those triggers appear to be actually executed:

- `OnInit()` executes as the Request Form opens. This is a good place to initialize any Request Form variables.

- `OnOpenForm()` executes immediately after the `OnInit()` Request Form trigger.

- `OnActivateForm()` executes when the **Options** tab of the Request Form is activated.

- `OnDeactivateForm()` executes when the **Options** tab of the Request Form is deactivated by either returning to a Data Item tab or by exiting the request form.

- `OnQuesryCloseForm()` and `OnCloseForm()` execute (in that order) when the report completes.

Request Form Controls

Although when you call up the Toolbox while in Request Form Designer, it appears that all the controls we reviewed in the chapter on Forms are available, most of them don't operate in this context. The controls that are available to you are the ones that allow you to display or enter data that can logically be used to control the report you are about to run. The controls that are useful in the Request Form are:

- Label
- Text Box
- Check Box
- Option Button

The operation and properties for each of these controls are essentially the same as they would be for a standard form (see the Forms chapter for more information on form controls' behavior).

Request Form Control Triggers

In the chapter on forms, you were cautioned not to place C/AL code within a form if there was a way to avoid doing so. In the case of Request Forms, the only way to validate control information input in unbound controls is within the form. There are a number of triggers available for Request Form controls, but the most common (and most logical to use) is the OnValidate() trigger. This trigger executes when data has been entered into a control and completed with an *Enter* or *Tab* key.

Processing-Only Reports

One of the report properties we reviewed earlier was **ProcessingOnly**. If that is set to **Yes**, then the report object will not output a report, but will simply do whatever processing you program it to do. The beauty of this capability is that you can use the built-in processing loop of the NAV report object along with its sorting and filtering capabilities to create a variety of data updating routines with a minimum of programming. Use of the report objects also gives you access to the Request Form to allow user input and guidance for the run. You could create the same functionality using Codeunit objects and programming all the loops, the filtering, the user-interface Request Form, etc., yourself. But with a Processing-Only Report, NAV takes the load off you.

When running a Processing-Only object, you see very little difference as a user. You see that there is no visible output at the end of processing, of course. And at the beginning, the Processing-Only Request Form looks very much as it would for a printing report. Just a little earlier in the section on Request Forms, we saw a sample Request Form for one of our multi-table C/ANDL reports. The following is a screenshot of that same report structure, but now it is set up for Processing Only.

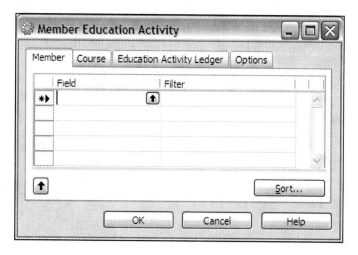

As you can see, comparing this Request Form screenshot to the one shown earlier for a standard report run, the differences are that the **Print** and **Preview** buttons missing in this screenshot, with an **OK** button in their place. Everything else looks the same.

Revising a Generated Report

In Chapter 1, we created Report 50000 Member List, using the Report Wizard. Look at the sections for that report, recalling that all this came from the Report Wizard.

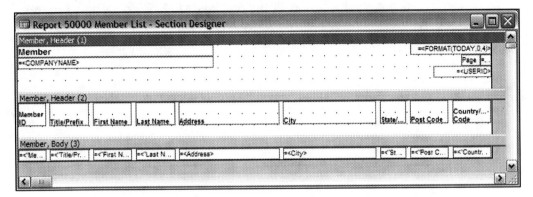

The first section is **Member, Header (1)**. While this section is designed to be the effective "report header", you can see that it is really a header for the Data Item for which the Wizard generated the report. This is often the case, as there is no way to have a section that isn't tied to a specific Data Item.

As a default for this header the Wizard uses the name of the primary Data Item (the only one that the Wizard will ever "know" about) as the Report Title (see "Member" in the first Label Control). That Label Control is left justified with a subheading below of a text box Control containing the **COMPANYNAME** field, a system variable based on the name of the company open in the database at the time this report is being run (when you open the database, you see a list of the Companies available, by Company Name).

On the right side of this first section, the Wizard puts fields for the **Date** the report is being run, the page number, and the ID of the user running the report. The positioning of these fields at the right side of the **Header (1)** section is right justified at the right margin of the page based on the default printer page setup at the time of the report generation.

Now look at the **Header (2)** and **Body** sections. See how the data fields extend beyond (to the right of) the right end of the **Header (1)** controls. If in fact the report date and page number are at the right side of the page, then it would seem these fields are off the edge of the paper. Let's find out.

If you haven't entered any sample Member data, now would be a good time to enter at least a few Member records, filling in all the fields on at least some of the records. Now run Report 50000, selecting the **Preview** option so that you can see the results on your screen. What is the right edge of the displayed data? If your report looks like the following screenshot, your rightmost fully displayed field is **Post Code**. But the rightmost field in our layout was **Country/Region Code**.

Member								A
CRONUS International Ltd.								
Member								Co
ID	Title/Prefix	First Name	Last Name	Address	City	State/Pr	Post Code	Co
42	Mr.	David	Smith	2007 Maple Street	Chicago	IL	60611	US
101	Mrs.	Karen	Jones	1444 Ellison Way	Green Bay	WI	54308	US
406	Ms.	Rebecca	Martin	111 Biringham Road	Atlanta	GA	30305	US
1003	Mr.	Christopher	Longfellow	921 Ogden Avenue	Naperville	IL	60540	US
15000	Dr.	Juan	Lopez	18 Newport Road	Canton	OH	44612	US

What you see is the result of the Wizard creating the layout it was told to create. It doesn't matter whether or not it would work properly in an operational situation. Of course, if you decided to change your page setup from Portrait to Landscape, then your printed page would be wide enough for the report as currently laid out.

Revision—First Design

Let's try that. Open Report 50000 in the Designer, highlight the first empty Data Item line and click on **View | Properties**. Click on the **Orientation** property and change it to **Landscape**. Exit, save, and compile the object. Run the report in again **Preview** mode. This time you should see all of the data in the **Header (2)** and **Body** sections on your screen. Of course, your user could have used his/her page setup to accomplish the same thing, but if your report was always going to require landscape orientation, it only makes sense for you as developer to set it once rather than every user setting it themselves.

Another alternative would be to change the report layout so it will fit on the page in portrait mode. Because the Wizard uses the maximum size of each field to position fields and because the Wizard only places fields in a single row, its layout creativity is pretty low. You, on the other hand, can be much more creative. To save time, you start with the Wizard. When the Wizard has done its work, guided by you, you take over and improve the result.

To experiment with that approach, let's first change the Report **Orientation** property from Landscape back to Portrait. Once that's done, you should save and compile your report. Now we're going to revise the generated report in a couple of simple ways just so you can get an idea of what can be done. After that, it'll be up to you to explore these and other options.

First, copy the generated report so we can work on it without fear of losing what we have done successfully so far. Open the report in Designer, then select **File | Save As** and save the report as ID **50003** with **-1** appended to the name. We're just trying to select an **ID** that isn't in use and to which we have access. NAV doesn't allow two objects of the same type to have the same name, so we've changed the name enough to take care of that requirement. You should have a screen similar to the following screenshot:

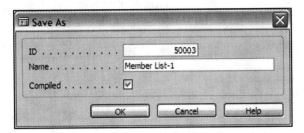

The first approach we're going to try is to put the data onto two lines. This is a several-step process, which you can approach in a variety of ways. We'll talk about one approach, but you should experiment with different methods and, over time, choose the approach that is most comfortable and efficient for you. We'll do our work on the copied object, 50003.

You can use either a visual "painter" mode or you can work strictly "by the numbers" using the properties. If you want perfect alignment and very fine control of positioning of controls, you will use the **XPos** and **YPos** properties in the end, whether or not you start with the "paint" drag-and-drop approach. Many find the combination approach easier because using drag-and-drop allows you to see the approximate layout, but setting the **XPos** and **YPos** properties lets you fine-tune the result.

In this case, we will move the **State/Province**, **Postal Zone**, and **Country** controls to a second line in the **Body** section, below the **City** control. We will move the three controls together just as they are originally positioned, but will locate them on a second line of the section, left justified with the **City** control. You can highlight all three controls at once, drag them over and drop them into the position. You can use the group movement to align them by eye to the best of your ability.

Some of the things that seem intuitive to do just can't be done. It isn't possible to use the align tool to left align the group of three controls with another control. The tool would just left align all four controls and that wouldn't be useful as the three controls on one line would end up stacked on top of one another (i.e. the group would not be left aligned, but each of the individual controls would be left aligned to the same position). You can't access properties for the three controls as a group, only for each control individually.

So once you get your control positioning approximated by eye, then you must check the **XPos** and **YPos** figures and align each control individually. After you get done with the data controls, you have to reduce the height of the label (header) controls to one line (423 mm/100) and then position them the same way. When you're all done, your sections should look somewhat similar to the following screenshot. It may take you a little practice to get the hang of this combined "left brain–right brain" approach, using both visual and data-oriented tools.

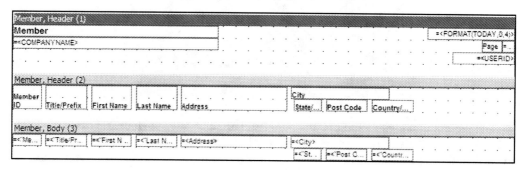

When you save, run and preview this version (Repot 50003), you should see a report result similar to the following screenshot:

Member						City			
	ID	Title/Prefix	First Name	Last Name	Address		State/Pr	Post Code	Country/Re
	42	Mr.	David	Smith	2007 Maple Street	Chicago	IL	60611	US
	101	Mrs.	Karen	Jones	1444 Ellison Way	Green Bay	WI	54306	US
	406	Ms.	Rebecca	Martin	111 Biringham Road	Atlanta	GA	30305	US
	1003	Mr.	Christopher	Longfellow	921 Ogden Avenue	Naperville	IL	60540	US
	15000	Dr.	Juan	Lopez	16 Newport Road	Canton	OH	44612	US

CRONUS International Ltd.   April 1, 2008   Page   1

Revision—Second Design

The other design approach we could easily use is to reduce the size of some of the fields where it appears the size allowed by the Wizard's generated layout is larger than the size we really need. In this case, by observation (and experience), it looks like we could squeeze down the **Title/Prefix**, the **Address** Line, the **City**, and the **State/Province** fields somewhat. Doing all these isn't necessary, so decide which ones will get you the most space with the least effort and let's go to work.

As before, we want to work on a copy of our original and, as before, we have to give it a unique name. So we'll use the same essential technique as before (highlight **Report 50000**, go to **Design | File | Save As**, set **ID** to **50004**, and set **Name** to **Member List-2**) to create the copy. Since we're going to be shortening some data controls and we would like to have the end result look as well positioned as what the Wizard does, we need to check what the Wizard does for inter-field spacing. If we check the properties of the first three or four controls on a row in a section, we'll find that the Wizard spaces controls 150 mm/100 apart. So when you re-position controls, you'll want to do the same.

The first step is to shorten the **City** field. Highlight the data control in the Body section, and then use the layout paint function to grab a handle on the right side of the control and drag it to the left, thus shortening the control. When you think you've got it resized appropriately, then it's time for a test run. One way to really test your new sizing is to enter a **Test** Member record with each field filled in to its maximum size. Those fields that are numeric, text, or code, can be filled in with the repeating string '**1234567890134567890....**'. With that test data, you can clearly see in a test run how well your control sizes fit your defined field sizes.

Member								
CRONUS International Ltd.							Page	1
Member ID	Title/Prefix	First Name	Last Name	Address	City	State/Pr	Post Code	
42	Mr.	David	Smith	2007 Maple Street	Chicago	IL	60611	
101	Mrs.	Karen	Jones	1444 Ellison Way	Green Bay	WI	54308	
408	Ms.	Rebecca	Martin	111 Biringham Road	Atlanta	GA	30305	
1003	Mr.	Christopher	Longfellow	921 Ogden Avenue	Naperville	IL	60540	
15000	Dr.	Juan	Lopez	18 Newport Road	Canton	OH	44612	
999999	Test	TestTestTest	TestTestTest	123456789012345678901234567 8	1234567890123456789 01234	1234567	1234567890	

Member report dated April 1, 2008.

In this screenshot you can see that our shortened **City** field control will display 24 characters out of the 30 the field can hold. If you think that size will work well enough for our report, we can move on to the next step. Otherwise you should resize the field and test again.

Once that field size is acceptable, then adjust the next field size, and test again. Continue this cycle until you have your fields shrunk down so that you can fit your Body section data onto a single print line. Once that is done, the next step is to move the reduced-size controls into their final position on the line. This can be done, as in the earlier design revision effort, by first using drag-and-drop, then fine-tuning the position by adjusting the **XPos** and **YPos** properties. It's probably just as easy to determine by inspection and simple math what the proper **XPos** for each control should be, and then set it accordingly. Yes, it's somewhat tedious to go step by step through each control's properties, rounding the adjusted lengths to logical figures, and calculating the proper **XPos** for the next control, using the formula:

Control N Xpos + Control X Width + 150 control separator = Control N+1 Xpos.

When you've got the Text controls in the Body Section all moved to their desired positions, then you need to resize and move the Label controls in the Header section so that they each match their respective Text controls. When you're all done, your redesigned report layout should look similar to the following screenshot:

Member								
CRONUS International Ltd.							April 1, 2008	
							Page 1	
Member ID	Title/ Prefix	First Name	Last Name	Address	City	State/ Province	Post Code	Country/Re Code
42	Mr.	David	Smith	2007 Maple Street	Chicago	IL	60611	US
101	Mrs.	Karen	Jones	1444 Ellison Way	Green Bay	WI	54306	US
406	Ms	Rebecc	Martin	111 Biringham Road	Atlanta	GA	30305	US
1003	Mr.	Christo	Longfellow	921 Ogden Avenue	Naperville	IL	60540	US
15000	Dr.	Juan	Lopez	16 Newport Road	Canton	OH	44612	US
999999	Test	TestTes	TestTestTestTest	12345678901234567890123456	12345678901234567890123 4	1234567	1234567890	1234567890

Once you like the result and decide this is the copy of the report that you want to keep for production use, it's time to wipe out the development copies and replace the original copy with the new version. One choice is to **Design** the final copy, then use **File | Save As** and assign the ID and name to overwrite the original ID of 50000 and Member List. Then delete the development Report objects 50003 and 50004. Or you could delete report objects 50000 and 50003, then renumber object 50004 to 50000 and rename it to Member List. The result is the same; you should do whatever feels more comfortable to you.

Creating a Report from Scratch

Even when you're going to create a report that cannot be done with the Report Wizard, it's still a good idea to use the Report Wizard as a starting point, if feasible. Choose the primary table in terms of data flow and layout, then rough out the report using the Wizard. Once that is done, begin modifying the report using the Designer to add parent and child data items, to add additional total levels, etc.

If your final target report is to be an Invoice format, for example, you could begin the report development by using the Wizard to lay out the Invoice Detail line. You would then use the Designer to create the Invoice Header sections and the appropriate Footer sections.

Let's start a simple Invoice example. A good designer defines the goal before starting development. To work the other way around is known as the "Ready, Fire, Aim" approach.

A simple **INVOICE** layout might look like the following:

```
                              INVOICE

Billing Company Name                        Document Number
Address
Address 2
City, State/Province
Post Zone


Member Name
Member Address
Member Address 2
Member City, State/Province
Post Zone

                                                        Amount
   Charge
   Date      Description            Amount     Tax      incl. Tax
   MM/DD/YY  XXXXXXXXXXXXXXXXXXXXX  999,999.99  99,999.99  9,999,999.99


                                          Total       9,999,999.99
```

The first thing we need to create is a table listing the charges to be invoiced. We'll create a `Member Charge` table for our C/ANDL system. Remember, this is just an example and a lot simpler than the Invoice data in the NAV standard system.

See the following screenshot for the data fields with which you could start:

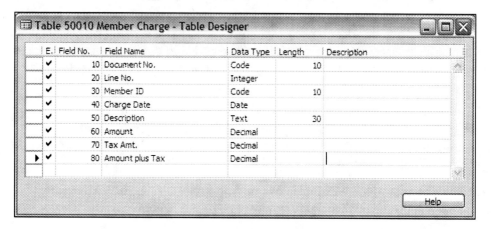

We'll give the **Member ID** a relationship to the Member table as shown in the next screenshot:

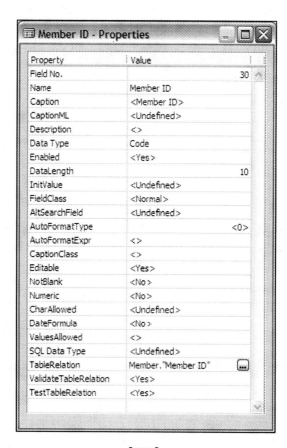

Now we'll define some **Keys**. The **Document No.**, **Line No.** fields will provide us with a unique key combination, so we'll use that as our primary key. Then we'll add a couple more keys based on what we as developers think the users will find useful (or, if this were real rather than an exercise, we would add keys based on how the users told us they would use the data in this table).

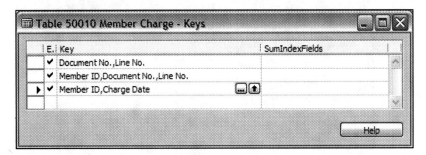

Now, let's populate the table with enough data that we can do a simple test. At this point, rather than creating a form, we will just **Run** the table and use the automatically generated temporary form to enter our sample data.

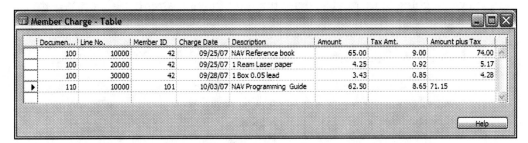

The next step in our example is to use the Report Wizard to create a first draft Invoice report based on the Member Charge table. This is what we've been trying to get to. The other work so far was a matter of building the foundation on which we could construct a report. This Wizard-generated report structure can then be a starting point for the full **Invoice** layout creation. We will save this as Report 50020 – Member Invoice.

Step 1 is to call up the Report Wizard, give it the name of the target table, the `Member Charge` table, and tell it to create a **Tabular-Type** report.

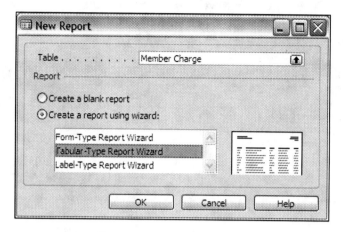

Step 2 is to choose the fields to be displayed, based on the layout we created earlier. Remember, we are using the **Report Wizard** to layout the basic Invoice Line section, and then we're going to manually revise the report layout after the Report Wizard does its magic.

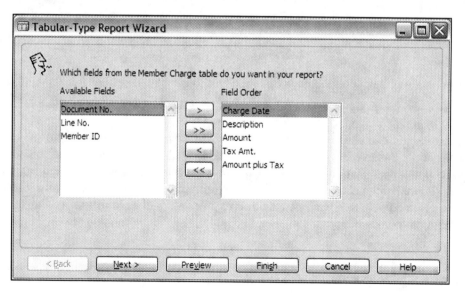

Step 3 is to define the data sequence we want to use. In this case, we don't want to allow the user to define a sequence at report print time, because we want to define the sequence based on the table's primary key as shown in the following screenshot. We will choose the Document No., Line No. key for our predefined sort sequence.

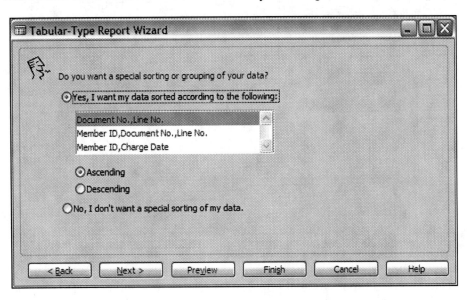

Step 4 is to define our data grouping. This tells the Report Wizard to create totals based on this data grouping. This will cause the Report Wizard to generate the C/AL code for our **Invoice Totals** based on the **Document No. Line No.** keys.

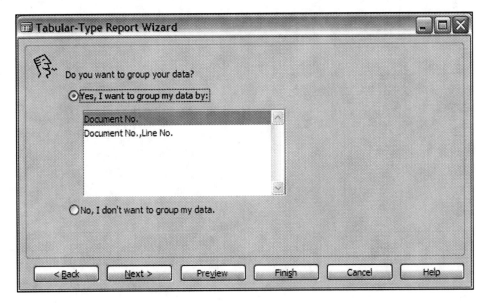

Step 5 is to choose the field(s) to be totaled from those eligible. We are allowed to pick from the integer and decimal fields. By choosing **Amount plus Tax**, we will have a total for the whole document.

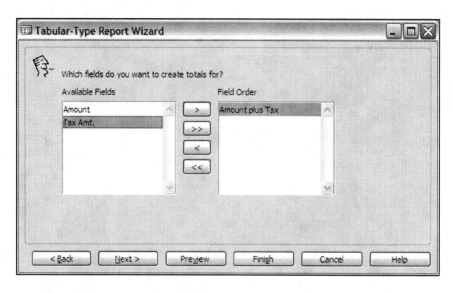

Step 6 is to choose a report style. If you don't already know which style you want when you get to this point, the best way to choose is to pick one, then **Preview** what it will look like, then exit the preview display, pick the other one, and preview what it will look like. You can go back and forth between the options until you decide which is closest to your target layout, then choose that one and proceed.

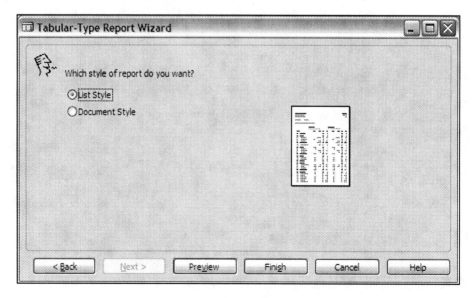

Step 7 is to save your generated report with a unique number and name.

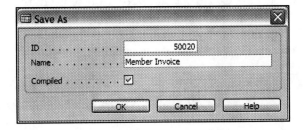

At this point, it is a good idea to preview the generated report to see what you've got. In fact, you probably will want to print it out, so that you can more easily compare the generated result to your original layout and identify what remains to be done.

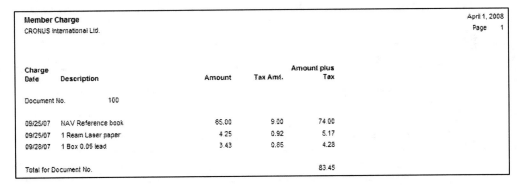

It's always useful at this point to also compare the printout of the generated report to the sections, to see what controls were used for each of the displayed fields. From that information, you can begin to plan how you want to manually change the sections to make the final report look like your original design layout.

Often, it is also useful to look at two or three of the standard NAV reports for similar functions to see how they are constructed. There is no sense in re-inventing the wheel (i.e. a report of a particular type) when someone else has not only invented a version of it already but provided you with the plans (i.e. the ability to peer into the C/AL code and the complete structure of the existing report object).

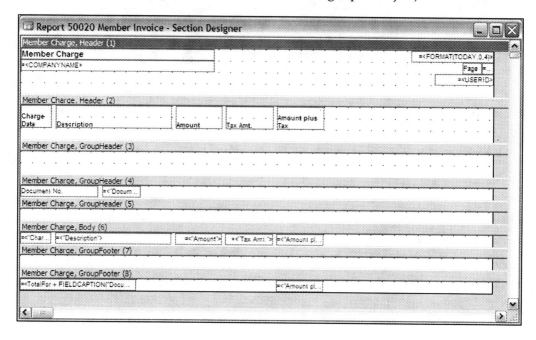

After you have moved some fields around, and added some header fields that your layout calls for, your in-process report design may look similar to the following screenshot. It's still not complete, but it's beginning to take shape. Note that to populate the **Company Address** fields shown here, C/AL code will also have to be added to read the Company Information table (Table 79).

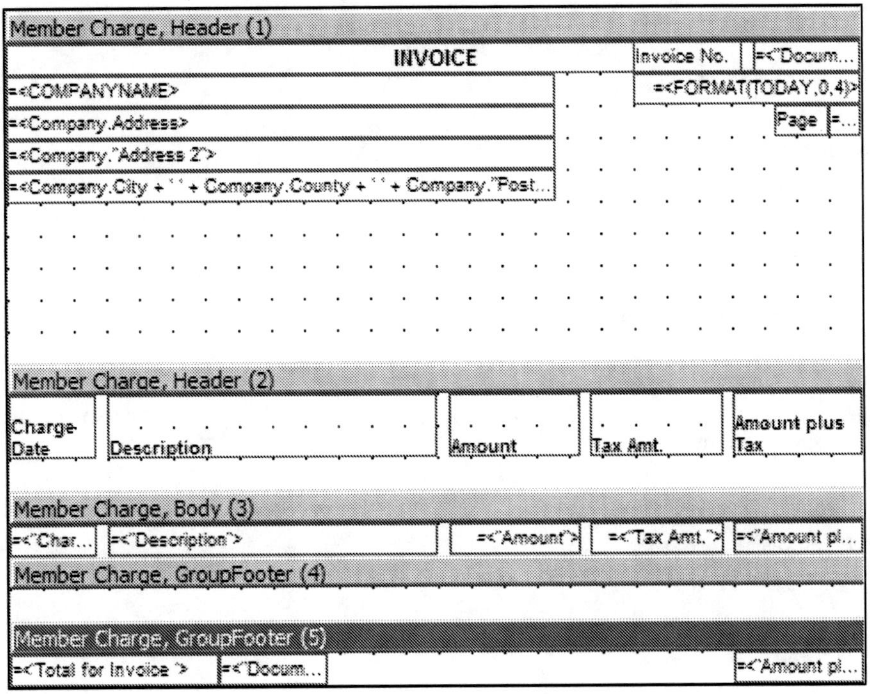

```
Member Charge, Header (1)
                                    INVOICE              Invoice No.   =<"Docum...
=<COMPANYNAME>                                          =<FORMAT(TODAY,0,4)>
=<Company.Address>                                                    Page  =...
=<Company."Address 2">
=<Company.City + ' ' + Company.County + ' ' + Company."Post...

Member Charge, Header (2)
Charge-                                                              Amount plus
Date        Description                    Amount      Tax Amt.      Tax

Member Charge, Body (3)
=<"Char...  =<"Description">              =<"Amount">  =<"Tax Amt.">  =<"Amount pl...
Member Charge, GroupFooter (4)

Member Charge, GroupFooter (5)
=<"Total for invoice ">   =<"Docum...                                =<"Amount pl...
```

At frequent intermediate points, it is very helpful in C/SIDE development to do test runs. This is particularly true when developing forms or reports. If we do a preview run of our report at the point of the sections layout in the preceding screenshot and select **Document No. 100,** we will get the **INVOICE** shown in the following screenshot:

	INVOICE		Invoice No.	100
CRONUS International Ltd.				April 1, 2008
5 The Ring				Page 1
Westminster				
London W2 8HG				

Charge Date	Description	Amount	Tax Amt.	Amount plus Tax
09/25/07	NAV Reference book	65.00	9.00	74.00
09/25/07	1 Ream Laser paper	4.25	0.92	5.17
09/28/07	1 Box 0.05 lead	3.43	0.85	4.28
Total for Invoice	100			83.45

Obviously the job is not done yet, but we are well on the way. To finish this particular example, we need some C/AL programming tools that we won't learn about until a later chapter. So we might want to lay this example aside and experiment with something else for a little while.

A key point of all this is to realize that even though the Wizards are of limited capability, they still can be used to make the work a lot easier. This is especially true for relatively straightforward forms and reports.

Of course there will be occasions when using the Report Wizard is simply not useful, in which case you will begin with a totally blank slate. There will also be cases where you do start out with the Wizard's output and strip out some of what the Wizard puts in. The reason for using the Wizard is not the high quality of the code it generates (it's adequate, but not very elegant), but for the time it saves you.

Creative Report Plagiarism

Just as we talked about in the chapter on Forms, when you want to create a new report of a type that you haven't done recently (or at all), it's a good idea to find another report that is similar in an important way and study it. At the minimum, you will learn how the NAV developers solved a data flow or totaling or filtering challenge. In the best case, you will find a model that you can follow closely, respectfully plagiarizing a working solution, thus saving yourself much time and effort.

When it comes to modifying a system such as NAV, plagiarism is a very effective research and design tool. In the case of reports, your search for a model may be based on any of several key elements. You might be looking for a particular data flow approach and find that the NAV developers used the Integer table for some Data Items (as many reports do).

You may need a way to provide some creative filtering similar to what is done in an area of the standard product. You might want to provide user options to print either detail or a couple of different levels of totaling, with a layout that looks good no matter which choice the user makes. You might be dealing with all three of these design needs in the same report. In such a case, you are likely to be using multiple NAV reports as your models, one for this feature, another for that feature, and so forth.

More likely, if you have a complicated, application-specific report to create, you won't be able to directly model your report on something that already exists. But quite often, you can still find ideas in standard reports that you can apply to your new report design. Most of the time, you'll be better off if you are only required to develop a modest amount of new design concept rather than inventing a totally new approach.

Too often, if your design concept is too big a leap from what has been done before by others you will find the tools available have built-in constraints that make it difficult for you to achieve your goal. In other words, generally you should build on the obvious strengths of C/AL. Creating entirely new approaches may be very satisfying (when it works), but too often it doesn't work well and costs a lot.

Special Output Issues

This section discusses some issues related to report output.

Printing PDF Files

Creating reports as electronic PDF (Adobe Portable Document Format) files allows reports to be stored, shared, transmitted, and used as searchable source documents. Fortunately, there is no particular barrier to creating PDF reports from NAV. All you need to do is install one of the many available PDF printer driver emulators and select that device when printing.

Printing HTML Formatted Output

This capability is even simpler than printing PDF formatted files. HTML formatted printing is built into NAV. In fact, you not only can print to HTML formatted files, but there is also a built-in option supporting the creation of HTML formatted report output and attaching it to an email ready to send. Both of these options are available on the **File** menu after you have printed a report in Preview mode. The print to HTML option is shown in the following screenshot as **Save as HTML** the print to HTML and attach to an email option is shown in the following screenshot as **Send | Report by E-Mail...**.

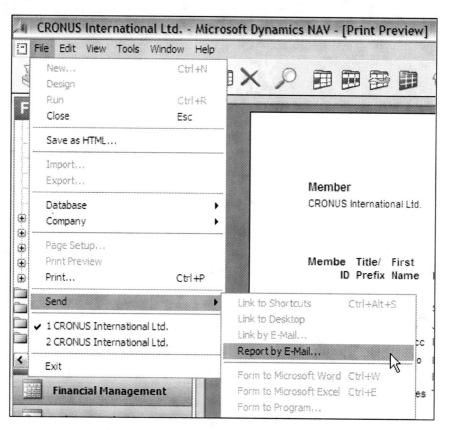

Printing to an Impact Printer

The first advice you will likely receive when considering printing to an impact printer (typically a dot-matrix printer) from NAV, is "don't do it". Because NAV and Windows really want to consider all output devices as graphic devices, some inherent conflicts are set up with a fixed format device such as a dot-matrix printer. If you don't design your report sections and controls in exactly the correct fashion, dot-matrix output will either be a mess or incredibly slow or both. Fortunately, there are some techniques that are not too difficult to apply.

First, because the print-line height on an impact printer is a function of the print head and paper tractor mechanism, there is generally only one "natural" line height, often this equates to either six lines per inch or eight lines per inch. When you lay out your report sections, make sure that all lines are exact multiples of a single line height. The normal default for NAV is a line height of 423 mm/100. This height works well for six lines per inch impact printing.

The other technique you must use is to ensure that all controls are ID numbered in sequence left to right on each line and top to bottom, line by line, section by section. In other words, if you were to take a copy of your physical page layout showing each print control on the layout, the numeric sequence would have to follow the same pattern going down the page as your eyes are following when reading this paragraph, left to right on a line, then down from the right end of one line to the left end of the next line. If you do not do this, Windows attempts to output to the printer in a graphics mode and the results are quite unpredictable, sometimes even varying from page to page within a report. Control ID numbers do not need to be contiguous, do not need to be in any particular number ranges. They simply need to be in ascending order in the pattern described.

Summary

In this chapter, we have focused on the structural and layout aspects of NAV Report objects. We have studied those primary structural components, data and format, along with the Request Form. We have experimented with some of the tools and modestly expanded our C/ANDL application.

In the next chapter, we are going to begin exploring the key tools that pull the other pieces together, the C/SIDE development environment and the C/AL programming language.

6

Introduction to
C/SIDE and C/AL

*Language is a process of free creation; its laws and principles are fixed, but
the manner in which the principles of generation are used is free and infinitely
varied – Noam Chomsky*

In the preceding chapters, we introduced the basic building block objects of NAV
tables, forms, and reports. In each of these we reviewed the triggers within various
areas such as the overall object, controls, data items, the Request Form, and so on.
The purpose of each trigger is to be a container in which C/AL code can reside. The
triggers are "fired", i.e. invoked or executed, when certain pre-defined events occur.

In this chapter, we're going to begin learning more about the C/AL programming
language. We'll start with the basics, but we won't spend a lot of time on those. Many
things you already know from programming in other languages apply to C/AL. In
addition, many of the basic definitions can be found in the Application Designer's
Guide and in the online C/AL Reference Guide that is part of the NAV **Help**.

Our goal here is to make it faster for you to learn how to navigate and productively
use the C/SIDE development environment as well as to be comfortable in C/AL.
We'll focus on the tools and processes that you use most often. Hopefully, you will
also learn concepts that you can apply in more complex tasks down the road.

As with most programming languages, you have considerable flexibility for defining
your own model for your code structure. However, when you are inserting new code
within existing code, there's a strong argument for utilizing the model that already
exists in the original code. When you feel compelled to improve on the model of the
existing code, do so in small increments.

Essential Navigation

All development for NAV normally takes place within the C/SIDE environment. The only exceptions are the possibility of doing development in Text mode using any text editor or the Developer's Toolkit. That approach is generally only appropriate for simple modifications to existing objects. In general, the recommendation is "don't do it that way".

As an Integrated Development Environment, C/SIDE provides you with a reasonably full set of tools for your C/AL development work. C/SIDE is not nearly as fully featured as Microsoft's Visual Studio, but the features it does have are quite useful. C/SIDE includes a smart editor (it knows something about C/AL, though sometimes not as much as you would like), the one and only C/AL compiler, integration with the application database, and tools to export and import objects both in compiled format and as formatted text files.

We'll explore each of these C/SIDE areas in turn. Let's start with an overview of the Object Designer.

Object Designer

All the NAV object development work can be done within the C/SIDE **Object Designer**. The **Object Designer** is accessed by selecting **Tools | Object Designer** or pressing *Shift+F12*, as shown in the following screenshot:

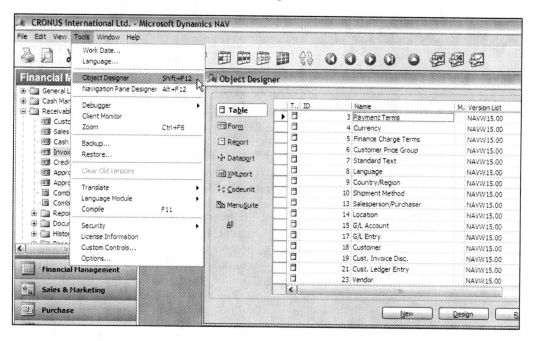

The type of object on which you're going to work is chosen by clicking on one of the buttons on the left side of the **Object Designer** screen. The choices match the seven object types **Table, Form, Report, Dataport, XMLPort, Codeunit**, and **MenuSuite**. When you click on one of these, the **Object Designer** screen display is filtered to show only that object type. There is also an **All** button, which allows objects of all types to be displayed on screen.

No matter which object type has been chosen, the same four buttons appear at the bottom of the screen: **New, Design, Run**, and **Help**. But, depending on which object type is chosen, the effect of selecting one of these options changes. When you select **Design**, you will open the object that is currently highlighted in a Designer specifically tailored to work on that object type. When you select **Run**, you will be requesting the execution of the currently highlighted object. The results of that, of course, will depend on the internal design of that particular object. When you select **Help**, you will be presented with the overall C/SIDE **Help** screen, positioned at the general Object Designer **Help**.

Starting a New Object

When you select **New**, the screen you see will depend on what type of object has focus at the time you make the **New** selection. In each case, you will have the opportunity to begin creating a new object and you will be presented with the Designer for that particular object type.

The **New** Designer screens for each of the object types are as follows:

The **Table Designer** screen is shown in the following screenshot:

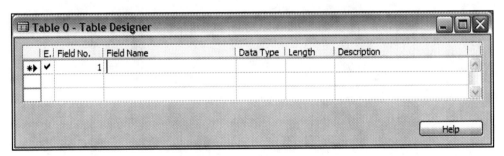

The **Table Designer** invites you to begin defining data fields. All the associated C/AL code will be embedded in the underlying triggers and developer-defined functions.

For the **Form Designer** the first screen is as follows:

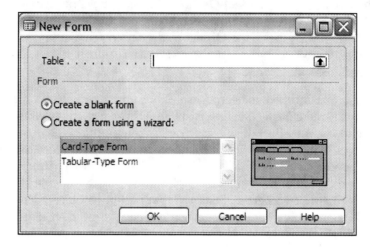

Any **New Form** effort begins with the choice of using the Wizard. If you wish not to use the Wizard and want to begin designing your form from scratch, you will select the **Create a blank form** option and then will see the following screen, which is your form layout screen:

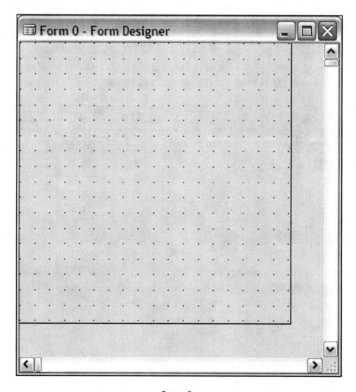

For **Report Designer** you first see the following screen:

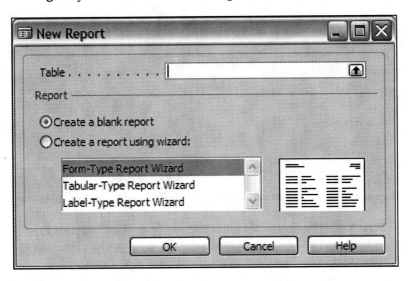

Any new report effort begins with the choice of using the Wizard. If you wish not to use the Wizard and want to begin designing your report from scratch, you will select the **Create a blank report** option. You'll then see the following screen where you can begin by defining the primary **DataItem** for your report.

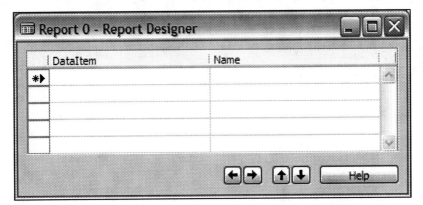

The **Dataport Designer** is as seen in the following screenshot:

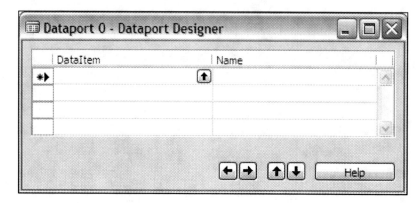

There is no Wizard for Dataports, so you go directly to the **Dataport Designer** screen. Notice that just like in the **Report Designer** screen, the **Dataport Designer** screen is set up for you to enter the **DataItem**(s) that your Dataport will process. We'll go into Dataports in more depth later, but it's interesting to note the basic similarity between Reports and Dataports. They both provide a predefined processing cycle that loops through the records of the input data.

Codeunits have no superstructure or surrounding framework around the single code trigger. Codeunits are primarily a shell in which you can place your own functions and code so that it can be called from other objects.

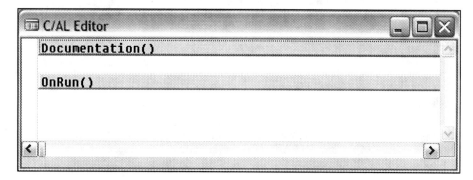

XMLports are tools for defining and processing XML data structures. XML is a set of data formatting rules for dissimilar applications to exchange data. In NAV, XMLports must be executed from other code (preferably Codeunits) as they cannot be run directly.

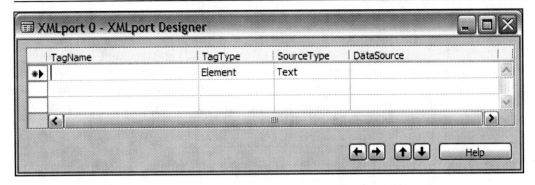

It was possible to define and process XML data prior to the addition of XMLports in V4.0, but it was a lot harder. The XML Designer provides considerable assistance in defining the hierarchical data structures of XML. XMLports are not essential to basic C/AL work and so far, most enhancements don't require XML interfaces, so we won't be spending much time on this object type. Once you become comfortable using C/SIDE and C/AL, you will want to learn about XML and XMLports because XML is becoming more and more important for inter-system data exchanges.

MenuSuites were also (along with XMLports) introduced in V4.0 of NAV. The initial screen that comes up when you ask for a new MenuSuite asks you to choose what MenuSuite Design Level you are preparing to create. The following screenshot shows all 14 available **Design Level** values:

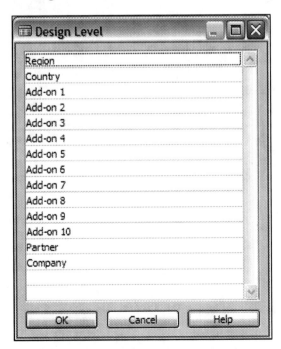

When one of those design levels has been used (i.e. created as a MenuSuite option), that design level will not appear in this list the next time **New** is selected in the MenuSuite Designer. MenuSuites can only exist at the 14 levels shown. Only one instance of each level is supported. Once you have chosen a level to create, NAV shifts to the MenuSuite Designer mode, which looks similar to a MenuSuite in production mode except for the heading at the top. The following screenshot shows a **Navigation Pane** (the MenuSuite displayed) ready for production use:

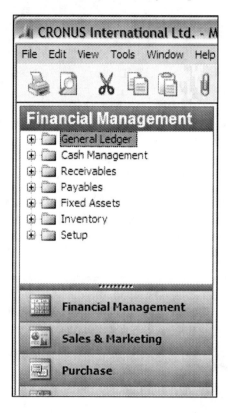

The following screenshot shows the same **Navigation Pane** in Designer mode:

As you can see, the main visible differences are the change in the heading to indicate what MenuSuite Level is being Designed (**Company** in this case) and the chevrons to the left of each menu bar icon.

Pressing *Alt+F12* or selecting **Tools | Navigation Pane Designer** will also take you into the Navigation Pane (MenuSuite) Designer. The only way to exit this Designer is by pressing *Esc* with focus on the Navigation Pane or by right-clicking on the Navigation Pane Designer heading and selecting the **Close Navigation Pane Designer** option that displays. There are a number of basic look and feel differences between the MenuSuite Designer and the other object designers. Some of these are simply due to the ways MenuSuites are different from other NAV objects and some are undoubtedly due to design decisions made by the Microsoft developers of the tool.

We will discuss what you can do with MenuSuite development more in Chapter 10.

Some Designer Navigation Pointers

In many places in the various designers, standard NAV data entry keyboard shortcuts apply. For example:

- *F3* to create a new empty entry.
- *F4* to delete an entry.
- *F8* to copy the preceding entry.
- *F5* to access the **C/AL Symbol Menu,** which shows you a symbol table for the object on which you are working. But this isn't just any old symbol table; this is a programmer's assistant. We'll go into how this works after we learn more about C/AL.
- *F9* to access underlying C/AL Code.

These last two (*F5* and *F9*) are particularly useful because sometimes the icons that you might normally use to access these areas disappear (a long standing system idiosyncrasy). The disappearing icons are disconcerting, but only a minor problem if you remember *F5* and *F9*.

- *F11* to do an on-the-fly compile (very useful for error checking code as you write it).
- *Shift+F4* to access properties.
- *Ctrl+Alt+F1* to bring up a **Help** screen showing all the available **Function Key** actions.
- *Ctrl+X, Ctrl+C,* and *Ctrl+V* in normal Windows mode for deletion (or cut), copy, and paste, respectively.

    You can cut, copy, and paste C/AL code relatively freely within an object or from object to object, much as if you were using a text editor. The source and target objects don't need to be of the same type.

- *Ctrl+F8* while highlighting any data record to zoom in on a display of the contents of all the fields in that record. This works for users and their data as well as for developers.

When you are in a list of items that cannot be modified, for example the C/AL Symbol Menu or a Zoom display on a record, you can focus on a column, click on a letter, and jump to the next field in sequence in the column starting with that letter. This works in a number of places where search is not supported, so it acts as somewhat of a search substitute.

The easiest way to copy a complete object in order to create a new version is to:

1. Open the object in Design mode.
2. Click on **File | Save As** object, assign a new object number, and change the object name (no duplicate names are allowed). A quick (mouseless) way to do a **Save As** is *Alt+F*, *Alt+A*, continuously holding down the Alt key while pressing first F, then A.

Don't ever delete an object or a field numbered in a range where your license doesn't allow creation of an object. If you don't have a compiled back-up copy of what you've deleted available for import, you will lose the ability to replace the deleted item. If you want to use an object or field number for a different purpose than the standard system assignment (not a good idea), make the change in place. Don't try a delete, followed by add; it won't work.

Exporting Objects

Object Export can be accessed for backup or distribution purposes via **File | Export**. Choosing this option brings up a standard Windows file-dialog screen with the file type options of `.fob` (NAV object) or `.txt` as shown in the following screenshot. The safer, more general purpose format for exporting is as a compiled object, created with a file extension of `.fob`. But the alternative is available to export an object as a text file with a file extension of `.txt`. An exported text file is the only way to use an external tool such as a third-party text editor to do before and after comparisons of objects or to search objects for the occurrences of strings (such as variable names).

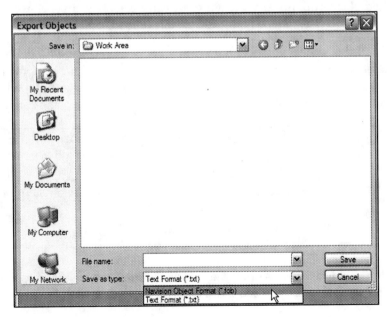

A compiled object can be shipped to another system as a patch to install with little fear that it will be corrupted midstream. The system administrator at the other system simply has to import the new object with some directions from you. Exported compiled objects also make excellent backups. Before changing or importing any working production objects, it's always a good idea to export a copy of the "before" object images into a .fob file, labeled so you can easily find it for retrieval. Any number of objects can be exported into a single .fob file. You can later selectively import any one or several of the individual objects from that group .fob.

Importing Objects

Object Import is accessed via **File | Import**. The import process is more complicated than the export process because there are more possibilities and decisions that are to be made. Since we've already mentioned exporting both text and compiled versions of an object, you might assume we can import both formats and you would be correct. The difference is that when you import a compiled version of an object, the Object Designer allows you to make decisions about importing and provides you with some information to help you.

However, when you import a text version of an object, the new version is brought in regardless of what it overwrites and regardless of whether or not the incoming object can actually be compiled. In other words, by importing a text-formatted object, you could actually replace a perfectly good, modified production object with some trash that only had a passing resemblance to a text object. The moral of this story is "Be very, very careful when importing" or "Look before you leap". It is best if text-formatted objects are never used when sending objects to an end user for installation.

When you import a compiled object (i.e. from a .fob file), you will get one of two decision-message screens, depending on what the Object Designer Import finds when it checks for existing objects. If there are no existing objects that the Import logic identifies as matching and modified, then you will see the following dialog:

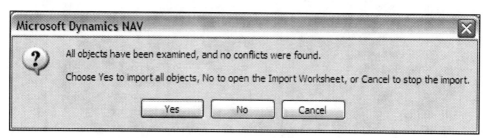

The safest thing to do is always open the **Import Worksheet** by clicking on the **No** button. Then examine what you see there before proceeding with the import.

If the `.fob` file you are importing is found to have objects that could be in conflict with existing objects that have been previously modified, then you will see the following dialog:

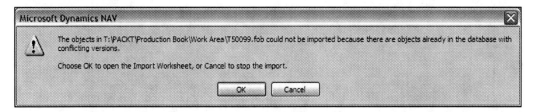

In this case, you will definitely want to click **OK** to open the **Import Worksheet** and examine the contents.

An example of what you might see in the **Import Worksheet** is shown in the following screenshot:

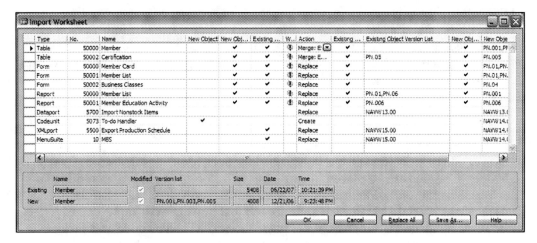

While all of the information presented is useful at one time or another, usually you can focus on just a few fields. The basic question, on an object-by-object basis, is "Do I want to replace the old version of this object with the new copy?" In the case of tables, import also allows you to merge the incoming and existing table versions. Only very sophisticated developers should attempt to use this feature.

The rest of us should always either choose the Import Action **Replace** or **Skip** (or **Create**, if it is a new object). This latter statement applies to all the object types.

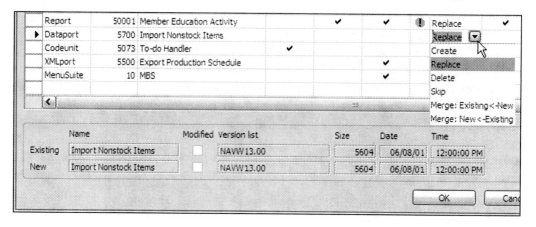

At the bottom of the preceding screenshot, you can see the comparison of the **Existing** object and the **New** object information. You must use this information to help you decide whether or not to accept the import of this object (action of **Create** or **Replace** or action of **Skip**). More information on using the **Import Worksheet** and the meaning of various Warnings and Actions can be found in C/SIDE Reference Guide **Help** under **Import Worksheet**.

Text Objects

A text version of an object is especially useful for a few development tasks. C/AL code or expressions can be placed in a number of different nooks and crannies of objects. In addition, sometimes object behavior is controlled by Properties. Consequently, it's not always easy to figure out just how an existing object is accomplishing its tasks. But an object exported to text has all its code and properties flattened out where you can use your favorite text editor to search and view. Text copies of two versions of an object can easily be compared in a text editor. In addition, a few tasks, such as renumbering an object, can be done more easily in the text copy than within C/SIDE.

Object Numbers

In Chapter 1 we reviewed some object numbering practices followed in NAV. The object number range for general purpose custom objects (those not part of an add-on) starts at 50000. If your client has purchased the license rights to **Table Designer**, the rights to 10 table objects are included, numbered 50000 to 50009. With **Form Designer** come the rights to 100 forms objects, numbered 50000 to 50099. With the **Report Designer** and **Dataport Designer** come the rights to 100 report objects and 100 dataport objects respectively, each numbered 50000 to 50099. With the **XMLport Designer** come the rights to 100 XMLport objects, numbered 50000 to 50099. Codeunit objects must be licensed separately. As part of the standard system, the customer has access to the MenuSuite Designer, not to add new levels, but just to modify the Company level.

Some Useful Practices

Liberally make backups of objects on which you are working. Always make a backup of the object before you start changing it. Do the same regularly during the development process. In addition to power outages and the occasional system crash, once in a while you may do something as a developer that upsets C/SIDE and it will go away without saving your work.

Use *F11* to test-compile frequently. You will find errors more easily this way.

When developing forms or reports, use *Alt+F, Alt+R* to do test runs of the objects relatively frequently. Whenever you reach a stage of having a working copy, save it.

Never design a modification that places data directly in or changes data directly in a Ledger table without going through the standard Posting routines. It's tempting to do, but doing so is an almost sure path to unhappiness. If you are creating a new Ledger for your application, for the sake of consistency with the NAV standard flow, design your process with a Journal table and a Posting process.

It at all possible, try to avoid importing modifications into a production system when there are users logged into the system. If a logged in user has an object active that is being modified, they will continue working with the old version (courtesy of NAV's Versioning feature) until they exit and re-enter. Use of the old object version may cause confusion or possibly even more serious problems.

Whenever possible try to test modifications in a reasonably current copy of the production system. Do your final testing using real data (or at least realistic data) and a copy of the customer's production license.

If you wish to reduce the likelihood that a change to a production system is incompatible with the rest of the system, recompile all the objects in the system after importing changes. You must have all referenced Automation or OCX routines registered in your system for this to work well. Note that, in systems in which developers have left inoperable or obsolete "temporary" objects (i.e. systems that have not had proper "housekeeping"), you may uncover serious problems this way, so be prepared.

Changing Data Definitions

The integration with the application database is particularly handy when you are making changes to an application that is already in production use. C/SIDE is good about not letting you make changes that are inconsistent with existing data. For example, let's presume you have a text field that is defined as being 30 characters long and there is already data in that field in the database, one instance of which is longer than 20 characters. If you attempt to change the definition of that field to 20 characters long, you will get an error message when you try to save and compile the table object. You will not be able to force the change until you adjust either the data in the database or you adjust the change so that it is compatible with all existing data.

Saving and Compiling

Whenever you exit the Designer for an object, if you have changed anything, by default NAV wants to save and compile the object on which were working. You will see a dialog similar to the following screenshot:

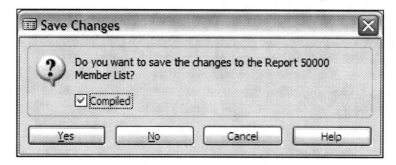

If you want to save the changed material under a new object number, you must **Cancel** this option and exit after using the **File | Save As** option. If your object under development is at one of those in-between stages where it won't compile, you can uncheck the **Compiled** check box and just **Save** without compiling. You should not complete a development session without getting a clean compile.

On occasion, you may make changes that you think it will affect other objects. In that case, from the **Object Designer** screen, you can select a group of objects to be compiled. One relatively easy way to do that is to mark each of the objects to be compiled, then use the **View | Marked Only** function to select just those marked objects. That allows them to be compiled *en masse*. Marking an object is done by putting focus on the object and pressing *Ctrl+F1*. The marked object is then identified with a bullet in the left screen column for that object's row.

See the four marked objects in the following screenshot:

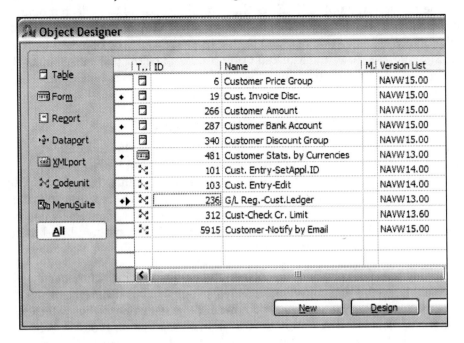

Selecting **View | Marked Only** yields the following screenshot:

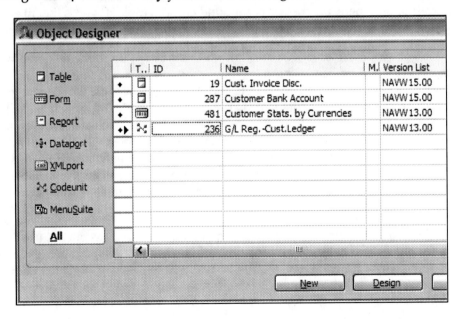

Select all the entries, press *F11*, and respond **Yes** to the question "**Do you want to compile the selected objects?**" Once the compilation of all the selected objects is completed, you will get a message indicating how many of the objects had compilation errors. After you respond to that message, only the objects with errors will remain marked. Since the **Marked Only** filter will be on, just those objects that need attention will be shown on the screen.

Some C/AL Naming Conventions

In the previous chapters, we have discussed naming conventions for tables, forms, and reports. In general, the naming guidelines for NAV objects and C/AL encourage consistency, common sense, and intelligibility. It is good to use meaningful names. These makes the system more intuitive to the users and more self-documenting to those who must maintain and support the system. If you have access to a copy of the document **C/AL Programming Guide**, you will find there a section on NAV Naming Conventions that covers the basics.

When naming internal variables, try to keep the names as self-documenting as possible. Make sure you differentiate between similar, but different, values such as **Cost** (cost from the vendor) and **Amount** (selling price to the customer). Embedded spaces, periods, or other special characters must be avoided. When you are defining multiple instances of a table, either differentiate clearly by name (e.g. Item and NewItem) or by a suffix number (e.g. Item1, Item2, Item3). In the very common situation where a name is a compound combination of words, begin each abbreviated word with a capital letter (e.g. NewCustBalDue).

Avoid creating variable names that are common words that might be reserved words (e.g. Page, Column, Number, and Integer). C/SIDE will *not* warn you that you have done so and you may find your logic and the automatic logic working at very mysterious cross purposes. Do not start variables with a suffix "x", which is used in some automatically created variables (such as xRec). Be sure to clearly differentiate between internal variable names and those originating in tables. C/SIDE will allow you to have a global name, local name, and/or record variable name, all with the same literal name. If you do this, you are practically guaranteeing a variable misidentification bug where the compiler uses a different variable than what you intended to be referenced.

When defining a temporary table, preface the name with Temp. In general, use meaningful names that help identify the type and purpose of the item being named. When naming a new function, you should be reasonably descriptive. Don't name two functions located in different objects with same name. It will be too easy to get confused later.

In summary, be careful, be consistent, be clear, and use common sense.

Variables

As we've gone through our examples showing various aspects of C/SIDE and C/AL, we've seen and referred to variables in a number of situations. Some of the following is likely obvious, but for clarity's sake we'll summarize here.

In Chapter 3, *Fields*, we reviewed the various Data Types that can be defined for variables defined within objects (referred to in Chapter 3 as *Working Storage Data Types*). Working Storage consists of all the variables that are defined for use within an object, but whose contents disappear when the object closes. The Data Types discussed there are those that can be defined in either the **C/AL Global Variables** or **C/AL Local Variables** tabs. Variables can be defined in these and several other places in an NAV object.

Global Variables

Global Variables are defined on the **C/AL Globals** form **Variables** tab, which we have just accessed in our function creation exercise.

Global Text Constants are defined on the **Text Constants** tab section of the **C/AL Globals** form. The primary purpose of the Text Constants area is to allow easier translation of messages from one language to another. By putting all message text in this one place in each object, a standardized process can be defined for language translation. There is a good explanation in the Application Designer's Guide on how to create Text Constants.

Global Functions are defined on the **Functions** tab of that same form.

Local Variables

Local Variables can only exist defined within the range of a trigger. This applies whether the trigger is a developer-defined function or one of the default system triggers or standard application-supplied functions.

Function Local Variables

Function **Local Variables** are defined on one or another of the tabs on the **C/AL Locals** form that we use for defining our function.

Parameters and **Return Value** are defined on their respectively named tabs.

The **Variables** and **Text Constants** tabs for **C/AL Locals** are exactly similar to the **C/AL Globals** tabs.

Other Local Variables

Trigger Local Variables are also defined on one or another of the tabs on the **C/AL Locals** form. The difference between trigger Local Variables and those for a function is that the first two tabs, **Parameters** and **Return Value**, are disabled for triggers that are not defined as functions. The use of the **Variables** and **Text Constants** tabs are exactly the same for triggers as for functions. When you are working within a trigger, you can access the Local Variables through the menu option **View | C/AL Locals**.

Special Working Storage Variables

These are those variables that can be defined within an object for use within that object only.

Temporary Tables

Temporary tables were discussed in Chapter 2. Now let's take a quick look at how one is defined. Defining a Global Temporary table starts just like any other Global Variable definition of the Record data type. Select **View | C/AL Globals**, enter a variable name, data type of **Record**, and choose as the **Subtype** the table whose definition is to be replicated for this temporary table. With focus on the new Record variable, click on the **Properties** icon (or press *Shift+F4*). Set the **Temporary** property to **Yes**. That's it, you've defined a Temporary Table..

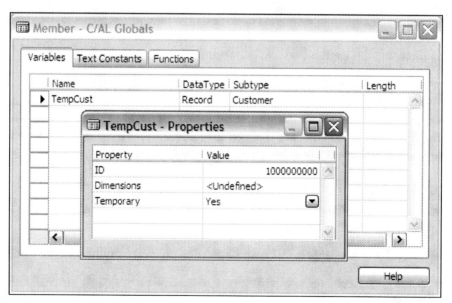

Now you can use the temporary table just as though it were a permanent table with some specific differences:

- The table contains only the data you add to it during this instance of the object in which it resides.

- You cannot change any aspect of the definition of the table in any way, except by changing the permanent table (which was its template) using the Table Designer, then recompiling the object containing the associated temporary table.

- Processing for a temporary table is done wholly on the client system and is therefore inherently single user.

- A temporary table creates no additional network traffic and is therefore faster than processing the same data in a permanent, database-resident table.

Sometimes it is a good idea to copy database table data into a temporary table for repetitive processing within an object. This can give you a significant speed advantage for a particular task.

Arrays

Arrays of up to 10 dimensions containing up to a total of 1,000,000 elements in a single variable can be created in an NAV object. Defining an array is done simply by setting the **Dimensions** property of a variable to something other than the default **<Undefined>**. An example is shown in the following screenshot:

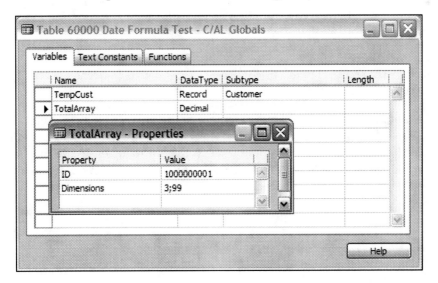

The semicolon separates the dimensions of the array. The numbers indicate the maximum sizes of the dimensions. This example is a two dimensional array which has three rows of 99 elements each. An array variable like **TotalArray** is referred to in C/AL as follows:

- The 15th entry in the first row would be `TotalArray[1,15]`
- The last entry in the last row would be `TotalArray[3,99]`

Initialization

When an object is initiated, all the variables within the object are automatically initialized. Booleans are set to false. Numeric variables are set to zero. Text and code data types are set to the empty string. Dates are set to 0D (the undefined date) and Times are set to 0T (the undefined time). The system also automatically initializes all system-defined variables.

Of course, once the object is active, you can do whatever initialization you wish. And if you wish to initialize variables at intermediate points during processing, you can use any of several approaches. Initialize a Record variable (for example, our TempCust temporary table) with the `INIT` function in a statement in the form:

```
TempCust.INIT;
```

In that case, all the fields, except those in the primary key, are set either to their **InitValue** property value or to their data type default value. Primary key fields must be explicitly set by C/AL code.

For other types of data, you can initialize fields with the `CLEAR` function in a statement in the form:

```
CLEAR(TotalArray[1,1]);
CLEAR(TotalArray);
CLEAR("Shipment Code");
```

The first example would clear a single element of the array, the first element in the first row. Since this variable is a Decimal data type, the element would be set to 0.0 when cleared. The second example would clear the entire array. In the third example a variable defined as a Code data type would simply be set to an empty string.

System-Defined Variables

NAV also provides you with some variables automatically. What variables are provided is dependent on the object in which you are operating:

System defined Variables				
Table	Form	Report	Dataport	XMLport
Rec	Rec			
xRec	xRec			
CurrFieldNo				
	CurrForm			
		CurrReport		
		RequestOptionsForm	RequestOptionsForm	
			CurrFile	
			CurrDataport	
				CurrXMLport

A Definition of Programming in C/SIDE

Many of the things that we do during development in C/SIDE might not properly be called programming. But so long as these activities contribute to the definition of the object and affect the processing that occurs, we'll include them in our broad definition of C/SIDE programming.

These activities include setting properties at the object and Data Item levels, creating Request Forms in Reports, defining Controls and their properties, defining Report Sections and their properties, creating Source Expressions and, of course, writing C/AL statements in all the places that you can put C/AL. Our study will include C/SIDE programming primarily as it relates to tables, reports, and Codeunits. We will touch on C/SIDE programming for forms and dataports, but not for XMLports because that is a relatively advanced C/AL topic and because, at this time, XMLport programming requires additional knowledge that we will not address in this book. And, since there can be no programming done with MenuSuites, we obviously will omit those objects from the programming part of our discussions.

There is considerable similarity across NAV objects, just as you would expect. Most have some kind of properties and triggers. Two, forms and reports, have controls. Two, reports and dataports, have built-in data item looping logic. All five object types that we are considering can contain C/AL code in one or more places. All five of these can have functions defined that can then be called either internally or externally, though good coding design says that any functions that are designed as "library" functions should be placed in a Codeunit. Don't forget, your fundamental coding work should focus on tables as much as possible, the foundation of the NAV system.

Functions

A function is a defined set of logic that performs a specific task. Similarly to many other programming languages, C/AL includes a set of prewritten functions that are available to you to perform quite a wide variety of different tasks. The underlying logic for some of these functions is hidden, invisible, and not modifiable. These functions are properly considered part of the programming language. Some simple examples:

- DATE2DMY: Supply a date, and depending on how you call this function, it will give you back the integer value of either the day, the month, or the year of that date.

- STRPOS: Supply a string variable and a string constant; the function will return the position of the first instance of that constant within the variable, or a zero if the constant is not present in the string contained in the variable.

- GET: Supply a value and a table, and the function will read the record in the table with a primary key equal to the supplied value, if one exists.

- INSERT: Add a record to a table.

- MESSAGE: Supply a string and optional variables; the function will display a message to the operator.

Such functions are the heart of the C/AL language. There are over 100 of them. On the whole, they are designed around the essential purpose of an NAV system: business and financial applications data processing. As these functions are not modifiable, they operate according to their predefined rules.

As a point of information, a trigger is a combination of a defined event and a function that is performed when the event occurs. In the case of the built-in functions, NAV supplies the logic and the processing/syntax rules. In the case of triggers, as the developer, you supply the processing rules.

In addition to the pre-written "language component" functions, there are a large number of pre-written "application component" functions. An example might be one to handle the task of processing a Customer Shipping Address to eliminate empty lines and standardize the layout based on user-defined setup parameters. This function would logically be placed in a Codeunit and thus made available to any routine that needs this capability. In fact, this function exists. It is called SaleHeaderShipTo and is located in the **Format Address** Codeunit. You can explore the following Codeunits for some functions you might find useful to use or from which to borrow logic. This is not an all-inclusive list, as there are functions in other Codeunits that you will also likely find useful in some future development project.

Some Codeunits containing useful functions are shown in the following table:

Object number	Name
1	ApplicationManagement
356	DateComprMgt
358	DateFilter-Calc
359	PeriodFormManagement
365	Format Address
397	Mail
412	Common Dialog Management
5053	TAPIManagement
5054	WordManagement
6224	XML/COM Management
99000755	Calendar Management

The pre-written application functions generally have been provided to address the needs of the NAV developers working at Microsoft. But you can use them too. Your challenge will be to find out that they exist and to understand how they work. There is very little documentation of these "application component" functions.

One significant aspect of these application functions is the fact that they are written in C/AL and their construction is totally exposed. In theory, they could be modified, though that is not advisable. If you decide to change one of these functions, you should make sure your change is compatible with existing uses of that function. A useful "trick" to find all the locations of use for a function is to add a dummy calling parameter to the function (temporarily) and then compile all objects in the system. You will get errors in all objects that call the changed function (don't forget about having all Automation and OCX functions registered before compiling and don't forget to remove the dummy calling parameter when you're done with testing).

We can also create our own functions for any needed purpose. There are several reasons for creating new functions. The most common reason is to create a single, standardized instance of the logic to perform a specific task. Just about any time you need to use the same logic in more than one place, you should be considering creating a callable function. If you need to create a customized variation on one of NAV's existing functions, rather than change the original function, you should copy the original into your own Codeunit and modify it as needed there.

Another occasion when you should be creating functions is when you're modifying standard NAV processes. One recommended rule of thumb is that whenever more than one line of code is needed for the modification, the modification should be created as a function in an external (i.e. modification-specific) Codeunit. That way the modification to the standard process can be limited to a call out to the new function. Though that approach is great in concept, it's often difficult to implement in practice. If, for example, you're not just adding logic, but you want to revise the way existing logic works, sometimes it is very convoluted to try to implement the change through just a call and an external (to the mainline process) function. Perhaps a more realistic approach is to set the threshold for creating an external function at some higher level such as 20 lines or 50 lines of new or changed code.

Let's take a quick look at how a function can be created. We're going to add a new Codeunit to our C/ANDL application, Codeunit 50000. Since this is where we will put any callable functions we need for our Member-oriented application, we will simply call it Member Management. In that Codeunit, we're going to create a function to calculate a new date based on a given date. If that seems familiar, it's the same thing we did in Chapter 3 to illustrate how a **DateFormula** data type works. This time, our focus is going to be on the creation of the function.

Our first step is to copy **Table 60000**, which we created for testing, and then save it as table **60001**. As a reminder, we do that by opening Table 60000 in the Table Designer, then selecting **File | Save As**, changing the object number to 60001 and the **Name** to **Date Formula Test-2** (see the following screenshot), then exiting and compiling.

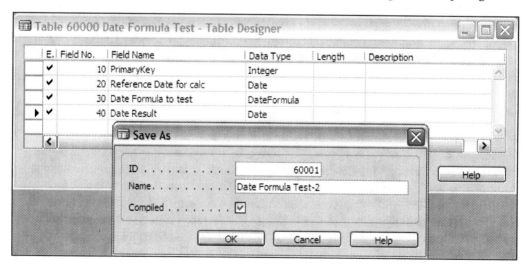

Once that is done, it would be good to change the Version List to show that this table has been modified. If you used the coding of PN for Programming NAV and .06 for a Chapter 6 change, then the Version List change would be to add PN.06 to whatever was there previously.

We can create our new Codeunit by simply clicking on the **Codeunit** button, then on the **New** button, and then choosing **File | Save As**, and entering the Object ID of **50000** and **Name** as **Member Management**.

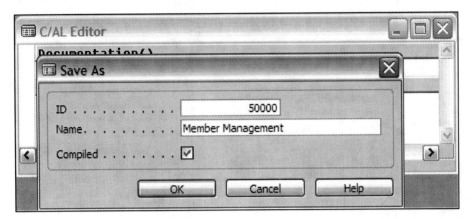

Now to the hard part, designing our new function. When we had the function operating as a local function inside the table where it was called, we didn't have to worry very much about passing data back and forth. We simply used the data fields that were already present in the table and treated them as global variables (which, in effect, they were). Now that we're going to have our function be external to the object from which it's called, we have to worry about passing data values back and forth. Here's the basic logic of our function:

```
Output = Function (Input Parameter1, Input Parameter2)
```

In other words, we need to feed two values into our new callable function and accept one value back on completion of the function's processing.

Our first step is to click on **View | C/AL Globals,** then the **Functions** tab. Enter the name of the new function following the guidelines for good names, (ApplyDateFormula), and then click on the **Locals** button. This will allow us to define all the variables that will be local to the new function. The first tab on the **Locals** screen is **Parameters**, i.e. input variables.

Again, in keeping with good naming practice, we will define two input parameters, as shown in the following screenshot:

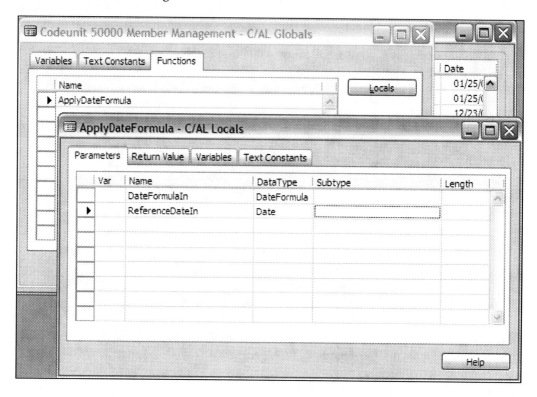

An important note regarding the **Var** column at the left of the **Parameters** tab form: If we check that column, then the parameter is passed by reference to the original calling routine's copy of that variable. That means when the called function (this one) changes the value of an input parameter, the original variable value gets changed. Because we've specified the input parameter passing here with no **Var** checkmark, changes in the value of that input parameter will be local to the copy of the data passed in to this function and will not affect the calling routine. Checking the **Var** control on one or more parameters is a way to effectively have more than one result passed back to the calling routine.

Now we need to select the **Return Value** tab and define our output variable. That will look like the following:

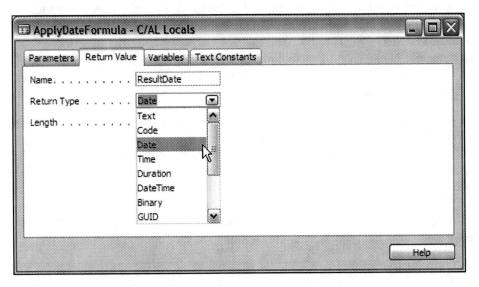

Once we complete the definition of our function and its local variables, we can exit via the *Esc* key and the results will be saved. One way to view the effect of what we just defined is to view the **C/AL Symbol Menu**. From the **Codeunit Designer** screen, with your new Codeunit 50000 in view and your cursor placed in the code area for our new function, click on **View | C/AL Symbol Menu** (or just press *F5*) and you will see the following image:

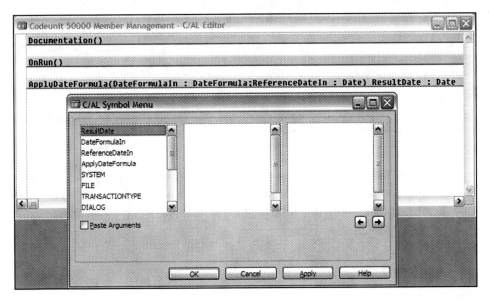

You can see that our `ApplyDateFormula` function has been defined with two parameters and a result. Now, press *Esc* or select **OK**, move your cursor to the `OnRun` trigger code area and again press *F5* to view the **C/AL Symbol Menu**. You won't see the two parameters and result. Why? Because those are local variables, which only exist in the context of the function and are not visible outside the function. We'll make more use of the C/AL Symbol Menu a little later, as it is a very valuable C/AL development tool. But right now we need to finish our new function and integrate it with our test Table **60001**.

Move your cursor back to the code area for our new function. Then click on the menu item **Window | Object Designer | Table** button, then on Table **60001 | Design**, and press *F9*. That should take you to the **C/AL Code** screen for Table 60001. Highlight and cut the code line from the local `CalculateNewDate` function. Admittedly this will not be a particularly efficient process this time, but hopefully it will make the connection between the two instances of functions easier to envision. Using the **Window** menu option, move back to our Codeunit function and paste the line of code we just cut from Table **60001**. You should see the following on screen:

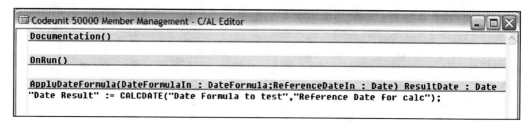

Now edit that line of code so the variable names match those shown in our function trigger above. This should give you the following display:

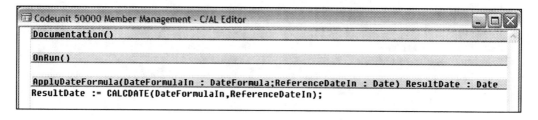

Press *F11* to check to see if you have a clean compile. If you get an error, do the traditional programmer thing. Find it, fix it, recompile. Repeat until you get a clean compile. Then exit and **Save** your modified **Codeunit 50000**.

Finally we must return to our test Table **60001**, to complete the changes necessary to use the external function rather than the internal function. The two lines of code that called the internal function `CalculateNewDate` must be changed to call the external function. The syntax for that call is:

```
Global/LocalVariable :=
    Local/GlobalObjectName.FunctionName[Parameter1,Parameter2,…].
```

Based on that, the new line of code should be:

```
"Date Result" := MemMgmnt.ApplyDateFormula("Date Formula to test,
    "Reference Date for calc");
```

Copy that line of code in place of the old function calls as shown in the following screenshot. To finish your housekeeping for this change, you should go to **View | Globals | Functions** tab and delete the now unused local function. Return to the **Globals** tab and add the variable as shown in the following screenshot:

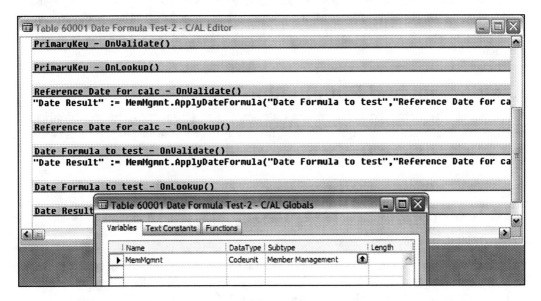

If all has gone well, you should be able to save and compile this modified table. When that works successfully, then **Run** the table and experiment with different Reference Dates and Date Formulas, just like you did back in Chapter 3. You should get the same results for the same entries.

You might ask "Why couldn't I just replace the logical statement in the existing local function with a call to the new external function?" The answer is "You could". The primary reason for not doing that is the fact that the program would then be making a two-level call, a less efficient procedure. On the other hand, this approach might create a sturcture that is easier to understand or easier to maintain, a relatively subjective decision. In the end, such a decision comes down to a matter of understanding what the best criteria are on which to judge the available design decisions, then applying those criteria.

You should now have a good feeling for the basics of constructing both internal and external functions and some of the optional design features available to you for building functions.

Basic C/AL Syntax

C/AL syntax is relatively simple and straightforward. The basic structure of most C/AL statements is essentially similar to what you learned with other programming languages. C/AL is modeled on Pascal and tends to use many of the same special characters in the same fashion as does Pascal. Some examples are as follows:

Assignment and Punctuation

Assignment is represented with a colon followed by an equal sign, the combination being treated as a single symbol. The evaluated value of whatever expression is to the right of the assignment symbol is assigned to the variable on the left side.

```
CustRec."Phone No." := '312-555-1212';
```

All statements are terminated with a semi-colon (see the preceding line as an example). Multiple statements can be placed on a single program line, but that makes your code hard for human beings to read.

Fully qualified data fields are prefaced with the name of the record variable of which they are part (see the preceding code line as an example where the record variable is named `CustRec`). Essentially the same rule applies to fully qualified function references; the function name is prefaced with the name of the object in which they are defined.

Single quotes are used to surround string literals (see the preceding code line for a phone number string).

Double quotes are used to surround a variable name that contains any characters other than numerals or upper and lower case letters. For example, the Phone No. field name in the preceding code line is constructed as "Phone No." because it contains a space and a period). Other examples would be "Post Code"(contains a space), "E-Mail" (contains a dash) and "No." (contains a period).

Parentheses are used much the same as in other languages, to indicate sets of statement elements to be interpreted according to their parenthetical groupings.

Brackets "[ ]" are used to indicate the presence of subscripts for indexing of array variables. On occasion a text string can be treated as an array of characters and you can use subscripts with the string name to access individual character positions within the string. For example, Address[1] represents the first or left-most character in the Address variable contents.

Statements can be continued on multiple lines without any special punctuation. The example below shows two instances that are interpreted exactly the same by the compiler.

```
CustRec."Phone No." := '312' + '-' + '555' + '-' + '1212';
CustRec."Phone No." := '312' +
   '-' + '555' +
   '-' + '1212';
```

Wild Cards

A **Wild Card** is a character that can be used in place of one or many other characters. There are two wild cards in C/AL. They are the question mark (?) and the asterisk (*). The question mark is a wild card representing one character. If you search in NAV for a match for the string 'a??ke', you will be rewarded with results such as the following: **appke, aaake, abake, adeke, afike, azoke, a37ke, a%#ke**, and many more possibilities.

The asterisk is a wild card representing a string of zero or more characters. If you search a field in NAV for the string **a*** you will get all the instances with strings starting with the letter **a**. If you search for the string **a*e**, you will get all the strings that start with the letter **a** and end with the letter **e** and have anything in between, including all the possibilities shown for our **?** search. Please be very cautious in using wildcards in your code. They can lead to unexpected results, and on certain occasions, cause severe performance degradation.

Expressions

Expressions in C/AL are made up of four elements: Constants, Variables, Operators, and Functions. Actually you could include a fifth element, Expressions, because an Expression may include within it a subordinate expression. As you become more experienced in coding C/AL, you will find that the capability of nesting expressions can be either a blessing or a curse.

You can create complex statements that will conditionally perform important control actions. These can allow you to create a code statement that operates in much the way that a person would think about the task.

You can also create complex statements that are very difficult for a human to understand. These are tough to debug and sometimes almost impossible to deal with in a modification.

One of your responsibilities over time will be to learn to tell the difference so you can do the former without doing the latter.

According to the Application Designer's Guide, "*a C/AL Expression is a group of characters (data values, variables, arrays, operators, and functions) that can be evaluated with the result having an associated data type*". We just looked at two code statements that accomplish the same result, namely that of assigning a literal string to a text data field. In each of these, the right side of the assignment symbol (i.e. to the right of the : =) is an expression. In each of these, the whole statement is also an expression. These statements are repeated below:

```
CustRec."Phone No." := '312-555-1212';
CustRec."Phone No." := '312' + '-' + '555' + '-' + '1212';
```

Operators

We're going to review C/AL operators grouped by category. Depending on what data types you are using with a particular operator, you may need to know what the type conversion rules are (i.e. what the allowed combinations of operator and data types are in an expression). The Application Designer's Guide provides good information on type conversion rules in two different sections of the manual, particularly in the section headed **Type Conversion**.

Before we discuss the operators that can be categorized, let's discuss some operators that don't fit any of the categories. Included in this grouping are the following:

Other Operators	
Symbol	**Evaluation**
.	Fields in Records Controls in Forms Controls in Reports Functions in Objects
( )	Grouping of elements
[ ]	Indexing
::	Scope
..	Range

The first symbol, a single dot or period, doesn't have a given name in the NAV documentation, so we'll call it the Member symbol. It indicates that a field is a member of a table (`TableName.FieldName`) or that a control is a member of a form (`FormName.ControlName`) or report (`ReportName.ControlName`) or that a function is a member of an object (`Objectname.FunctionName`).

We discussed parenthetical grouping and indexing earlier.

The Scope operator is a two character sequence `::`, two colons in a row. The Scope operator is used to allow C/AL code to refer to a specific Option value using the text descriptive value rather than the integer value that is actually stored in the database. For example, in our C/ANDL database `Member` table, we have an Option field defined that is called **Status** with Option string values of **Inactive** and **Active**. Those values would be stored as integers 0 and 1, but we would like to use the strings to refer to them in code, so that our code would be more self-documenting. The Scope operator allows us to refer to `Status::Inactive` (rather than 0) and `Status::Active` (rather than 1). These constructs are then translated by the compiler to 0 and 1, respectively. If you want to type fewer characters when entering code, you can just enter enough of the Option string value to be unique, then let the compiler automatically fill in the rest when you next save and compile the object.

The Range operator is a two character sequence `".."`, two dots in a row. This operator is very widely used in NAV, not only in your C/AL code, but also in the filters entered by users. The English lower case alphabet could be represented by the range `a..z`; the set of single digit numbers by the range `-9..9`; all the entries starting with the letter *a* (lower case) by `a..a*`. Don't underestimate the power of the range operator.

Arithmetic Operators and Functions

The Arithmetic operators include the following:

Arithmetic Operators		
Symbol	**Action**	**Data Types**
+	Addition	Numeric, String (concatenation), Date, Time
-	Subtraction	Numeric, Date, Time
*	Multiplication	Numeric
/	Division	Numeric
DIV	Integer Division (provides only the integer portion of the quotient of a division calculation)	Numeric
MOD	Modulus (provides on the integer remainder of a division calculation)	Numeric

As you can see by the data type column, these operators can be used on various data types. Numeric includes Integer, Decimal, Boolean, and Character data types. String includes Text and Code data types. Sample statements using DIV and MOD follow where BigNumber is an integer containing 200:

```
DIVIntegerValue := BigNumber DIV 60;
```

The contents of DIVIntegerValue after executing the preceding statement would be 3.

```
MODIntegerValue := BigNumber MOD 60;
```

The contents of MODIntegerValue after executing the preceding statement would be 20.

The syntax for these DIV and MOD statements is:

```
IntegerQuotient := IntegerDividend DIV IntegerDivisor;
IntegerModulus := IntegerDividend MOD IntegerDivisor;
```

Boolean Operators

Boolean operators only operate on expressions that can be evaluated as Boolean. They are as follows:

Boolean Operators	
Symbol	**Evaluation**
NOT	Logical NOT
AND	Logical AND
OR	Logical OR
XOR	Exclusive Logical OR

The result of an expression based on a Boolean operator will in turn be Boolean.

Relational Operators and Functions

The Relational Operators are listed in the following screenshot. Each of these is used in an expression of the format:

```
Expression RelationalOperator Expression
```

For example: `(Variable1 + 97) > ((Variable2 * 14.5) / 57.332)`

Relational Operators	
Symbol	**Evaluation**
<	Less than
>	Greater than
<=	Less than or Equal
>=	Great than or Equal
=	Equal to
<>	Not equal to
IN	IN Valueset

We will spend a little extra time on the IN operator, both because this can be very handy and because it is not documented elsewhere. The term valueset in the Evaluation column for IN refers to a list of defined values. It would be reasonable to define a valueset as a container of a defined set of individual values, or expressions, or other valuesets. Some examples of IN as used in the standard NAV product code are as follows:

```
GLEntry."Posting Date" IN [0D,WORKDATE]
Description[I+2] IN ['0'..'9']
"Gen. Posting Type" IN ["Gen. Posting Type"::Purchase,
                        "Gen. Posting Type"::Sale]
SearchString IN ['','=><']
No[i] IN ['0'..'9']
"FA Posting Date" IN [01010001D..12319998D]
```

Here is another example of what IN used in an expression might look like:

```
TestString IN ['a'..'d','j','q','l'..'p'];
```

If the value of TestString were 'a' or 'm', then this expression would evaluate to TRUE (Yes). If the value of TestString were 'z', then this expression would evaluate to FALSE (No).

Precedence of Operators

When expressions are evaluated by the C/AL compiler, the parsing routines use a predefined precedence hierarchy to determine what operators to evaluate first, what to do second, and so forth. That precedence hierarchy is provided in the Application Designer's Guide, but for convenience the information is repeated here.

C/AL Operator Precedence Hierarchy		
Sequence	**Symbols**	
1	.	Member (Fields in Records, etc)
	[ ]	Indexing
	( )	Parenthetical Grouping
	::	Scope
2		Unary instances of:
	NOT	Logical Not
	+	Positive value
	-	Negating value
3	*	Multiplication
	/	Division
	DIV	Integer division
	MOD	Modulus
	AND	Logical AND
	XOR	Logical Exclusive OR
4	+	Addition or Concatenation
	-	Subtraction
	OR	Logical OR
5	>	Greater than
	<	Less than
	>=	Greater than or equal to
	<=	Less than or equal to
	<>	Not equal to
	IN	IN Valueset
6	..	Range

Some Basic C/AL

It's time for us to learn some more of the standard functions provided for our convenience by C/SIDE. We will focus on those most frequently found useful.

MESSAGE, ERROR, CONFIRM, and STRMENU Functions

There is a group of functions in C/AL called **dialog functions**. The purpose of these functions is to allow for communications (i.e. dialog) between the system and the user. There are eleven different dialog functions available. At least three of those are easy to use as tools in testing and debugging. In order to make it easier for us to proceed with our next level of C/AL development work, we're going to take time now to learn about those three dialog functions.

In each of these functions, data values can be inserted through use of a substitution string. The substitution string is the % (percent sign) character followed by the digit 1 through 9, located within a message text string. That could look like the following:

```
MESSAGE('A message + a data element to display = %1',OrderAmount);
```

If the `OrderAmount` value was $100.53, the output from the preceding would be:

```
A message + a data element to display = $100.53
```

You can have up to nine substitution strings in one dialog function. In all cases, the use of substitution strings and their associated display values is optional. You can also use any one of the dialog functions simply to display a completely predefined text message with nothing variable.

MESSAGE Function

`MESSAGE` is the most commonly used dialog function. It is easy to use for the display of transient data and can be placed almost anywhere in your C/AL code. All it requires of the user is acknowledgement that the message has been read. The disadvantage of messages is that they are not displayed until either the object completes its run or pauses for some other external action. Plus, if you should inadvertently create a situation that generates hundreds or thousands of messages, there is no graceful way to terminate their display once they begin displaying.

It's common to use `MESSAGE` as the poor man's trace tool. You can program the display of messages to only occur under particular circumstances and use them to view either the flow of processing (by outputting simple unique codes from different points in your logic) or to view the contents of particular data elements through multiple processing cycles.

`MESSAGE` has the following syntax: `MESSAGE (String [, Value1] , ...])`, where there are as many ValueX entries as there are %X substitution strings (up to nine).

Here is a sample debugging message:

```
MESSAGE('Loop %1, Item No. %2',LoopCounter,"Item No.");
```

The output would look like the following (when the counter was **12** and the **Item No.** was **I0123**):

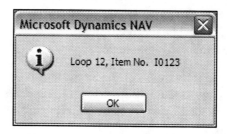

ERROR Function

ERROR is formatted almost exactly like MESSAGE except, of course, the function name is obviously different and, of course, ERROR behaves differently. When an ERROR function is executed, the execution of the current process terminates, the message is immediately displayed and the database remains unchanged as though the process calling the ERROR function had not run at all.

Sometimes you can use the ERROR function in combination with the MESSAGE function to assist in repetitive testing. MESSAGE functions can be placed in code to show what is happening with an ERROR function placed just prior to where the process would normally complete. Because the ERROR function rolls back all database changes, this technique allows you to run through multiple tests against the same data without any time-consuming backup and restoration of your test data. This isn't likely to be the original intended purpose of this function, but it turns out to be a very useful one.

ERROR has the following syntax:

ERROR (String [, Value1] , ...]) where there are as many ValueX entries as there are %X substitution strings (up to nine).

If the preceding MESSAGE was an ERROR function instead, the code line would be:

```
ERROR('Loop %1, Item No. %2',LoopCounter,"Item No.");
```

The output would look like the following screenshot:

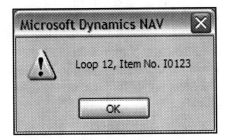

Except for the exclamation point in a triangle symbol, you couldn't tell this was an ERROR message, although your process would terminate, which would be a clue. A better way of communicating would be to let the users know that they had just received an ERROR message, for example by including the word ERROR in your message, something like the following:

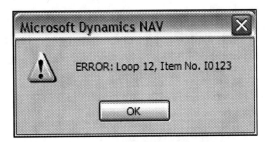

Even in the best of circumstances, it is difficult for the system to communicate clearly with the users. Sometimes our tools, in their effort to be flexible, make it too easy for developers to take the easy way out and communicate poorly or not at all. In fact, an ERROR statement of the form ERROR('') will terminate the run and roll back all processing without even displaying any message at all. An important part of your job as a developer is to ensure that your system communicates clearly and completely.

CONFIRM Function

A third dialog function is the CONFIRM function. A CONFIRM function call causes processing to stop while the user responds to the dialog. In a CONFIRM, you would likely include a question in your text because the function provides Yes and No button options.

In a debugging situation, it's sometimes useful to use CONFIRM to control the path processing will take. You can display the status of data or processing flow and then allow the operator to make a choice (Yes or No) that can then be used to influence what happens next. This is exactly what CONFIRM is designed for in normal processing. But execution of a CONFIRM function will also cause any pending MESSAGE outputs to be displayed before the CONFIRM function displays. Consequently, combined with MESSAGE and ERROR, creative use of CONFIRM can add to your debugging/diagnostic toolkit.

CONFIRM has the following syntax:

BooleanValue := CONFIRM(String [, Default] [, Value1] ,…) where Default choice is TRUE or FALSE and there are as many ValueX entries as there are %X substitution strings (up to nine).

If you just code CONFIRM(String), the Default choice will be false. Note that true and false appear onscreen as **Yes** and **No** (an interesting feature that is consistent throughout NAV for Boolean values).

A CONFIRM function call with a similar content as the preceding examples might look like this for the code and the display:

```
CONFIRM('Loop %1, Item No. %2\OK to continue?',
    TRUE,LoopCounter,"Item No.");
```

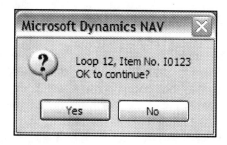

In typical usage, the CONFIRM function is part of or referred to by a conditional statement that uses the Boolean value returned by the CONFIRM function.

An additional feature to note here is the use of the backslash (\) which forced a new line in the displayed message. This works throughout NAV screen display functions; to display a backslash, you must put two of them in your string, i.e. \\.

STRMENU Function

A fourth dialog function is the STRMENU function. A STRMENU function call also causes processing to stop while the user responds to the dialog. The advantage of the STRMENU function is the ability to provide several choices, rather than just two. Unfortunately, in a STRMENU, you cannot include a question in your text but must rely on either the phrasing of your choices and context, or some other mechanism to make it clear to what the user is responding. Perhaps for this reason, STRMENU is not heavily used. A common use is to provide an option menu in response to the user pressing a command button.

STRMENU has the following syntax:

```
IntegerValue := STRMENU(StringVariable of Options separated by commas
[, OptionDefault])
```

where the OptionDefault is an integer representing which of the options will be selected by default when the menu displays. If you do not provide an OptionDefault, 1 will be used (i.e. the first option listed will be the default).

Here is an example of STRMENU:

```
OptionNo := STRMENU('Red,Yellow,Black
            Stripes,Show more options...',4);
```

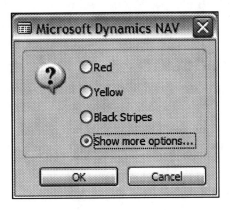

Setting the default to 4 caused the fourth option (**Show more options...**) to be the default selection when the menu was displayed.

If the user responds **Cancel** or presses *Esc,* the value returned by the function is 0.

Use of the STRMENU function eliminates the need to use a Form object when asking the user to select from a limited set of options. The STRMENU can also be utilized from within a report or Codeunit when calling a Form would restrict processing choices.

SETCURRENTKEY Function

The SETCURRENTKEY function behaves considerably differently when using the C/SIDE database than when using the SQL Server database. The explanation that follows focuses on the C/SIDE database behavior. On SQL Server, SETCURRENTKEY only determines the order in which the data will be presented to the processing, but the actual key choice is made by the SQL Server Query Analyzer.

The SETCURRENTKEY function allows you to select the specific key to be used for subsequent processing, thus defining the sort order to be used. The syntax is:

```
[BooleanValue :=] Record.SETCURRENTKEY ( FieldName1,
                                        [FieldName2], … )
```

The BooleanValue is optional. If you do not specify it and no matching key is found, a run-time error will occur. This may not be a bad thing, as generally your key specification in code is fixed (not variable) and you would want to know during initial testing that you had not specified an existing key. In addition, if keys are later changed, you will want to make sure that either you have allowed for that in your error handling or that you have allowed the run-time error to identify a problem and stop processing until it is corrected.

If the key structure you specify is a partial structure, for example only one field, and that structure matches multiple keys, C/AL may not select the key you intended. Therefore it is good to provide a complete key specification.

SETRANGE Function

The SETRANGE function provides the ability to set a simple range filter on a field. SETRANGE syntax is as follows:

```
Record.SETRANGE(FieldName [,From-Value] [,To-Value]);
```

Prior to applying its range filter, the SETRANGE function removes any filters that were previously set for the defined field. If SETRANGE is executed without any From or To values, it will clear the filters on the field.

[If SETRANGE is executed with only one value, that will act as both the From and To values.]

Some examples of the SETRANGE function in code are as follow:

Filter to get only members with ID from 100 through 499, or from the variable values LowVal through HiVal:

```
Member.SETRANGE("Member ID",100,499);
```

```
Member.SETRANGE("Member ID",LowVal,HiVal);
```

Clear the filters on Member ID:

```
Member.SETRANGE("Member ID");
```

Filter to allow all records with dates up through the contents of the field "Volunteer ActivityLedger"."Activity Date":

```
ActRate.SETRANGE("Effective Date",0D,
        "Volunteer ActivityLedger"."Activity Date");
```

GET Function

GET is the basic data retrieval function in C/AL. GET retrieves a single record, based on the primary key only. GET has the following syntax:

```
[BooleanValue :=] Record.GET ( [KeyFieldValue1]
                        [,KeyFieldValue2] ,…)
```

The parameter(s) for the GET function are the primary key value (or values, if the primary key consists of more than one field).

Assigning the GET function result to a BooleanValue is optional. If the GET function is not successful, i.e. no record is found, and the statement is not handled by code or assigned, the process will terminate with a run-time error. Typically, therefore, the GET function is encased in an IF statement structured something like the following:

```
IF Customer.GET(NewCustNo)  THEN …
```

 GET data retrieval is not constrained by filters. If there is a matching record in the table, GET will retrieve it.

FIND–NEXT Functions

The FIND function is the general purpose data retrieval function in C/AL. It is much more flexible than GET, therefore more widely used. GET may have the advantage of being faster as it operates only on an unfiltered direct access via the primary key, looking for a single uniquely keyed entry. FIND has the following syntax:

```
[BooleanValue :=] RecordName.FIND ( [Which] )
```

Just as with the GET function, assigning the FIND function result to a Boolean value is optional. But in almost all cases, FIND is embedded in a condition that controls subsequent processing appropriately.

FIND differs from GET in several important ways:

FIND operates under the limits imposed by whatever filters are applied on the subject field.

FIND uses whatever key is currently selected.

There are also special versions of the FIND function for use with the SQL Server database. The intent is to allow C/AL coding to be optimized for SQL Server compatibility as these instructions are especially designed for use with SQL Server. The SQL Server-related FIND functions are:

- FINDSET: Allows defining the standard size of the read record cache; defaults to 500.

- FINDFIRST: Finds the first record in a table that satisfies the defined filter and current key. Conceptually equivalent to the FIND('-') but much better for SQL Server.

- FINDLAST: Finds the last record in a table that satisfies the defined filter and current key. Conceptually equivalent to the FIND('+') but much better for SQL Server.

Through the [Which] parameter, FIND allows the specification of what record is searched for relative to the defined key values. The defined key values are the set of values currently in the fields of the active key in the memory-resident record of table RecordName.

The following table lists the `Which` parameter options and prerequisites. The results are always relative to the selected set (i.e. they respect applied filters).

FIND Which parameter	FIND action	Search and primary key value prerequisite before FIND
=	Match the search key values exactly	All must be specified
>	read the next record with key values larger than the search key values	All must be specified
<	read the next record with key values smaller than the search key values	All must be specified
>=	read the first record found with key values equal to or larger than the search key values	All must be specified
<=	read the next record with key values equal to or smaller than the search key values	All must be specified
-	read the first record in the selected set	No requirement
+	read the last record in the selected set	No requirement

The FIND function is quite often used as the first step in the course of reading a set of data, for example, reading all the Sales Invoices for a single Customer. In such a case, the NEXT function is used to trigger all the data reads after the sequence is initiated with a FIND.

The typical read loop is as follows:

```
IF MyData.FIND('-') THEN
  REPEAT
    Processing logic here
UNTIL MyData.NEXT = 0;
```

We will discuss the REPEAT-UNTIL control structure in more detail in the next chapter. Essentially, it does what it says; "**repeat** the following logic **until** the defined **condition** is **true**". In the case of the FIND-NEXT, the NEXT function provides both the definition of how the read loop will advance through the table and provides the exiting condition.

When `DataTable.NEXT = 0`, that means there are no more records to be read. We have reached the end of the data, based on the filters and other conditions that apply to our reading process.

The specific syntax of the NEXT function is `DataTable.NEXT(Step)`. `DataTable` is the name of the table being read. `Step` defines the number of records NAV will move ahead (or back) per read. The default `Step` is 1, meaning NAV moves ahead one record at a time, reading every record. A `Step` of 0 is ignored. If the `Step` were 2, NAV would move ahead two records at a time and the process would only be presented with every other record. Step can also be negative, in which case NAV moves backwards through the table. This would allow you to do a FIND('+') or FINDLAST for the end of the table, then a NEXT(-1) to read backwards through the data. This is very useful if, for example, you need to read a table sorted by date and want to access the most recent entries first.

BEGIN–END Compound Statement

In C/AL, there are instances where the syntax rules only allow for use of a single statement. But your design may require the execution of several code statements. C/AL provides at least two ways to address this need. One method is to have the single statement as a call to a function that contains multiple statements.

On the other hand, in-line coding is often more efficient to run and significantly easier to understand. So C/AL provides a tool to define a **Compound Statement** or **Block** of code. A compound statement containing several, or even many, statements can be used in place of a single code statement

A compound statement is enclosed by the reserved words BEGIN and END. The compound statement structure looks like this:

```
BEGIN
    <Statement 1>;
    <Statement 2>;
    ..
    <Statement n>;
END
```

IF–THEN–ELSE Statement

IF is the basic conditional statement of most programming languages. It operates in C/AL similar to other languages. The basic structure is: IF a conditional expression is true, THEN execute Statement-1 ELSE (if conditional not true) execute Statement-2. The ELSE portion is optional. The syntax is:

```
IF <Condition> THEN <Statement-1> [ ELSE <Statement-2> ]
```

As with other languages, IF statements can be nested so that you have conditionals dependent on the evaluation of other conditionals. Obviously one needs to take care with such constructs, as it is easy to end up with convoluted code structures that are difficult to debug and difficult for your successor developer (i.e. the next person that works on this system) to understand.

As you work with NAV C/AL code, you will see that often the <Condition> is really an expression built around a standard C/AL function. This approach is often used when the standard syntax for the function is Boolean value, function expression. Some examples are:

- `IF Customer.FIND('-') THEN...`
- `IF Update.CONFIRM('OK to update?',TRUE) THEN...`
- `IF TempData.INSERT THEN...`
- `IF Customer.CALCFIELDS(Balance,Balance(LCY)) THEN...`

Indenting Code

Because we have just discussed BEGIN-END compound statements and IF conditional statements, which also are compound (i.e. containing multiple expressions), this seems a good time to discuss indenting code.

In C/AL, the standard practice for indenting subordinate, contained, or continued lines is relatively simple. Always indent such lines by two characters except where there are left and right parentheses to be aligned.

Some examples are:

```
IF (A <> B) THEN
    A := A + Count1
ELSE
    B := B + Count2;
```

Or:

```
IF (A <> B)
THEN
    A := A + Count1;
```

Or:

```
IF (A <> B)
THEN BEGIN
    A := A + Oount1;
    B := A + Count2;
    IF C > (A * B) THEN
      C := A * B;
END
ELSE
    B := B + Count2;
```

Some Simple Coding Modifications

Now we're going to actually add some C/AL code to some objects we've created for our C/ANDL application.

Adding a Validation to a Table

Let's start with some code in the `Validation` triggers of our Table 50005–`Volunteer Activity Ledger`. When a new record is added to this table, we would like all the fields to be filled in. The description should be copied from the `Volunteer Activity` table. We can do that at the time the Volunteer Activity Code is validated. We also want to calculate the number of **Volunteer Hours** worked times the **Points per Hour** for the appropriate activity.

The basic logic is defined by the following pseudo-code:

In the Activity Code `OnValidate` trigger:

- GET the Volunteer Activity record; allow for a no-match lookup.
- Copy `VolunteerActivity.Description` to `VolunteerActivityLedger.Description`

In the `Hours OnValidate` trigger:

- GET the Volunteer Activity record; allow for a no-match lookup.
- Assign the result of the expression `VolunteerActivityLedger.Hours` times `VolunteerActivity.PointsPerHour` to `VolunteerActivityLedger.Points`.

In reality, the actual code is simpler than the pseudo-code. That's often the case with NAV code. Once you have figured out a good process flow design, C/AL coding is usually a relatively quick process. Much more of your time is likely to be spent designing and testing than actually coding.

You should now open up the Table Designer, Design Table 50005, and translate the preceding pseudo-code into C/AL. Then save and compile the table. Now enter some data to see if your modifications work. If they do not, then your job is to figure out what you did wrong and fix it.

As with almost any coding task, there are multiple correct ways to write the code. In this case for example, we need to GET the Volunteer Activity record associated with this data item from two different OnValidate triggers. Should we write essentially the same code in both triggers, or should we create a new function that does the GET and call that function from each of the triggers? At this point in our application design, either answer is a reasonable one. It might be a good idea if you try both ways so you can understand the differences in the ways you would structure the code for each. We'll step through the option of adding code to both triggers.

Adding a Table Validation Coding Option

The first thing is to define a global variable allowing us to reference the Volunteer Activity table from C/AL code within the Volunteer Activity Ledger table.

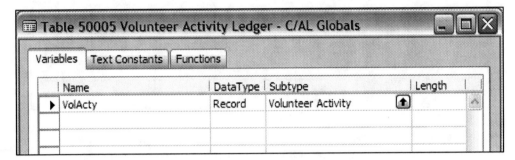

When an Activity Code entry is made into a Volunteer Activity Ledger record, we will want to access the related Volunteer Activity record using a GET statement. An easy way to begin that coding is to use a tool built into C/SIDE. That tool is the **C/AL Symbol Menu**, which is accessed via the screen's top menu **View | C/AL Symbol Menu**.

All objects, records, and data fields, whether defined by the developer or automatically by the system, are listed in the leftmost column of the **C/AL Symbol Menu** display. In the next chapter we'll explore this tool some more.

Right now we just want to use it very simply to help us enter our **VolActy** variable and the related GET function in the correct format and with the correct spelling.

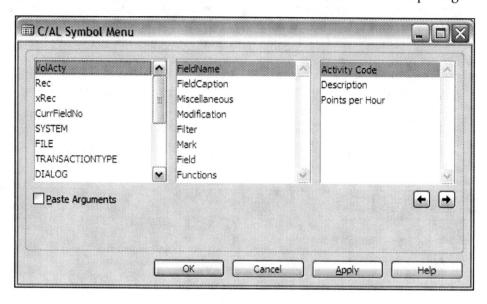

We can just use this screen as a reference tool or we can use it to populate our code. In this case, let's do the latter. Once we've highlighted the elements we want (as shown in the preceding screenshot), working in the columns from left to right, we can double-click on the rightmost element and it will be inserted into our development screen (as shown in the following screenshot).

```
Activity Code - OnValidate()
[Ok :=] VolActy.GET([Value] ,...)

Activity Code - OnLookup()
```

What has been pasted into our code is not workable. It is just a template that we can begin with to create the code we want. In this case, referring back to our pseudo-code, we see that we want our GET function embedded in a condition, followed by an action expression to be executed if the condition is true. That code can be structured as shown in the following screenshot:

```
Activity Code - OnValidate()
IF VolActy.GET("Activity Code") THEN
  Description := VolActy.Description;

Activity Code - OnLookup()
```

Time to test. Exit the table and compile. Enter some test data. Does the description copy in from the Volunteer Activity record as you wanted it to? If not, it's now time to figure out why. If it does work (or when it does), congratulations!

Our next modification has a very similar structure, except for the action expression. To create the IF + GET portion of our statement, we could do a copy and paste, or a view and type, or go through the same process we went through for the first instance. Once we've done that, then we must type in our expression to do the math. We have the names of two of the variables at hand because they are part of the table in which we are coding. But it just might be easiest to look up the third variable (Points per Hour) in the **C/AL Symbol Menu** and click it in.

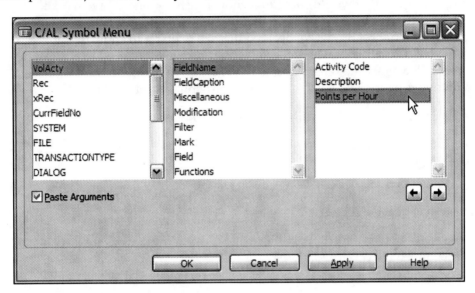

As you can see in the following screenshot, the selected field variable pops in complete with the qualifying record variable name **VolActy**.

```
Hours - OnValidate()
IF VolActy.GET("Activity Code") THEN
   Points := Hours * VolActy."Points per Hour";


Hours - OnLookup()
```

Once again, it's time to test our work. Exit and save, and compile. Test entry of some Hours in the Volunteer Activity Ledger. Does the new code properly calculate and store the Points? Before you move on, make sure this part works correctly.

Adding Code to Enhance a Report

As you may recall, our C/ANDL members' volunteer activities serve two purposes. One is simply to provide direct benefits through the volunteer work. The other is to "earn" the promised payments from our sponsor company, BigC. Originally BigC agreed to pay $5 per point for the work done. But there have been some discussions going on and BigC has decided to raise the rate for work done on or after Jan 1, 2008 to $6 per point and is going to provide a special holiday bonus rate for work done during December 2007 of $10 per point.

So we've got some work to do on our application. We haven't gotten around to creating our report that would show BigC how much members have worked and therefore earned. It's time for us to do that. While we could just hard-code these rate changes in that report, we've decided that we're going to allow for more user-oriented flexibility than hardcoding would provide. We need to create a new table that will contain the rates along with the effective dates. Because we need a good unique primary key, we'll include a record entry number as well.

Table 50008 – `Activity Rate` will contain the entries as:

- Entry No.: Integer
- Effective Date: Date
- Rate: Decimal

Create your new table.

Now we're going to use the Report Wizard to create a framework for a report to show how much we've earned.

Layout for Report 50002 – Volunteer Activity Earnings

Data Element	Source Table
Member ID	Volunteer Activity Ledger
Activity Code	Volunteer Activity Ledger
Description	Volunteer Activity Ledger
Date	Volunteer Activity Ledger
Hours	Volunteer Activity Ledger
Points	Volunteer Activity Ledger
Rate	Activity Rate
Amount Earned	calculated in Report 50002

Since the first set of fields come from the same table, we can readily drive the Report Wizard with that table (Table 50005 – `Volunteer Activity Ledger`), then add in the rest of the fields and necessary processing.

Create the basic version of Report 50002. While you're at it, create totals on the **Hours** and **Points** columns.

Add the controls for the **Rate** and **Amount Earned** fields to the generated report. Make the column header control for **Amount Earned** print on two lines. Looking at the logic that was generated to calculate totals for **Hours** and **Points**, you'll see that it's tied to the Data Item that is driving the report. You also want to calculate a total for the **Amount Earned** column, but you'll have to handle that in manual code. Since the generated report doesn't calculate and print grand totals, add that feature too.

Add the logic into the `OnAfterGetRecord` trigger to look up the applicable **Activity Rate** for each Volunteer Activity Ledger record. Now code the calculation for Amount Earned. Don't forget to define the necessary global variables. Test your report and fix any problems.

In case you're having some problems, here are some screenshots showing one solution to this task along with brief descriptions of the developer work done along the way.

First we need to define the new table:

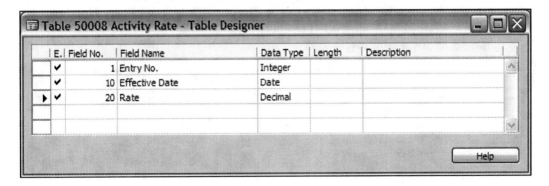

As part of the definition process we will set the minimum and maximum number of decimal places on the Rate variable to two (i.e. **DecimalPlaces** property of **2:2**).

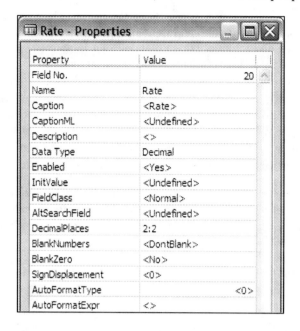

In order to select data based on the **Effective Date** field, we need to have a key on that field. We want the effective sort to be **Effective Date**, then **Entry No.**, but because the primary key is appended to every other key we don't need to explicitly add that field to our secondary key.

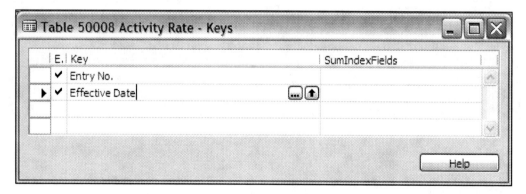

Now we can use our previous experience and generate a List format report based on the `Volunteer Activity Ledger`. We will select all the fields, order it by **Member**, group it by **Member**, and total both the available fields. The following screenshot is from a generated report with no modifications:

```
Volunteer Activity Ledger                                                    March 4, 2008
CRONUS International Ltd.                                                     Page    1



                     Activity      Activity
  Member ID          Code          Date        Description         Hours        Points


  Member ID                        406


  406                IPAINT        04/06/08     Inside Painting      2.00         8.00
  406                MOW           06/13/08     Mowing               2.50         7.50
  406                OPAINT        07/01/08     Outside Painting     3.00        15.00
  406                OPAINT        07/13/08     Paint the trim       2.00        10.00


  Total for Member ID                                               9.50        40.50



  Member ID                        1003


  1003               MOW           06/23/08     Mowing               1.50         4.50
  1003               MOW           06/24/08     Mowing               1.00         3.00


  Total for Member ID                                               2.50         7.50
```

The following is the same report in **Section Designer**:

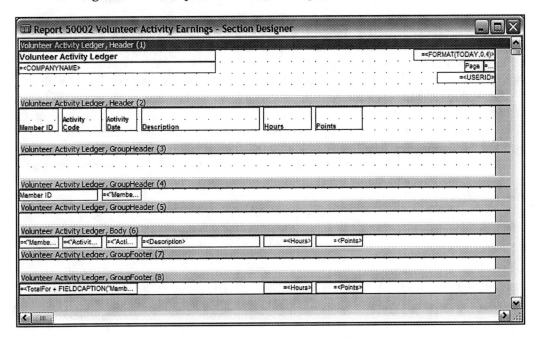

Once we have a generated basic version of Report 50002, we can start polishing it for production use. The first thing we should do is to add the new working storage (i.e. global) variables to support our lookup code and the totalling. In actuality, the process of writing the C/AL code and defining the new variables is a back and forth process, doing first one, then the other, and then back to the first. We'll just show the final results here. These are the final set of globals:

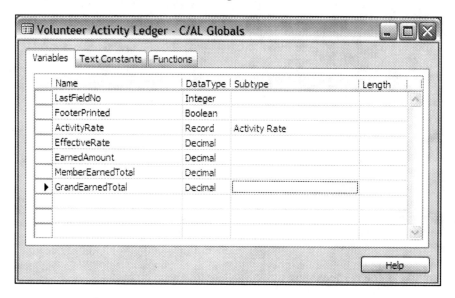

The next screenshot is a snapshot of the final mainline C/AL code. First an intermediate variable (`EffectiveRate`) is cleared to 0 and the `Activity Rate` table key tied to Effective Date is assigned as the active key. When the Volunteer Activity Ledger record is read in, the Activity Date in that record is used to act as a High Value for a filter on the Activity Rate table so we can find the applicable Rate record. Next, a `FIND('+')` is performed to find the last entry (highest date). Assuming one is found, `EffectiveRate` is calculated, `EarnedAmount` is calculated, and the `EarnedAmount` totals are calculated. By the way, the expression `Variable1 += Variable2` gives the same results as `Variable1 := Variable1 + Variable2`, and the expression `Variable1 -= Variable2` gives the same results as `Variable1 := Variable1 - Variable2`.

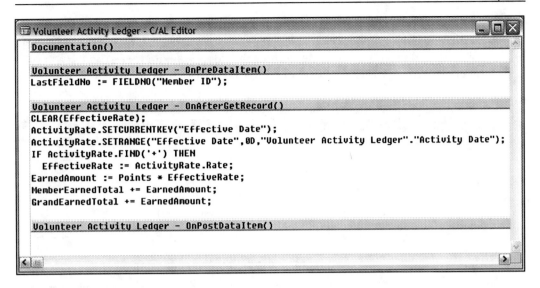

```
Volunteer Activity Ledger - C/AL Editor                                    _ □ X
Documentation()

Volunteer Activity Ledger - OnPreDataItem()
LastFieldNo := FIELDNO("Member ID");

Volunteer Activity Ledger - OnAfterGetRecord()
CLEAR(EffectiveRate);
ActivityRate.SETCURRENTKEY("Effective Date");
ActivityRate.SETRANGE("Effective Date",0D,"Volunteer Activity Ledger"."Activity Date");
IF ActivityRate.FIND('+') THEN
  EffectiveRate := ActivityRate.Rate;
EarnedAmount := Points * EffectiveRate;
MemberEarnedTotal += EarnedAmount;
GrandEarnedTotal += EarnedAmount;

Volunteer Activity Ledger - OnPostDataItem()
```

In the preceding screenshot, because the variable "Volunteer Activity Ledger"."Activity Date" refers to a data field within the table that is the focus of the current record trigger, the table name is not required. For unqualified variable names, the compiler will look first to the currently in-focus table, then to the global and local variables. So that line of code could just as easily be:

```
ActivityRate.SETRANGE("Effective Date",0D, "Activity Date");
```

In fact that latter style is the preferred method of coding variables for the current data item. However, if you happen to use the Symbol Menu to fill in a variable name, it will include the full table qualification as shown in the preceding screenshot.

Quite a bit more work was required in the Sections portion of the report to get to our desired result. Going from the top down the following changes were made:

- The Report label was changed from the default to one better representing the intended report usage.

- A Group Header section was subjectively judged unnecessary. The C/AL code contained in its trigger was reviewed and was not found to have any effect outside that section. So the section was deleted.

- Two new report columns were added i.e. Rate and EarnedAmount. The controls were created by copying existing controls, then modifying properties. The new controls were positioned carefully by examining the relative position of the generated controls, then mimicking their spacing.

- A Group Footer Section (5) was added for the sole purpose of including the horizontal line graphic control for appearance's sake. A Group Footer Section (7) was added to contain code to reset the `MemberEarnedTotal` value after it was printed. A screenshot of that code follows the **Section** screenshot:

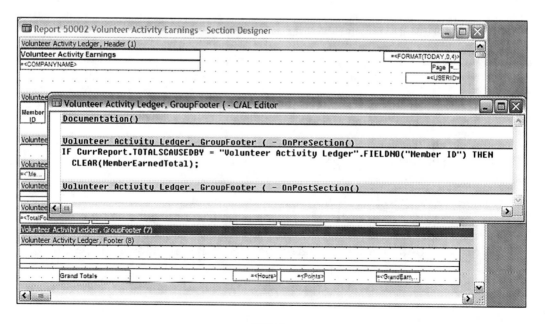

- Finally a Footer Section was added to print the report grand totals.

Of course, as this development proceeded, various sets of tests needed to be run. As with any development effort, there were some "oops" along the way and minor changes in direction. The final data input for testing purposes for the `Volunteer Activity Ledger` table is as shown:

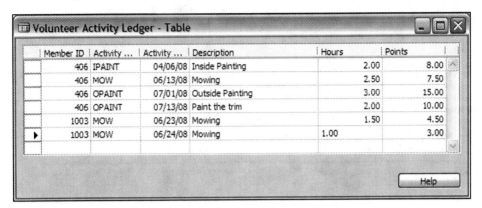

And the test data for the `Activity Rate` table is as shown in the following screenshot:

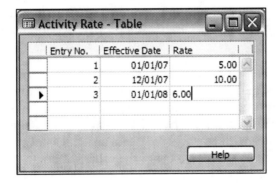

After all this work, we are finally ready for a test run of our modified report. A screenshot of that is as follows:

Member ID	Activity Code	Description	Activity Date	Hours	Points	Rate	Amount Earned
Volunteer Activity Earnings							March 4, 2008
CRONUS International Ltd.							Page 1
406	IPAINT	Inside Painting	04/06/08	2.00	8.00	6.00	48.00
406	MOW	Mowing	06/13/08	2.50	7.50	6.00	45.00
406	OPAINT	Outside Painting	07/01/08	3.00	15.00	6.00	90.00
406	OPAINT	Paint the trim	07/13/08	2.00	10.00	6.00	60.00
Total for Member ID	406			9.50	40.50		243.00
1003	MOW	Mowing	06/23/08	1.50	4.50	6.00	27.00
1003	MOW	Mowing	06/24/08	1.00	3.00	6.00	18.00
Total for Member ID	1003			2.50	7.50		45.00
Grand Totals				12.00	48.00		288.00

Note that we didn't have to do anything to calculate the totals for the two generated columns. That is because those columns contain data from a Data Item and in the properties for that Data Item, the **TotalFields** property contained the field names of **Hours** and **Points**.

There are many different ways to accomplish essentially the same result as this particular Report 50002. Some of those paths would be indistinguishable to the user. Some would not even be meaningfully different to the next developer who has to work on this report. What is important is that the result works reliably, provides the desired output, operates with reasonable speed, and does not cost much to create or maintain. If all those goals are met, most of the other differences are generally not terribly important.

Summary

Thought is the blossom; language the bud; action the fruit behind it
— Ralph Waldo Emerson

In this chapter we've covered topics including Object Designer navigation as well as more specific navigation of individual Object (Table, Form, Report) Designers.

We covered a number of C/AL language areas in relative detail including functions and how they may be used, variables of various types (both development and system), basic C/AL syntax, and discussion of C/AL expressions and operators. Some of the essential C/AL functions we covered included dialogs for communication with the user, SETRANGE filtering, GET and FIND, and related functions, BEGIN-END for code structures, plus IF-THEN-ELSE for basic process flow control.

Finally, we got some hands-on experience by adding validation code to a table and adding code to significantly enhance a generated report.

In the next chapter, we will expand our exploration and practice in the use of the tools of C/AL.

7

Intermediate C/AL

A language that doesn't have everything is actually easier to program in than some that do — Dennis Ritchie

In the last chapter, we learned enough C/AL to create a basic operational set of code. In this chapter, we will learn more about C/AL functions and pick up a few good habits along the way. The C/AL functions represent a significant portion of knowledge that you will need on a day-to-day basis, as you are getting started as a professional C/AL Developer.

Our goal is to understand more complex C/AL statement types, to be able to competently manage I/O, to create moderately complex program logic structures, and to understand data filtering and sorting as handled in NAV and C/AL. Since the functions and features in C/AL are designed for business and financial applications, you can do a surprising amount of work with a relatively small number of language constructs.

Keep in mind that anything discussed in this chapter will not relate to MenuSuites, as they contain no C/AL.

Development

All NAV development is done in C/AL and all C/AL development is done in C/SIDE. As an Integrated Development Environment, C/SIDE contains a number of tools designed to make our C/AL development effort easier, among which is the C/AL Symbol Menu.

C/AL Symbol Menu

When you are in one of the Object Designers, the **C/AL Symbol Menu** is accessed from either the menu option **View | C/AL Symbol Menu** or just by pressing *F5*. The default three-column display has variables and function categories in the left column. If the entry in the left column is a system function or a variable of function type, then the center column contains subcategories for the highlighted left-column entry. Finally, the right column contains the set of functions that are part of the highlighted center-column entry. In a few cases (such as subforms or BLOB fields or Matrix controls), there is additional information displayed in columns further to the right. Those columns are accessed through the arrows displayed just below the rightmost display column, as shown in the following screenshot:

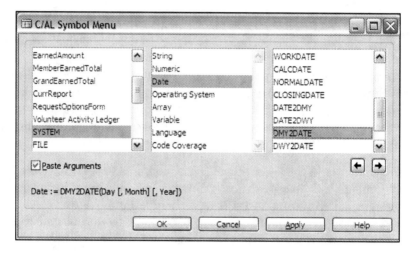

The **C/AL Symbol Menu** is a very useful multi-purpose tool for the developer. You can use it as a quick reference to see what C/AL functions are available to you, to access **Help** on those functions, and to view what other systems would refer to as the Symbol Table. You can also use the **C/AL Symbol Menu** to paste variable names or code structures into your code.

The reference use is most helpful when you are starting as a C/AL developer. It is a very useful guide to the inventory of available code tools. This reference has some very handy features. The first one is the general syntax for the highlighted function shown at the bottom left of the screen, as shown in the previous screenshot.

You have also quick and focused access to C/SIDE Reference Guide **Help**. When you put focus on an entry in the right (third) column and press *F1*, you will be taken directly to the **Help** for that function. If focus is in the left or center column, pressing *F1* may just bring up the general C/SIDE Reference Guide **Help** rather than a specific entry.

The second use of the C/AL Symbol Menu is as a symbol table. The symbol table for your object is visible in the left column of the **C/AL Symbol Menu** display. The displayed symbol set (i.e. variable set) is context sensitive. It will include all system-defined symbols, all your **Global** symbols, and **Local** symbols from the function that had focus at the time you accessed the C/AL Symbol Menu. Though it would be useful, there is no way within the Symbol Menu to see all Local variables in one view. The Local symbols will be at the top of the list, but you have to know the name of the first Global symbol to determine the scope of a particular variable (i.e. does it appear in the symbol list before or after the first Global?).

The third use for the C/AL Symbol Menu is as a code template with a paste function enabled. Paste is initiated by pressing either the **Apply** button or the **OK** button. In both the cases, element with focus will be pasted into your code. **Apply** will leave the Symbol Menu open and **OK** will close it (*double-clicking* on the element has the same effect as clicking on OK).

If the element with focus is a simple variable, then that variable will get pasted into your code. If the element is a function whose syntax appears at the lower left of the screen, the result of the paste action (i.e. **Apply** or **OK** or *double-click*) depends on whether or not **Paste Arguments** (just below the leftmost column) is checked or not. If **Paste Arguments** is not checked, then only the function itself will be pasted into your code. If **Paste Arguments** is checked, then the complete syntax string, as shown, will be pasted into your code. This can be a very convenient way to create a template to help you more quickly enter the correct parameters with the correct syntactical punctuation.

When you are in the C/AL Symbol Menu, you can focus on a column, click on a letter and jump to the next field in sequence in the column starting with that letter. This acts as a limited Search substitute, a sort of assisted browse.

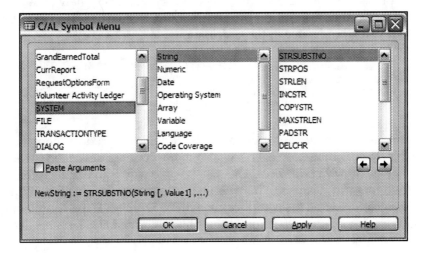

Internal Documentation

When you are creating or modifying software, it is always a good thing to document what you have done. It is often difficult for developers to spend much time (i.e. money) on documentation because most never enjoy doing it and the benefits are uncertain. A reasonable goal is to provide enough documentation so that a smart person following you, working on the same code, can understand the reason behind what you have done. It is true that if you choose good variable names, the C/AL code will tend to be self-documenting in terms of the logic flow. But you need to add comments to describe the functional reason for the change.

In the case of a brand-new function, a simple statement of purpose is all that is necessary. In the case of a modification, it is very useful to have comments providing a definition of what the change is intended to accomplish from a functional point of view and a description of what has been changed. If there is good external documentation of the change, then the comments in the code can refer back to this external documentation. In any case, the primary focus should be on the functional reason for the change, not just the technical reason.

In the following example, the documentation is for a brand-new report. The comments are in the Documentation trigger, where there are no format rules, except for those you impose. This is a new report, which we created in the previous chapter. The comment is coded to indicate the organization making the change (we are crediting our book "Programming NAV") and a sequence number for this change. In this case we are using a two digit number (**06**) for the change, plus the version number of the change, **00**, hence **PN.06.00**, followed by the initials of the developer (**DAS**) and the date of the change as shown in the following screenshot.

You can make up your own standard format that will identify the source and date of the work, but do have a standard and use it. When you add a new data element to an existing table, the **Description** property should receive the same modification identifier that you would place in the code comments.

When you make a subsequent change to an object, you should document that change in the Documentation trigger and also in the code, as described earlier. Inline comments can be done in two ways. The most visible way is to use a // character sequence (two forward slashes). Whatever text follows the slashes on that line will be treated as a comment by the compiler, i.e. will be ignored. If the comment spans two physical lines, the second portion of the comment must also be preceded by two forward slashes.

In the following screenshot we have used // to place comments inline in code to identify a change:

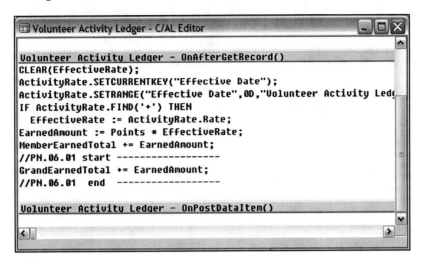

In this case, we have made the modification version number to **01**, resulting in **PN.06.01**. In the following code, modifications are traced by bracketing the additional code with comment lines containing the modification identifier, and **start** and **end** indicators. The NAV published standards do not include the dashed lines, as shown here, but doing something like that often makes it easier to spot modifications when you are scanning code rapidly. Don't forget, you can create your own standards, but then you should follow them consistently.

The second way to place a comment within code is to surround the comment with a matched pair of braces { }. Because braces are less visible than the slashes, you should always use // when your comment is relatively long. If you want to use { }, it wouldn't be a bad idea to insert a // comment at the beginning and end of the material inside the braces, to make the existence of the comments more readily identifiable. For example:

```
{//PN.06.02 start deletion -------------
//PN.06.02 replace validation with a call to an external function
...miscellaneous C/AL validation code
//PN.06.02 end deletion   ------------- }
```

When you delete code, you should always leave original statement in place, but commented so that it is inoperative. When you change existing code, you should leave the original code in place, but commented out, with the new version being inserted as shown in the following screenshot:

```
      added appropriate globals, inline logic and footer section
PN.06.02 DAS 2/15/08 Refine the Current Key selection to always have latest entry for a date
              last in order and therefore be the one used


Volunteer Activity Ledger - OnPreDataItem()
LastFieldNo := FIELDNO("Member ID");


Volunteer Activity Ledger - OnAfterGetRecord()
CLEAR(EffectiveRate);
//PN.06.02 start -----------------
//ActivityRate.SETCURRENTKEY("Effective Date");
ActivityRate.SETCURRENTKEY("Effective Date","Entry No.");
//PN.06.02  end  -----------------
ActivityRate.SETRANGE("Effective Date" AND "Volunteer Activity Ledger"."Activity Date");
```

Don't forget to update the external version numbers located in the Version List field on the Object Designer screen.

From previous experience, you know that it is not the format of the internal documentation that is critical. It is the fact that it exists in a consistent and reliable fashion that accurately describes the code changes that have occurred.

Computation—Validation Utility Functions

C/AL includes a number of utility functions designed to facilitate data computations and validation or initiation of field contents. The following are some of the Validation Utility Functions:

TESTFIELD

The TESTFIELD function is widely used in standard NAV code. With TESTFIELD, you can test a variable value and, if necessary, issue an error message in a single statement. The syntax is as follows:

```
Record.TESTFIELD (Field, [Value] )
```

If a Value is specified and the field does not contain that value, an error condition is raised (i.e. the process terminates) and the associated error message is issued. If no Value is specified, the condition evaluated is relative to zero or blank. If no Value is specified and the field is zero or blank, then that is an error.

The advantage of TESTFIELD is ease of use and consistency in code. The disadvantage is that the error message, although not as hard to understand as others, is not as informative as you might provide as a careful developer.

FIELDERROR

Another function very similar to the TESTFIELD function is the FIELDERROR function. But where TESTFIELD performs a test and terminates with either an error or an OK result, FIELDERROR presumes that the test was already performed and the field failed the test. The FIELDERROR is designed to display an error message, and then trigger a run-time error, thus terminating the process. The syntax is as follows:

```
TableName.FIELDERROR(FieldName[,OptionalMsgText]);
```

If you include your own message text, for example:

```
Member.FIELDERROR("Member Type",': The data is not like it should be');
```

you will see an error message from FIELDERROR similar to the following screenshot:

The error message begins with the name of the field, which is the FieldName parameter in the function call (in this case **Member**), followed by your specified MsgText (**The data is not like it should be**), which is in turn followed by the word "**in**", the qualified name of the first table field (**Member.Member ID**) and the value in that field (**42**).

If you do not include your own message text, your function call will look like the following screenshot:

```
Member.FIELDERROR("Member Type");
```

If you don't specify your own message text, the default message comes in two flavors. The first instance is the case where the referenced field is not empty, such as in the following screenshot. In this case, the contents of the field are the option text **Retired**.

The error message logic presumes that the error is due to a wrong value.

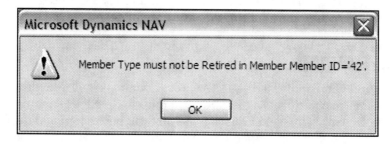

Following is another instance of a FIELDERROR function call with no message text supplied.

```
Member.FIELDERROR("Business Class");
```

In this case the field was empty. The resulting error message logic presumes that the error is the due to empty field, shown in the following screenshot:

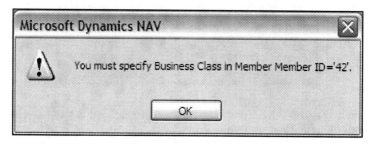

VALIDATE

The syntax of the VALIDATE function is as follows:

```
Record.VALIDATE ( Field [, Value] )
```

VALIDATE will fire the OnValidate trigger of Record.Field. If you have specified a Value, then that Value is assigned to the field and the field validations are invoked. If you don't specify a Value, then the field validations are invoked using the field value that already exists in the field. This function allows you to easily centralize your code design around the table, a definite advantage and one of NAV's strengths.

ROUND

The ROUND function lets you control the rounding precision for a decimal expression. The syntax for the ROUND function is as follows:

```
DecimalResult := ROUND (Number [, Precision] [, Direction] )
```

where Number is what is being rounded, Precision spells out the number of digits of decimal precision, and Direction indicates whether to round up, round down, or round to the nearest number. More specifically, some examples of Precision values are as follows:

Precision value	Rounding effect
100	To a multiple of 100
1	To an integer value
.01	To two decimal places (the US default)
0.01	Same as .01
.0001	To four decimal places

As noted, if no Precision value is specified, the US Localization will default to two decimal places, the standard for US currency. Default options in other localizations may differ.

The options available for the Direction value are shown in the following table:

Direction value (a text value)	Rounding effect
'='	Round to the nearest (mathematically correct)
'>'	Round up
'<'	Round down

The following statement:

```
DecimalValue := ROUND (1234.56789,0.001,'<')
```

would result in a DecimalValue containing 1234.567 whereas the statements:

```
DecimalValue := ROUND (1234.56789,0.001,'=')
DecimalValue := ROUND (1234.56789,0.001,'>')
```

would each result in a DecimalValue containing 1234.568.

TODAY, TIME, and CURRENTDATETIME Function

TODAY retrieves the current system date as set in the operating system. TIME retrieves the current system time as set in the operating system. CURRENTDATETIME retrieves the current date and time in the DATETIME format, which is stored in UTC international time and then displayed in local time. The syntax is as follows:

```
DateField := TODAY;
TimeField := TIME;
DateTimeField := CURRENTDATETIME;
```

These are useful for date- and time-stamping transactions or for filling in default values in fields of the appropriate data type. For data entry purposes, the current system date can be entered by simply typing a letter **t** or **T** or the word **TODAY** in the date entry field. NAV will automatically convert that entry to the current system date.

WORKDATE Function

A useful feature of NAV is the Work Date. Many standard NAV routines default dates to WorkDate rather than to the system date. When a user log into the system, the **Work Date** is initially set equal to the system date. But at any time, the operator can set the Work Date to any date by accessing **Tools | Work Date**, and then entering the desired new Work Date as shown in the following screenshot:

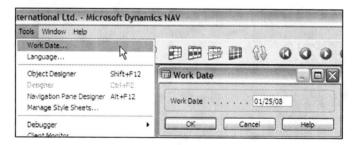

The syntax for using the WorkDate is as follows:

```
DateField := WORKDATE;
```

For data entry purposes, the current system date can be entered by the operator simply typing a letter **w** or **W** or the word **WORKDATE** in the date entry field. NAV will automatically convert that entry to the current system date.

Data Conversion Functions

Some data type conversions are handled in process by NAV without any particular attention on part of the Developer (e.g. Code to Text, Char to Text). Some data type conversions can only be handled through C/AL functions. Formatting is included as a data type conversion.

FORMAT Function

The FORMAT function provides for the conversion of an expression of any data type (e.g. integer, decimal, date, option, time, Boolean, etc.) into a formatted string. The syntax is as follows:

```
StringField := FORMAT( ExpressionToFormat [, OutputLength]
[, FormatString or FormatNumber])
```

The formatted output of the ExpressionToFormat will be assigned to the output StringField. The optional field controls the conversion according to a complex set of rules. These rules can be found in the C/SIDE **Help** file for the FORMAT function. Whenever possible, you should always apply FORMAT in its simpler form. The best way to determine the likely results of a FORMAT expression is to test it through a range of the values to be formatted. Make sure to include the extremes of the range of possible values in your testing.

The optional OutputLength field can be zero (which is the default), a positive integer, or a negative integer. The typical OutputLength value is either zero, in which case the defined format is fully applied, or it is a figure designed to control the maximum character length of the formatted string result.

The last optional parameter has two totally separate sets of choices. One set, represented by an integer FormatNumber, allows the choice of a particular predefined (i.e. standard) format, of which there are four to nine choices depending on the ExpressionToFormat data type. The other set of choices allows you to build your own format expression. The **Help** information for the FORMAT property provides a relatively complete description of the available tools from which you can build your own format expression. The FORMAT property **Help** also provides a complete list of the predefined format choices.

Note that a FORMAT function which cannot be executed will create a run-time error that will terminate execution of the process. Thus the importance of thorough testing to avoid production crashes.

EVALUATE Function

The EVALUATE function is somewhat the reverse of the FORMAT function. It allows you to convert a string field into the defined data type. The syntax of the EVALUATE function is as follows:

```
[ BooleanField := ] EVALUATE ( ResultField, StringToBeConverted [, 9]
```

The handling of a run-time error can be done by specifying the BooleanField. The ResultField data type will determine what data conversion the EVALUATE function will attempt. The data type of the ResultField must be one of the following: integer, Boolean, date, time, code, option, text constant, or GUID. The format of the data in StringToBeConverted must be compatible with the data type of ResultField otherwise a run-time error will occur. The optional parameter, number 9, only applies for XMLport data exporting.

DATE Functions

In order to convert numeric data to Date data types and Dates to numeric data, C/AL uses a series of Date functions.

DATE2DMY Function

DATE2DMY allows you to extract the sections of a date (Day, Month, and Year) from a Date field. The syntax is as follows:

```
IntegerVariable := DATE2DMY ( DateField, ExtractionChoice )
```

The fields IntegerVariable and DateField are just as their names imply. The ExtractionChoice parameter allows you to choose which value (day, month, or year) will be assigned to the IntegerVariable. The following table provides the DATE2DMY extraction choices:

DATE2DMY Extraction Choice	Integer Value Result
1	2 digit day (1 – 31)
2	2 digit month (1 – 12)
3	4 digit year

DATE2DWY Function

DATE2DWY allows you to extract the sections of a date (Day of the week, Week of the year, and Year) from a Date field. The syntax is as follows:

```
IntegerVariable := DATE2DWY ( DateField, ExtractionChoice )
```

The fields `IntegerVariable` and `DateField` are just as their names imply. The `ExtractionChoice` parameter allows you to choose which value (day, week, or year) will be assigned to the `IntegerVariable`.

The following table provides the `DATE2DWY` extraction choices:

DATE2DWY Extraction Choice	Integer Value Result
1	2 digit day (1 – 7 for Monday – Sunday)
2	2 digit week (1 – 53)
3	4 digit year

DMY2DATE and DWY2DATE Functions

`DMY2DATE` allows you to create a date from integer values (or defaults) representing the Day of the month, Month of the year and four digit Year. If an optional parameter (Month or Year) is not specified, the corresponding value from the system date is used. The syntax is as follows:

```
DateVariable := DMY2DATE ( DayValue [, MonthValue] [, YearValue] )
```

The only way to have the function use Work Date values for Month and Year would be to extract those values and then use them explicitly. An example is as follows:

```
DateVariable := DMY2DATE(22,DATE2MDY(WORKDATE,2),DATE2MDY(WORKDATE,3))
```

 This example also illustrates how expressions built upon functions can be nested.

`DWY2DATE` operates similarly; allowing you to create a date from integer values representing the Day of the week (1 to 7, i.e. Monday to Sunday), Week of the year (from 1 to 53) and four digit Year. The syntax is as follows:

```
DateVariable := DWY2DATE ( DayValue [, WeekValue] [, YearValue] )
```

An interesting result can occur if the specified week spans for two years. In that case the year of the result will vary depending on the day of the week in the parameters (i.e. the year of the result may differ from the year specified in the parameters).

CALCDATE Function

`CALCDATE` allows you to calculate a date value to be assigned to a Date data type variable based on a Date Expression applied to a Base or Reference Date. If you don't specify a `BaseDateValue`, the default date used is the current system date. Otherwise the `BaseDateValue` can be supplied either in the form of a variable of data type Date or as a Date constant.

The syntax for CALCDATE is as follows:

```
DateVariable := CALCDATE ( DateExpression [, BaseDateValue])
```

There are a number of ways by which you can build a DateExpression. The rules for the CALCDATE function DateExpression are similar to the rules for DateFormula described in Chapter 3.

If there is a CW, CM, CP, CQ, or CY (Current Week, Current Month, Current Period, Current Quarter, Current Year) parameter in an expression, then they will be evaluated based on the BaseDateValue. If you have more than one of these in your expression, the results are unpredictable.

If your Date Expression is stored in a DateFormula variable (or a Text or Code variable with the **DateFormula** property set to **Yes**), then the Date Expression will be language independent. If you create your own Date Expression in the form of a string constant within your inline C/AL code, surrounding the constant with < > delimiters as part of the string, that will make the constant language independent. Otherwise, the Date Expression constant will be language dependent.

Regardless of how you have constructed your DateExpression, it is important to test it carefully and thoroughly before moving on. One easy way to test it is by using a Report whose sole task is to evaluate your expression and display the result. If you want an easy way to try different Base Dates, then you can use the Request Form, accept the Base Date as input, then calculate and display the DateVariable in the OnValidate trigger.

Some sample CALCDATE expression evaluations are as follows:

- ('<CM>',031008D) will yield 03/31/2008, i.e. the last day of the Current Month for the date 3/10/2008.
- ('<-WD2>',031007D) will yield 03/06/2007, i.e. the WeekDay #2 (the prior Tuesday) before the date 3/10/2007.
- ('<CM+1D>',BaseDate) where BaseDate equals 03/10/08, will yield 04/01/2008, i.e. the last day of the month of the Base Date plus one day (the first day of the month following the Base Date).

FlowField-SumIndex Functions

In the chapter on Fields, we discussed SumIndexFields and FlowFields. To recap briefly, SumIndexFields are defined in the screen where Keys are defined. They allow very rapid calculation of values in filtered data. SumIndexFields are the basis of FlowFields; a FlowField must refer to a data element that is defined as a SumIndexField.

When you access a record that has a SumIndexField defined, there is no visible evidence of the data sum that SumIndexField represents. When you access a record that contains FlowFields, the FlowFields are empty virtual data elements until they are calculated. When a FlowField is displayed in a form, it is automatically calculated by NAV; the developer doesn't need to do so. But in any other scenario, the developer is responsible for calculating FlowFields before they are used.

CALCFIELDS Function

The syntax for CALCFIELDS is as follows:

```
[BooleanField := ] Record.CALCFIELDS ( FlowField1 [, FlowField2] ,…)
```

Executing the CALCFIELDS function will cause all the specified FlowFields to be calculated (i.e. updated). Specification of the BooleanField allows you to handle any run-time error that may occur. The run-time errors for CALCFIELDS usually result from a coding error or a change in a table key structure.

The FlowField calculation takes into account the filters that are currently applied to the Record. After the CALCFIELDS execution, the included FlowFields can be used similarly to any other data fields. The CALCFIELDS must be executed for each cycle through the subject table.

CALCSUMS Function

The CALCSUMS function is conceptually similar to CALCFIELDS. But the CALCFIELDS operates on FlowFields and CALCSUMS differs by operating directly on the record and field where the SumIndexField is defined. That difference means that you must specify the proper key plus any filters to apply (the applicable key and filters to apply are already defined in the properties for FlowFields).

The syntax for CALCSUMS is as follows:

```
[ BooleanField := ] Record.CALCSUMS ( SIFTField1 [,SIFTField2] ,…)
```

Prior to this statement, you must have specified a key and that key must have the SIFTFields defined. And before executing the CALCSUMS function, you need to specify any filters that you want to apply to the record data from which the sums are to be calculated. The SIFTField calculations take into account the filters that are currently applied to the Record.

Executing the CALCSUMS function will cause all the specified SIFTField totals to be calculated. Specification of the BooleanField allows you to handle any run-time error that may occur. The run-time errors for CALCSUMS usually result from a coding error or a change in a table key structure.

Before the execution of CALCSUMS, SIFTFields contain only the data that originated with the individual record that was read. After the CALCSUMS execution, the included SIFTFields contain the totals that were calculated by the CALCSUMS function (these totals only affect the data in memory, not that on the disk). These totals can then be used the same as data in any field, but if you want to access the individual record's original data for that field, you must either save a copy of the record before executing the CALCSUMS or you must re-read the record. The CALCSUMS must be executed for each cycle through the subject table.

The CALCSUMS function operates somewhat differently in the SQL Server environment. If you are using CALCSUMS in code designed for use with SQL Server, you should review the differences, as they can have a significant affect on performance.

Flow Control

The structures defined for flow control are as follows:

REPEAT–UNTIL Control Structure

REPEAT-UNTIL allows you to create a repetitive code loop REPEATing a block of code UNTIL a specific conditional expression evaluates to TRUE. In that sense REPEAT-UNTIL defines a block of code, operating like the BEGIN-END compound statement structure which we covered in the previous chapter. In this case, the REPEAT tells the system to keep reprocessing the block of code, while the UNTIL serves as the exit doorman, checking if the conditions for ending the processing are true. Because the exit condition is not evaluated until the end of the loop, a REPEAT-UNTIL structure will always process at least once through the contained code.

REPEAT-UNTIL is very important in NAV because it is frequent part of the data input cycle with FIND-NEXT structure, which will be covered shortly.

An example of the REPEAT-UNTIL structure to process data in a 10-element array is as follows:

```
LoopCount := 0;

REPEAT

  LoopCount := LoopCount + 1;

  TotCustSales := TotCustSales + CustSales[LoopCount];

UNTIL LoopCount = 10;
```

WHILE–DO Control Structure

A WHILE-DO control structure allows you to create a repetitive code loop DOing a block of code WHILE a specific conditional expression evaluates to TRUE. WHILE-DO is different from REPEAT-UNTIL, both in the possible need for a BEGIN-END structure to define a block of code and in the timing of the evaluation of the exit condition.

The syntax of the WHILE – DO control structure is as follows:

```
WHILE <Condition> DO <Statement>
```

The Condition can be any Boolean expression, which evaluates to TRUE or FALSE. The Statement can be a simple expression or the most complex possible compound BEGIN-END statement. Most WHILE-DO loops will contain a BEGIN-END block of code. The Condition will be evaluated at the beginning of the loop. When it evaluates to FALSE, the loop will terminate, meaning that a WHILE-DO loop can be exited without processing.

An example of the WHILE-DO structure to process data in a 10-element array is as follows:

```
LoopCount := 0;
WHILE LoopCount < 10
DO BEGIN
   LoopCount := LoopCount + 1;
   TotCustSales := TotCustSales + CustSales[LoopCount];
END;
```

CASE–ELSE Statement

The CASE-ELSE statement is a conditional expression very similar to IF-THEN-ELSE except that it allows for more than two choices of outcomes for the evaluation of the controlling expression. The syntax of the CASE-ELSE statement is as follows:

```
CASE <ExpressionToBeEvaluated> OF
 <Value Set 1> : <Action Statement 1>;
 <Value Set 2> : <Action Statement 2>;
 <Value Set 3> : <Action Statement 3>;
 . . .
 . . .
 <Value Set n> : <Action Statement n>;
 [ELSE <Action Statement n + 1>;
END;
```

The `ExpressionToBeEvaluated` must not be a record. The data type of the `Value Set` must be compatible with (i.e. able to be automatically converted to) the data type of the `ExpressionToBeEvaluated`. Each `Value Set` must be an expression, a set of values or a range of values. The following example illustrates a typical instance of a CASE-ELSE statement:

```
CASE Customer."Salesperson Code" OF
   '2','5','9': Customer."Territory Code" := 'EAST';
   '6'..'8': Customer."Territory Code" := 'WEST';
   '3': Customer."Territory Code" := 'NORTH';
   '1'..'4': Customer."Territory Code" := 'SOUTH';
   ELSE Customer."Territory Code" := 'FOREIGN';
END;
```

In this example, you can see several alternatives for the `Value Set`. The first line (EAST) `Value Set` is a list of values. If the "Salesperson Code" is equal to '2' or equal to '5' or equal to '9', the value EAST will be assigned to the `Customer."Territory Code"`. The second line (WEST) `Value Set` is a range, any value from '6' through '8'. The third line (NORTH) `Value Set` is just a single value ('3'). Looking at the bulk of standard code, you will see that the single value is the norm for CASE structures. The fourth line (SOUTH) `Value Set` is again a range ('1'..'4'). If nothing in any `Value Set` matches `ExpressionToBeEvaluated`, then the ELSE clause will be executed.

An example of an IF-THEN-ELSE statement equivalent to the preceding CASE-ELSE statement is as follows:

```
IF Customer."Salesperson Code" IN ['2','5','9'] THEN
   Customer."Territory Code" := 'EAST'
ELSE IF Customer."Salesperson Code" IN ['6'..'8'] THEN
    Customer."Territory Code" := 'WEST'
  ELSE IF Customer."Salesperson Code" = '3' THEN
      Customer."Territory Code" := 'NORTH'
    ELSE IF Customer."Salesperson Code" IN ['1'..'4'] THEN
        Customer."Territory Code" := 'SOUTH'
      ELSE Customer."Territory Code" := 'FOREIGN';
```

The following is a more creative, somewhat less intuitive example of the CASE-ELSE statement. In this instance, the `ExpressionToBeEvaluated` is a simple TRUE and the `Value Set` statements are all conditional expressions. The first line containing a `Value Set` expression that evaluates to TRUE will be the line whose `Action Statement` is executed. The rules of execution and flow in this instance are same as the previous example.

```
CASE TRUE OF
   Salesline.Quantity < 0:
```

```
   BEGIN
     CLEAR(Salesline."Line Discount %");
     CredTot := CredTot - Salesline.Quantity;
   END;
 Salesline.Quantity > QtyBreak[1]:
     Salesline."Line Discount %" := DiscLevel[1];
 Salesline.Quantity > QtyBreak[2]:
     Salesline."Line Discount %" := DiscLevel[2];
 Salesline.Quantity > QtyBreak[3]:
     Salesline."Line Discount %" := DiscLevel[3];
 Salesline.Quantity > QtyBreak[4]:
     Salesline."Line Discount %" := DiscLevel[4];
ELSE
     CLEAR(Salesline."Line Discount %");
END;
```

WITH–DO Statement

When you are writing code referring to fields within a record, the most specific syntax for field references is the fully qualified reference. When referring to the field **City** in the record **Customer**, use the reference `Customer.City`.

In many C/AL instances, the record name qualifier is implicit, i.e. the compiler assumes a default record qualifier based on context within the code. This happens automatically for variables within a form that is bounded to a table. The bound table becomes the implicit record qualifier for fields referenced in the Form object. In a Table object, the table is the implicit record qualifier for fields referenced in the C/AL internal to that object. In Report and Dataport objects, the Data Item record is the implicit record qualifier for the fields referenced within Data Item-specific triggers (e.g. `OnAfterGetRecord`, `OnAfterImportRecord`, etc.).

In all other C/AL code, the only way to have an implicit record qualifier is to use the `WITH-DO` statement. `WITH-DO` is widely used in Codeunits and processing Reports. The `WITH-DO` syntax is as follows:

```
WITH <RecordQualifier> DO <Statement>
```

Typically, the `DO` portion of this statement will be followed by a `BEGIN-END` code block, i.e. the `Statement` will be a compound statement. The scope of the `WITH-DO` statement is terminated by the end of the `DO Statement`.

When you execute a `WITH-DO` statement, `RecordQualifier` becomes the implicit record qualifier used by the compiler until the end of the `Statement` or until it is overridden by a nested `WITH-DO` statement. Where fully qualified syntax would require the following form:

```
Customer.Address := '189 Maple Avenue';
Customer.City := 'Chicago';
```

the `WITH-DO` syntax takes advantage of the implicit record qualification making the code easier to write, and hopefully easier to read, for example:

```
WITH Customer DO
BEGIN
  Address := '189 Maple Avenue';
  City := 'Chicago';
END;
```

Nested `WITH-DO` statements are valid, but not generally used, and are not recommended because they can easily lead to developer confusion and therefore result in programming bugs. The same comments apply to nesting a `WITH-DO` statement within a function where there is an automatic implicit record qualifier, such as in a table, bound form, report, or dataport. Of course, wherever the references to other record variables occur within the scope of a `WITH-DO`, you must include the specific qualifiers. This is particularly important when there are variables with the same name (e.g. `City`) in multiple tables that might be referenced in the same set of C/AL logic.

QUIT, BREAK, EXIT, SKIP, and SHOWOUTPUT Functions

There is a group of C/AL functions that can be used to control the flow and affect the processing under different circumstances. Each acts to interrupt flow in different places and with different results.

QUIT Function

The `QUIT` function is the ultimate processing interrupt for Report, Dataport or XMLport objects. When a `QUIT` is executed, processing immediately terminates even for the `OnPostObject` triggers. The syntax of the `QUIT` function is as follows:

```
CurrReport.QUIT;
CurrDataport.QUIT;
CurrXMLport.QUIT;
```

BREAK Function

The effect of a BREAK function depends on the context in which it executes. If the BREAK is within a loop structure such as a WHILE-DO or REPEAT-UNTIL loop, BREAK exits the loop as if the loop exit condition had been satisfied except it exits at the point of the BREAK. If the BREAK function is not in a loop, then its execution will exit the trigger. BREAK can only be used in Data Item triggers in Reports, Dataports, and XMLports.

The BREAK syntax is one of the following:

```
CurrReport.BREAK;
CurrDataport.BREAK;
CurrXMLport.BREAK;
```

EXIT Function

EXIT is used to end the processing within a C/AL trigger. EXIT works the same whether it is executed within a loop or not. EXIT can be used simply to end the processing of the trigger or to pass a return parameter from a local function. If EXIT is used without a return parameter then a default parameter of zero is returned. The syntax for EXIT is as follows:

```
EXIT([<ReturnValue>])
```

EXIT could be considered as an acceptable substitute for the dreaded GOTO.

SKIP Function

When executed, the SKIP function will skip the remainder of the processing in the current cycle in the current trigger. Unlike BREAK, it does not terminate processing in the trigger. It can be used only in the OnAfterGetRecord trigger of a Report, Dataport, or XMLport object. The SKIP syntax is one of the following:

```
CurrReport.SKIP;
CurrDataport.SKIP;
CurrXMLport.SKIP;
```

SHOWOUTPUT Function

SHOWOUTPUT can be used only in the OnPreSection trigger of Report objects. If it is set to FALSE, then the section is not outputted, but any other processing is performed. The syntax of SHOWOUTPUT is as follows:

```
[ BooleanValue := ] CurrReport.SHOWOUTPUT ( [ BooleanExpression ] )
```

If there is no explicit SHOWOUTPUT function, the implicit value will be TRUE, i.e. the section will be outputted.

Input and Output Functions

In the previous chapter, we learned a little about the basics of the FIND function. We learned about FIND('-') to read the beginning of the selected records and FIND('+') to begin reading at the far end of the selected records. Now we will review additional functions that are generally used with FIND in typical production code. While designing the code by using the Modify and Delete record functions, you need to consider the possible interactions with other users on the system. There might be someone else modifying and deleting records in the same table in which your application is working.

You will likely want to utilize the LOCKTABLE function to gain total control of the data briefly, while updating the data. You can find more information on LOCKTABLE in both the Application Designer's Guide and in the on-line C/AL Reference Guide (i.e. C/SIDE **Help**). Be aware that LOCKTABLE performs quite differently in the C/SIDE database from how it performs in the SQL Server database.

NEXT Function (with FIND)

The syntax defined for the NEXT function is as follows:

```
IntegerValue := Record.NEXT ( ReadStepSize )
```

The full assignment statement format is rarely used to set an IntegerValue. In addition, the rules for the resulting IntegerValue are not clear in the available documentation.

If the ReadStepSize value is negative, the file will be read in reverse; if that value is positive (the default), then the file will be read forward. The size of the value in ReadStepSize controls which records are read. For example, if ReadStepSize is 2 or -2, then every second record will be read. If ReadStepSize is 10 or -10, then every tenth record will be read. The default value is zero, in which case every record will be read (the same as if it were 1 or +1) and the read direction will be forward.

In a normal data input loop, the first read is instigated by a FIND function followed by a REPEAT–UNTIL loop with the exit condition for that loop being a NEXT expression similar to UNTIL Record.NEXT = 0;.

The full C/AL syntax would look like the following:

```
IF CustRec.FIND('-') THEN
REPEAT
 Block of C/AL logic
UNTIL CustRec.NEXT = 0;
```

INSERT Function

The purpose of the INSERT function is to insert (i.e. add) records into the table. The syntax for the INSERT function is as follows:

        [BooleanValue :=] Record.INSERT ([TriggerControlBoolean])

If the BooleanValue is not used and the INSERT function fails (if, for example, inserting would result in a duplicate primary key condition), then the process will terminate with an error statement. Any detected error should either be handled or should terminate the process.

The TriggerControlBoolean value is a TRUE or FALSE entry, which controls whether or not the table's OnInsert trigger fires when this INSERT occurs. The default value is FALSE. If you let the default FALSE control, you run the risk of not running error checking that the table's designer assumed would be run when a new record was added.

> If you are reading a table and you need to also INSERT records in that table, the INSERTs should be done to a separate instance of the table, either a global or local variable.

MODIFY Function

The purpose of the MODIFY function is to modify (i.e. update) existing data records. The syntax for MODIFY is as follows:

        [BooleanValue :=] Record.MODIFY ([TriggerControlBoolean])

If the BooleanValue is not used and the MODIFY fails (if, for example, the modification would result in a duplicate primary key condition), then the process will terminate with an error statement. Any detected error should either be handled or should terminate the process. The TriggerControlBoolean value is a TRUE or FALSE entry, which controls whether or not the table's OnModify trigger fires when this MODIFY occurs. The default value is FALSE.

MODIFY cannot be used to cause a change in a primary key field. In that case, the RENAME function must be used.

Rec and xRec

In Table and Form objects, the system automatically provides you with the system variables Rec and xRec. After a record has been modified, Rec represents the current record data in process and xRec represents the record data before it was modified. By comparing field values in Rec and xRec, you can determine if changes have been made to the record in the current process cycle. When any table is updated through a MODIFY, the data in xRec is updated to what was in Rec followed by the change. Rec and xRec records have all the same fields in the same structure as the table to which they relate.

DELETE Function

The purpose of the DELETE function is to delete existing data records. The syntax for DELETE is as follows:

```
[BooleanValue :=] Record.DELETE ( [ TriggerControlBoolean ] )
```

If the BooleanValue is not used and the DELETE fails, then the process will terminate with an error statement. Any detected error should either be handled or should terminate the process.

The TriggerControlBoolean value is a TRUE or FALSE entry, which controls whether or not the table's OnDelete trigger fires when this DELETE occurs. The default value is FALSE. If you let the default FALSE prevail, you run the risk of not running error checking that the table's designer assumed would be run when a record was deleted.

MODIFYALL Function

MODIFYALL is the high-volume version of the MODIFY function. If you have a group of records in which you wish to modify one field in all of them to the same new value, you should use MODIFYALL. MODIFYALL is controlled by the filters that apply at the time of invoking. MODIFYALL does not do any error checking, such as checking for an empty set.

The other choice for doing a mass modification would be to have a FIND-NEXT loop in which you modified each record one at a time. The advantage of MODIFYALL is that it allows the system to optimize processing for the volume update.

The syntax for MODIFYALL is as follows:

```
Record.MODIFYALL (FieldToBeModified,NewValue [,TriggerControlBoolean ] )
```

The TriggerControlBoolean value is a TRUE or FALSE entry, which controls whether or not the table's OnModify trigger fires when this MODIFY occurs. The default value is FALSE.

In a typical situation, a filter or series of filters would be applied to a table followed by the MODIFYALL function. A simple example where we are going to reassign all the Territory Codes for a particular Salesperson to NORTH is as follows:

```
CustRec.SETRANGE("Salesperson Code",'DAS');
CustRec.MODIFYALL("Territory Code",'NORTH',TRUE);
```

DELETEALL Function

DELETEALL is the high volume version of the DELETE function. If you have a group of records that you wish delete, use DELETEALL. The other choice would be to have a FIND-NEXT loop in which you delete each record one at a time. The advantage of the DELETEALL is that it allows the system to optimize processing for the volume deletion.

The syntax for DELETEALL is as follows:

```
Record.DELETEALL (FieldToBeModified,NewValue [,TriggerControlBoolean] )
```

The TriggerControlBoolean value is a TRUE or FALSE entry that controls whether or not the table's OnDelete trigger fires when this DELETE occurs. The default value is FALSE. If the TriggerControlBoolean value is TRUE, then the OnDelete trigger will fire for each record deleted. In that case, there is no speed advantage for DELETEALL versus the use of a FIND-DELETE-NEXT loop.

In a typical situation, a filter or series of filters would be applied to a table followed by the DELETEALL function, similar to the preceding example. Like MODIFYALL, DELETEALL respects the filters that have been set and does not do any error checking.

Filtering

We have talked about the fact that the filtering capabilities built into NAV provide a significant additional level of power to the system. This power is available to the users and to the developer as well. It is true that other systems provide filtering of data for inquiry, reporting, or analysis. But few other systems have filtering implemented as pervasively as does NAV nor do they have it tied to the detailed retention of historical data. The result of NAV's features is that even the most elementary implementation of NAV includes very powerful data analysis capabilities for end-user use.

You as the developer should appreciate the fact that you cannot anticipate every need of any user, let alone anticipate every need of every user. For that reason, you should give the user as much freedom as you can. Wherever feasible, the user should be given the opportunity to apply their own filters so that they can determine the optimum selection of data for their particular situation. On the other hand, freedom, here as everywhere else, is a double-edged sword. With the freedom to decide just how to segment one's data, comes the responsibility for figuring out what constitutes a good segmentation to address the problem at hand.

Since you, as the experienced systems designer and developer, presumably have considerable insight into good ways to analyze and present the data, it may be best for you to provide some predefined selections. And in some cases, the data structure means that only a very limited set of options make sense (maybe just one). The end result is that in most cases you should provide one or more specific accesses to data (forms and/or reports), but then, if possible, also provide the more sophisticated users access to manipulate the data creatively on their own.

When applying filters using any of the options, be very conscious of the table key that will be active when the filter takes affect. In a table containing a lot of data, filtering on a field that is not represented very high in the currently active key may result in poor (or very poor) response time for the user. Conversely, in a system suffering from poor response time during processing, you should first investigate the relationships of active keys to applied filters.

SETRANGE Function

SETRANGE allows you to set a simple range filter on your data. The syntax is as follows:

```
Record.SETRANGE (Field [,LowValue] [,HighValue] );
```

If both the optional parameters are omitted, any filtering that was previously applied to Record.Field will be cleared. In fact, this is the recommended way for clearing filters on a single field. If only one parameter is specified, it becomes both the high and low range values. In other words, you will be filtering on a single value in this field. If you specify both a low and high range value, the filter will be logically the same as: LowValue less than or equal to Field less than or equal to HighValue. If you happen to specify a HighValue that is greater than the LowValue, you will exclude all data, resulting in selecting an empty set.

SETFILTER Function

SETFILTER allows you to apply any Filter expression that could be created manually, including various combinations of ranges, C/AL operators, and even wild cards. SETFILTER syntax is as follows:

```
Record.SETFILTER ( Field, FilterString [, FilterValue1], . . . ] );
```

FilterString can be a literal such as '1000..20000' or 'A*|B*|C*'. Optionally, you can use variable tokens in the form of %1, %2, %3, and so forth, representing variables (but not operators) FilterValue1, FilterValue2, and so forth to be substituted in the filter string at run time. This construct allows you to create dynamic filters whose data values can be defined dynamically at run time. A pair of SETFILTER example is as follows:

```
CustRec.SETFILTER("Salesperson Code",'DAS'|'EFF'|'TKW');
CustRec.SETFILTER("Salesperson Code",'%1|%2|%3',SPC1,SPC2,SPC3);
```

If SPC1 equals' DAS', SPC2 equals 'EFF', and SPC3 equals 'TKW', these two examples would have the same result. But obviously the second option allows flexibility not allowed by the first option.

COPYFILTER and COPYFILTERS Functions

These functions allow copying the filters on a single field or all the filters on a record (table) and applying what is copied to another record. The syntaxes are as follows:

```
FromRecord.COPYFILTER(FromField, ToRecord.ToField)
ToRecord.COPYFILTERS(FromRecord)
```

Note that the COPYFILTER structure begins with the FromRecord variable while that of COPYFILTERS begins with the ToRecord variable.

GETFILTER and GETFILTERS Functions

These functions allow you to retrieve the filters on a single field or all the filters on a record (table) and assign the result to a text variable. The syntaxes are as follows:

```
ResultString := FilteredRecord.GETFILTER(FilteredField)
ResultString := FilteredRecord.GETFILTERS
```

The text contents of the ResultString will contain an identifier for each filter and the currently applied value of the filter. GETFILTERS is often used to retrieve the filters on a table and print them as part of a report heading. The ResultString will look similar to the following:

Customer:: No.: 10000..999999, Balance: >0

MARK Function

A Mark on a record is an indicator that disappears when the current session ends and which is only visible to the process setting the mark. The MARK function sets the Mark. The syntax is as follows:

```
[BooleanValue := ] Record.MARK ( [SetMarkBoolean] )
```

If the optional BooleanValue and assignment operator (:=) is present, the MARK function will give you the current Mark status (TRUE or FALSE) of the Record. If the Optional SetMarkBoolean parameter is not present, the Record will be Marked (or unmarked) according to that value (TRUE or FALSE). The default for SetMarkBoolean is FALSE. The MARK functions are a little tricky to use, so should be used carefully, only when a simpler solution is not readily available. MARKing records can cause significant performance problems for SQL Server installations.

CLEARMARKS Function

CLEARMARKS clears all the marks from the specified record (i.e. from the particular instance of the table in this instance of the object). The syntax is as follows:

```
Record.CLEARMARKS
```

MARKEDONLY Function

MARKEDONLY is a special filtering function that can apply a Mark-based filter.

The syntax for MARKEDONLY is as follows:

```
[BooleanValue := ] Record.MARKEDONLY ( [SeeMarkedRecordsOnlyBoolean] )
```

If the optional BooleanValue parameter is defined, it will be assigned a value TRUE or FALSE to tell you whether or not the special MARKEDONLY filter is active. Omitting the BooleanValue parameter, MARKEDONLY will set the special filter depending on the value of SeeMarkedRecordsOnlyBoolean. If that value is TRUE, it will filter to show only Marked records; if that value is FALSE, it will remove the Marked filter. Though it may not seem logical, there is no option to see only the unmarked records. The default value for SeeMarkedRecordsOnlyBoolean is FALSE.

RESET Function

This function allows you to RESET (i.e. clear) all filters that are currently applied to a record. The syntax is as follows:

```
FilteredRecord.RESET;
```

RESET also sets the current key back to the primary key, removes any marks, and clears all internal variables in the current instance of the record.

InterObject Communication

There are several ways for communicating information between objects during NAV processing.

Via Data

The most widely used and simplest, is through data tables. For example, the table No. Series is the central control for all document numbers. Each object that assigns numbers to a document (e.g. Order, Invoice, Shipment, etc.) accesses the No. Series table for the next number to use, and then updates the table so that the next object demanding to assign a number to the same type of document will have the correct information.

Via Function Parameters

When one object calls a function in another object, information is generally passed through the calling and return parameters. The calling and return parameter specifications were defined when the function was originally coded. The generic syntax for a function call is as follows:

```
[ReturnValue := ] FunctionName ( [ Parameter1 ] [ ,Parameter2 ] ,…)
```

The rules for including or omitting the various optional fields are specific to the local variables defined for each individual function. When you as a developer design the function, you define those rules and thereby determine just how communications with the function will be handled.

Via Object Calls

Sometimes you need to create an object which in turn calls other objects. You may simply want to allow the user to be able to run a series of processes and reports but only enter their controlling parameters once. Your user interface object is then responsible for invoking the subordinate objects after having communicated setup and filter parameters. There is a significant set of standard functions designed for various modes and circumstances of invoking other objects. Examples of these functions are SETTABLEVIEW, SETRECORD, and GETRECORD (there are others as well). There are also instances where you will need to build your own data passing function.

In order to properly manage these relatively complex processes, you will have to be familiar with the various versions of RUN and RUNMODAL functions. You will also need to understand the meaning and effect of a single instance or multiple instances of an object. Briefly, key differences between invoking an object from within another object via RUN versus RUNMODAL are as follows:

- RUN initiates a new instance of the invoked object every time, which means all internal variables are initialized.

- RUNMODAL does not initiate a new instance of the invoked object, nor are internal global variables reinitialized each time the object is called. The object can be re-initialized with CLEAR(Object).

- RUNMODAL does not allow any other object to be active while it is running, whereas RUN does.

Covering these topics in more detail is too advanced for this book, but once you have mastered the material covered here, you should study the information in the C/SIDE **HELP** and reference manuals relative to this topic.

Use the New Knowledge

Now we are going to take some of the knowledge that we have gained in this and preceding chapters and do some development work for the C/ANDL system.

A Development Challenge for You

We are going to create a Member Volunteer Statistics report. As we have gone through the various development efforts for the C/ANDL system, most have been at least moderately real-life in approach, and in addition focused on illustrating material covered in this volume.

In this particular case, we are going to stray a little in the sense that while the overall goal is reasonably real-life, our approach will be aimed more at using our new knowledge than creating the best possible code. Where appropriate, we should take note of our compromises. For example, normally a Statistics function like that which we are going to create would be done via a form rather than a report (e.g. see Form 151 Customer Statistics).

The Member Volunteer Statistics report will have the following layout:

```
Member Volunteer Statistics - rough layout                              ①
[Standard generated report heading              including date, page #, etc]
Activity for the Year To Date YYYY using As Of Date [Work Date]


Member No.  Name                            Area of                     ②
                                            Responsibility
   9999     xxxxxxxxxxxxxxxxxxxxxxxxxxxxxx   xxxxxxxxxxxxx


Volunteer Activities                                                    ③
   Code        Date     Description              Hours       Points
xxxxxxxxxx   mm/dd/yy   xxxxxxxxxxxxxxxxxxxxxxxxx  99.99       99.99

                                                                        ④
                          Grand Totals          999.99      999.99
                          YTD Totals            999.99      999.99
                          QTD Totals            999.99      999.99
```

This layout is split into four sections. The top section, marked ①, is the report header. We will generate some of this with the Report Wizard and create our own code for the rest. The next section, marked ②, is the Member information. The existence of that section will be generated using the Report Wizard, but we will add code for both the **Name** field and the **Area of Responsibility**. Section ③ will be generated completely manually. The same will be true for section ④.

If you are willing, it would be a good exercise to try creating this report on your own. If you are done and want to look at another approach, we will walk through an example approach together. Or you might just prefer to walk through the example first, and then experiment on your own. First, let us define the steps that we need to take to create this report. They are as follows:

Phase 1

1. Create a new report 50003 using the Report Wizard. Focus the report on the Member table to get started.

2. Create logic to properly display the Member Name.

3. Create logic using a CASE statement to fill a text description for the work Area of Responsibility (Executive, Technical Manager, Developer, Sales, Consulting, or Training).

4. Create logic to display the date-specific heading based on the Work Date.

Phase 2

5. Add the Volunteer Activity Ledger Data Item.

6. Create Header and Body Sections for this Data Item.

Phase 3

7. Create a Footer Section to hold Report totals.

8. Create logic to calculate Report totals using one approach.

9. Add a second Footer Section for a new set of Report totals.

10. Create logic to calculate Report totals using a different approach.

Now you can either go to work (good experience) or read on for one way to address the task.

A Sample Approach to the Challenge

There are many ways to solve a programming task; the illustration that follows is one of them. If your approach is significantly different, but works well, it's excellent. You may have come up with a better approach than this one. The measures of quality should be reliablility and speed when in production, along with clarity of the design, which should also be easy to maintain.

Phase 1

We will address the first four steps described earlier as follows:

Step 1

Our first step will be to use the Report Wizard to create a report structure for the heading and the specified Member data. From our Report Wizard, we get a basic report structure with a single Data Item for the Member table as shown in the following screenshot:

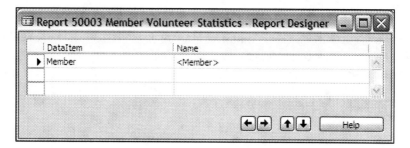

We will adjust the properties of the Member Data Item to add a value (**Member ID**) to the **ReqFilterFields**, shown in the following screenshot, to force a Selection Tab to appear for the Report Request Form.

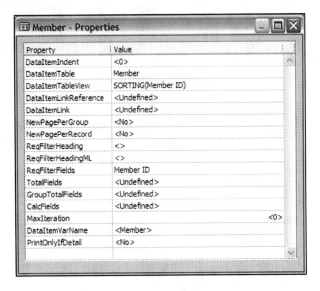

Since the **Name** and **Area of Responsibility** fields will need to be filled in manually, only the **Member No.** field will be part of the Report Wizard report layout results.

The **Section** layout is a good start, but we need to create the **Name** field and the **Area of Responsibility** field with their associated headings as shown in the following screenshot. We also need to add another heading line showing date information as per our report design layout.

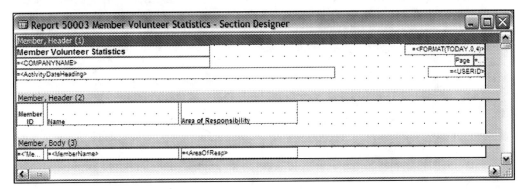

As we begin to build the pieces, we add fields as needed to the Global **Variables**. We need fields, as shown in the following screenshot, to build the concatenated **Name**, to build the heading line (**ActivityDateHeading** and **AsOfYear**), and to store the **Area of Responsibility** description field for printing as shown in the following screenshot:

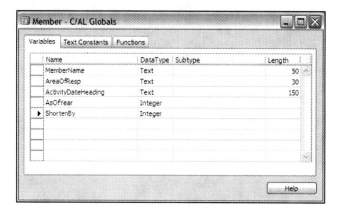

Step 2

Since the **MemberName** exists in the **Member** table in its component parts (first name, last name, etc.), we have to build the **Name** field by using string concatenation (i.e. similar to "First Name" + "Last Name"). As we start to build the logic to do the Name concatenation, it becomes obvious that this is a somewhat complex piece of logic that would be suited to be placed in its own function for clarity. So we have created a function, which is invoked with the simplest possible expression ConcatenateName;. When we are writing the logic to concatenate the components of name fields, we realize that we want to protect against overflow, thus the addition of a work field (**ShortenBy**) to our **Globals** will make the string manipulation code a little easier to understand.

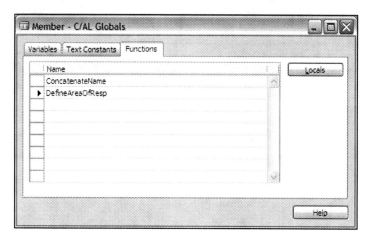

Step 3

Since the **Area of Responsibility** field in our `Member` table is several discrete fields, we will use a CASE statement to choose a description for this field. To make the code clearer for debugging and future maintenance, we put the **CASE** statement in its own function as well, as shown in the following screenshot:

```
Member - C/AL Editor                                                      _ □ ✕
 Member - OnAfterGetRecord()
ConcatenateName;
DefineAreaOfResp;

 Member - OnPostDataItem()

 ConcatenateName()
WITH Member DO
BEGIN
//Concatenate the first and last names into one string
//If the combined name is longer than the print string, calculate the amount to truncate
IF (STRLEN("First Name" + ' ' + "Last Name")) > MAXSTRLEN(MemberName) THEN
  BEGIN
    ShortenBy := (STRLEN("First Name" + ' ' + "Last Name") - MAXSTRLEN(MemberName)) + 1;
    MemberName := COPYSTR(("First Name" + ' ' + "Last Name"),ShortenBy,MAXSTRLEN(MemberName))
  END ELSE
//If the combined name is not too long, use it
    MemberName := "First Name" + ' ' + "Last Name";
END;


 DefineAreaOfResp()
WITH Member DO
BEGIN
//Based on the Member field marked, choose description for Area of Responsibility
  CASE TRUE OF
      Executive           : AreaOfResp := 'Executive';
      "Technical Manager" : AreaOfResp := 'Technical Manager';
      Developer           : AreaOfResp := 'Developer';
      Sales               : AreaOfResp := 'Sales';
      Consulting          : AreaOfResp := 'Consulting';
      Training            : AreaOfResp := 'Training';
    ELSE AreaOfResp := 'Undefined';
  END;
END;
```

Our **CASE** statement (and previously our report design) presumes that only one of the various Area of Responsibility options will be TRUE. When we review the `Member` table definition, we realize that constraint is not part of our basic design, in other words we have just found a logic hole that needs to be patched. We might as well take care of that, while making these other changes.

As we make this change, we realize that if we only want one of six possible values to be true, we should have defined the table originally with a single option field rather than six separate fields. But, as often happens as a system evolves, that is an earlier design flaw that we are not going to fully correct at this point. In a production system, resolving such a problem might require a brief system shutdown, some data conversion processing, perhaps even some minor user training, and documentation changes. At the moment, though, we will just add the editing capability to properly constrain the data as shown in the following screenshot:

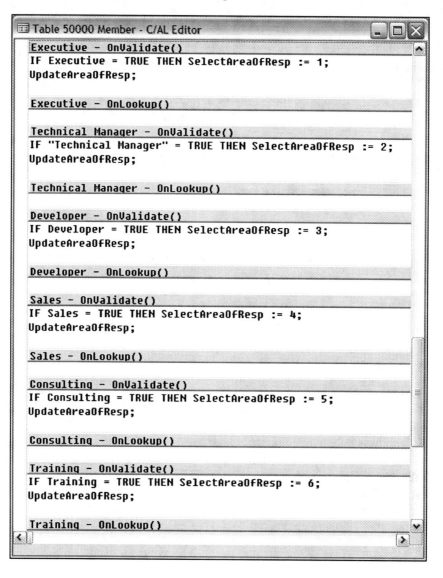

```
Table 50000 Member - C/AL Editor               _ □ ✕
  Member since - OnLookup()                              ^

  UpdateAreaOfResp()
  CLEAR(Executive);
  CLEAR("Technical Manager");
  CLEAR(Developer);
  CLEAR(Sales);
  CLEAR(Consulting);
  CLEAR(Training);
  CASE SelectAreaOfResp OF
    1: Executive := TRUE;
    2: "Technical Manager" := TRUE;
    3: Developer := TRUE;
    4: Sales := TRUE;
    5: Consulting := TRUE;
    6: Training := TRUE;
  END;
                                                         v
  <                                                   >
```

Step 4

Rather than using the System Date for the report, we will use the Work Date. This will allow the user to set the Work Date and create a report showing the appropriate data **as of** a particular date. So we need to access the Work Date, manipulate it, and apply the results as a filter to limit the Volunteer Activity records processed.

```
Report - OnPreReport()
AsOfYear := DATE2DMY(WORKDATE,3);
ActivityDateHeading := 'Activity for the year to date '+ FORMAT(AsOfYear) +
                       ' using As Of Date ' + FORMAT(WORKDATE);
YTDStart := DMY2DATE(1,1,AsOfYear);
//The preceding could also be CALCDATE('CY-1Y+1D',WORKDATE) or CALCDATE('CY+1D-1Y',WORKDATE)
QTDStart := CALCDATE('CQ+1D-1Q',WORKDATE);
//The preceding formula won't work in the form 'CQ-1Q+1D' for all quarters


Report - OnPostReport()
```

Phase 2

In Phase 2, we need to add the **Volunteer Activity Ledger** Data Item, link it with the Member Data Item, and create the related Header and Body report Sections. The visual appearance of the resulting report layout is a very important and subjective task. In most cases, this being no exception, several test runs and some manual adjusting of various layout aspects is necessary. The steps included in this phase are as follows:

Step 5

Add the **Volunteer Activity Ledger** Data Item as shown in the following screenshot:

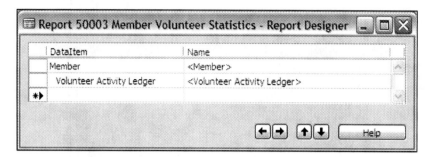

Link the new Data Item to the Member Data Item. Also add a Key definition to the **DataItemTableView** property, as shown in following screenshot, so that the Request form will not show a default Selection Tab.

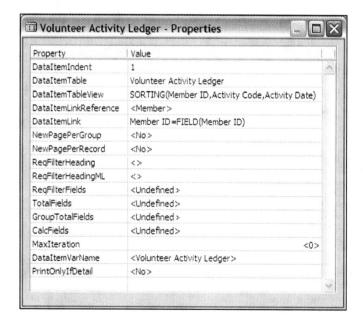

Step 6

Create the Header and Body report Sections for the **Volunteer Activity Ledger** data as shown in the following screenshot:

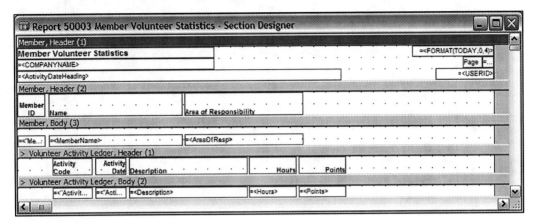

Use *Alt+F* | **Run** | **Preview** to see the sample output. This sample used a Work Date of **9/25/08** and filtered on **Member ID = 406**. The following screenshot displays the output:

Phase 3

Steps 7 and 9

We add the working storage variables to collect our totals and to hold our filters. The totaling variables are all arrays of two entries, [1] for Hours and [2] for Points.

We create two sets of variables, one for each of the approaches to totaling that we want to implement.

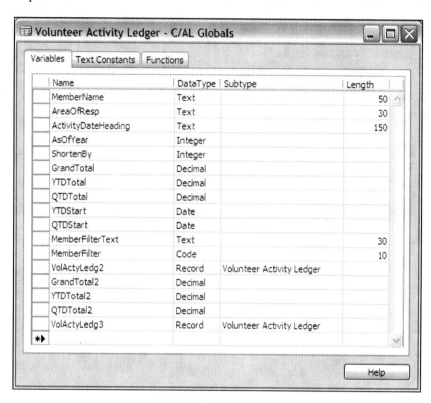

If our approach is to use functions for clarity of structure, we need to create new ones for each of our two totaling routines.

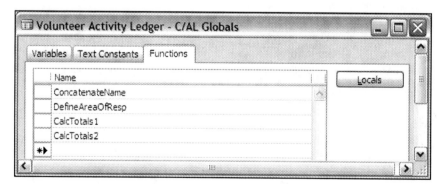

Add the new Footer Section as shown in the following screenshot. Since our reason for having two sets of totals was simply for the experience and to compare the results, we put both set of totals in the same Footer Section. We could just easily have used two Footer Sections.

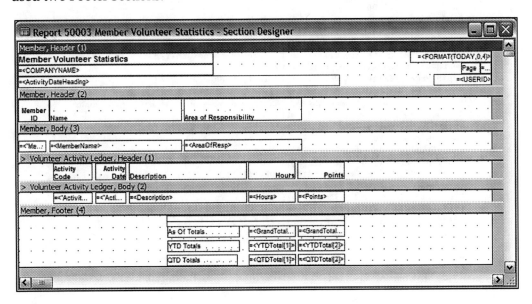

Steps 8 and 10

One totaling function uses a READ-REPEAT-UNTIL-NEXT loop to process filtered Activity data and to accumulate totals.

```
CalcTotals1()
WITH VolActyLedg2 DO
BEGIN
//Capture filter on Member."Member ID"
  MemberFilterText := Member.GETFILTER("Member ID");
//Apply Member Filter to Volunteer Activity Ledger for Read loop
  SETFILTER("Member ID",'%1',MemberFilterText);
//For a single value (one member), this could also be done with a SETRANGE
//Apply Date Range based on WorkDate
  SETRANGE("Activity Date",0D,WORKDATE);
  IF FIND('-') THEN
  REPEAT
    GrandTotal[1] := GrandTotal[1] + Hours;
    GrandTotal[2] := GrandTotal[2] + Points;
    IF "Activity Date" >= YTDStart THEN
    BEGIN
      YTDTotal[1] := YTDTotal[1] + Hours;
      YTDTotal[2] := YTDTotal[2] + Points;
    END;
    IF "Activity Date" >= QTDStart THEN
    BEGIN
      QTDTotal[1] := QTDTotal[1] + Hours;
      QTDTotal[2] := QTDTotal[2] + Points;
    END;
  UNTIL NEXT = 0;
END;
```

The second totaling function applies filters and uses the CALCSUMS function to accumulate the same totals so that we can vividly see how each approach works.

```
CalcTotals2()
WITH VolActyLedg3 DO
BEGIN
//Capture filter on Member."Member ID"
  MemberFilterText := Member.GETFILTER("Member ID");
//Convert string version of filter to integer to be applied
  EVALUATE(MemberFilter,MemberFilterText);
//Apply Member Filter to Volunteer Activity Ledger for Read loop
  SETFILTER("Member ID",'%1',MemberFilter);
//For a single value (one member), this could also be done with a SETRANGE
//Apply Date Range based on WorkDate
  SETRANGE("Activity Date",0D,WORKDATE);
  CALCSUMS(Hours,Points);
  GrandTotal2[1] := GrandTotal2[1] + Hours;
  GrandTotal2[2] := GrandTotal2[2] + Points;
  SETRANGE("Activity Date",YTDStart,WORKDATE);
  CALCSUMS(Hours,Points);
  YTDTotal2[1] := YTDTotal2[1] + Hours;
  YTDTotal2[2] := YTDTotal2[2] + Points;
  SETRANGE("Activity Date",QTDStart,WORKDATE);
  CALCSUMS(Hours,Points);
  QTDTotal2[1] := QTDTotal2[1] + Hours;
  QTDTotal2[2] := QTDTotal2[2] + Points;
END;
```

At the end of processing detail data, we call the totaling functions. Once they have done their work, we compare the results to make sure that our code is working as expected.

```
Volunteer Activity Ledger - OnPostDataItem()
CalcTotals1;
CalcTotals2;
//Error checking to see if both sets of totals are equal
IF (GrandTotal[1] <> GrandTotal2[1])
  OR(GrandTotal[2] <> GrandTotal2[2])
  OR (YTDTotal[1] <> YTDTotal2[1])
  OR (YTDTotal[2] <> YTDTotal2[2])
  OR (QTDTotal[1] <> QTDTotal2[1])
  OR (QTDTotal[2] <> QTDTotal2[2])
  THEN
    ERROR(Text000);
```

In the interest of the multi-language capability of NAV, we put the string literal for our error message in the **Text Constants** area, as shown in the following screenshot:

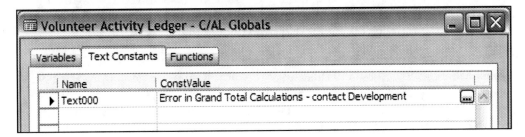

Finally, after debugging is complete, we can run a successful test. The output will be similar to the following screenshot:

Member Volunteer Statistics

CRONUS International Ltd.

Activity for the year to date 2008 using As Of Date 09/25/08

Member

ID	Name			Area of Responsibility		
406	Rebecca Martin			Consulting		

Activity Cod	Activity D	Description	Hours	Points
IPAINT	04/06/08	Inside Painting	2.00	8.00
MOW	06/13/08	Mowing	2.50	7.50
OPAINT	07/01/08	Outside Painting	3.00	15.00
OPAINT	07/13/08	Paint the trim	2.00	10.00
		As Of Totals	9.50	40.50
		YTD Totals	9.50	40.50
		QTD Totals	5.00	25.00

Summary

In this chapter, we have covered a number of practical tools and topics regarding C/AL coding and development. We started with reviewing methods and then dove into a long list of functions that you will need on a frequent basis.

We started this chapter by covering development assisted by use of the C/AL Symbol Menu, followed by a discussion of development documentation. Then we covered a variety of selected data-centric functions, including some for Computation and Validation, Data Conversion, and Date handling. Next, we reviewed functions that affect the flow of logic and the flow of data, including Flowfields and SIFT, Processing Flow Control, Input and Output, and Filtering.

In the next chapter, we will move from the details of the functions to the broader view of C/AL development including models of code usage in the standard product code, integration into the standard NAV code, and some debugging techniques.

Advanced NAV Development

You think you know when you can learn, are more sure when you can write, even more when you can teach, but certain when you can program – Alan Perlis

Once you have achieved some mastery in the basics of C/AL programming, you are ready to start creating your own C/AL in NAV. But it is important that you get some familiarity with NAV C/AL code in the standard product first. You may recall the advice in a previous chapter that the new code you create should be visually and logically compatible with what already exists. If you think of your new code as a guest being hosted by the original system, you will be doing what any thoughtful guest does – fitting smoothly into the host's environment.

An equally important aspect of becoming familiar with the existing code is to increase the likelihood of being able to take advantage of its features and components to address some of your application requirements. There will be at least two groups of material that you can use.

One group is the Callable Functions that are used liberally throughout NAV. There is no documentation for most of those functions so you must either learn about them here or through doing your homework (i.e. studying NAV code). The second group includes the many code snippets that you can copy when you face a problem similar to something the NAV developers have already addressed.

The code snippets differ from the callable functions in two ways. Firstly, they are not structured as coherent and callable entities. Secondly, they may only apply to your problem as a model, code that must be modified to fit the situation (e.g. changing variable names, adding or removing constraints, etc.).

In this chapter, we will look at some of the code structures. We will also discuss techniques for working with the code, for debugging, and as a developer, taking advantage of the strengths of the C/SIDE and NAV environment. Following this chapter, you should have enough tools in your NAV toolkit to start doing basic development projects.

Callable Functions

There are many callable functions in the standard NAV product. Most of these are designed to handle a very specific set of data or conditions and have no general-purpose use (e.g. the routines for updating Check Ledger entries during a posting process are likely to apply only to that specific function). If you are making modifications to a particular application area within NAV, you may find functions in that area that you can utilize either as they exist or as models for new similar functions which you have to create.

However, there are also some functions within NAV that are relatively general purpose. They either act on data that is common in many different situations (e.g. dates) or they perform processing tasks that are common to many situations (e.g. provide access to an external file). We will review a number of such functions that you may find usable at some point. If nothing else, they are useful as study guides for "here is how NAV does it". Example functions follow.

Codeunit – 358 Date Filter-Calc

This codeunit contains two functions you could use in your code to create filters based on the Accounting Period Calendar. The first is `CreateFiscalYearFilter` which has syntax of:

```
CreateFiscalYearFilter.DateFilterCalc
                    (Filter,Name,BaseDate,NextStep)
```

The calling parameters are `Filter` (text, length 30), `Name` (text, length 30), `BaseDate` (date) and `NextStep` (integer).

The second such function is `CreateAccountingPeriodFilter` which has syntax of:

```
CreateAccountingPeriodFilter.DateFilterCalc
                    (Filter,Name,BaseDate,NextStep)
```

The calling parameters are `Filter` (text, length 30), `Name` (text, length 30), `BaseDate` (date) and `NextStep` (integer).

In the following code screenshot from Form 151 – Customer Statistics, you can see how NAV calls these functions. Form 152 – Vendor Statistics, Form 223 – Resource Statistics, and a number of other `Master` table statistics forms also use this set of functions.

```
Form - OnAfterGetRecord()
SETRANGE("No.");

IF CurrentDate <> WORKDATE THEN BEGIN
  CurrentDate := WORKDATE;
  DateFilterCalc.CreateAccountingPeriodFilter(CustDateFilter[1],CustDateName[1],CurrentDate,0);
  DateFilterCalc.CreateFiscalYearFilter(CustDateFilter[2],CustDateName[2],CurrentDate,0);
  DateFilterCalc.CreateFiscalYearFilter(CustDateFilter[3],CustDateName[3],CurrentDate,-1);
END;
```

In the next code screenshot, NAV uses the filters stored in the `CustDateFilter` array to constrain the calculation of a series of Flowfields for the Customer Statistics form.

```
FOR i := 1 TO 4 DO BEGIN
  SETFILTER("Date Filter",CustDateFilter[i]);
  CALCFIELDS(
    "Sales (LCY)","Profit (LCY)","Inv. Discounts (LCY)","Inv. Amounts (LCY)","Pmt. Discounts (LCY)",
    "Pmt. Disc. Tolerance (LCY)","Pmt. Tolerance (LCY)",
    "Fin. Charge Memo Amounts (LCY)","Cr. Memo Amounts (LCY)","Payments (LCY)",
    "Reminder Amounts (LCY)","Refunds (LCY)","Other Amounts (LCY)");
```

When one of these functions is called, the `Filter` and `Name` fields are updated within the functions so you can use them effectively as Return parameters allowing the function to return a workable filter and a name for that filter. The filter is calculated from the `BaseDate` and `NextStep` you supply.

The returned filters are supplied back in the format of a range filter string, `'startdate..enddate'` (e.g. 01/01/07..12/31/07). If you call `CreateFiscalYear`, the `Filter` will be for the range of a fiscal year, as defined by the system's `Accounting Period` table. If you call `CreateAccountingPeriodFilter`, the `Filter` will be for the range of a fiscal period, as defined by the same table.

The dates of the Period or Year filter returned are tied to the `BaseDate` parameter, which can be any legal date. The `NextStep` parameter says which period or year to use, depending on which function is called. A `NextStep` = 0 says use the period or year containing the `BaseDate`, `NextStep` = 1 says use the next period or year into the future, and `NextStep` = -2 says use the period or year before last (i.e. step back 2 periods or years).

The `Name` value returned is also derived from the `Accounting Period` table. If the call is to the `CreateAccountingPeriodFilter`, then `Name` will contain the appropriate Accounting Period Name. If the call is to the `CreateFiscalYearFilter`, then `Name` will contain `'Fiscal Year yyyy'`, where yyyy will be the four digit numeric year.

Codeunit 359 – Period Form Management

This codeunit contains three functions that can be used for date handling. They are as follows:

- `FindDate` function
    - Calling Parameters (`SearchString` (text, length 3), `CalendarRecord` (Date table), `PeriodType` (Option, integer))
    - Returns `DateFound` Boolean

        `FindDate(SearchString,CalendarRec,PeriodType)`

This function is often used in Matrix forms to assist with the date calculation. The purpose of this function is to find a date in the `CalendarRecord` table based on the parameters passed in. The search starts with an initial record in the `CalendarRecord` table. If you pass in a record that has already been initialized (i.e. you positioned the table to some date), then that will be the base date, otherwise the Work Date will be used.

The `PeriodType` in the function is an Option field with the option values of 'day, week, month, quarter, year, accounting period'. For ease of coding you could call the function with the integer equivalent (0, 1, 2, 3, 4, 5) or set up your own equivalent Option variable.

Finally, the `SearchString` allows you to pass in a logical control string containing =, >, <, <=, >=, etc. FindDate will find the first date starting with the initialized `CalendarRecord` date that satisfies the `SearchString` logic instruction and fits the `PeriodType` defined. E.g. if the `PeriodType` is day and the date 01/25/08 is used along with the `SearchString` of >, then the date 01/26/08 will be returned in the `CalendarRecord`.

- `NextDate` function
    - Calling Parameters (`NextStep` (integer), `CalendarRecord` (Date table), `PeriodType` (Option, integer))
    - Returns `NextStep` integer

        `NextDate(NextStep,CalendarRec,PeriodType)`

`NextDate` will find the next date record in the `CalendarRecord` table that satisfies the calling parameters. The `CalendarRecord` and `PeriodType` calling parameters for `FindDate` have the same definition as they do for the `FindDate` function. However, for this function to be really useful, the `CalendarRecord` must be initialized before calling `NextDate`, otherwise the function will calculate the appropriate next date from day 0. The `NextStep` parameter allows you to define the number of periods of `PeriodType` to move, so as to obtain the desired next date. For example, if you start with a `CalendarRecord` table positioned on 01/25/08, a `PeriodType` of quarter (i.e. 3), and a `NextStep` of 2, the `NextDate` will move forward two quarters and return with `CalendarRecord` focused on Quarter, 7/1/08 to 9/30/08.

- `CreatePeriodFormat` function
    - Calling Parameters (`PeriodType` (Option, integer), `DateData` (date))
    - Returns `FormattedPeriod` (Text, length 10)

        `FormattedDate := CreatePeriodFormat(PeriodType,DateData)`

`CreatePeriodFormat` simply allows you to supply a date and specify which of its format options you want via the `PeriodType`. The function's return value is a 10-character formatted text value, e.g. mm/dd/yy or ww/yyyy or mon yyyy or qtr/yyyy or yyyy.

Codeunit 365 – Format Address

The functions in the `Format Address` codeunit, as the name suggests, serve the purpose of formatting addresses. The address data in any master record (Customer, Vendor, Sales Order Sell-to, Sales Order Ship-to, Employee, etc.) may contain embedded blank lines, e.g. the Address 2 line may be empty. When you print out the address information on a document or report, it will look better if there are no blank lines. These functions take care of that.

In addition, NAV provides setup options for multiple formats of City – Post Code – County – Country combinations. The `Format Address` functions also take care of formatting your addresses according to what was chosen in the setup or has been defined in the Countries/Regions form for different Postal areas.

There are over 50 data-specific functions in the `Format Address` codeunit. These data-specific functions allow you to pass a record parameter for the record containing the raw address data (such as a Customer record, a Vendor Record, a Sales Order, etc.). These function calls also require a parameter of a one-dimensional Text array with 8 elements of length 90. Each function extracts the address data from its specific master record and stores it in the array. The function passes that data to a general-purpose function, which does the actual work of re-sequencing and compressing the data according to the various setup rules.

The following is an example of function call format for these functions for `Company` and the `Sales` Ship-to addresses. In each case `AddressArray` is Text, Length 90, and one-dimensional with 8 elements.

```
"Format Address".Company(AddressArray,CompanyRec);
"Format Address".SalesHeaderShipTo(AddressArray,SalesHeaderRec);
```

The result of the function's processing is returned in the `AddressArray` parameter.

In addition to the data-specific functions in the `Format Address` codeunit, you can also directly utilize the more general-purpose functions contained therein and called by the data-specific functions. If you have added a new address structure as part of an enhancement you have coded, it is likely that you would want to create your own data-specific address formatting function in your own codeunit. But you might as well design your function to call the general purpose functions that already exist (and are debugged).

The primary general-purpose address formatting function (and the one you are most likely to call directly) is FormatAddr. This is the function that does most of the work in this codeunit. The syntax for the FormatAddr function is as follows:

```
FormatAddr(AddressArray,Name,Name2,ContactName,Address1,Address2,
           City,PostCode,County,CountyCode)
```

The calling parameters of AddressArray, Name, Name2 and ContactName are all text, length 90. Address1, Address2, City and County are all text, length 50. PostCode and CountryCode are code, length 20.

Your data is passed into the function in the individual Address fields. The results are passed back in the AddressArray parameter for you to use.

There are two other functions in the Format Address codeunit that can be called directly. They are FormatPostCodeCity and GeneratePostCodeCity. The FormatPostCodeCity function serves the purpose of finding the applicable setup rule for PostCode + City + County + Country formatting. It then calls the GeneratePostCodeCity function, which does the actual formatting.

If you are going to use functions from Codeunit 365, take care that you truly understand how they operate. In this case, as well as all others, you should study a function and test with it before assuming you understand how it works. There is no documentation for these functions, so their proper use is totally up to you.

Codeunit 396 – NoSeriesManagement

Throughout NAV, master records (e.g. Customer, Vendor, Item, etc.) and activity documents (Sales Order, Purchase Order, Warehouse Transfer Orders, etc.) are controlled by the unique identifying number assigned to each one. This unique identifying number is assigned through a call to a function within the NoSeriesManagement codeunit. That function is InitSeries. The calling format for InitSeries is as follows:

```
NoSeriesManagement.InitSeries(WhichNumberSeriesToUse,
  LastDataRecNumberSeriesCode, SeriesDateToApply, NumberToUse,
  NumberSeriesUsed)
```

The parameter WhichNumberSeriesToUse is generally defined on a **Numbers** Tab in the Setup record for the applicable application area. The LastDataRecNumberSeriesCode tells the function what Number Series was used for the previous record in this table. The SeriesDateToApply parameter allows the function to assign ID numbers in a date-dependent fashion. The NumberToUse and the NumberSeriesUsed are return parameters.

The following screenshots show examples for first Table 18 - Customer and then Table 36 - Sales Header:

```
OnInsert()
IF "No." = '' THEN BEGIN
  SalesSetup.GET;
  SalesSetup.TESTFIELD("Customer Nos.");
  NoSeriesMgt.InitSeries(SalesSetup."Customer Nos.",xRec."No. Series",0D,"No.","No. Series");
END;
```

```
OnInsert()
SalesSetup.GET;

IF "No." = '' THEN BEGIN
  TestNoSeries;
  NoSeriesMgt.InitSeries(GetNoSeriesCode,xRec."No. Series","Posting Date","No.","No. Series");
END;
```

With the exception of GetNextNo (used in assigning unique identifying numbers to each of a series of transactions), you are not likely to use other functions in the NoSeriesManagement codeunit. They are principally used either by the InitSeries function or other NAV routines whose job it is to maintain Number Series control information and data.

Codeunit 397 – Mail

This codeunit contains a series of functions for interfacing with Microsoft Outlook as an Automation Controller. Since the complexity of both Automation Controllers and the APIs for various products, including Outlook, are beyond the scope of this book, we will not cover the functions of this codeunit in any detail. Suffice it to say that if you are going to create code that deals with Outlook in any way, you should start with this codeunit either for functions you can use directly or as a model for what you need to do.

In older versions of Dynamics NAV (then called Navision), codeunit 397 contained logic for interfacing with a MAPI mail client through the OCX interface. If you need an SMTP interface in Version 4.x, you should seek out a copy of Codeunit 397 prior to Version 4.0 of NAV. In Version 5.0, Codeunit 400 provides SMTP mail access.

Codeunit 408 – Dimension Management

Codeunit 408 – Dimension Management is of general interest because dimensions are so widely used (and useful) throughout NAV. Dimensions are a user-definable categorization of the data. There are two **Global Dimensions**, which are carried as values in the primary data records. Any dimensioned data can also have up to six additional categorizations (**Shortcut Dimensions**), which are stored in subordinate tables. Each dimension can have any number of possible values. More detailed information about Dimensions in NAV is available in the **Help** and in printed documentation about the functional application. A good place to start is the `Dimension` Table **Help**.

When you move, process, post, delete, or otherwise manipulate many different types of NAV data, you must also deal with the associated Dimensions data. The functions in Codeunit 408 support that activity. You would be wise not to be particularly creative in your use of the Dimension Management functions, but to simply find and study existing code used in a situation that you feel is similar to that on which you are working.

If you are manipulating standard system records (records that are part of the system as delivered from Microsoft), then you would most likely be calling functions in Codeunit 408 directly, perhaps even cloning existing code from another routine for your calling routines. If you are creating new tables that contain Dimensions, you may need to create your own Dimensions handling functions to reside in your codeunit. In this case, you would be wise to model your new functions as closely as possible on the standard code in Codeunit 408. Take note that in most of NAV, any posting of Dimensions initially uses temporary table in order to avoid degrading performance by locking critical `Dimensions` tables. This is one of those times where creativity is not likely to pay off.

Codeunit 412 – Common Dialog Management

The Common Dialog Management codeunit contains just one function, the `OpenFile` function. This function provides the system's access to the OCX module for the Microsoft Common Dialog Control, which is a standard part of Windows. The Common Dialog Control provides a user interface function for accessing external files.

The following screenshot appears when the Common Dialog Control is executed:

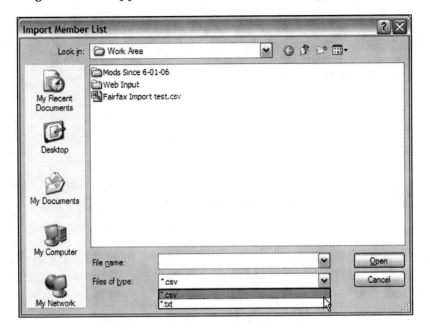

The code that invoked this dialog is as follows:

```
CDM.OpenFile('Import Member List','',4,'*.csv|*.csv|*.txt|*.txt',0);
```

The syntax for the OpenFile function is as follows:

```
OpenFile (ScreenTitle,DefaultFileName,FileTypeOption,FileTypeFilterSt
ring,Action)
```

The calling parameters are `ScreenTitle` (text, length 50), `DefaultFileName` (text, length 250), `FileTypeOption` (option choices of ' ', Excel, Word, Custom), `FileTypeFilterString` (text, length 250), `Action` (option choices of Integer, Open, Save).

In this instance the `ScreenTitle` is defined, the `DefaultFileName` is omitted, there is a `FileTypeOption` of Custom, which allows the `FileTypeFilterString` to be specified for `*.csv` and `*.txt` (see **Files of type** in preceding screenshot), and an `Action` of 0 (zero), which defines what Action button (**Open** or **Save**) will be displayed (**Open** is chosen here).

The syntax rule for the `FilterTypeFilterString` is a string sequence consisting of the Filter Type description followed by a pipe symbol followed by the Filter Mask. Each subsequent filter option description+mask sequence is separated from the preceding one by another pipe symbol.

The default filter options in **Codeunit 412** are defined as **Text** strings as shown in the following screenshot:

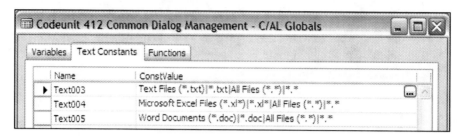

Sampling of Function Models to Review

It is very helpful when you're creating new code to have a model that works that you can study (or clone). This is especially true in NAV where there is little or no "how to" documentation available for many different functions. One of the more challenging aspects of learning to develop in the NAV environment is learning how to address the wide variety of common issues in the "NAV way".

A list of objects that contain functions that you may find useful as models, and certainly find useful as subjects for study follows. Here is how "it's" done in NAV ("it" obviously varies depending on the function's purpose). When you build your function modeled on one of NAV function, that code should reside in a customer licensed codeunit.

 It is not a good practice to add custom functions to the standard NAV codeunits. Keeping customizations well segregated makes both maintenance and upgrades easier.

Codeunit 228 – Test Report-Print

This codeunit contains a series of functions to invoke the printing of various Test Reports. These functions are called from various data entry forms, typically Journal forms. You can use these functions as models for any situation where you want to allow the user to print a test report from a form menu or command button.

Although all of the functions in this codeunit are used to print Test Reports, there isn't any reason you couldn't use the same logic structure for any type of report. The basic logic structure is to create an instance of the table of interest, apply any desired filters to that table instance, execute other appropriate setups for the particular report, and then call the report with a code line similar to the following:

```
REPORT.RUN(ReportID,TRUE,FALSE,DataRecName)
```

The first Boolean option will enable the Report Request form if TRUE. Use of the RUN function will invoke a new instance of the report object. In cases where a new instance is not desired, RUNMODAL is used.

Codeunit 229 – Print Documents

This codeunit is very similar to Codeunit 228 in the structure of its internal logic. It contains a series of functions for invoking the printing of document formatted reports. An NAV document is generally a report formatted such that a page is the basic unit (e.g. invoices, orders, statements, checks). For those documents printed from the Sales Header or Purchase Header, a basic "calculate discounts" function is called for the header record prior to printing the chosen document.

In some cases, there are several reports (in this case, documents) all generated from the same table such as the Sales Quote, Sales Order, Sales Invoice and Sales Credit Memo. For such situations, the function has a common set of pre-processing logic followed by a CASE statement to choose the proper report object call. In the case where there is only one report-table combination (e.g. Bank Checks), the function is simpler but still basically has the same structure (just without the CASE statement).

Some other Objects to Review

Some other Codeunits that you might productively review for an insight into how NAV manages certain activities and interfaces are:

- Codeunit 80 – Sales-Post: For posting journal data into a ledger
- Codeunit 90 – Purch. Post: For posting journal data into a ledger
- Codeunit 5053 – TAPI Management: For Telephone API handling
- Codeunit 5054 – Word Management: For interfacing to Microsoft Word
- Codeunit 6201 – Conventions: For a number of data format conversion functions
- Table 330 – Currency Exchange Rate: Contains some of the key currency conversion functions

Management Codeunits

There are approximately 100 codeunits with the word Management as part of their description name. Each of these codeunits contains functions whose purpose is the management of some specific aspect of NAV data. Most of these are very specific to a narrow range of data. Some can be considered more general because they contain functions that you can reuse in another application area (such as the functions in Codeunit 396 – NoSeriesManagement).

The key point here is that when you are working on an enhancement in a particular functional area, you should check to see what Management Codeunits are utilized in that area. Several possibilities exist. You may be able to use some function(s) directly. This will have the benefit of reducing the code you have to create and debug. Of course, when a new version is released, you will have to check to see if the function(s) on which you relied have changed in any meaningful way that might affect relative to your code.

If you can't use any of the existing material as is, in many cases you will find functions that you can use as models for similar tasks in the area of your enhancement. And, even if that is not true, by researching and studying the existing code, you will learn more about how the data is structured and the processes flow in the standard system.

Documenting Modifications

We have discussed many of the good documentation practices that you should follow, when modifying an NAV system. We will briefly review those here.

Identify and document your modifications. Assign a unique project ID and use it for version tags and all internal documentation tags. Assign a specific number range for any new objects.

Wrap your customizations in code with tagged comments. Place an identifying "Mod starts here" comment before any modification and a "Mod ends here" comment at the end. Retain any replaced code inside comments. Depending on the amount of replaced or deleted code, it should be commented out with either slashes or braces (// or { }).

 No matter how much or what type of standard NAV C/AL code is affected, the original code should remain intact as comments.

Always include explanatory documentation in the Documentation Trigger of modified objects. In the case of changes that can't be documented in-line such as changes to properties, the Documentation Trigger may be the only place you can easily create a documentation trail describing the changes.

If your modification requires a significant number of lines of new code or code that can be called from more than one place, you should strongly consider putting the body of the modification into a separate new codeunit (or codeunits) or at least in a new separate function (or functions). This approach allows you to minimize the footprint of your modifications within the standard code making. Generally that will make both maintenance and upgrading easier.

Where feasible to do so, create new versions of standard objects and modify those rather than modifying the original object. This works well for many reports and some forms but often doesn't work well for tables, codeunits, and many forms.

Maintain an external document that describes the purpose of the modification and a list of what objects were affected. Ideally this documentation should begin with a Change Request or Modification Specification and then be expanded as the work proceeds. The description should be relatively detailed and written so that knowledgeable users (as well as trained C/AL developers) can understand what has been done and why.

Multi-Language

The NAV system is designed as a multi-language system, meaning it can interface with users in more languages than just English. The base product is distributed with American English as the primary language, but each local version comes with one or more other languages ready for use. Because the system can be set up to operate from a single database displaying user interfaces in several different languages, NAV is particularly suitable for firms operating from a central system serving users in multiple countries. NAV is used by businesses all over the world, operating in dozens of different languages. It is important to note that when the application language is changed, that has no affect on the data in the database and, in fact, does not multi-language enable the data.

The basic elements that support the multi-language feature include:

- Multi-Language Captioning properties (e.g. **CaptionML**) supporting definition of alternative language captions for all fields, button labels, titles, etc.

- Application Management codeunit logic that allows language choice on login.

- `fin.stx` files supplied by NAV, which are language specific and contain texts used by C/SIDE for various menus such as File, Edit, View, Tools, etc. (`fin.stx` cannot be modified except by the Microsoft NAV Development Team).

- The Text Constants property **ConstantValueML** supporting definition of alternative language messages.

Before embarking on creating modifications that need to be multi-language enabled, be sure to review all the available documentation on the topic. It would also be wise to do some small scale testing to ensure you understand what is required and that your approach will work (always a good idea for any potentially significant compatibility issue).

Multi-Currency

NAV was one of the first ERP systems to fully implement a multi-currency system. Transactions can start in one currency and finish in another. For example, you can create the order in US dollars and accept payment for the invoice in Euros. For this reason, where there are money values, they are generally stored in the local currency (e.g. **LCY**) as defined in setup. But there is a set of currency conversion tools built into the applications and there are standard (by practice) code structures to support and utilize those tools. A couple of example of code segments from the `Sales Line` table illustrating handling of money fields follow:

```
GetSalesHeader;
IF SalesHeader."Currency Code" <> '' THEN BEGIN
  Currency.TESTFIELD("Unit-Amount Rounding Precision");
  "Unit Cost" :=
    ROUND(
      CurrExchRate.ExchangeAmtLCYToFCY(
        GetDate,SalesHeader."Currency Code",
        "Unit Cost (LCY)",SalesHeader."Currency Factor"),
      Currency."Unit-Amount Rounding Precision")
END ELSE
  "Unit Cost" := "Unit Cost (LCY)";
```

```
"Line Discount Amount" :=
  ROUND(
    ROUND(Quantity * "Unit Price",Currency."Amount Rounding Precision") *
    "Line Discount %" / 100,Currency."Amount Rounding Precision");
```

As you can see, before you get too far into creating any modification that has money fields, you would want to familiarize yourself with the NAV currency conversion feature and the code that supports it. A good place to start is the C/AL code within Table 37 - Sales Line, Table 39 - Purchase Line, and Table 330 – Currency Exchange Rate.

Code Analysis and Debugging Tools

The tools and techniques that you use with NAV to determine what code to modify and to debug modifications are essentially the same. The goal in the first case is to focus your modifications so that you have the minimum effect on the standard code. This results in multiple benefits. Smaller pieces of well focused code are easier to debug, easier to document, easier to maintain, and easier to upgrade. Because of NAV's relatively tight structure and unique combination of features, it is not unusual to spend significantly more time in determining the right way to make a modification than it actually takes to code the modification. Obviously this depends on the type of modification being made. Unfortunately the lack of documentation regarding the internals of NAV also contributes to an extended analysis time required to design modifications. The following sections review some of the tools and techniques you can use to analyze and test.

Developer's Toolkit

To paraphrase the introduction in the NAV Developer's Toolkit documentation, the Toolkit is designed to help you analyze the source code and make it easier to design and develop application customizations and perform updates. The Developer's Toolkit is not part of the standard product distribution, but is available to all Microsoft Partners for NAV for download from the Partner website. While it takes a few minutes to set up the Developer's Toolkit for the database on which you will be working, the investment is still worthwhile. You should follow the instructions in the Developer's Toolkit manual for creating and loading your Toolkit database. The Help files in the Developer's Toolkit are also generally useful.

The NAV Developer's Toolkit has two major categories of tools, the Compare and Merge Tools, and the Source Analyzer. The Compare and Merge Tools are useful anytime you want to compare a production database's objects to an unmodified set of objects to identify what has been changed. This might be in the process of upgrading the database to a new version or simply to better understand the contents of a database when you are about to embark on your own modification adventure.

The Source Analyzer tools are the more general-purpose set of tools. Once you have loaded the source information for all your objects into the Developer's Tools database, you will be able to quickly generate a host of useful code analyses. The starting point for your code analyses will be the **Object Administrator** view as shown in the following screenshot:

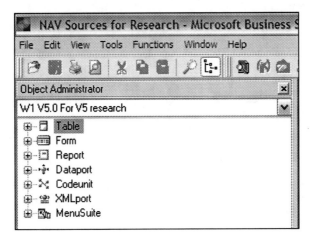

When you get to this point, it's worthwhile experimenting with various menu options and various objects just to get comfortable with the environment and how the tools work. Not only are there several tool options, but also several viewing options. Some will be more useful to you than others depending on your working habits as well as the specifics of the modification task you are addressing.

Relations to Tables

With rare exceptions, table relations are defined between tables. The Toolkit allows you to select an object and request analysis of the defined relations between elements in that object and various tables. As a test of how the **Relations to Tables** analysis works, we will expand our **Table** entry in the **Object Administrator** to show all the tables. Then we will choose the **Location** table, right-click, and choose the option to view its **Relations to** other **Tables** with the result shown in the following screenshot:

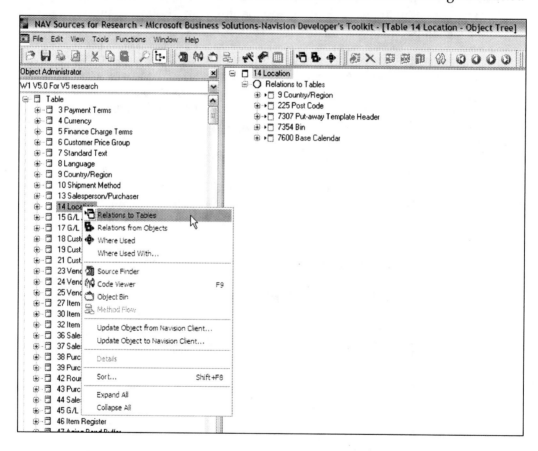

If we want to see more detail, we can right-click on the **Location** table name in the right window, choose the **Expand All** option, and see the results as shown in the following screenshot:

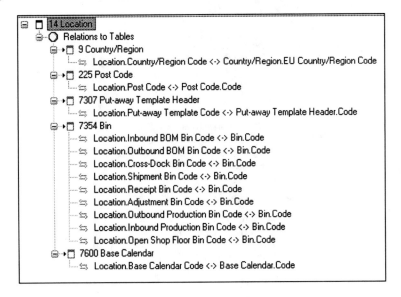

This shows us the **Relations to Tables**, with the relating (from) field and the related (to) field both showing in each line.

Relations from Objects

If you are checking to see what objects have a relationship pointing back to a particular table (i.e. the inverse of what we just looked at), you can find that out in essentially the same fashion. Right-click on the table of interest and choose the **Relations from Objects** option. If you wanted to see both sets of relationships in the same display, you could then right-click on the table name in the right window and choose the **Relation to Tables** option.

At that point your display would show both sets of relationships as shown in the following screenshot for the table `Sales Line`:

Source Access

On any of these screens you could select one of the relationships and drill down further into the detail of the underlying C/AL code. There is a search tool, the **Source Finder**. When you highlight one of the identified relationships and access the **Code Viewer**, the Toolkit will show you the object code where the relationship is defined.

Where Used

The Developer's Toolkit contains other tools that are no less valuable to you as a developer. The idea of **Where Used** is fairly simple: list all the places where an element is used within the total library of source information. There are two different flavors of **Where Used**. The Toolkit's **Where Used** is powerful because it can search for uses of whole tables or key sequences or individual fields. Many developers use other tools (primarily developer's text editors) to accomplish some of this. But the Developer's Toolkit is specifically designed for use with C/AL and C/SIDE.

The second flavor of Where Used is **Where Used With**. This version of the Toolkit Where Used tool allows you to focus the search. Selecting the **Where Used With Options** bring up the screen in the following screenshot. As you can see, the degree of control you have over the search is extensive.

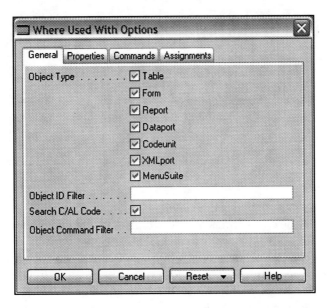

Screenshots of the other three tabs of the **Where Used With Options** form follow:

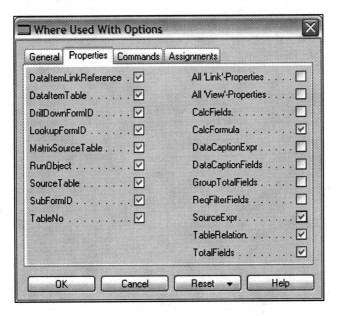

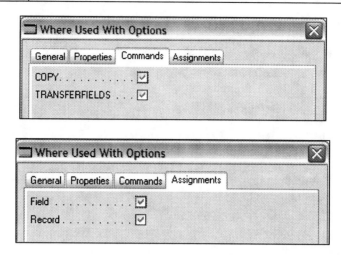

Try it Out

To really appreciate the capabilities and flexibilities of the Developer's Toolkit, you must work with it to address a real-life task. For example, what if your firm was in a market where merger of firms was a frequent occurrence? In order to manage this, the manager of accounting decides that the system needs to be able to merge the data for two customers, including accounting and sales history under a single customer number. You decide that to do that, you must first find all the instances of the **Customer No.** referenced in keys of other tables. The tool to do this in the Developer's Toolkit is the **Source Finder**.

Calling up the **Source Finder**, first you **Reset** all fields by clearing them. Then you enter what you are looking for i.e. **Customer No.** as shown in the following screenshot:

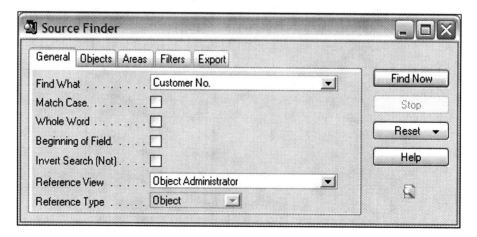

Then you specify that you are only looking for information contained in **Tables**, as shown in the following screenshot:

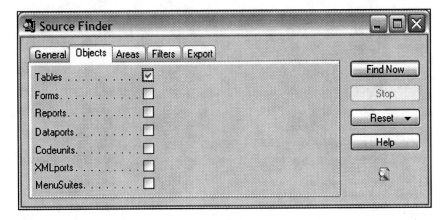

and only in **Keys**, as shown in the following screenshot:

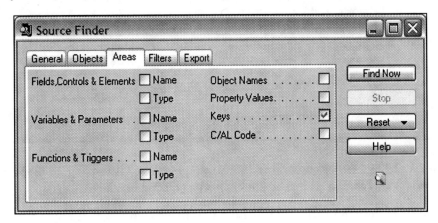

Your initial results will look like the following screenshot:

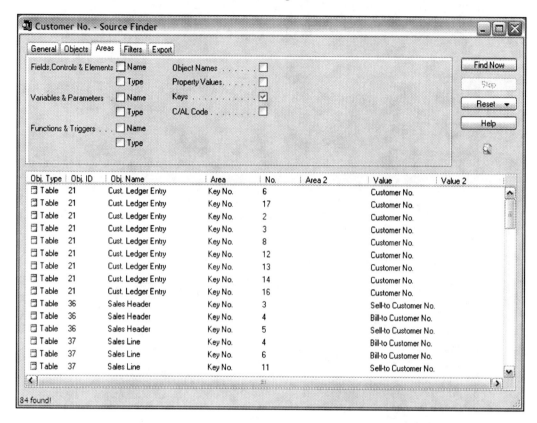

This data could be further constrained through the use of **Filters** (e.g. to find only Key 1 entries) and can be sorted by clicking on a column head.

Of course, as mentioned earlier, it will help you to experiment along the way. Don't make the mistake of thinking the Developer's Toolkit is the only tool you need to use, but also don't make the mistake of ignoring this one just because it won't do everything.

Working in Exported Text Code

As mentioned a little earlier, some developers export objects into text files then use a text editor to manipulate them. Let us take a look at an object that has been exported into text and imported into a text editor.

We will use one of the tables that are part of our C/ANDL development, the Volunteer Activity table, **50003** as shown in the following screenshot:

```
OBJECT Table 50003 Volunteer Activity
{
  OBJECT-PROPERTIES
  {
    Date=01/11/08;
    Time=[ 4:55:46 PM];
    Modified=Yes;
    Version List=PN.05;
  }
  PROPERTIES
  {
    LookupFormID=Form50004;
    DrillDownFormID=Form50004;
  }
  FIELDS
  {
    { 10  ;   ;Activity Code      ;Code20         }
    { 20  ;   ;Description        ;Text30         }
    { 30  ;   ;Points per Hour    ;Integer        }
  }
  KEYS
  {
    {     ;Activity Code                          ;Clustered=Yes }
  }
  CODE
  {

    BEGIN
    END.
  }
}
```

The general structure of all exported objects is similar, with differences that you would expect for the different objects. For example, Table objects have no Sections, but Report objects do. You can also see here that this particular table contains no C/AL-coded logic, as those statements would be quoted in the text listing.

You can see by looking at this table object text screenshot that you could easily search for instances of the string **Activity Code** throughout the text export of the entire system, but it would be more difficult to look for references to the **Volunteer Activity** form, **Form50004**. And, while you can find the instances of **Activity Code** with your text editor, it would be quite difficult to differentiate those instances that relate to the Volunteer Activity table from those in the Volunteer Activity Ledger from those simply defined as Global Variables. But the Developer's Toolkit could do that.

If you were determined to use a text editor to find all instances of "Volunteer Activity". "Activity Code", you could do the following:

Rename the field in question to something unique. C/SIDE will rename all the references to this field. Then export all the sources to text followed by using your text editor (or even Microsoft Word) to find the unique name. You must either remember to return the field in the database to the original name or you must be working in a temporary "work copy" of the database, which you will shortly discard.

One task that needs to be done occasionally is to renumber an object or to change a reference inside an object that refers to a no longer existing element. The C/SIDE editor may not let you do that easily, or in some cases, not at all. In such a case, the best answer is to export the object into text, make the change there and then import it back in as modified. Be careful though. When you import a text object, C/SIDE does not check to see if you are overwriting another instance of that object number. C/SIDE makes that check when you import a fob (i.e. a compiled object).

Theoretically, you could write all your C/AL code with a text editor and then import the result. Given the difficulty of such a task and the usefulness of the tools embedded in C/SIDE, such an approach would be foolish. However, there are occasions when it is very helpful to simply view an object "flattened out" in text format. In a report where you may have overlapping logic in multiple data items and in several section triggers as well, the only way to see all the logic at once is in text format.

You can use any text editor you like, Notepad or Word or one of the visual programming editors; the exported object is just text. You do need to cope with the fact that when you export a large number of objects in one pass, they all end up in the same text file. That makes the exported file relatively difficult to deal with. The solution to that is to split that file into individual text files, named logically, one for each NAV object. There are several freeware tools available to do just that. Check one of the NAV forums on the Internet.

 Two excellent NAV forums are www.mibuso.com and www.dynamicsuser.net.

Using Navigate

Navigate is an often under-appreciated tool both for the user and for the developer. We will focus here on its value to the developer. We will also mention how you might enhance your extension of the NAV system by expanding the coverage of the Navigate function.

Testing with Navigate

Navigate is a form object (Form 344) that searches for and displays the number and types of all the associated entries for a particular posting transaction. The term "associated" in this case is defined as those entries having the same **Document Number** and **Posting Date**.

Navigate can be called from the **Navigate** button, which appears on each screen that displays any of the entries that a Navigate might find and display. It can also be called directly from various Navigate entries in the user Menu. These are generally located within History menu groups.

If you invoke the Navigate form using the menu, you must actually enter the **Posting Date** and **Document Number** of the entries you wish to find. Or, alternately you can enter a **Business Contact Type** (Vendor or Customer), a **Business Contact No.** (Vendor No. or Customer No.), and optionally, an **External Document No.** There are occasions when this option is useful, but the **Posting Date + Document No.** option is much more frequently useful.

Instead of seeking out a Navigate form and entering the critical data fields, it is much easier to call Navigate from a **Navigate** button on a form showing data. In this case you just highlight a record and click on **Navigate** to search for all the related entries. In the following example, the first **General Ledger Entry** displayed is highlighted.

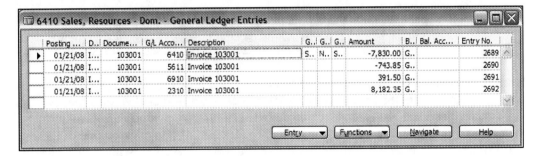

After clicking on the **Navigate** button, the **Navigate** form will pop up, filled in, with the completed search, and will look similar to the following screenshot:

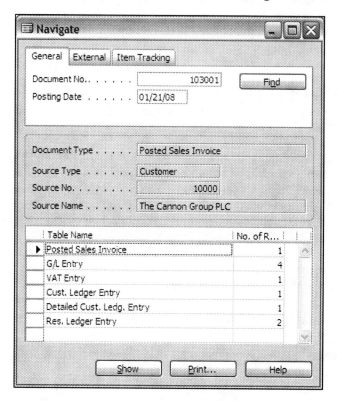

Had we accessed the **Navigate** form through one of the menu entries, we would have filled in the **Document No.** and **Posting Date** fields and clicked on **Find**. As you can see here, the **Navigate** form shows a list of related, posted entries including the one we highlighted to invoke the Navigate function. If you click on one of the items in the **Table Name** list at the bottom of the form, you will see an appropriately formatted display of the chosen entries.

For the `G/L Entry` table in this form, you would see a result like the following screenshot. Note that all the `G/L Entry` are displayed for same **Posting Date** and **Document No.**, matching those specified at the top of the **Navigate** form.

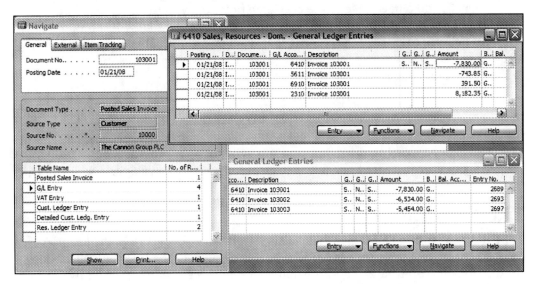

You may ask "Why is this application form being discussed in a section about C/AL debugging?" and the answer would be: "When you have to test, you need to check the results. When it is easier to do a thorough check of your test results, your testing will go faster and be of higher quality." Whenever you make a modification that will affect any data that could be displayed through the use of **Navigate**, it will quickly become one of your favorite testing tools.

Modifying for Navigate

If your modification creates a new table that will contain posted data and the records contain both Document No. and Posting Date fields, you can include this new table in the **Navigate** function.

The C/AL Code for **Posting Date + Document No.** Navigate functionality is found in the `FindRecords` function trigger of Form 344 – Navigate. The following screenshot illustrates the segment of the Navigate `CASE` statement code for the `Item Ledger Entry` table:

```
IF ItemLedgEntry.READPERMISSION THEN BEGIN
  ItemLedgEntry.RESET;
  ItemLedgEntry.SETCURRENTKEY("Document No.");
  ItemLedgEntry.SETFILTER("Document No.",DocNoFilter);
  ItemLedgEntry.SETFILTER("Posting Date",PostingDateFilter);
  InsertIntoDocEntry(
    DATABASE::"Item Ledger Entry",0,ItemLedgEntry.TABLECAPTION,ItemLedgEntry.COUNT);
END;
```

The code checks the READPERMISSION. If that is enabled for this table, then the appropriate filtering is applied. Next, there is a call to the InsertIntoDocEntry function, which fills the temporary table that is displayed in the **Navigate** form. If you wish to add a new table to the Navigate function, you must replicate this code for your new table. In addition, you must add the code that will call up the appropriate form to display the records that Navigate found. This code should be inserted in the ShowRecords function trigger of the **Navigate** form similar to the lines in the following screenshot:

```
DATABASE::"Item Ledger Entry":
    FORM.RUN(0,ItemLedgEntry);
```

Making a change like this, when appropriate, will not only provide a powerful tool for users, but will also provide a powerful tool for you as a developer.

The Debugger

C/SIDE has a built-in **Debugger** that is very helpful in tracking down the location of bugs. There are two basic usages of the available debugger. The first is identification of the location of a run-time error. This is fairly simple process, accomplished by setting the debugger (from the **Tools** Menu) to **Active** with the **Break on Triggers** option turned off as shown in the following screenshot. When the run-time error occurs, the debugger will be activated and display exactly where the error is occurring.

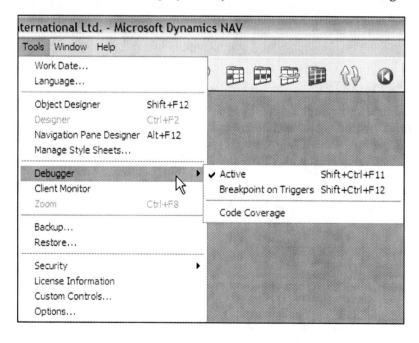

The second option is the support of traditional tracing of logic. Use of the Debugger for this purpose is hard work. It requires that you, the developer, have firmly in mind how the code logic is supposed to work, what the values of variables should be under all conditions, and the ability to discern when the code is not working as intended.

The Debugger allows you to see what code is being executed, either on a step-by-step basis (using *F8*) or trigger by trigger (using *F5*). You can set your own **Breakpoint** (using *F9*), points at which the Debugger will break the execution so you can examine the status of the system. The method by which execution is halted in the Debugger doesn't matter (so long as it is not by a run-time error); you have a myriad of tools with which to examine the status of the system at that point.

Other development environments have more flexible and more sophisticated debugging tools than the one in C/SIDE. Many debuggers allow a person to set the value of operating variable mid-stream in processing at a breakpoint, but the C/SIDE Debugger does not. Regardless, the C/SIDE Debugger is quite a useful tool and it is the only debugger that works in C/SIDE. It will pay you to learn to use it. The only way to do that is through hands-on practice. The Debugger is documented reasonably well in the Application Designer's Guide. Beyond studying that documentation, the best way to learn more about the C/SIDE debugger is to experiment using it.

The Code Coverage Tool

Code Coverage is a tool that tracks what code is executed and logs that information for your review and analysis. Code Coverage is accessed from the **Tools | Debugger** option. When you invoke Code Coverage, all that happens is you are opening the Code Coverage form. You then start Code Coverage by clicking on Start, and stop it by returning to the form. That's done through the Windows menu option as the Code Coverage form will remain open while it is running. The Application Designer's Guide provides some information on how to interpret the information collected.

Just like the Debugger, there is no substitute for experimenting to learn more about using Code Coverage. Code Coverage is a tool for gathering a volume of data about the path taken by the code while performing a task or series of tasks. This is very useful for two different purposes. One is simply to determine what code is being executed (another valuable debugging tool). But this tracking is done in high speed with a log file, whereas if you do the same thing in the debugger, the process is excruciatingly slow and you have to log the data manually.

The second use is to identify the volume of use of routines. By knowing how often a routine is executed within a particular process, you can make an informed judgement about what routines are using up the most processing time. That, in turn, allows you to focus any speed-up efforts on the code that is used the most. This approach will help you to realize the most benefit for your code acceleration work.

Dialog Function Debugging Techniques

In previous chapters, we have discussed some of the other simpler debugging techniques that you can productively use when developing in C/AL and C/SIDE. Sometimes these simpler methods are more productive than the more sophisticated tools because you can set up and test quickly, resolve the issue (or answer a question) and move on. The simpler methods all involve using one of the C/AL DIALOG functions such as MESSAGE, CONFIRM, DIALOG, or ERROR.

Debugging with MESSAGE

The simplest method is to insert MESSAGE statements at key points in your logic. It is very simple and, if structured properly, provides you a simple "trace" of the code logic path. You can number your messages to differentiate them and can display any data (in small amounts) as part of a message.

The disadvantage is that MESSAGE statements do not display until processing either terminates or is interrupted for user interaction. If you force a user interaction at some point, then your accumulated messages will appear prior to the interaction. The simplest way to force user interaction is a CONFIRM message in the format as follows:

```
IF CONFIRM ('Test 1',TRUE) THEN;
```

Debugging with CONFIRM

If you want to do a simple trace but want every message to be displayed as it is generated (i.e. have the tracking process move at a very measured pace), you could use CONFIRM statements for all the messages. You will then have to respond to each one before your program will move on, but sometimes that is what you want.

Debugging with DIALOG

Another tool that is useful for certain kinds of progress tracking is the DIALOG function. This function is usually set up to display a window containing a small number of variable values. As processing progresses, the values are displayed in real time. This can be useful in several ways. A couple of examples follow:

- Simply tracking progress of processing through a volume of data. This is the same reason you would provide a DIALOG display for the benefit of the user. The act of displaying does slow down processing somewhat. During debugging that may or may not matter. In production it is often a concern, so you may want to update the DIALOG display occasionally, not on every record.

- Displaying indicators for processing reaching certain stages. This can be used either as a very basic trace with the indicators showing the path taken or so that you may gauge the relative speed of progress through several steps. E.g., you might have a six-step process to analyze. You could define six tracking variables and display them all in the DIALOG.

  Each tracking variable would be initialized with values that would be dependent on what you are tracking, but each would likely be different (e.g. A1, B2000, C300000, etc.). At each step of your process, you would update the contents and display the current state of one of the variables (or all of the variables). This can be a very visual and intuitive guide for how your process works internally.

Debugging with Text Output

You can build a very handy debugging tool by outputting the values of critical variables or other informative indicators of progress either to an external text file or to a table created just for this purpose. This approach allows you to run a considerable volume of test data through the system, tracking some important elements while collecting data on the variable values, progress through various sections of code, etc. You can even timestamp your output records so that you can use this method to look for processing speed problems.

Following the test run, you can analyze the results of your test more quickly than if you were using displayed information. You can focus on just the items that appear most informative and ignore the rest. This type of debugging is fairly easy to set up and to refine as you identify the variables or code segments of most interest. This approach can be combined with the following approach using the ERROR statement if you output to an external text file, then close it before invoking the ERROR statement, so that its contents are retained following the termination of the test run.

Debugging with ERROR

One of the challenges of testing is maintaining repeatability. Quite often you need to test several times using the same data, but the test changes the data. If you have a small database, you can always back up the database and start with a fresh copy each time. But that that can be inefficient and, if the database is large, impractical. One alternative is to conclude your test with an ERROR function.

The ERROR function forces a run-time error status, which means the database is not updated (i.e. it is rolled back to the status at the beginning of the process). This works well when your debugging information is provided by using the Debugger or by use of any of the DIALOG functions just mentioned. If you are using MESSAGE, you could execute a CONFIRM immediately prior to the ERROR statement and be assured that all messages were displayed. Obviously this method won't work well when your testing validation is dependent on checking results using Navigate or your test is a multi-step process such as order entry, review, and posting. But in applicable situations, it is a very handy technique for repeating a test with minimal effort.

When testing the posting of an item, it can be useful to place the test-concluding ERROR function just before the point in the applicable Posting codeunit where the process would otherwise complete successfully.

Summary

In this chapter, we have reviewed a number of tools and techniques aimed at making your life as an NAV developer easier and more efficient. Many of these topics require more study and some hands-on practice by you. Among the topics we covered are functions that you can use "as is" and functions that you can use as models for your own code. We have reviewed some guidelines for documenting your modifications and briefly discussed dealing with Multi-Language and Multi-Currency compatibility. Finally we have gone over a host of handy code analysis and debugging techniques including use of the Developer Toolkit, working in objects exported as text, using Navigate, using the Debugger and associated tools, and some handy tips on other creative techniques.

By this point in the book, we have covered many of the core elements of NAV development. You should be just about ready begin your own development project. In the next chapter we are going to consider a number of important concepts that need to be considered when designing and creating modifications to an NAV system.

Designing NAV Modifications

When I am working on a problem, I never think about beauty. I think only of how to solve the problem. But when I have finished, if the solution is not beautiful, I know it is wrong. — attributed to R. Buckminster Fuller

In this chapter we are going to discuss a number of issues that must be considered when designing and developing modifications for Microsoft Dynamics NAV. We will also consider the differences between a minor enhancement and the creation of a new subsystem. Further, we will explore the NAV processing flow and explain how to design modifications compatible with the unique NAV structure.

Starting a New NAV Enhancement Project

Whenever you start a new project, you must define the goals and boundaries for the project. Some of them are as follows:

- What are the functional requirements and what flexibility exists within these?
- What are the user interface standards?
- What are the coding standards?
- What are the budgets, both time and financial?

Before starting a modification project, you must also determine which end goals are compatible with the base product you are proposing to modify. You probably don't want to use Microsoft Dynamics NAV as the basis for a modification to control a submarine's atomic reactor or as the basis for modification to create CAD drawings.

When you are making modifications to a system, the defined goals and boundaries must be flexible enough not only for the basic functional design and development to operate properly but also to fit the result of that work within the existing system. Modification project budgets must allow for the effort necessary to properly integrating the new material with the original.

Now that you have good insight into the workings of the NAV C/SIDE Development Environment and C/AL, it is a good time to review how you deal with software design for NAV. Most developers feel that designing for NAV enhancements and modifications requires more forethought and knowledge of the specifics of the application than we have needed with other systems. So let us explore what is special about designing NAV modifications.

Design of NAV Modifications

New material should be as compatible and as consistent with the original as possible. After you are done, it should be difficult (or impossible) for a new user to tell what's original and what's a modification. Otherwise you may end up with a Frankenstein system, where it is easy to identify new patched-on parts because you can see all the stitches and the bolts that (barely) hold them together.

Take a look at the following two examples of form modifications. The bad example is the first one. Hopefully its flaws are obvious (e.g. it does not follow Microsoft NAV GUI standards, has bad positioning of a new field, non-standard use of shape, garish use of color, and is ugly). The example of difficult-to-detect modification is the second form, where the **Date Added** field is added to the bottom right column of the standard form layout, shown in the second of the following screenshots:

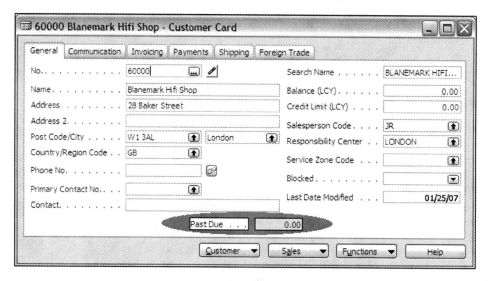

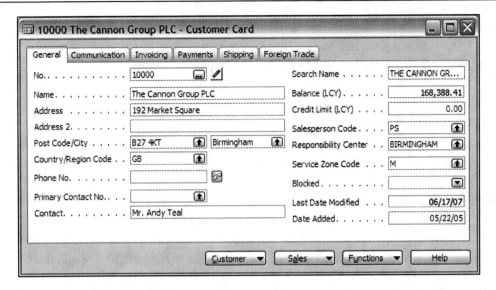

Another approach to adding new fields to a form is to put them all on a new tab. This keeps the modifications clearly identified. However, it may make use of the new fields awkward. Obviously there is no single best answer. The right design decision will depend on the specific situation.

New code should be modeled onto the code that is already present. You might feel that you know how to write better code than the code on which you are working. May be you are right. But when you modify an existing system you should respect the structure and design of the code that makes up the system you are changing. That does not mean you can't or shouldn't be creative, but that you should put rather strict boundaries on that creativity.

For example, the standard code structure for issuing an ERROR message looks like the following:

```
IF CheckLedgEntry.FIND('-') THEN
   ERROR(Text006,"Document No.");
```

With the following defined Text variable:

```
Text006   Check %1 already exists for this Bank Account.
```

Therefore you shouldn't be coding an ERROR message that looks similar to the following, where the message is hard-coded in-line, making it difficult to enable multilanguage capabilities.

```
IF CheckLedgEntry.FIND('-') THEN
   ERROR('Check %1 already exists for this Bank Account.',"Document
         No.");
```

This approach of having all messages in Text variable supports the multi-language capabilities of NAV.

Knowledge is Key

In order to respect the existing system being modified, you have to understand and appreciate the overall structure and design philosophy of that system. Among other things, NAV has unique data structure tools (SIFT and FlowFields), quite a number of NAV specific decimal and date functions which make it easier to program business applications, and a data structure (journal, ledger, etc.) which is inherently accounting structured.

The object base of NAV the and specific built-in function set of C/SIDE also add to its differences. Overall, because NAV is philosophically different from most other ERP application systems, learning NAV is challenging. A big part of your job will be to learn how NAV is different from other systems you have modified in the past so that the material you create will fit well within NAV.

If you are like most other developers, after a while you will learn to really appreciate NAV differences because with NAV you have lots of tools and capabilities you haven't had before. Nevertheless, the learning curve is significant, both because of the differences between NAV and other business software packages, and also (unfortunately) because there is a lack of product design documentation to help you over that learning curve. Hopefully, this book is making your leap into NAV easier than it would have been otherwise.

No matter which type of modification you are developing, you should resist the temptation to imprint your personality and your knowledge of "better ways to do it" on the system. If you have a totally irresistible urge to do it "your way", you should probably create your own system, not support and enhance NAV (or any other package product).

Creating a New Functional Area

The first thing to consider is whether you are creating software for a new functional area or creating an integrated modification of existing NAV functionality. Based on your experience with other systems, you will likely appreciate how and why these two project types are significantly different from each other. Or you may ask "How should I differentiate?"

One way would be that if you are adding an entry to the main menu or adding at the top level of one of the primary submenus, then your modification is likely to be a new functional area. If there is no menu entry at all involved in your enhancement, then almost certainly it is not a new functional area. To make sure we all are on the same wavelength here, let us discuss briefly some of the issues that make working on these two task types different from one another.

Advantages of Designing New Functionality

When creating new functionality, you have a lot more leeway in the design of your data structure, forms, processing flow, and user interface subtleties than you do when you are enhancing existing functionality. Nevertheless, you still have a strong responsibility for consistency with the design of the original system.

Menu structure, form navigation, invoking of reports, indeed, the whole user experience needs to be designed and implemented in a manner consistent with the out-of-the-box product. If you don't do that, you will significantly increase training requirements, error rates, and overall user frustration within the application. When there are significant user interface design inconsistencies from one portion of the system to another, it is unnecessarily challenging (and expensive) for users.

New functionality will likely have a relatively full representation of new instances of NAV objects, almost certainly including one or more tables, reports, and forms along with a menu entry or two. You may also have dataports or XMLports as well.

Some developers find that designing new functionality is generally an easier task than modifying existing functionality. There are several reasons for this. One reason is that you have more freedom in your user interface design. Of course, those aspects of the new application that are similar to functionality within the base system should be modeled on the NAV standard approach.

A second reason is that much of what you are creating will involve completely new objects. Creating a new object may be easier because you don't have to study, understand, and integrate with all the complexities of an existing object. Even documenting a new object is easier because you can put most, if not all, of your internal documentation comments in one place, rather than having to identify and comment individual modifications in place.

A third reason is that it is much easier to provide ease of upgrading. A new object can often be moved to an upgraded version with little or no change. In fact, this aspect of system maintainability sometimes leads to utilizing new objects (and justifying their use) for modifications even when they are not otherwise required. This possibility of easier upgrading should not be interpreted to mean that custom objects don't need to be carefully examined during an upgrade. There is always the possibility that the data structure or flow on which the modification design was built has been changed in the new version. In that case, the custom object will need to be revised just as would the embedded customization.

Enhancing an Existing Functional Area

When you are modifying existing functionality, you should operate with a very light touch, changing as little as possible to accomplish your goals. Your new code will look like NAV code and your user interface will work like the standard product interface. Of course, you will leave behind a well documented trail. Your new fields will fit neatly and tightly on the forms. Your new function will operate so similarly to existing standard NAV functions that little or no user training will be required except to inform users that the new function exists and what it does.

In contrast to the pros and cons of creating a new functional area with your modification, there is a different set of pros and cons when your modification is localized and tightly integrated into existing NAV structure and code. Because your modification should closely resemble the design and structure of what already exists, which means you don't have nearly as much creative freedom as to how to do what you're going to do.

Modifying an existing function means you may not need to learn as much about optional approaches. Plus, while you should be intimately familiar with the processes and logic in the parts of the system you are affecting, you can usually focus your study on a relatively small segment of the original system, thus reducing the breadth of your study of the existing system. Finally, when you are modifying an existing function, you have the distinct advantage of knowing that the base on which you are building is already debugged and working.

Testing can be easier in a smaller modification. Often you will have your choice of testing using the Cronus demo database or using a test copy of the production database. Depending on exactly what your modification does of course, you may be able to use existing setups, master table data, perhaps even existing in-process transactions to test your modification. Since the creation of a consistent set of test data can be a very time-consuming process, this is a significant advantage.

Advantages of using a copy of the live database for testing include having a fully set up system that matches the customer's production environment as well as data that matches the real production world. This can make it quite a bit easier to compare new results to previous results and to spot speed bottlenecks that relate to historical data volumes. This applies to any type or scope of modification.

NAV Development Time Allocation

For many years, those responsible for software development technology have been promising to increase the ratio of design time and effort to the coding time and effort. But, very few systems or toolsets have fulfilled that promise, particularly in the business application marketplace. In a majority of customization cases, a lot more time and effort is spent writing and debugging code than in the design of that code.

The NAV structure, code functions, and IDE tool set actually begin to fulfill that long-delayed promise of significantly reducing the code coding effort to design effort ratio. It is not unusual, while making an NAV modification, to spend several hours studying existing code, testing logic and flow with a variety of data samples, before making a code change of just two, three, or four lines to effect a significant change.

You might work on the design side of the task for a half day, and then spend a half hour on the actual implementation of your design. This is due to the combination of the very tight code structure and the powerful set of language functions NAV provides. That is not enough to say that NAV is perfectly assembled and has no places where the code could be significantly improved. But if it were perfect, there wouldn't be much work left for us to do, would there?

Data-Focused Design for New Functionality

Any new application design must begin with certain basic analysis and design tasks. That is just as applicable when our design is for new functionality to be integrated into an existing standard software package such as NAV. Before we dig into what needs to be done in an NAV system, let us briefly consider some of what has to happen in any system when you are designing and developing a new area of application functionality.

Define the Big Picture: The End Goals

What capability is the new application functionality intended to accomplish? This needs to be spelled out in sufficient detail so that the designers will know when they are done. Not only do the end goals need to state what the new functional expectations are, they also need to state what they are not, and what resource constraints must be taken into account. There is no sense in allowing the system designers to take advantage of the latest computing technology if the application must operate on five-year-old computer systems.

A Simple Sample Project

This example is intended to illustrate the concepts discussed here, not to represent a complete system design. Let us assume we are working with a firm that has NAV installed and operating. It distributes electronic consumer goods. Several of its equipment vendors provide significant rebates based on the volume of certain products purchased and sold in specific geographic areas. Reporting is to be done on a monthly basis. To keep our example simple, we will assume the geographic areas are defined by **Postal Zone Code** ranges. The report we will print for each vendor will look similar to the following **Vendor Rebate Report draft layout**. If you can provide the same information in a more attractive layout, you should feel free to revise this design to fit your improved approach.

```
Vendor Rebate Report draft layout – use standard report heading

Vendor: xxNo.xxxxx   XXXXXXXXXNAMEXXXXXXXXXXXXXXXXX
Sales during: mm/dd/yyyy1 – mm/dd/yyyy2
Report Filter: xxxxxxxxxxxxxxxxxxxxxxxxxxxxxxxxxxxxxxxxxxxxxxxxxxxxxxxxxxxxxxxx

Item No.           Description                          Qty        Purchase Cost
Sales for the area: axxxxxxxx - bxxxxxxx

xxxxxxxxxxxx    xxxxxxxxxxxxxxxxxxxxxxxxxxxxxxxxxxxx    99,999,999    99,999,999.99
xxxxxxxxxxxx    xxxxxxxxxxxxxxxxxxxxxxxxxxxxxxxxxxxx    99,999,999    99,999,999.99
xxxxxxxxxxxx    xxxxxxxxxxxxxxxxxxxxxxxxxxxxxxxxxxxx    99,999,999    99,999,999.99

Area axxxxxxxx - bxxxxxxx Total                                    999,999,999.99

Sales for the area: cxxxxxxxx - dxxxxxxx

xxxxxxxxxxxx    xxxxxxxxxxxxxxxxxxxxxxxxxxxxxxxxxxxx    99,999,999    99,999,999.99
xxxxxxxxxxxx    xxxxxxxxxxxxxxxxxxxxxxxxxxxxxxxxxxxx    99,999,999    99,999,999.99
xxxxxxxxxxxx    xxxxxxxxxxxxxxxxxxxxxxxxxxxxxxxxxxxx    99,999,999    99,999,999.99
xxxxxxxxxxxx    xxxxxxxxxxxxxxxxxxxxxxxxxxxxxxxxxxxx    99,999,999    99,999,999.99

Area cxxxxxxxx - dxxxxxxx Total                                    999,999,999.99


Vendor Total                                                      999,999,999.99
```

Then Define the Little Pictures

What information must the new application functionality make available to the users in order to accomplish those lofty goals? How do the users expect that data to be presented? What type of constraints exist due to practice or practicality? Define what actions are to be performed by the system when presented with the appropriate and expected data or user actions.

Sample Project Continued—1

Our end goal is to create an easy-to-maintain small subsystem. It should allow the user to maintain data on what products, vendors, and geographic areas are to be reported. This will keep the new functional application flexible. The reporting process should be a simple report run with a time period parameter. Normal filtering should be enabled to allow flexibility. The processing will not change any data. This will minimize its impact on the system. If possible, the design should not change any standard data structures. This will make it easier to debug, maintain, and upgrade.

Define What Data is Required to Create the Pictures

In order to accomplish the stated goals, we must determine what data is required. What will it take to construct the material the users need to see? With what level of detail and in what structural forms must the data be stored and how it must be retrieved? In light of the actions that the new system must perform, what data are required to support them?

Sample Project Continued—2

First we must define the data that determine what transactions will be considered. In this case, it is pretty simple. We need a list of the vendors to whom we will report. We need a list of the products on which rebates will be paid for each vendor, as these are the product sales that we will count. We need a list of the definitions of the geographic areas on which each vendor is focusing, i.e. a list of **Postal Zone Code** ranges.

The system activity data we need includes all the individual sales transactions for the products in question along with the applicable **Post Codes**. Since the rebates are calculated on the price paid to the vendor for the product, we will need our cost for the product for each sale. Before we go further, we need to clarify whether the rebate is paid based on the post code of the location that buys the item or the location to which the item is shipped. Let us assume we asked the question and found it is the location to which the item is shipped. That means we will use the **Ship-to Post Code**.

Define the Sources for the Data

Having defined what data and other inputs are required to be able to provide the required outputs and system actions, we have to define the sources of all this material. Some may be input manually, some may be forwarded from other systems, some may be derived from historical accumulations of data, and some will be computed from combinations of all these, and more. In any case, every component of the information needed must have a clearly defined point of origin, schedule of arrival, and format.

Sample Project Continued—3

Part of our control information should be a list of product (i.e. Item) codes by rebating **Vendor**. If this list is built by making sure that the **Vendor – Item** combinations match available combinations in the standard `master` table data. Then, in our new application, we can use the **Item No.** as the first point of control for data gathering. We should create one table keyed on **Vendor + Item No.** and a second table keyed on **Vendor + From Post Code + To Post Code**. We will call these, respectively, the **Vendor Rebate Totaling** table and the **Vendor Post Code Range** table.

If, in the first table, we include work fields (not filled in the permanent data table) for the **From Post Code** and **To Post Code**, we will have a table structure that matches the report structure. We will also include variables in which we can sum up totals. In processing we can then use this table as the definition template for a `Temporary` table where the totals are accumulated for reporting. The following screenshots show what those table designs might look like: first the **Vendor – Item** table and **Keys**, and then the **Vendor – Post Code** table.

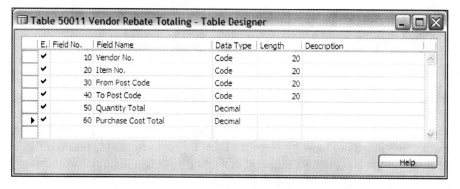

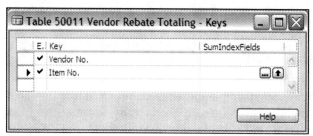

The first place we might look at as a possible primary data source is the Item Ledger Entry table. That table contains an entry for every sale transaction and every purchase transaction and it is organized by **Item**, i.e. by product. An alternative location would be the Sales Invoice Line table, which would also have all the product sales detail. A third possible data source would be the Sales Shipment Line table. That table also contains the product quantity shipped and cost data. These records are child records of the Sales Shipment Header records, where the necessary **Ship-to** address information is located.

After studying the three options, we see that they all can be filtered by **Item No.**, all have cost information (which equates to what we paid the vendor for the product) and all have a way to get to the shipment document where the **Ship-to** address information is located. To decide which to use, we must investigate the relationships for each of the detail data tables to the Sales Shipment Header.

At first it appears the Sales Shipment Line data would be the easiest to use and the Sales Invoice Line data would be the hardest to use. These judgements are based on the ease with which all the related data can be accessed from the intended primary data source. But our study determines that the Item Ledger Entry cost information is the most fully updated of the choices. In addition, the Item Ledger Entry records have a field, **Document No.**, that points directly at the related Sales Shipment Header.

The Item Ledger Entry cost information is "best" because all adjustments get applied to the Item Ledger, but previously posted Invoice and Shipment cost data is not updated by adjustments subsequent to the posting. Therefore our design choice depends on whether or not it is necessary to use the most accurate possible cost information. At this point in our example, we will assume that it was determined that the cost information in the Sales Shipment Line table will be sufficiently accurate as it would be accurate as of the time of shipment.

Define the Data "Views"

Based on all the definitions spelled out in the preceding steps, define how the data should be presented. How does it need to be "sliced and diced"? What levels of detail and summary? What sequences and segmentations? What visual formats? What media? This definition must be wholly in the context of the original big picture goals. Success isn't going to be measured by the sophistication of the tools but by how well the system serves its masters, the users for whom it was originally intended.

Sample Project Continued—4

The visual format requirements for our sample project are pretty simple. We will use the draft layout as the model for our report. In this particular example, the report layout essentially provides the required levels of detail and summary. We need to sum up product costs for the individual sales transactions by **Item No.** within **Post Code** range within a **Transaction Date** range within **Vendor**. The **Transaction Date** range will be a report filter. Exactly how we construct the logic and internal global variables to collect and print the data will depend on factors such as whether we are doing this for multiple vendors at one time or only one vendor at a time. Since the new tables are very simple in their structure, we just use default formatting for a tabular form to maintain and view those tables.

Other Factors Must Always be Considered

Of course, many other issues need to be considered in the full design of a system, including user interface specifications, data and access security, accounting standards and controls, etc. In this discussion and the associated example, the focus is on the data and its handling.

NAV Processing Flow

The steps in reviewing the flow of data through the NAV system are as follows:

1. Prepare all the Master data, reference data, and control and setup data. Much of this preparation is done initially when an application is first set up for production usage.

2. Enter transactions into a `Journal` table; preliminarily validating data as it is entered, referencing auxiliary data tables as appropriate.

3. Provide for additional test validations of data prior to submitting the Batch to Posting.

4. Post the Journal Batch, finally validating the transaction data, adding entries as appropriate to one or more Ledgers and, perhaps a Register and a document history.

5. Access the data via Forms and/or Reports of various types as appropriate. At this point, total flexibility exists. Whatever tools are available and are appropriate to provide system users with what they need should be used. There are some very good, but somewhat limited (in terms of visual technologies) tools built into NAV for data manipulation, extraction, and presentation. In the past, these capabilities were considered good enough to be widely accepted as full OLAP (Online Analytical Processing) tools.

6. Continue maintenance of Master data, reference data, and setup and control data, as appropriate. The loop returns to Step 1 of this data flow sequence.

Data Preparation

Prepare all the Master data, reference data, and control and setup data. Much of this preparation is done initially when an application is first set up for production usage.

Naturally, this data must be maintained as new Master data becomes available, as various system operating parameters change, etc. The standard approach for NAV data entry is to allow records to be entered that have just enough information to define the primary key fields, but not necessarily enough to support processing. This allows a great deal of flexibility in the timing and responsibility assignment for entry and completeness of new data.

On the other hand, it allows initial and incomplete data entry by one person, with validation and completion to be handled later by someone else. For example, a sales person might initialize a new customer entry with name, address, and phone number, saving the entry when the data to which they have access is entered. At this point, there would not be enough information recorded to process orders for this new customer. At a later time, someone in the accounting department might set up Posting Groups, Payment Terms, and other control data that should not be controlled by the sales department. This new entry could make the new customer record ready for production use. Given that in many instances data comes into an organization on a piecemeal basis, the NAV approach allows the system to be updated on an equally piecemeal basis providing a certain flexible, user friendliness that many accounting-oriented systems lack.

Enter Transactions

Enter transactions into a `Journal` table; preliminarily validating data as it is entered, referencing auxiliary data tables as appropriate.

NAV uses a relational database design approach that could be referred to as a "rational normalization". NAV resists being constrained by the concept of a Normalized data structure, where any data element appears only once. The NAV data structure is normalized so long as that principle doesn't get in the way of processing speed. Where processing speed or ease of use for the user is improved by duplicating data across tables, NAV does so. For the sake of a label, this could be called "rational normalization".

At the point where Journal transactions are entered, a considerable amount of data validation takes place. Most, if not all, of the validation that can be done based on the combination of the individual transaction entry plus the related Master records and associated reference tables (e.g. lookups, application or system setup parameters, etc.) is done when a Journal entry is made. Still, the practice continues of allowing entries to be made that are incomplete and not totally ready for processing.

Provide for Additional Data Testing

Provide for additional test validations of data prior to submitting the Batch to Posting.

Any additional validations that need to be done to ensure the integrity and completeness of the transaction data prior to being Posted are done both in pre-Post routines and directly in the course of the Posting processes. When a Journal Entry is Posted, it becomes a part of the permanent accounting record in the system. In general, NAV follows the standard accounting practice of requiring Ledger corrections to be made by Posting reversing entries, rather than deletion of problem entries. That makes NAV a very auditable system, a key requirement for a variety of government, legal, and certification requirements for information systems.

Depending on the specific application function, when Journal transactions don't pass muster during this final validation stage, either the individual transaction is bypassed while acceptable transactions are Posted, or the entire Journal Batch is rejected until the identified problem is resolved.

Post the Journal Batch

Post the Journal Batch, finally validating the transaction data and adding entries as appropriate to one or more Ledgers and, perhaps a Register and a document history.

As mentioned earlier, Ledgers are handled as permanent records of what transactions have been processed. Most data cannot be changed or deleted once it is resident in a Ledger except by a subsequent Posting process.

Related data recorded during the Posting process is not necessarily considered permanent data. For example document histories such as Posted Invoices, Posted Shipments, Posted Receipts and such, while useful information, can be deleted.

Access the Data

Access the data via Forms and/or Reports of various types as appropriate, assuming total flexibility. Whatever tools are available and are appropriate should be used. There are some very good, tools in NAV for data manipulation, extraction, and presentation. These include, among other things, the SIFT/FlowField functionality, the pervasive filtering capability (including the ability to apply filters to subordinate data structures), the Navigate function, and even the Form and Report Wizards.

There are a number of methods by which data can be pushed or pulled from an NAV database for processing and presentation outside NAV. This allows use of more graphically oriented outputs or use of other specialized data analysis tools such as Microsoft Excel or others. Even given NAV's lack of graphical presentation capabilities, NAV still provides a very respectable set of user data review and analysis tools through use of the very flexible filtering toolset combined with the truly unique SIFT technology.

Continuing Maintenance

Maintenance of Master data, reference data, and setup and control data as appropriate. The loop returns to the first Step of this data flow sequence, Data Preparation.

Designing a New NAV Application Functionality

Given the preceding top-down view how an NAV application works in general, let us now discuss how we should go about designing a modification. Our view once again will be data centred. At this point, we will only consider the design issues for new functionality. Our design process will presume that the overall goals for the new functionality have already been clearly and completely defined (the "big picture").

When one is designing a much more limited "tweak" modification, the design process is extremely dependent on exactly what is being done, and is very difficult to generalize. Some of the following will apply in such a case, but very selectively.

Define the Data Tables

This definition includes the data fields, the keys to control the sequence of data access and to ensure rapid processing, frequently used totals (which are likely to be set up as SumIndex Fields), references to lookup tables for allowed values, and relationships to other primary data tables. It is important not to just define the primary data tables (e.g. those holding the data being processed in the course of business activity). The design definition activity at this point must also include any related lookup tables and controlling "setup" information tables. Finally, it is appropriate to consider what "backward looking" references to these new tables will be added to the already existing portions of the system. These connections are often the finishing touch that makes the new functionality operate in a truly seamlessly integrated fashion with the original system.

Design the User Data Access Interface

Design the forms and reports to be used to display or interrogate the data. Define what keys are to be used or available to the users. Define what fields will be allowed to be visible, what are the totaling fields, how the totaling will be accomplished (e.g. FlowFields, on-the-fly), and what dynamic display options will be available. Define what type of filtering will be needed. Some filtering needs may be beyond the ability of the built-in filtering function and may require auxiliary code functions. Determine whether external data analysis tools will be needed and will therefore need to be interfaced. Design considerations at this stage often result in returning to the previous data structure definition stage to add additional data fields, keys, SIFT fields, or references to other tables.

Design the Data Validation

Define exactly how the data must be validated before it is accepted upon entry into a table.

There are likely to be multiple levels of validation. There will be a minimum level, which defines the minimum set of information required before a new record is accepted. The minimum may be no more than an identifying number or it may include several data fields. At the least, it must include all the fields that make up the primary key to the table.

Subsequent levels of validation may exist relating to particular subsets of data, which are in turn tied to specific optional uses of the table. For example in the base NAV system, if the manufacturing functionality is not being used, the manufacturing-related fields in the `Item Master` table do not need to be filled in. But if they are filled in, then they must satisfy certain validations.

As mentioned earlier, the sum total of all the validations that are applied to data when it is entered into a table may not be sufficient to completely validate the data. Depending on the use of the data, there may be additional validations performed during the processing, reporting, or inquiries.

Appropriate Data Design Sequence

Perform the above three steps for the permanent data (Masters and Ledgers) and then for the transactions (Journals). As a general rule, once all the supporting tables and references have been defined for the permanent data tables, there are not likely to be many, if any, such new definitions required for the `Journal` tables. If any significant new supporting tables or totally new table relationships are identified during the definition of `Journal` tables, you should go back and re-examine the earlier definitions. Why? Because there is a high likelihood that this new requirement should have been defined for the permanent data and was overlooked.

Design Posting Processes

First define the final data validations, then define and design all the ledger and auxiliary tables (e.g. Registers, Posted Document tables). At this point you are determining what the permanent content of the Posted data will be. if you identify new supporting table or table reference requirements at this point, you should go back to the first step to make sure this requirement didn't need to be included at that earlier design definition stage.

Whatever variations in data are permitted to be Posted must be assumed to be acceptable in the final instance of the data. Any information or relationships that are necessary in the final Posted data must be ensured before Posting is allowed to proceed.

Part of the Posting design is to determine whether data records will be accepted or rejected individually or in complete batches. If the latter happens, you must also define what constitutes a batch. If the former, it is quite likely that the makeup of a Posting Batch will be flexible.

Design Support Processes

Design the processes necessary to validate, process, extract, and format data for the desired output. In earlier steps, these processes may be assumed to exist. That way they can be defined as "black boxes" in terms of the available inputs and required outputs without overdue regard for the details of the internal processes. That allows the earlier definition and design steps to proceed without being sidetracked into the inner-working detail of these processes.

These processes are the cogs and gears of the functional application. They are necessary, but often not pretty. By leaving design of these processes in the application design as late as possible, you increase the likelihood that you will be able to create common routines and to standardize how similar tasks are handled across a variety of parent processes. At this point you may identify opportunities or requirements for improvement in material defined in a previous design step. In that case, you should return to that step relative to the newly identified issue. In turn, you should also review the effect of such changes for each subsequent step's area of focus.

Double-Check Everything

Do one last review of all the defined reference, setup, and other control tables to make sure that the primary tables and all defined processes have all the information available when needed. This is a final double-check step.

Summary

By now it will be exceedingly obvious that this design approach is an iterative approach. At each step there are opportunities to discover things that ideally would have been dealt within a previous step. When such discoveries are made, the design work should return to that previous step and proceed methodically back to where the discovery was made.

It is important to realize that returning to a previous step to address a previously unidentified issue is not a failure of the process, it is a success. A paraphrase of a quote attributed to *Frank Lloyd Wright* says,

> *"You can use an eraser on the drafting table or a sledge hammer on the construction site."*

It is much cheaper and more efficient to find and fix design issues during the design phase rather than after the system is in testing or, worse yet, in production (it's quieter too).

Now that we have reviewed the flow of information through an NAV system and discussed an overview of how we should design creation of a new functional area as a modification, we will continue exploring auxiliary tools and features that contribute to the power and flexibility of NAV.

10

External Interfaces

A picture is worth a thousand words. An interface is worth a thousand pictures—Ben Shneiderman

In this chapter, we will look at how your NAV processes can interface with outside data sources or targets from NAV and how the outside world (systems and users) can interface with NAV data and objects. Users of the system must communicate with the system by finding the location of the tool that they wish to use. The Menu, provided in NAV by means of the MenuSuites, provides access to the tools.

NAV must also accommodate communication with other software or hardware. Sometimes that communication is either Inside-Out (i.e. instigated by NAV) or Outside-In (i.e. triggered by the outside connection). When we consider system-to-system communications, it's not unusual for the process to be a two way street, a meeting of peers.

To make it easier for our users to meet their needs, we have to understand the features and limitations of MenuSuites. To supply, receive, or exchange information with other systems (hardware or software), we need at least a basic understanding of the interface tools that are part of NAV.

 It is critical to understand that because of the way some data is retrieved from the NAV database, particularly FlowFields, it is very risky for an external system to access NAV data directly without using one or more C/AL based routines as an intermediary.

MenuSuites

MenuSuite objects were added to NAV with the release of V4.0 to provide a user interface very similar to that of Microsoft Office products. The obvious goal was to make the learning curve for new users shorter by leveraging familiarity. The effect is limited by the fact that NAV is nothing like a standard Office application, but the commonality of appearance was achieved.

One major advantage of **MenuSuites** is the fact that the Menus can be modified by users. There is a predefined Menu Section called Shortcuts. Users can copy menu items from the location where they appear in the standard system to the Shortcuts section. In this way, users (or the user IT staff) can build their own menu section containing their personal frequently used menu entries. Another significant feature of **MenuSuites** is the fact that they automatically adapt to show the functions currently enabled by the active license and the user permissions. In other words, if you are not allowed to use a particular NAV function, you won't see it on your menu.

MenuSuite Levels

There are 15 levels of menu objects. They go from level 1 to 15, 1 being a "lower" level than level 2, etc. The displayed set of menus is built up by first using the lowest level, then amending it by applying next higher level, and so forth until all defined levels have been applied. Wherever a higher level redefines a lower level, the higher level definition takes precedence.

The available menu levels are **MBS, Region, Country, Add-on 1** through **Add-on 10, Partner**, and **Company**. The lowest level that can be modified in Design mode without a special license is the **Partner** Level (you can open lower levels but you cannot save changes). The lower levels are reserved to the NAV corporate developers and the ISVs who create Add-ons. The following screenshot shows a **MenuSuite** with the original Microsoft master **MenuSuite** object (**MBS**), a regional localization object (**Region**), a **Partner**-created object (**Partner**), and an end-user Administrator-created MenuSuite object (**Company**).

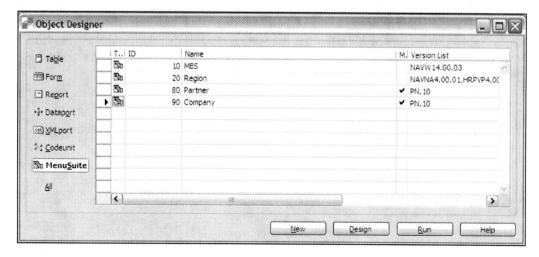

MenuSuite Structure

The Menu displayed when you enter NAV is a roll-up of the contents of all the menu objects, filtered based on your license and your assigned permissions. Each level has the ability to override the lower levels for any entry with the same **GUID number**. (Globally Unique Identifier (GUID) numbers are unique numbers that can be used for the identification of database objects, data records, etc. The value of each GUID is generated by Microsoft developed algorithm. The standard GUID representation is {12345678-1234-1234-1234-1234567890AB}).

A changed Menu entry description is a higher-level entry overriding a lower-level entry. The lower-level entry isn't really changed. A deleted lower-level entry is not really deleted. Its display is blocked by the existence of a higher-level entry indicating the effective deletion.

The changes that are made to one **MenuSuite** object level are stored as the differences between the effective result and the entries in the lower-level objects. On the whole this doesn't really make any difference in how you maintain entries, but if you export menu objects to text and study them, it may help explain some of what you see there and what happens when changes are made to MenuSuite entries. Some examples are as follows:

The following screenshot shows the user view of the **Financial Management** menu in its original form as shipped by Microsoft.

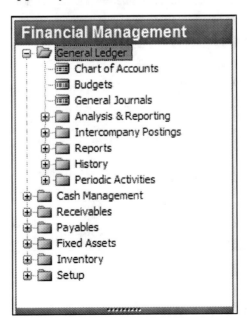

The following screenshot shows the developer view of the same menu with two modifications. The first modification is a change in the description of the **Chart of Accounts** menu item to **NEW TEST Chart of Accounts**. The second modification is an added menu entry, **New Form for Menu Test**, immediately below the first modification.

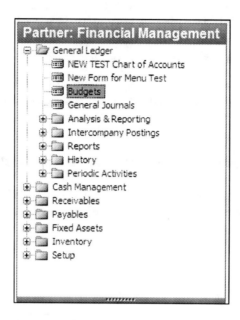

MenuSuite Internal Structure

The following screenshot shows the exported text for the unmodified **Chart of Accounts** and **Budgets** menu items.

```
{ MenuItem      ;[{8AC7917D-2C91-457D-88D6-A24B42F71AE7}] ;Name=Chart of Accounts;
                                                           CaptionML=ENU=Chart of Accounts;
                                                           MemberOfMenu=[{F8D2429D-834B-4C58-9B5E-81BE962DB1BC}];
                                                           RunObjectType=Form;
                                                           RunObjectID=16;
                                                           ParentNodeID=[{B12180CF-8EFB-43AD-9118-7765E953AAFD}];
                                                           Visible=Yes;
                                                           NextNodeID=[{92F88635-48B9-47EA-98CF-7D2E6A9447BE}] }
{ MenuItem      ;[{92F88635-48B9-47EA-98CF-7D2E6A9447BE}] ;Name=Budgets;
                                                           CaptionML=ENU=Budgets;
                                                           MemberOfMenu=[{F8D2429D-834B-4C58-9B5E-81BE962DB1BC}];
                                                           RunObjectType=Form;
                                                           RunObjectID=113;
                                                           ParentNodeID=[{B12180CF-8EFB-43AD-9118-7765E953AAFD}];
                                                           Visible=Yes;
                                                           NextNodeID=[{A0228F75-6AE8-489F-A9AF-E0F544B72976}] }
```

The next screenshot shows the exported text for the **Partner** object. You can also see the modification for the **Chart of Accounts** entry containing enough information to have the new description override the original along with the GUID number of the original entry. The added menu entry (**New Form for Menu Test**) contains all of the necessary information to completely define that entry. By examining the entry GUIDs and the NextNodeID values, you can see that the menu is constructed as a simple, singly linked list.

```
{               ;[{8AC7917D-2C91-457D-8006-A24B42F71AE7}]  ;CaptionML=[ENU=NEW TEST Chart of Accounts;
                                                             FRC=Plan comptable;
                                                             ENC=Chart of Accounts];
                                                            NextNodeID=[{84F60F25-A5A2-4389-B72F-30D9E9555CC6}] }
{ MenuItem      ;[{84F60F25-A5A2-4389-B72F-30D9E9555CC6}]  ;Name=New Form for Menu Test;
                                                            CaptionML=ENU=New Form for Menu Test;
                                                            MemberOfMenu=[{F8D2429D-034B-4C58-9B5E-81BE962DB1BC}];
                                                            RunObjectType=Form;
                                                            RunObjectID=1;
                                                            ParentNodeID=[{B12180CF-8EFB-43AD-9118-7765E953AAFD}];
                                                            Visible=Yes;
                                                            NextNodeID=[{92F88635-48B9-47EA-90CF-7D2E6A9447BE}] }
```

Now, if we open the MenuSuite Designer at the **Company** level, we can reverse the two changes we earlier made at the **Partner** level so that the displayed menu will look as though no changes had ever been made. What actually happens? Entries in the **Company**-level **MenuSuite** object are overriding the entries in the **Partner**-level object, which are in turn are overriding the entries in the **MBS**-level object. The following screenshot shows the entries that were added to the **Company** level object when we "restored" the menu appearance by changing the first entry description back and by deleting the added entry.

```
{           ;[{84F60F25-A5A2-4389-B72F-30D9E9555CC6}]  ;Deleted=Yes }
{           ;[{8AC7917D-2C91-457D-8006-A24B42F71AE7}]  ;CaptionML=[ENU=Chart of Accounts;
                                                         FRC=Plan comptable;
                                                         ENC=Chart of Accounts] }
```

If you are faced with working on a MenuSuite containing several levels and you want to start by analyzing what menu entries are touched at each level, your only good option is to export each of the levels to text and analyze the text.

MenuSuite Development

The **MenuSuite Designer** can be accessed through two paths. Users with appropriate permissions (and developers) can access the MenuSuite Designer through the **Tools** menu as shown in the following screenshot. This path will only allow access to the **Company**-level menu, the highest of the levels.

Access to the other levels of **MenuSuite** objects is through **Tools | Object Designer | MenuSuite** in a fashion essentially similar to accessing other NAV objects for development purposes.

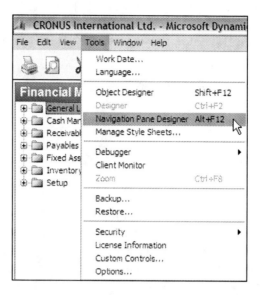

To exit MenuSuite Designer, right-click on the open **MenuSuite** object heading. You will see the **Close Navigation Pane Designer** option as shown in the following screenshot (**Navigation Pane Designer** is an alternative name for the MenuSuite Designer). Click on that option to close the Designer. You will have the usual opportunity to respond to "**Do you want to save the changes**".

Once you have opened the MenuSuite Designer at the desired level (typically **Partner** or **Company**), your next step is to create menu modifications. As mentioned in Chapter 1, the development tools for MenuSuites are quite different in form than those of other NAV objects. To access the development options for a MenuSuite, highlight an item (e.g. a menu or menu entry) and right-click. After highlighting a menu, you will see the display similar to the following screenshot:

If you select the **Create Menu** option, you will see the form in the following screenshot. This allows you to create a new Menu. For example, you might want to create a new menu allowing access to a limited set of inquiry forms.

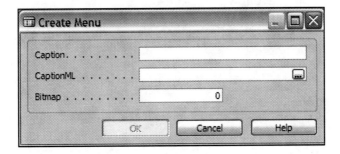

In this form, you can enter whatever the new Menu's **Caption** is to be and choose a **Bitmap** to be displayed as the icon at the left of the caption string when the MenuSuite is displayed.

If you highlight a menu entry and right-click, you will see the option list shown in the following screenshot:

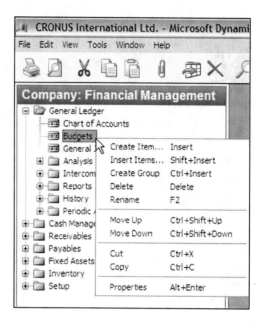

The options shown on this menu are the total set available for a MenuSuite item. The first set of options allows you to **Create**, **Delete**, or **Rename** items. The **Move Up** and **Move Down** are the principal positioning tools. If you click on **Properties**, you will see a display similar to the following screenshot:

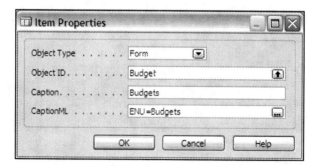

The only object types allowed are Table, Form, Report, Dataport, and Codeunit. Once you have chosen an object type, you can specify the particular object of that type to be executed and what the **Captions** are to be. And that's all that you can do as a developer in a MenuSuite. An appropriately authorized user can do exactly the same things, but only in the Company level MenuSuite.

If you are creating a new Menu containing menu items that exist in other Menus, you can populate it very quickly and easily. Create a new Menu, and just copy and paste menu items into it from other Menus.

There is no allowance for any type of embedded C/AL code in a MenuSuite item to handle control, filtering, special validation, or other logic. You cannot invoke a specific function within an object. If you want to include any such customized capability, you must put that logic in an object, such as report, dedicated to handle the control task. Your MenuSuite item can then execute that control object, which will apply your enhanced control logic and then invoke another object.

NAV Menus before V4.0

Versions of NAV (aka Navision) prior to V4.0 had a menu system made from Forms objects. The appearance of the menu was quite different from MenuSuites (see the following screenshot from a V3.7 US-localized database).

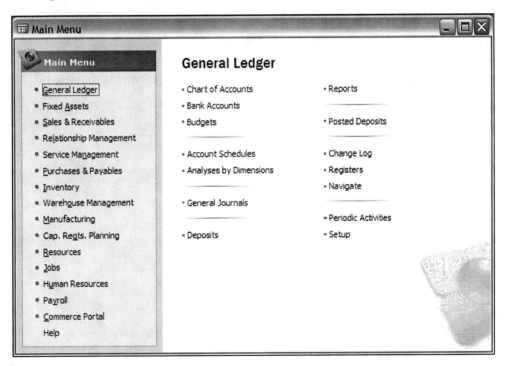

Clicking on an entry in the left-hand panel would change the display in the right-hand panel. This was accomplished by a series of forms, one for each functional menu (e.g. **General Ledger, Fixed Assets**, etc.). These forms were stacked one on top of the other, with the **Visible** property being used to determine which specific menu form was visible at any point in time.

When an entry in the left panel was clicked, it would set its designated menu form **Visible** and set all the others as **Not Visible**. Because each menu was a form, any desired C/AL logic could be embedded in that form. But this approach had the disadvantage of not allowing users to modify or create their own Shortcut menus. In addition, it did not fit the desired Microsoft model of the Office menu format.

Dataports

Dataports are objects specifically designed for the purpose of importing and exporting external text files. Dataports for text files in standard format, such as .csv files, are quickly and easily created. Conversely, Dataports can be quite complex, manipulating, filtering, and otherwise processing the data. Dataports can be designed to include user involvement to specify filters or the external data file name and path. Or they can be set up to operate totally in the background with no direct user interaction.

Dataport Components

The basic structure of a Dataport is quite similar to that of a report. An NAV Dataport structure may include any or all the following elements. A particular Dataport might utilize only a small number of the possible elements, but many different combinations are possible.

- Dataport Properties
- Dataport Triggers
- Data Items
    ◦ Data Item Properties
    ◦ Data Item Triggers
    ◦ Dataport Fields
        ◦ Field Properties
        ◦ Field Triggers
- Request Form
    ◦ Request Form Properties
    ◦ Request Form Triggers
    ◦ Request Form Controls
        ◦ Request Form Control Properties
- Request Form Control Triggers

Dataports can be either **Import** (reading a text file and updating one or more NAV tables) or **Export** (reading one or more NAV tables and creating a text file output). Depending on whether a Dataport is importing or exporting, different properties and triggers come into play. As a developer you must determine whether your Dataport design is to be used just for **Import**, just for **Export**, or if you will allow the user to dynamically choose **Import** or **Export**.

Dataport Properties

Dataport properties are shown in the following screenshot. A few of these properties are essentially similar to those of other object types such as Reports and Forms. We won't spend much time on these. We will delve into properties that are specific to Dataports.

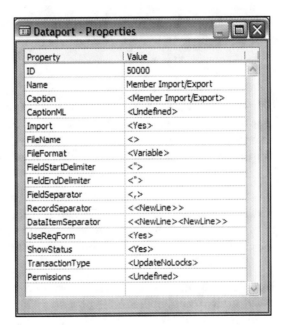

The description is as follows:

- **ID**: The unique dataport object number.
- **Name**: The name by which this dataport is referred to within C/AL code.
- **Caption**: The name that is displayed for this dataport; **Caption** defaults to **Name.**
- **CaptionML**: The **Caption** translation for a defined alternative language.

- **Import**: This can contain the default **<Yes>**, **Yes**, or **No**. It can also be set dynamically (i.e. at run time) in the `OnPreDataportTrigger`. If **Import** is equal to default **<Yes>**, then the user can choose on the Request Form **Options** tab whether the Dataport processing is going to be an **Import** or an **Export**. Otherwise, if **Import** is set to **Yes**, then processing will be an **Import**. If **Import** is set to **No**, then processing will be an **Export**.

  In the latter two cases, the Request Form **Options** tab will not display an option or otherwise hint whether an **Import** or an **Export** is about to be executed. In those cases, you need to make clear what is going to happen, either by properly naming the object or by a message or documentation. Screenshots displaying the two instances of the Request Form **Options** Tab will follow later in this chapter.

> Take note that if you test run a Dataport from within the Designer (using **File | Run**) and the run is an **Import**, then no data will be inserted into the database.

- **FileName**: This can be filled with the predefined path and name of a specific external text data file to be either the source (for **Import**) or target (for **Export**) for the run of the Dataport or this property can be set dynamically. Only one file at a time can be opened, but the file in use can be changed during the execution of the Dataport (a relatively tricky-to-use, seldom used feature).

- **FileFormat**: This specifies whether the file format is to be **Fixed** or **Variable**. It defaults to **<Variable>**. A **Fixed** format file will be processed based on fixed length fields of predefined sizes. A **Variable** format file will be processed based on field delimiters specifying the start and end of all fields, and the separator between each field.

- **FieldStartDelimiter**: This applies to **Variable** format external files only. It defaults to **<">** — double quote, the standard for so-called "comma-delimited" text files. This property supplies the string that will be used as the starting delimiter for each data field in the text file. If this is an **Import**, then the Dataport will look for this string and use the string following, until a **FieldEndDelimiter** string is found, as data. If this is an **Export**, the Dataport will insert this string at the beginning of each data field.

- **FieldEndDelimiter**: This applies to **Variable** format external files only. It defaults to **<">** — double quote, the standard for so-called "comma-delimited" text files. This property supplies the string that will be used as the ending delimiter for each data field in the text file. This string will be used in similar fashion just to that described for the **FieldStartDelimiter**.

- **FieldSeparator**: This applies to **Variable** format external files only. Defaults to **<,>** — a comma, the standard for so-called "comma delimited" text files. This property supplies the string that will be used as the delimiter between each data field in the text file (looked for on **Imports** or inserted on **Exports**).

- **RecordSeparator**: This defines the string that will be used as the delimiter at the end of each data record in the text file. If this is an **Import**, the Dataport will look for this string to mark the end of each data record. If this is an **Export**, the Dataport will append this string at the end of each data record output. The default is <NewLine> which represents any combination of CR (carriage return - ASCII value 13) and LF (line feed – ASCII value 10) characters.

- **DataItemSeparator**: This defines the string that will be used as the delimiter at the end of each Data Item (e.g. each text file). The default is <NewLine><NewLine>.

- **UseReqForm:** This determines whether a Request Form should be displayed to allow the user choice of Sort Sequence, entry of filters, and other requested control information. The options are **Yes** and **No**. The default is <Yes>.

- **ShowStatus**: This determines whether the processing status and a user-accessible **Cancel** button are shown or not. The options are **Yes** and **No**. The default is <Yes>.

- **TransactionType**: This identifies the Dataport processing Server Transaction Type as **Browse, Snapshot, UpdateNoLocks**, or **Update**. This is an advanced and seldom used property. For more information, you can refer to **Help** files and SQL Server documentation. The default is <UpdateNoLocks>.

- **Permissions**: This provides report-specific setting of permissions, which are rights to access data, subdivided into **Read, Insert, Modify**, and **Delete**. This allows the developer to define report and processing permissions that override the user-by-user permission security setup.

For more information on each of these properties, please look them up in the C/SIDE Reference Guide (i.e. online C/SIDE **Help**). There is a good description of various options and their effects for each of these properties.

Dataport Triggers

The Dataport triggers, shown in the following screenshot, are a relatively simple set. Their description is as follows:

- `Documentation()` is for your documentation comments.
- `OnInitDataport()` executes once when the Dataport is loaded.
- `OnPreDataport()` executes once after the Request Form has completed, after table views and filters have been set. Those can be reset here.

- `OnPostDataport()` executes once after all the data is processed, if the Dataport completes normally.

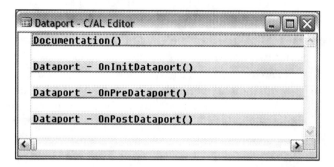

Data Item

Most Dataports have only a single Data Item. A Dataport can have multiple Data Items, but they can only be processed sequentially. Dataport Data Items cannot be nested (i.e. indented) even though the Data Item screen has the indentation buttons visible and active. The one exception is Dataports which create User Portal XML files. It is very rare for a Dataport to have more than one Data Item.

Data Item Properties

Data Item properties are shown in the following screenshot. Most of these are similar to a Report Data Item.

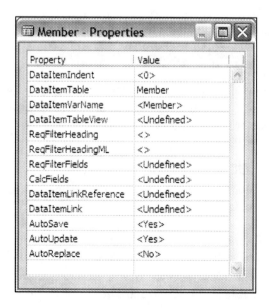

Their description is as follows:

- **DataItemIndent**: This shows the position of referenced data item in the hierarchical structure of the Dataport, but cannot be used for Dataports.

- **DataItemTable**: This names the table assigned to this Data Item.

- **DataItemTableView**: This defines the fixed limits that are to be applied to the Data Item (what key to use, ascending or descending sequence, what filters to apply, etc.).

- **ReqFilterHeader, ReqFilterHeadingML**: The heading that will appear at the top of the Request Form tab for this Data Item.

- **ReqFilterFields**: This allows you to choose certain fields to be named on the appropriate Dataport Request Form tab to make it easier for the user to use those as filter fields.

- **CalcFields**: This names the FlowFields that are to be calculated for each processed record. Because FlowFields do not contain data, they have to be calculated to get exported.

- **DataItemLinkReference**: This names the Data Item in the hierarchy above the Data Item to which this one is linked. Generally not used in Dataports.

- **DataItemLink**: This identifies field-to-field linkage between the data item and its parent data item. Generally not used in Dataports.

- **AutoSave, AutoUpdate,** and **AutoReplace**: All these are only meaningful for **Import**. In an **Import**, they control what the automatic processing defaults are for our data.
    - If **AutoSave** is **No,** then the only processing that occurs for our data is what we do in C/AL code. The default is **Yes**
    - If **AutoSave** is **Yes** and:
        - If **AutoUpdate** is **No** and **AutoReplace** is **No,** then imported data will be inserted in the database unless a duplicate primary key is identified. In that case, a run-time error occurs and processing is terminated.
        - If **AutoUpdate** is **Yes** and **AutoReplace** is **No,** then imported data is inserted in the database with duplicate key items updating existing records. Updating means filled fields in the import data will overwrite existing data; empty fields in the import data will have no effect. This is the default setting.
        - If **AutoReplace** is **Yes,** then imported data is inserted in the database with duplicate key items overwriting existing records. In this case, the **AutoUpdate** value doesn't matter.

Data Item Triggers

The following screenshot shows the Data Item triggers:

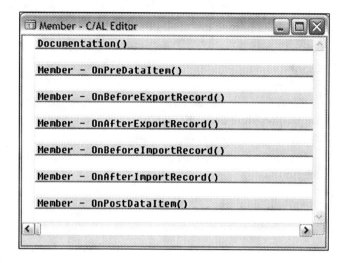

Their description is as follows:

- `OnPreDataItem()`: the logical place for pre-processing to take place that wasn't handled in `OnInitDataport()` or `OnPreDataport()`.

- `OnBeforeExportRecord()`: for **Export** only. This trigger is executed after the NAV record has been retrieved from the database, but not yet exported. This is where you can make decision about exporting a particular record or not. The retrieved record is available in the Data Item at this point for examination or manipulation.

- `OnAfterExportRecord()`: for **Export** only. This trigger is executed after the data has been written out to the text file. In the case where you need to do some type of post-output processing on a per-record basis, that code can be put in this trigger.

- `OnBeforeImportRecord()`: for **Import** only. This trigger is executed before the next external record is read in, allowing you to manipulate the external file before reading it.

- `OnAfterImportRecord()`: for **Import** only. This trigger is executed after the next external record has been read and mapped into the input fields, but before it has been written out to the database. This allows you to do whatever pre-processing or exception processing you need to do (including skipping or exiting records).

Dataport Fields

Dataport fields can be added in several ways. Each of them is called by the **Field Designer** screen, accessed from **View | Dataport Fields**. For our example, we will create a Dataport with one **DataItem,** our `Member` table. After calling the **Field Designer,** it will look similar to the following screenshot:

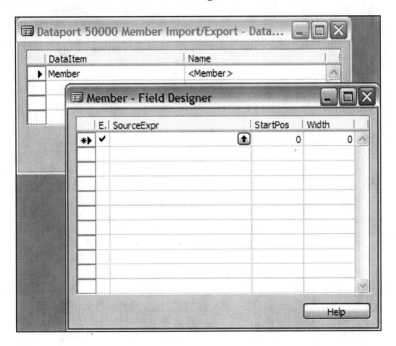

The first, and most obvious, method of defining Dataport fields would be to click on the **Lookup arrow** in the **SourceExpr** column. This will bring up a field list for the highlighted **DataItem** (in this example, a list of the fields in the Member table).

You can highlight and select (via the **OK** button) fields one at a time to be inserted in the **Field Designer** list.

A second method of defining Dataport fields is to call up the **Field Menu** by clicking on the icon at the top of the **Object Designer** form, as shown in the following screenshot:

On the **Field Menu**, you can highlight any number of fields from the **DataItem**, and then right-click in the first empty **Field Designer SourceExpr** line. You will be presented with the message shown in the following screenshot. If you respond **Yes**, the highlighted fields will be added to the **Field Designer** list (duplicate entries are allowed). Using this method you can load the **Field Designer** with any number of the **DataItem** fields with a minimum amount of effort. In fact, with just four quick clicks, you can insert all the fields at once (click on the **Field Menu** icon, click on the upper left corner of the **Field Menu** list, right-click on the empty **SourceExpr** line, and finally click on **Yes**).

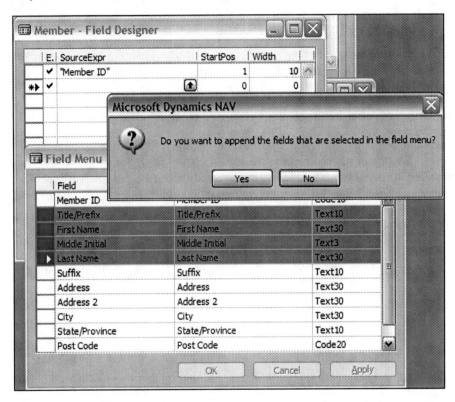

The third method relates to referencing Global variables rather than fields within a **DataItem**. Often when you want to manipulate data you are importing, rather than having the initial import directly into **DataItem** fields, you will import into working storage (Global) variables. In this case, you cannot look up the variables. You must simply type the variable name into the **SourceExpr** field. Error-checking of these entries only occurs when the object is compiled. Therefore it's a good idea to press *F11* every time you enter a Global variable. This will compile the Dataport object to catch typos or missing variable definitions.

Some examples of instances where you might want to import into Global variables are:

- When an incoming text field might be longer than the defined field in the database

- When you need to replace the incoming data element with other information, e.g. the incoming data has text for **Yes** or **No** and your data field is a Boolean to which you need to assign TRUE or FALSE

- When you need to do a format conversion of the data, e.g. the incoming data is dates in the text format of 'mm/dd/yy', including the slashes, and your data field has a Data Type of Date

- When there is data in the incoming record that you will use for computation or decision making in a preprocess mode, but which will not be imported to the Data Item

A wide variety of other instances are certainly possible based on your specific situation.

In the **Field Designer**, there are two columns headed **StartPos** and **Width** (shown in the following screenshot). These columns are only meaningful for Dataports whose **FileFormat** is **Fixed**. If the **FileFormat** is **Variable**, any data in the **StartPos** and **Width** columns is ignored.

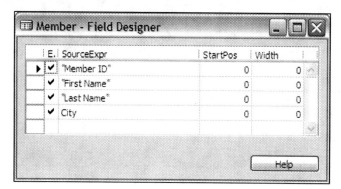

Dataport Field Properties

Dataport Field properties are shown in the following screenshot:

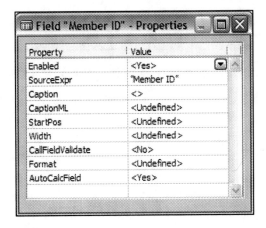

Their description is as follows:

- **Enabled**: This indicates whether data will be placed in the field for **Export** or data in the field will be transferred to the database for **Import.**

- **SourceExpr**: This must be a valid C/AL variable name for **Import**, either from the **DataItem** or a Global variable. For **Export**, this can be any C/AL expression, i.e. you could export the result of a formula or a constant.

- **Caption** and **CaptionML**: The field name displayed, depending on the language option in use.

- **StartPos**: The position of the leftmost character of this data field in the external text record format—for **Fixed FileFormat** only.

- **Width**: The number of characters in this data field in the external text record format—for **Fixed FileFormat** only.

- **CallFieldValidate**: This applies to **Import** and **DataItem** fields only. If this property is **Yes**, then whenever the field is imported into the database, the OnValidate() trigger of the field will be executed.

- **Format**: This applies to **Export** only. This property can contain any NAV Format expression, standard or custom, compatible with the data type of this field.

- **AutoCalcField**: It applies to **Export** and Flowfield Data Fields only. If this property is set to **Yes**, the field will be calculated before it is retrieved from the database. Otherwise, a Flowfield would export as an empty field.

Dataport Field Triggers

There are two Dataport Field triggers as shown in the following screenshot:

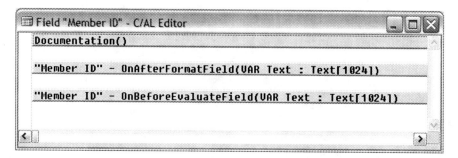

Their description is as follows:

- `OnAfterFormatField` applies to **Export** only. This trigger allows access to the data field being exported after it has been formatted for export, but before it has been written to the external text file. The data will be in the System variable `Text` with a maximum length of `1024` characters.

- `OnBeforeEvaluateField` applies to **Import** only. This trigger allows access to the data field being imported from the external text file before it has been processed in any way. The data will be in the System variable `Text` with a maximum length of `1024` characters.

XMLports

XML is eXtensible Markup Language, a structured text format that was developed specifically to describe data to be shared by dissimilar systems. Because the manual creation and handling of XML-formatted data is rather tedious and very subject to error, NAV has XMLports, a data import/export function that processes XML-formatted data only. Use of XMLports allows the setup of XML-based communication with another system.

 XML is very important because in the future, most system-to-system communication will be built on XML documents.

XML data is text based, with each piece of information structured in one of two basic formats:

- `<StartTag>data value</EndTag>` (an **Element** format)
- `<Data Item Name = "data value">` (an **Attribute** format)

Single or double quotes can be used in an attribute. Elements are considered more general purpose than Attributes, probably because they are easier to parse and generate simpler data structures when there are multiple entries created for one level. Complex data structures are built up of combinations of these two formats. For example:

```
<Table='Sample XML format'>
    <Record>
            <Data Item 1>12345</Data Item 1>
            <Data Item 2>23456</Data Item 2>
    </Record>
    <Record>
            <Data Item 1>987</Data Item 1>
    </Record>
    <Record>
            <Data Item 1>22233</Data Item 1>
            <Data Item 2>7766</Data Item 2>
    </Record>
</Table>
```

In this case we have a set of data identified as a `Table` labeled `'Sample XML format'`, containing three `Records`, each `Record` containing data in one or two fields named `Data Item 1` and `Data Item 2`. The data is clearly structured and in text format so that it can be read and processed by any system that is prepared to read this particular XML format. If the field tags are well designed, the data becomes readily interpretable by normal humans as well. The key to successful exchange of data using XML is simply the sharing and common interpretation of the format between the transmitter and recipient of the information.

XML is a standard format in the sense that the data structure options are clearly defined. But it is very flexible in the sense that the identifying tag names in `<>` brackets and the related data structures that can be defined and handled are totally open ended. XML data structures can be as simple as a flat file consisting of a set of identically formatted records or as complex as an order structure with headers containing a variety of data items, combined with associated detail lines containing their own variety of data items.

XMLport Components

Although in theory XMLports can operate in both an import and an export mode, in practice individual XMLport objects tend to be dedicated to either import or export. In general, this allows the internal logic to be simpler. XMLports consist of fewer components than do Dataports or Reports.

XMLports have no Request Forms or Data Items (they cannot run, except by being invoked from another object type). The components of XMLports are as follows:

- XMLport Properties
- XMLport Triggers
- XMLport Lines
  - ° XMLport Line Properties (aka fields)
- XMLport Line Triggers

XMLport Properties

XMLport properties are shown in the following screenshot:

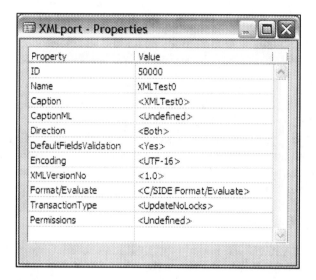

Their description is as follows:

- **ID**: The unique XMLport object number.
- **Name**: The name by which this XMLport is referred to within C/AL code.
- **Caption**: The name that is displayed for this XMLport; **Caption** defaults to **Name**.

- **CaptionML:** The **Caption** translation for a defined alternative language.

- **Direction:** This defines whether this XMLport can only **Import, Export,** or **<Both>** (default).

- **DefaultFieldsValidation:** This defines the default value (**Yes** or **No**) for the **FieldValidate** property for individual XMLport data fields. The default for this field is **Yes**, which would in turn set the default for individual field **FieldValidate** properties to **Yes**.

- **Encoding:** This defines the character encoding option to be used, **UTF-8** or **UTF-16**. **UTF-16** is the default. This is inserted into the heading of the XML document.

- **XMLVersionNo:** This defines to which version of XML the document conforms, **Version 1.0** or **1.1**. The default is **Version 1.0**. This is inserted into the heading of the XML document.

- **Format/Evaluation:** This can be **C/SIDE Format/Evaluate** or **XML Format Evaluate**. This property defines whether the external text data is (for imports) or will be (for exports) XML data types or C/SIDE data types. Default processing for all fields in each case will be appropriate to the defined data type. If the external data does not fit in either of these categories, then the XML data fields must be processed through a temporary table.

  This approach will have the external data read into text data fields with data conversion logic done in C/AL into data types that can then be stored in the NAV database. Additional information is available in the online C/SIDE Reference Guide (i.e. the **Help** files). The default value for this property is **C/SIDE Format/Evaluate**.

- **TransactionType:** This identifies the XMLport processing Server Transaction Type as **Browse, Snapshot, UpdateNoLocks,** or **Update**. This is an advanced and seldom-used property. For more information, you can refer to the **Help** files and SQL Server documentation.

- **Permissions:** This provides report-specific setting of permissions, which are rights to access data, subdivided into **Read, Insert, Modify,** and **Delete**. This allows the developer to define permissions that override the user-by-user permissions security setup.

XMLport Triggers

The XMLport has a limited set of triggers as shown in the following screenshot:

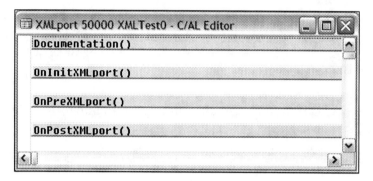

Their description is as follows:

- `Documentation()` is for your documentation comments.
- `OnInitXMLport()` is executes once when the XMLport is loaded.
- `OnPreXMLport()` is executes once after the table views and filters have been set. Those can be reset here.
- `OnPostXMLport()` is executes once after all the data is processed, if the XMLport completes normally.

XMLport Data Lines

An XMLport can contain any number of data lines. The data lines are laid out in a strict hierarchical structure, with the elements and attributes mapping exactly, one for one, in the order of the data fields in the external text file, the XML document.

The sample XMLport in the following screenshot shows data being extracted from the `Customer` table and `Country/Region` table to create an XML document file.

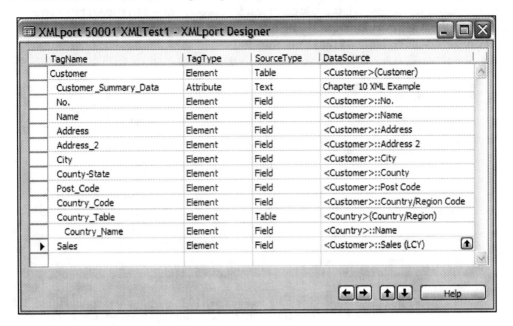

The last data line in the sample (**Sales**, referencing a FlowField) has the **AutoCalcField** property set to **Yes** (the default) so that the FlowField will be calculated before it is outputted (see the preceding screenshot).

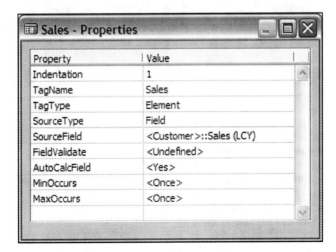

The following two screenshots show the C/AL code that is a part of this sample XMLport. The line of code in the first screenshot assigns a text literal value to the variable (**Chapter 10 XML Example**) defined by its placement in the **DataSource** column in the **XMLPort Designer**. The line of code in the second screenshot sets a filter on the Country table so that only the single Country Name associated with the Customer record's Country Code will be output.

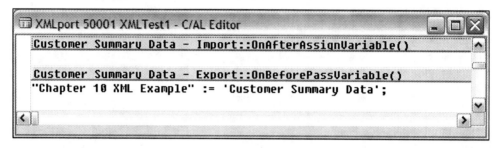

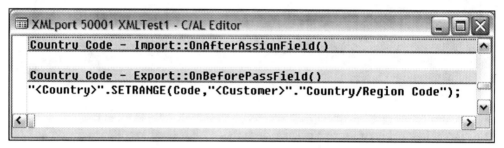

The XML document output from this sample XMLport is shown in the following screenshot. Note that the XML document is headed with a line showing the XML version and encoding type. That is followed by the text literal, which we coded, then the selected data.

```xml
<?xml version="1.0" encoding="UTF-16" standalone="no" ?>
<Customer Customer_Summary_Data="Customer Summary Data">
    <No.>10000</No.>
    <Name>The Cannon Group PLC</Name>
    <Address>192 Market Square</Address>
    <Address_2 />
    <City>Birmingham</City>
    <County-State />
    <Post_Code>B27 4KT</Post_Code>
    <Country_Code>GB</Country_Code>
    <Country_Table>
        <Country_Name>Great Britain</Country_Name>
    </Country_Table>
    <Sales>17120.16</Sales>
</Customer>
```

XMLports cannot run directly from a menu command, but must be executed by properly constructed C/AL code. XMLports run from C/AL code that calls the XMLport and streams data either to or from an XML document file. This code is typically written in a Codeunit but can be placed in any object that can contain C/AL code.

This example process is driven by C/AL code in a Codeunit, illustrated in the following screenshot. This is the minimum amount of code required to execute an exporting XMLport. The illustration is as follows:

- Line 1 – Creates the data file to contain the XML document. The variable **OutStreamObj** is defined as Data Type **OutStream**

- Line 2 – Creates an **OutputStream**.

- Line 3 – Executes the specific **XMLport**.

- Line 4 – Closes the text data file.

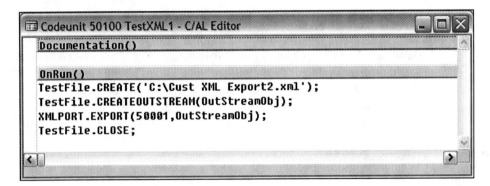

```
Codeunit 50100 TestXML1 - C/AL Editor

Documentation()

OnRun()
TestFile.CREATE('C:\Cust XML Export2.xml');
TestFile.CREATEOUTSTREAM(OutStreamObj);
XMLPORT.EXPORT(50001,OutStreamObj);
TestFile.CLOSE;
```

An equivalent Codeunit designed to execute an importing XMLport would look similar to the following screenshot. The **InStreamObj** variable is defined as Data Type **InStream**.

```
Codeunit 50101 TestXML2 - C/AL Editor

Documentation()

OnRun()
TestFile.OPEN('C:\Cust XML Export.xml');
TestFile.CREATEINSTREAM(InStreamObj);
XMLPORT.IMPORT(50002,InStreamObj);
TestFile.CLOSE;
```

XMLport Line Properties

The XMLport Line properties which are active on a line depend on the contents of **SourceType** property. The first four properties listed are common to all three **SourceType** values (**Text, Table,** or **Field**) and the other properties specific to each are listed below the screenshots showing all the properties for each **SourceType**.

- **Indentation**: This indicates at what subordinate level in the hierarchy of the XMLport this entry exists. Indentation **0** is the primary level, parent to all higher numbered levels. Indentation **1** is a child of indentation **0**, indentation **2** is a child of **1**, and so forth. Only one Indentation **0** is allowed in an XMLport (i.e. only one primary table).

- **TagName**: This defines the Tag that will be used in the XML document to open and close the data associated with this level. If the Tag is **Customer**, then the start and ending tags will be `<Customer>` and `</Customer>`. No spaces are allowed in a **TagName**; you can use underscores, dashes, periods.

- **TagType**: This defines if this data item is an **Element** or an **Attribute**.

- **SourceType**: This defines the type of data this field corresponds to in the NAV database. The choices are **Text, Table,** and **Field**. Text means that the value in the **SourceField** property will act as a Global variable and, typically, must be dealt with in embedded C/AL code. Table means that the value in the **SourceField** property will refer to an NAV table. Field means that the value in the **SourceField** property will refer to an NAV field within a table.

SourceType as Text

The following screenshot shows the properties for **SourceType** as **Text**:

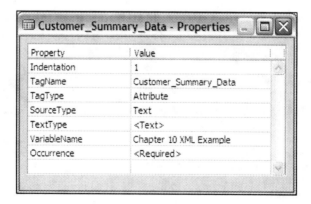

The description of the Text-specific properties is as follows:

- **TextType**: This defines the NAV Data Type as **Text** or **BigText**. Text is the default.
- **VariableName**: This contains the name of the Global variable, which can be referenced by C/AL code.

The **Occurrence** property is discussed later in this chapter.

SourceType as Table

The following screenshot shows the properties for **SourceType** as **Table**:

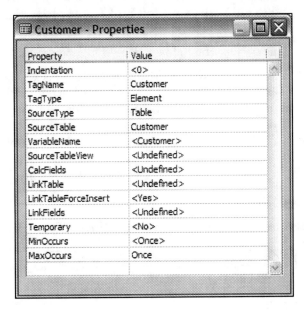

The description of the Table-specific properties is as follows:

- **SourceTable**: This defines the NAV table being referenced.
- **VariableName**: This defines the name to be used in C/AL code for the NAV table. Essentially, this is a definition of a Global variable.
- **SourceTableView**: This enables the developer to define a view by choosing a key and sort order or by applying filters on the table.
- **CalcFields**: This lists the FlowFields in the table that are to be automatically calculated.

- **LinkTable**: This allows the linking of a field in a higher-level item to a key field in a lower-level item. If, for example, you were exporting all the Purchase Orders for a Vendor, you might Link the Buy-From Vendor No. in a Purchase Header to the No. in a Vendor record. The **LinkTable** in this case would be Vendor and **LinkField** would be No.; therefore **LinkTable** and **LinkFields** work together. Use of the **LinkTable** and **LinkFields** operates the same as applying a filter on the higher-level table data so that only records relating to the defined lower-level table and field are processed. See the online C/SIDE Reference Guide **Help** for more detail.

- **LinkTableForceInsert**: This can be set to force insertion of the linked table data and execution of the related `OnAfterInitRecord()` trigger. This property is tied to the **LinkTable** and **LinkFields** properties. It also applies to **Import**.

- **LinkFields**: This defines the fields involved in a table + field linkage.

- **Temporary**: This defaults to **No**. If this property is set to Yes, it allows the creation of a Temporary table in working storage. Data imported into this table can then be evaluated, edited, and manipulated before being written out to the database. This Temporary table has the same capabilities and limitations as a Temporary table defined as a Global variable.

The **MinOccurs** and **MaxOccurs** properties are discussed later in this chapter.

SourceType as Field

The following screenshot shows the properties for **SourceType** as **Field**:

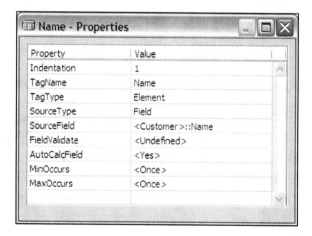

The description of the Field-specific properties is as follows:

- **SourceField**: This defines the data field being referenced. It may be a field in any defined table.
- **FieldValidate**: This applies to **Import** only. If this property is Yes, then whenever the field is imported into the database, the OnValidate() trigger of the field will be executed.
- **AutoCalcField**: This applies to **Export** and Flowfield Data fields only. If this property is set to **Yes**, the field will be calculated before it is retrieved from the database. Otherwise, a flowfield would export as an empty field.

The details of the **MinOccurs** and **MaxOccurs** properties are as follows:

Element or Attribute

An **Element** data item may appear many times but an **Attribute** data item may only appear (at most) once; the occurrence control properties differ based on the **TagType**.

TagType as Element

The Element-specific properties are as follows:

- **MinOccurs**: This defines the minimum number of times this data item can occur in the XML document. This property can be **Zero** or **Once** (the default).
- **MaxOccurs**: This defines the maximum number of times this data item can occur in the XML document. This property can be **Once** or **Unbounded**. Unbounded (the default) means any number of times.

TagType as Attribute

The Attribute-specific property is as follows:

- **Occurrence**: This is either **Required** (the default) or **Optional**, depending on the text file being imported.

XMLport Line Triggers

The XMLport line triggers are shown in the following screenshot:

```
Test Text - Export::OnBeforePassVariable()

Test Text - Import::OnAfterAssignVariable()

Test Table - Import::OnAfterInsertRecord()

Test Table - Export::OnPreXMLItem()

Test Table - Export::OnAfterGetRecord()

Test Table - Import::OnAfterInitRecord()

Test Table - Import::OnBeforeInsertRecord()

Test Field - Import::OnAfterAssignField()

Test Field - Export::OnBeforePassField()
```

The triggers appearing for the XMLport data line depend on the values of the **DataType** field. As you can see in the preceding screenshot, there are different triggers depending whether **DataType** is **Text**, **Table** or **Field**.

DataType as Text

The triggers for DataType as text are:

- `Export::onBeforePassVariable()`, for **Export** only. This trigger is typically used for manipulation of the text variable.

- `Import::OnAfterAssignVariable()`, for **Import** only. This trigger gives you access to the imported value in text format.

DataType as Table

The triggers for DataType as table are:

- `Import::OnAfterInsertRecord()`, for **Import** only. This trigger is typically used when the data is being imported into Temporary tables. This is where you would put the C/AL code to build and insert records for the permanent database table(s).

- `Export::OnPreXMLItem()`, for **Export** only. This trigger is typically used for setting filters and doing initializations before finding and processing the first database record.

- `Export::OnAfterGetRecord()`, for **Export** only. This trigger allows access to the data after the record is retrieved from the NAV database. This trigger is typically used to allow manipulation of table fields being exported and calculated depending on record contents.

- `Import::OnAfterInitRecord()`, for **Import** only. This trigger is typically used to check whether or not a record should be processed further or to manipulate the data.

- `Import::OnBeforeInsertRecord()`, for **Import** only. This is another place where you can manipulate data before it is inserted into the target table. This trigger is executed after the `OnAfterInitRecord()` trigger.

DataType as Field

The triggers for DataType as field are:

- `Import::OnAfterAssignField()`, for **Import** only. This trigger provides access to the imported data value for evaluation or manipulation before outputting to the database.

- `Export::OnBeforePassField()`, for **Export** only. This trigger provides access to the data field value just before the data is exported.

Advanced Interface Tools

NAV has a number of other methods of interfacing with the world outside its database. We will review those very briefly here. To learn more about these you should begin by reviewing the applicable material in the Application Designer's Guide and other documentation as well as the online C/SIDE **Help** material. You should also study any sample code, especially that in the standard system as represented by the Cronus Demonstration Database. And, of course, you should take advantage of any other resources available including the Internet forums focusing on NAV.

Automation Controller

One option for NAV interfacing is by connection to COM Automation servers. A key group of Automation servers are the Microsoft Office products. Automation components can be instantiated, accessed, and manipulated from within NAV objects using C/AL code. Data can be transferred back and forth between the NAV database and COM Automation components.

Limitations include the fact that only non-visual controls are supported. You cannot use a COM component as a control on an NAV Form object. However, a COM component can have its own window providing an interactive graphical user interface.

Some common uses of Automation Controller interfaces are to:

- Populate Word template documents to create more attractive communications with customers, vendors, and prospects (e.g. past due notices, purchase orders, promotional letters)

- Move data to Excel spreadsheets for manipulation (e.g. last year's sales data to create this year's projections)

- Move data to and from Excel spreadsheets for manipulation (e.g. last year's financial results out and next year's budgets back in)

- Use Excel's graphing capabilities to enhance management reports

- Access to and use of ActiveX Data Objects (ADO) Library objects to support access to and from external databases and their associated systems

NAV Communication Component

The NAV Communication Component is an automation server that provides a consistent API (Application Programming Interface) communications bus adapter. Adapters for use with Microsoft Message Queue, Socket, and Named Pipe transport mechanisms are supplied with NAV. Adapters for other transport mechanisms can be added.

The NAV Communication Component enables input/output data-streaming communication with external services. Function calls can be done on either a synchronous or asynchronous basis. The details on NAV Communication Component are available in the **Help** file devguide.chm.

Linked Server Data Sources

The two table properties, **LinkedObject** and **LinkedInTransaction**, are available when the NAV database is SQL Server. Use of these properties in the prescribed fashion allows data access, including views, in linked server data sources such as Excel, Access, another instance of SQL Server, and even an Oracle database. For additional information, see the Application Designer's Guide section on Linked Objects.

NAV ODBC

The NAV ODBC interface (referred to as N/ODBC) is an NAV-specific implementation of the standard ODBC (Open DataBase Connectivity) toolset. N/ODBC is simple to install and, once installed, can be made readily available to users to directly extract data from the NAV database. N/ODBC can only be used with the C/SIDE database, not with the SQL Server database option.

Because N/ODBC Write operations bypass all NAV's triggers (i.e. no business logic is processed), no N/ODBC writing should occur except under the most controlled conditions. In Read mode, N/ODBC operates very similarly to any other ODBC connection.

There is a separate N/ODBC Driver Guide for reference, which must be reviewed prior to installing N/ODBC. N/ODBC must be licensed separately.

C/OCX

NAV interfaces with properly installed and registered Custom Controls (i.e. .ocx routines) through the C/OCX interface granule. The interface and limitations are similar to those available for Automation Server Controls. Using C/OCX is one way, generally a relatively economical way, to interface between NAV and various other software products or hardware products. An excellent example would be to use Microsoft Common Dialog Control to invoke the standard File Open/Save dialog for user convenience.

C/FRONT

C/FRONT is a programming interface that supports connection between C language-compatible software and the NAV database. C/FRONT provides a library of functions callable from C programs. These functions provide access to all aspects of the NAV database with the goal of providing a tool to integrate external applications with NAV. There is a separate manual called C/FRONT Reference Guide.

Since its original development, C/FRONT has been enhanced to provide its API access to languages other than C and C++. Earlier, C/FRONT was made usable by additional languages such as Visual Basic. Now, it can be used by any .NET language.

NAV Application Server (NAS)

The NAV Application Server is a middle-tier server than runs as a service. It is essentially an automated user client. Because NAS was created primarily using components from the standard NAV C/SIDE client module, NAS can access all of NAV's business rules. NAS is a very powerful tool, but it can run only NAV Report and Codeunit objects and only those that do not invoke a graphical user interface of any type. Any error messages that are generated by an NAS process are logged in the Event Viewer or written to a file defined when NAS is started from a command line.

If there are processing tasks that need to be automated, NAS is a very good solution. However, NAS operates essentially the same as any other NAV C/SIDE client (except for being automated). It processes all requests in its queue one at a time, in the same manner as the GUI client. Therefore, as a developer, you need to limit the number of concurrent calls to an NAS instance as the queue should remain short to allow timely communications between interfaces. If necessary, additional NAV Application Servers can be added to the system configuration (with appropriate license purchases).

Summary

In this chapter, we have focused on interfaces with NAV. The initial area of interface we discussed was user management and accessing the system. The other interfaces we discussed tie to other systems or even hardware as well. Data is moved into and out of NAV, both on a batch and interactive basis, either in an automatic or a user-controlled mode. And some of the interfaces created can even facilitate controlling other systems from NAV or the other way around.

In this chapter we have covered MenuSuites, Dataports, XMLports, and advanced Interfaces. In the next chapter we will cover some additional advanced and broader topics related to overall system design and implementation.

11
Design to Succeed

Look, we'd get along much faster if we knew what we were doing — Doctor Who

Whatever we do to change or enhance an NAV system, whether developing a minor modification for a single site, or developing a full-blown system for many installations, we need to plan for the future. That means we need to consider the effect of our design and our code in variety of ways over and above the functionality we are initially attempting to achieve.

We should consider the fact that someone else can meet up with our code in the course of their maintenance activities. We should consider the fact that regardless of the database platform in use, Microsoft SQL Server is likely to be the choice in the relatively near future. We should also consider the fact that, if this system is performing well for the users, it needs to be upgraded to a new version at some point.

Before we begin writing code, we should have a firm definition of what we aim to accomplish and how it is going to be accomplished. We need to design our changes to the database and the process flow not only so that they work well for the intended purpose, but also so that they do not negatively impact on previously implemented code.

No matter how much effort we put into our designs creating clean and simple code, we must test it thoroughly and realistically. These systems are very complex and the results of our "simple" changes often have significant unintended consequences. *Isaac Asimov* once made a statement to the effect that many significant discoveries are preceded by the comment "That's funny…"

If this book has helped you feel that you are ready to move from the status of beginning C/AL Developer to intermediate or even advanced, there are quite a number of other issues that you will need to deal with that we haven't discussed yet. Fortunately, there are other resources available to use that can help you. In addition, if you rigorously apply the techniques you've learned here, you will have a good foundation on which to build advanced knowledge.

Design for Efficiency

Whenever you are designing a new modification, you not only need to design to address the defined needs, but also to provide a solution that processes efficiently. An inefficient solution carries unnecessary ongoing costs. Many of the things that you can do to design an efficient solution are relatively simple.

Disk I/O

The slowest thing in any computer system is the disk I/O. Disk I/O takes the most time, generally more time than any other system activity. Therefore, if you have to choose where to concentrate your efforts in designing with respect to efficiency, you should focus on minimizing the disk I/O.

The most critical elements are the design of the keys, the number of keys, the design of the SIFT fields, the number of SIFT fields, the design of the filters, and the frequency of accesses of data (especially FlowFields). If your system is going to have five or ten users, processing a couple of thousand order lines per day and not being heavily modified, then you probably won't have much trouble. But if you are installing a system with one or more of the following attributes, which can have a significant effect on the amount of disk I/O, you will need to be very careful with your design and implementation.

- Critical attributes
    - large number of users
    - high transaction volumes
    - large stored data volumes
    - significant modifications
- Very complex business rules

Locking

One important aspect of the design of an integrated system such as NAV, that is often overlooked until it rears its ugly head after the system goes into production, is the issue of "**Locking**". Locking occurs when one process has control of a data element, record, or group of records (e.g. table) for the purpose of updating the data within the range of the locked data and, at the same time, another process requests the use of some portion of that data but finds it to be locked by the first process.

In the worst case, there is a design flaw; each process has data locked that the other process needs and neither process can proceed. This is a **"deadlock"**. Your job as a developer or system implementer is to minimize the locking problems and eliminate any deadlocks.

Locking interference between processes in an asynchronous processing environment is inevitable. There are always going to be points in the system where one process instance locks out another one momentarily. The secret to success is to minimize the frequency of these and the time length of each lock. Locking becomes a problem when the locks are held too long and the other locked-out processes are unreasonably delayed.

You might ask "What is an unreasonably delay?" For the most part, a delay becomes unreasonable when the human beings, whom we call users, can tell it is happening. If the users see stopped processes or simply experience counter-intuitive processing time lengths (i.e. a process that seems ought to take 10 seconds actually takes two minutes), then the delays are probably unreasonable. Of course, the ultimate unreasonable delay is the one that does not allow the work to get done in the available time.

The obvious question is how to avoid locking problems. The best solution is simply to speed up the processing. That will reduce the number of lock conflicts that arise. Important recommendations for speed include:

- Restricting the number of active keys
- Restricting the number of active SIFT fields, eliminating them when feasible
- Carefully reviewing the keys, not necessarily using the "factory default" options
- Making sure that all disk accessing code is SQL Server optimized

Some additional steps that can be taken to minimize locking problems are:

- Always process tables in the same relative order.
- When a common set of tables will be accessed and updated, lock a "standard" master table first (e.g. when working on Orders, always lock the Order Header table first).
- Process data in small quantities (e.g. process 10 records or one order, then COMMIT, which releases the lock).
- In long process loops, process a SLEEP command in combination with an appropriate COMMIT command to allow other processes to gain control
- Shift long-running processes to off-hours.

For more information, refer to the relevant documentation. There are several NAV documents containing valuable SQL Server recommendations including:

- The Application Designer's Guide
- Installation & System Management: SQL Server Option for the C/SIDE Client
- Microsoft Business Solutions — Navision SQL Server Option Resource Kit Whitepaper.

C/SIDE versus SQL Server Databases

The issue of the two available databases for NAV creates an interesting set of tensions. The original C/SIDE database is so simple to use and is so low in cost, that it has many fans. On the other hand, SQL Server is considered as state-of-the-art technology, very powerful and flexible, deserving of full faith and trust. Let us take a look at some of the differences between the two database implementations as they affect NAV in a production environment. They are as follows:

Some important areas of difference between the two NAV database options		
Area of difference	**NAV C/SIDE database**	**Microsoft SQL Server**
Maximum database size	256 Gigabytes (128 GB practical)	1 Terabyte
Hardware resources required	Less than SQL	More than C/SIDE for both memory and disk
Disk configuration recommended (based on experience, not the manual)	Raid 1 (Mirrored)	Raid 1 for the OS and separately for the Log File. Raid 10 (Mirrored and Striped and Non-parity) for the data, as many drives as economics permit
Multiple processor support	No	Yes
Versioning	Embedded, behind the scenes, provides extremely fast and simple crash recovery	Simulated via datetime stamps, not built into the database system, more accessible in case of a problem
Backup/Restore	Simple, minimal options, relatively fast	Several options, some faster options provided but full scale restore slower than C/SIDE
SIFT	Integral, embedded in the database's index structure, very fast	Not part of the database, implemented as another table layer, slower
Object code design	Optimized for the C/SIDE database	Each succeeding version has improved SQL performance; still more possible and desirable. V5.0 is much improved.
Implementation effort	Very small	Any sizable installation requires significant setup and tailoring of the database, the tables and the I/O routines to assure a successful operation
Locking problem potential	Very low	High unless the implementation tailoring is well done

Some important areas of difference between the two NAV database options – cont'd		
Area of difference	**NAV C/SIDE database**	**Microsoft SQL Server**
Administrative tools	Minimal	Many
Tuning	Very little possible	Much possible, much required
Server locking and I/O choices	Simple	Complex and sometime surprising
Locking	At the table only	Row, multi-row, table
Typical I/O commands	Find('-'), Find('+')	FindFirst, FindLast, FindSet
Collation Sequence	Fixed	Choose one of two options
Data Security	Table Level	Record Level
Reporting capabilities	Relatively limited and technically difficult to use	Very many options now and more coming
Integration with other systems	Feasible through text files (including XML) or N/ODBC or C/OCX or C/FRONT interfaces; data insert must be through NAV C/AL to invoke business rules	Easy to extract data directly via SQL access, but not so easy to get the right data without going through NAV; data insert should be handled the same way as with the C/SIDE database
Administration	Very little required except to expand the database as needed	Requires a NAV knowledgeable DBA readily available and providing regular maintenance
Cost, both initial and ongoing	Less	More
Future	Limited future, no significant R&D investment	This is the option strongly recommended by Microsoft

It depends on your environment which of these differences is the most important. There is little doubt that at some point in the future of NAV, SQL Server will be the only real option. It is the product in which Microsoft is investing and which generates the most revenue. For example, to use the 3-tier structure and the new SharePoint-based client planned for V5.1, it will be necessary to operate on the SQL Server database.

Among the many challenging issues in current installations, there are some items that affect daily productivity of the system. According to specialists in NAV SQL Server installations, it is very important to set up the system correctly at the beginning, making whatever adjustments are appropriate relative to the maintenance of indexes and SIFT fields. Even after the system has been properly set up, it must receive regular, competent maintenance by a skilled NAV SQL Server expert. Some third-party tools are also available in the market to help address the NAV-specific issues of SQL Server installation maintenance. They still require expert hands at the controls.

Conversely, the C/SIDE database requires an absolute minimum of maintenance. Many C/SIDE database installations have operated for years with only rare attention from an experienced technician.

If, as a developer, you are targeting your code to run in a SQL Server environment, you need to make sure that you understand and appreciate the SQL Server-specific issues. You must take advantage of the SQL Server-specific I/O commands to make your functions more efficient. They should not cause problems if your code is also used in a C/SIDE database environment. If your code may be used in either environment, you should target SQL Server.

SQL Server I/O Commands

C/AL I/O statements are converted by the C/SIDE compiler into T-SQL statements to be directed to SQL Server. If you want to optimize your C/AL code for the SQL Server environment, you need to learn about how various C/AL code sequences are interpreted for SQL Server, how SIFT works in SQL Server, and how to optimize key handling in SQL Server. As stated earlier, the same C/AL code will almost always work for both C/SIDE and SQL Server database platforms. But it does not mean that the same code is the best choice for both.

There are several sources of information about NAV and SQL Server, but none of them is very complete yet. The sources include Application Designer's Guide and the SQL Server Resource Kit, especially the SQL Server Option Resource Kit whitepaper. You can also find additional information and assistance on www.mibuso.com and www.dynamicsuser.net. Finally, there are third party seminars and training programs available led by experts in this area.

Three commands, FINDFIRST, FINDLAST, and FINDSET, have been added to C/AL for helping the compiler optimize the generated SQL commands. In the C/SIDE database, the choices of how the data is accessed are relatively straightforward and simple (at least for the developer). But many more options are available for data access in SQL Server. When you properly use the tools and information available to you to allow (normally) or help (not often) SQL Server choose a better data access method, it can make a great deal of difference in processing efficiency. If you use these commands to improve your SQL Server code performance, they will just work fine in the C/SIDE database where they will be translated to work the same as FIND('+'), FIND('-'), and FIND('-') respectively.

FINDFIRST Function

The FINDFIRST function is designed to act the same as FIND('-') but with the advantage (for SQL Server code generation) of explicitly reading only the first record in a set. FINDFIRST is interpreted as a T-SQL statement of the form SELECT TOP 1 *. There are many instances when processing logic only wants to know if a record set has data or not, or wants to access just the first record in the set. FINDFIRST is the right choice in the SQL Server environment for those cases.

The syntax of FINDFIRST is as follows:

```
[BooleanValue :=] RecordName.FINDFIRST
```

FINDLAST Function

The FINDLAST function is designed to act the same as FIND('+') but with the advantage (for SQL Server code generation) of explicitly reading only the last record in a set. There are many instances when processing logic only wants to access just the last record in the set, perhaps to find an entry number in the last entry to be incremented for the next entry, such as when a table like G/L Entries is being updated. FINDLAST should be used in those cases in the SQL Server environment. FINDLAST is interpreted as a T-SQL statement of the form SELECT TOP 1 *, DESC.

The syntax of FINDLAST is as follows:

```
[BooleanValue :=] RecordName.FINDLAST
```

FINDSET Function

The FINDSET function is designed to act the same as FIND('-'), UNTIL NEXT = 0 but with the advantage (for SQL Server code generation) of generating code to read the requested data as a set. This obviously applies to the instances when processing logic wants to access all the records in a set, perhaps to update them. It is quite important for the sake of efficiency to use FINDSET for those situations in the SQL Server environment.

There is a database property, settable for an NAV SQL Server installation, called **Record Set**, which allows an installation to define the default number of records in a set.

The syntax of FINDSET is as follows:

```
[BooleanValue :=] RecordName.FINDSET(UpdateRecordsBoolean,UpdateKeyBo
olean)
```

The UpdateRecordsBoolean parameter must be set to TRUE if any of the data records will be updated during the loop through the set. The UpdateKeyBoolean must be set to TRUE if any of the Key fields will be updated. If UpdateKeyBoolean is TRUE, then UpdateRecordsBoolean must also be TRUE.

FINDFIRST, FINDLAST, and FINDSET

Just as with the earlier described FIND functions, assigning the result of any of these three FINDxxx functions to a BooleanValue is optional. But typically the FIND function is embedded in a condition, which controls subsequent processing appropriately.

FINDFIRST, FINDLAST, and FINDSET all operate under the limits imposed by whatever filters are applied on the subject field. However, in the SQL Server environment, they do not necessarily use whatever key is currently selected by the C/AL code. The T-SQL data request is constructed and SQL Server determines what index to use. It is important in the interest of efficient SQL Server processing to understand what happens and how to optimize the results.

Any FlowFields in the found records are set to zero and must be updated with CALCFIELDS.FINDSET to process the data in ascending sequence.

Design for Updating

One must differentiate between "updating" a system and "upgrading" a system. In general, most of the NAV development work we will do is modifying individual NAV systems to provide tailored functions for end-user firms. Some of those modifications will be created as part of an initial system configuration and implementation, i.e. before the NAV system is in production use. Other such modifications will be targeted at a system that is being used for day to day production. All these cases are "Updating".

Upgrading is when you implement a new version of the base code and port all the previously existing modifications into that new version. We will cover issues involved in upgrading later.

Any time you are updating a production system by applying modifications to it, a considerable amount of care is required. Many of the disciplines that should be followed in such an instance are the same for an NAV system as with any other production application system. But some of the disciplines are specific to NAV and the C/SIDE environment. We'll review a representative list of both types.

Customization Project Recommendations

Some of these recommendations may seem patently obvious. That might be a measure of your experience and your own common sense. Even so, it is surprising that the number of projects go sour because one (or many) of the following suggestions are not considered in the process of developing modifications.

- One modification at a time
- Design thoroughly before coding
- Multi-stage testing
  - ° Cronus for individual objects
  - ° Special test database for functional tests
  - ° Copy of production database for final testing as appropriate
  - ° Setups and implementation
- Testing full features
  - ° User interface tests
  - ° System load tests
  - ° User Training
- Document and deliver
- Follow up and move on

One at a Time

It is very important that changes made to the objects should be made in a very well organized and tightly controlled manner. In most situations, only one developer at a time will make changes to an object. If an object needs to be changed for multiple purposes, the first set of changes should be fully tested (at least through development testing) before the object is released to be modified for a second purpose.

If the project in hand is so large and complex or deadlines are so tight that this approach is not feasible, then you should consider use of a software development version control system such as Microsoft's Visual SourceSafe.

Similarly, as a developer working on a system, you really should only be working on one functional change at a time. That is not to say that you might not be working on changes in two different systems in parallel, but simply that you shouldn't be working on multiple changes in a single system in parallel. It's challenging to keep all the aspects of a single modification to a system under control without having incomplete pieces of several tasks, all floating around in the same system.

If multiple changes need to be made to a single system in parallel, then one approach would be to assign multiple developers, each with their own individual components to address. Another approach would be for each developer to work on their own copy of the development database, with a project librarian assigned to resolve overlapping updates. This is one area where we should learn from the past. In mainframe development environments, having multiple developers working on the same system at the same time was common. Then the coordination problems were addressed and well-documented in professional literature. Similar solutions would still apply.

Design, Design, Design

As mentioned much earlier in this book, the NAV system has made giant strides towards the long standing goal of creating an environment for the developers where the majority of their efforts are spent on design, not on writing code. Design in this case includes functional design (accomplishing the task), system design (the logic of our process), and code design (accomplishing the modification with the least effect on the original system).

It is not unusual, when making a small modification in the NAV environment, to spend several hours designing the modification then only writing a few lines of code. This ratio does not mean you've been wasting time just thinking and planning and not doing anything. In fact, it means you've been working hard to do the right thing. Remember, the less code changed means the less debugging effort required.

Test, Test, Test

As you know, there is no substitute for complete and thorough testing. Fortunately, NAV provides some useful tools to help you to be more efficient than you might be in some other environment.

Cronus-Based Testing

If your modifications are not tied to previous modifications and not tied to specific customer data, then you should use the Cronus database as a test platform. This works well when your target is a database that is not heavily modified in the area on which you are currently working. As the Cronus database is small, you will not get lost in deep piles of data. Most of the master tables are populated, so you don't have to create and populate this information. Setups are done and generally contain reasonably generic information.

If you are operating with an unmodified version of Cronus, you have both the pro and con that your test is not affected by other pre-existing modifications. The advantage is the absence of clouding factors (e.g. is some other modification tripping up your modification?) and the disadvantage, of course, is that you are not testing in a wholly realistic situation. You will generally not detect a potential performance problem when testing in a Cronus database.

Sometimes even when your modification is targeted at a highly modified system where those other modifications will affect what you are doing, it's useful to test a version of your modification initially in Cronus. This can allow you to determine that your change has internal integrity before you move on to testing in the context of the fully modified copy of the production system.

If the target database for your modifications is an active customer database, then there is no substitute for doing complete and final testing in a copy of the production database. You should also be using a copy of the customer's license. This way you will be testing the compatibility of your work with the production setup, the full set of existing modifications, and of course, live data content and volumes. The only way to get a good feeling for possible performance issues is to test in a copy of the production database.

Testing in Production

While it is always a good idea to thoroughly test before adding your changes to the production system, sometimes, if you're very careful, you can safely do your testing inside the production environment. If the modifications consist of functions that do not change any data and can be tested without affecting any ongoing production activity, you might decide to test within the production system.

The examples of such eligible modifications can range from a simple inquiry form or a new analysis report or export of data that is to be processed outside the system to a completely new subsystem that does not change any existing data. There are also situations where the only changes to the existing system are the addition of fields to existing tables. In such a case, you may be able to test just a part of the modification outside production (we'll discuss that mode of testing a little later), and then implement the table changes to complete the rest of the testing in the context of the production system.

If your modification includes changes that would be visible to production users, such as adding an option to a button menu on a form, that falls within the category of a change that affects production. Generally speaking, you should not test that type of change in place in the production system. Sometimes you can start with a test instance of the form, assigned to an object number that only a developer can access, and test it from there. At other times, because objects are interrelated and refer to each other only by their object number, that approach can't be used. Then you may be forced to do your testing in a test copy of the database.

Testing within the production environment can be done in at least two ways. The first is simply to run the test object from the Object Designer screen. If the intended production process is to run a form, from which you can then access other objects, you can just highlight that form object entry and **Run** it. The other way is to add the new functionality to the Company Menu Level, but assign it to Test User; or you may require certain privileges to access the new entries. Even this Menu change should be considered as a change to the production system and tested offline before implementing it in the production environment. In other words, be very careful and very methodical about what you change and how you implement changes.

Using a Testing Database

From a testing point of view, the most realistic testing environment is a copy of actual production database. There are often very good excuses about why it is just too difficult to test using a copy of the actual production database.

  Don't give in to excuses – use a Testing Database!

Remember, when you implement your modifications, they are going to receive the "test of fire" in the environment of production. If you haven't done everything to assure success, you need to surely find out what you did not consider. Let us review some of the problems involved in testing with a copy of the production database and how to cope with them.

"It's too big"—is not a good argument relative to disk space. With USB disk drives available for less than $0.20 US per GB, you can easily afford to have plenty of spare disk space.

"It's too big"—is a better argument if you are doing file processing of some of the larger files (e.g. Item Ledger, Value Entry, etc.). But NAV's filtering capabilities are so strong that you should relatively easily be able to carve out manageable size test data groups with which to work.

"There's no data that's useful"—might be true. But it would be just as true for a test database, probably even more so, unless it were created expressly for this set of tests. By definition, whatever data is in a copy of the production database is what you will encounter when you eventually implement the enhancements on which you are working. If you build useful test data within the context of a copy of the production database, your tests will be much more realistic and therefore of better quality. In addition, the act of building workable test data will help to define what will be needed to set up the production system to utilize the new enhancements.

"Production data will get in the way"—may be true. If this is especially true, then perhaps the database must be preprocessed in some way to begin testing or testing must begin with some other database, Cronus or a special testing-only mockup. But, as stated earlier, the production database must be dealt with when you put the enhancements into production. Therefore, it makes good sense for you to test in that environment. The meeting and overcoming of challenges will prepare you for doing a better job at the critical time of going live with the newly modified objects.

"We need to test repeatedly from the same baseline" or "We must do regression testing"—both are good points, but don't have much to do with what type of database you're using for the testing. Both cases are addressed by properly managing the setup of your test data and keeping incremental backups of your pre-test and post-test data at every step of the way. Disk space is not a valid excuse for not making every possible useful intermediate stage backup. Staying organized and making lots of backups may be time consuming, but done well and done correctly, it is less expensive to restore from a backup than to recover from being disorganized or having to redo the job. Most of all, doing the testing job well is much less expensive than implementing a buggy modification.

Testing Techniques

Since you are an experienced developer, you are already familiar with good testing practice. Even so, it never hurts to be reminded about some of the more critical habits to maintain.

First, any modification greater than trivial should be tested on one form or another by at least two people. The people assigned should not be a part of the team who created the design or code of the modification. It would be best if one of the testers is a sharp user because users seem to have a knack (for obvious reasons) of relating how the modification acts compared to how the rest of the system operates relative to the realities of the day-to-day work.

One of the testing goals is to supply unexpected data and make sure that the modification can deal with it properly. Unfortunately, those who were involved in creating the design will have a very difficult time being creative in supplying the unexpected. Users often enter data the designer or programmer didn't expect. For that reason, testing by experienced users is good. Another goal this approach addresses is that of obtaining meaningful feedback on the user interface before stepping into production.

Second, after you cover the mainstream issues (whatever it is that the modification is intended to accomplish) you need to plan your testing to cover all boundary conditions. Boundary conditions are the data items that are exactly equal to the maximum or minimum or other range limit. More specifically, boundaries are the points at which input data values change from valid to invalid. Boundary condition checking in the code is where programmer logic often goes astray. Testing at these points is often very effective for uncovering data-related errors.

Deliverables

Create useful documentation and keep good records of the complete testing. Retain these records for future reference. Identify the purpose of the modifications from a business point of view. Add a brief, but complete, technical explanation of what must be done from a functional design and coding point of view to accomplish the business purpose. Record briefly the testing that was done. The scope of the record keeping should be directly proportional to the business value of the modification being made and the potential cost of not having good records. All such investments are a form of insurance and preventative medicine. You hope they won't be needed but you have to allow for the possibility they will be needed.

More complex modifications will be delivered and installed by experienced implementers, maybe even by the developers themselves. With NAV, small modifications may even be transmitted electronically to the customer site for installation by a skilled super-user. Any time this is done, all the proper and normal actions must occur, including those actions regarding backup before importing changes, user instruction (preferably written) on what to expect from the change, and written instruction on how to correctly apply the change. As a responsible developer, whenever you supply objects for installation by others, you must make sure that you always supply .fobs (compiled objects), not text objects. This is because the import process for text objects simply does not have the same safeguards as does the import process for compiled objects.

Get It Done

Bring projects to conclusion, don't let them drag on through inaction and inattention—open issues get forgotten and then don't get addressed. Get it done, wrap it up, and then review what went well and what didn't, both for remediation and for application to future projects. Set up ongoing support services as appropriate and move on to the next project.

Plan for Upgrading

The ability to upgrade a customized system is a very important feature of NAV. Most complex corporate systems are very difficult to customize at the database-structure and process-flow levels. NAV readily offers that capability. This is a significant differentiation between NAV and the competitive products in the market.

Beyond the ability to customize is the ability to upgrade a customized system. While not a trivial task, at least it is possible with NAV. For other such systems, the only reasonable path to an upgrade is often to discard the old version and re-implement with the new version, recreating all customizations.

You may say, "That's nice. But I'm a developer. Why do I care about upgrades?" There are at least two good reasons you should care about upgrades. First, because how you design and code your modifications can have a considerable impact on the amount of effort require to upgrade a system. Second, because as a skilled developer doing NAV customizations, you might well be asked to be involved in an upgrade project. Since the ability to upgrade is important and because you are likely to be involved one way or another, we will review a number of factors that relate to upgrades.

Benefits of Upgrading

Just so we are on common ground about why upgrading is important to both the client and the MBS Partner, the following is a brief list of some of the benefits available when a system is upgraded:

- Easier support of a more current version
- Access to new features and capabilities
- Continued access to fixes and regulatory updates
- Improvements in speed, security, reliability, and user interface
- Assured continuation of support availability
- Compatibility with necessary infrastructure changes
- Opportunity to do needed training, data cleaning, and process improvement
- Opportunity to resolve old problems, to do postponed "housekeeping", create a known system reference point

This list is representative, not complete. Obviously, not every possible benefit will be realized in any one situation.

Coding Considerations

The toughest part of an upgrade is porting code and data modifications from the older version of a system to the new version. Sometimes the challenges inherent in that processes cannot be avoided. When the new version has major design or data structure changes in an area that you have customized, it is quite likely that your modification structure will have to be re-designed and perhaps even be re-coded from scratch.

On the other hand, a large portion of the changes that appear in a new version of a product such as NAV are relatively modest in terms of their effect on existing code, at least on the base logic. That means, if done properly, it is not too difficult to port well designed code from the older version into the new version. By applying what some refer to as "low-impact coding" techniques, you can make the upgrade job easier and thereby less costly.

Good Documentation

In earlier chapters, we discussed some documentation practices that are good to follow when making C/AL modifications. The following is a brief list of few practices that should be used:

- Identify every project with its own unique project tag.
- Use the project tag in all documentation relating to the modification.
- Include a brief but complete description of the purpose of the modification in a related `Documentation()` trigger.
- Include a description of the related modifications to each object in the `Documentation()` trigger of that object, including changes to properties, Global and Local variables, functions, etc.
- Add the project tag to the version code of all modified objects.
- Bracket all C/AL code changes with in-line comments so that they can be easily identified.
- Retain all replaced code within comments, using // or { }.
- Identify all new table fields with the project tag.

Low-Impact Coding

We have already discussed most of these practices in other chapters. Nevertheless, it is useful to review them relative to our focus here on coding to make it easier to upgrade. You won't be able to follow each and every one of these, but will have to choose the degree to which you can implement low-impact code and which options to choose.

- As much as feasible, separate, and isolate new code.
- Create functions for significant amounts of new code, using single code line function calls.
- Either add independent Codeunits as repositories of modification functions or, if that is overkill, place the modification functions within the modified objects.
- If possible, add new data fields, don't change the usage of existing fields.
- When the functionality is new, add new tables rather than modifying existing tables.
- For minor changes, modify the existing forms, else copy and change the clone.
- Create and modify copies of reports, dataports and XMLports rather than modifying the original versions in place.
- Don't change field names in objects, just change captions and labels if necessary.

In any modification, you will have conflicting priorities regarding doing today's job in the easiest, least expensive way versus doing the best you can do to plan for the future. The right decision is never a black and white choice, but must be guided by subjective guidelines as to which choice is really in the customer's best interest.

The Upgrade Process

We won't dwell here on the actual process of doing an upgrade except to describe the process at the highest level and the executables-only option.

Upgrade Executables Only

The executables are the programs that run under the operating system. They are individually visible in a disk directory and include .exe and .dll files. Since the Navision Windows product was first shipped in 1995, the executables delivered with each new version of NAV (or Navision) have been backward compatible with the previous versions of the objects. In other words, you could run any version of the database and objects under any subsequent version of the server and client executables.

This backward compatibility allows the option of upgrading only the executables for a client. This is a relatively simple process, which provides access to enhanced compatibility with infrastructure software (e.g. Windows desktop and server software, etc.), provides access to added features relating to communications or interfacing, and often provides faster and more reliable processing. Upgrading the executables will also provide access to the C/AL features and user-accessible features that are part of the new version. Some folks use the term "Technical Upgrade" for the act of upgrading the executables.

The process of upgrading the executables just requires replacing all the files related to the executables on the server and clients, typically through doing a standard installation from the distribution CD. This will include the server software, the client software, the executables, and libraries for auxiliary tools such as the Application Server, N/ODBC, and C/FRONT. Then convert the database to be compatible with the new version (preferably through a backup and restore into a new, empty database).

[Remember, upgrading the executables is a one-way process.]

Once done, it cannot be undone. So, like any other change to the production system that affects the data, it should be thoroughly tested before implementing in production.

Full Upgrade

A full upgrade includes the aforesaid executables upgrade, but that is the simplest part of the process. The full upgrade process consists of a clearly defined multi-step project, which is best handled by developers who are specifically experienced in the upgrade process. It is critical to keep in mind that the customer's business may be at stake based on how well and how smoothly an upgrade is carried out.

The following list is a summary of the steps involved in a full upgrade of an NAV system:

- Identify all modifications, enhancements, and add-ons by comparing the full production set of objects against an unmodified set of the same version of the objects as distributed by Microsoft. This is always done by exporting the objects to be compared with text, then importing the resulting text files into a comparison tool. The comparison tools that are specifically designed to work with C/AL provide capabilities that general-purpose programmer editors don't have, though these can also be used. C/AL-oriented tools include the Developer's Toolkit from Microsoft or the Merge Tool found at www.mergetool.com.

- Plan the upgrade based on what customizations need to be ported, which ones should be discarded because they have been superseded or made obsolete, which ones will need to be re-developed, what special data conversions and new setups and user training will be required, and what upgraded add-ons must be obtained, and identify any license issues.

- Beginning with a current copy of the production database and a distribution of the new version, create a set of new version objects containing all the customizations, enhancements and add-ons (as previously planned) that were contained in the old version.

- Create modifications to the standard data conversion routines as necessary.

- Convert a full set of (backup) production data, then combine it with the upgraded objects to create a Testing Database.

- Work with experienced customer super-users to set up, then test the upgraded system, identify any flaws, and resolve them. In parallel, address any training requirements.

- Continue testing until the system is certified ready to use by both client and Partner test team members.

- Do a final production data conversion, using the final upgraded object set to create a new production database for go-live use.

A typical upgrade will take two or three weeks, a lightly customized system may take a couple of months, and a highly customized system will take more than that. If multiple sites are involved, then it will significantly add to the complexity of the upgrade process, particularly those parts of the process where users are directly involved.

Tips for Small Successes

The following are some tips for success:

Cache Settings for Development

Go to the **Tools** menu and click on the **Options** menu button. Select **Option**, and you will get the from in the following screenshot:

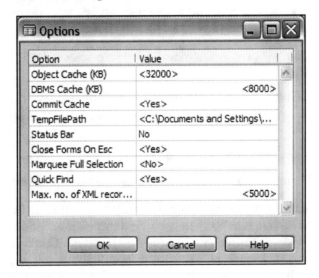

You can learn more about these **Option** fields through **Help**, but at least one or two of them are important to utilize. The first entry (**Object Cache (KB)**) controls the amount of memory on the client system that is allocated to hold objects in cache memory. A good figure to set is **40000**. This will allocate 40 MB to the **Object Cache** and provide you with quicker responsiveness during your development testing.

In the special case of an environment where multiple developers are working within the same database, a useful technique is to set the parameter to zero. That way, every time an object is read, it is read directly from the database rather than from the cache. This ensures that each time a developer reads an object, they are getting the latest version.

The second entry (**DBMS Cache (KB)**) only appears on the **Options** screen if:

- The database in use is the NAV C/SIDE database.
- The database connection is local (i.e. single user).

If both are true, then you should set this value to something in the range of 400000 to 800000 (400 MB to 800 MB) to maximize the speed of data processing. The largest figure that can be used is currently 1000000 (1 GB). You will notice the effect of this setting when you are processing large data volumes in a test. Some operating system configurations will cause NAV to crash with a DBMS Cache set above 800 MB.

Two Monitors

Often when you are doing development work, you will be accessing two sets of information in a back-and-forth fashion. The two sets of information could be any of the following:

- A set of code plus a reference manual or **Help** screen or documentation document
- A set of code plus a Word document where you are creating documentation
- Two or more sets of data being examined either in forms or by Running the tables
- Source or reference code plus a set of code in which you are actively working
- Two sets of code (e.g. old version and new version) that you are comparing

Undoubtedly you can think of many more examples. One way to be much more efficient and effective at such tasks is to use two independent monitors both connected to your system, sitting side by side on your desk. Since you won't have to flip back-and-forth between screens, this setup will allow you to work faster and more accurately. Such a setup will only cost $250 to $500 US (or even less). You can expect to get a good return on that investment within a few weeks in terms of increased productivity.

Simple System Administration

Some basic information and simple system administration can be accessed from **File | Database | Information** option. This will lead you to the form in the following screenshot:

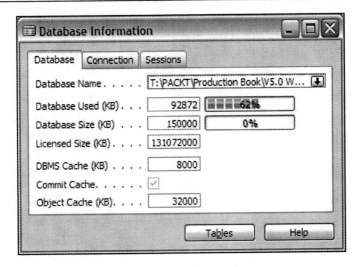

The **Database** tab obviously provides information about the status of the database. The **Connection** tab (next screenshot) shows you what you are connected to. In this instance, the connection is to a **Local** test database. If, in development or training, you are switching back-and-forth between **Local** and **Server** instances of a database, it is very important to check the tab in the following screenshot to confirm which database is active. The tab only shows for a C/SIDE database, not for a SQL Server database.

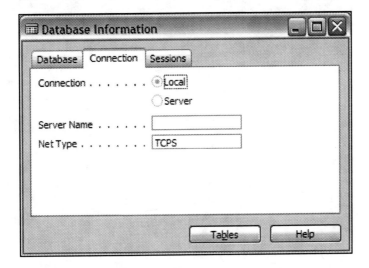

Finally, the **Sessions** tab (next) shows you how many user sessions are connected and how many are available in the currently active system license. A system administrator might use the tab in the following screenshot to drill down on the **Current Sessions** entry where they could see the user names of all the active logins.

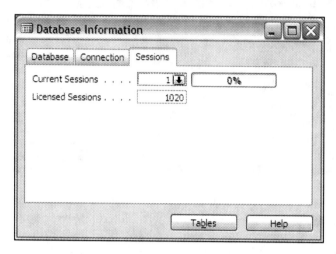

At the bottom of this form is the **Tables** button. Clicking on **Tables** will take you to the from shown in the following screenshot:

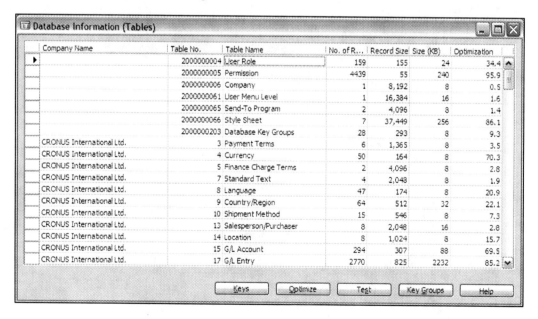

This is the C/SIDE database version; in the SQL Server version the **Keys** button at the bottom and the **Optimization** column at the right is missing. What you can get from this form is information about the relative size of various tables, in terms of physical size, number of records, and key information relative to the base data. You can also invoke the **Optimize** function from this form, which will clean zero-value records out of the SIFT data, freeing up the space and making processing more efficient. You can also use the **Test** function to check any or all of the tables for errors in structure. See the **Help** function for more information.

Careful Naming

Most programming languages have Reserved Words. These are the words or phrases that are reserved for use by the system, generally because they are used by the compiler to reference predefined functions or system-maintained values. C/AL is no exception to this general rule. But, no list of C/AL Reserved Words has been published.

If you choose a variable name which is the same as a C/AL Reserved Word, the compiler will generally recognize that fact. If, under some circumstance it does not, then it will provide unintended results. Such a possibility is slim, but it is relatively easy to avoid by prefacing all variable names with a two or three character string that will clearly identify the variable as part of your modification. You must be careful with this technique when naming variables to be used in conjunction with Automation Controllers. C/SIDE creates some of its own Automation Controller related variables by combining your variable names with suffixes. The combined names are then truncated to 30 characters, the maximum limit allowed for a C/SIDE variable name. If the names you have created are too long, this suffixing plus truncating process may result in some duplicate names.

Confusion can also result in the case of global and local variables with the same name or working storage and table variables of the same name. Two actions can minimize the possibility. First, minimize the instances where two variables have the same name. Second, whenever there is a possibility of name confusion, variable names should be fully qualified with the table name or the object name.

Tools

There are several special use tools available from Microsoft. You should review them to know what they do and when to use them.

Code Coverage

The Code Coverage tool provides lists in both summary and detail format showing what code has been executed. Code Coverage is accessed from **Tools | Debugger | Code Coverage**. The next screenshots shows a summary example first, followed by a detail example:

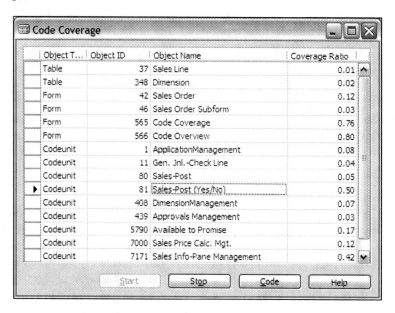

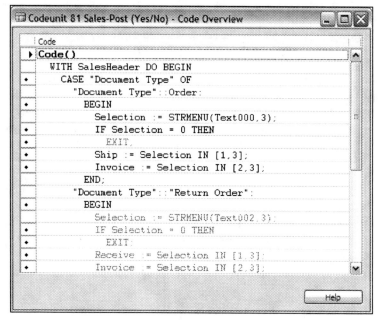

You could think of Code Coverage as the instant replay version of the Debugger, because you get to see where your program has been after the fact rather than stepping through it in the midst of processing. It is very useful to use the two tools together. Use Code Coverage to see all the code that is processed. Determine what you want to examine in detail by looking at the variables in process and set the Debugger break points. Then use the Debugger for a dynamic look at the execution.

Client Monitor

Client Monitor is a performance analysis tool. It can be very effectively used in combination with Code Coverage to identify what is happening, in what sequence, specifically how it is happening and how long it is taking. Before you start Client Monitor, there are several settings you can adjust to control its behavior, some specific to the SQL Server environment.

Client Monitor is accessed from **Tools | Client Monitor.** The **Client Monitor** output looks similar to the following screenshot:

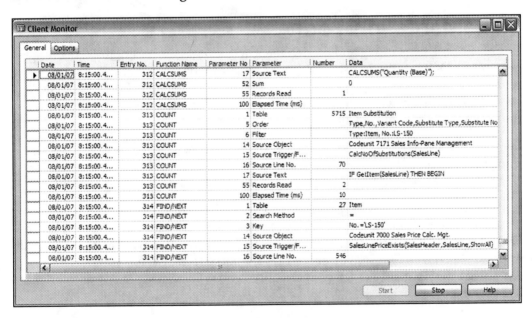

In both the database environments, **Client Monitor** helps you to identify the code that is taking the major share of the processing time so that you can focus on your code design optimization efforts. In the SQL Server environment, Client Monitor will help you to see what calls are being made by SQL Server and will clearly identify problems with improperly defined or chosen indexes and filters.

If you have knowledge about SQL Server calls, the Client Monitor output will be even more meaningful to you. In fact, you may decide to combine these tools with the SQL Server Error Log for an even more in-depth analysis of either speed or locking problems. Look at the **Performance Troubleshooting Guide** from Microsoft for additional information and guidance. This manual also contains instructions on how to use Excel pivot tables for analyzing the output from Client Monitor.

Creating Help for Modifications

There's no tutorial available, just the reference. The official documentation for creating new online **Help** files for modifications suggests the use of the **RoboHelp** product. There is a manual titled "**Online Help Guide for Microsoft Business Solutions**". Another alternative is available as freeware on the download section at www.mibuso.com or at www.mergetool.com. This solution, part of *Per Mogensen's Mergetool*, does not require the use of a commercial product to create or compile NAV **Help** files.

Implementation Tool

One of the time-consuming and moderately complex tasks, a part of implementing a new system, is the gathering and loading of data into the system. Generally master tables such as Customers, Vendors, and Items must be loaded before you can even begin serious system testing and training. Mostly, this data is loaded for testing and training and at final cutover for the production use.

In order to assist in this process, Microsoft provides a set of tools called the Rapid Implementation Methodology (RIM). The documentation for RIM is in the manual "**Dynamics NAV Rapid Implementation Methodology Toolkit Users Guide**".

Basically RIM consists of a set of questionnaires, some industry-specific data templates, and the associated Import and Export routines. The recommended process has initial data entry occurring in Excel spreadsheets, then exported to XML files and imported into NAV for use. You should review these tools. Even if you find the tools aren't the right answer for your situation, you will learn some useful techniques by studying them.

Other Reference Material

With every NAV system distribution there is an included set of reference guides. These are highly recommended. There are also a number of other guides available, but sometimes you have to search for them. Most of them are readily available to Partner development personnel, though that may be more by force of habit than as a policy.

In nearly every case you will find these documents a very good starting place, but you will be required to go beyond what is documented, experimenting, and figuring out what is useful for you. If you are working with a single system, you are likely to narrow in on a few things. If you are working with different systems from time to time, then you may find yourself working with one aspect of one tool this month and something entirely different next month.

Here is a list of some documentation you will be interested in (when you look for those with "Navision", they might have been changed to "Dynamics NAV"). A number of filenames are included, especially when they are not easy to interpret. For example, names starting with `w1` are from Worldwide product distribution.

- Application Designer's Guide (the C/AL "bible") — part of the system distribution — `w1w1adg.pdf`

- Terminology Handbook — part of the system distribution — `w1w1term.pdf`

- Installation & System Management of Application Server for Microsoft Dynamics™ NAV — part of the system distribution — `w1w1atas.pdf`

- Installation & System Management of C/SIDE Database Server for Microsoft Dynamics™ NAV — part of the system distribution — `w1w1ism.pdf`

- Installation & System Management of SQL Server Option for the C/SIDE Client — part of the system distribution — `w1w1sql.pdf`

- Microsoft Dynamics™ NAV ODBC Driver 5.0 Guide — part of the system distribution — `w1w1nocbc.pdf`

- Making Database Backups in Microsoft Dynamics™ NAV — part of system distribution — `w1w1bkup.pdf`

- C/FRONT Reference Guide — part of the system distribution — `w1w1cfront.pdf`

- Navision Developer's Toolkit

- NAV Tools CD

  ◦ Microsoft Business Solutions — Navision SQL Server Option Resource Kit — whitepaper

  ◦ Performance Troubleshooting Guide for Microsoft Business Solutions — Navision — `w1w1perftguide.pdf`

  ◦ Security Hardening Guide 5.00

  ◦ Application Benchmark Toolkit

  ◦ User Rights Setup

  ◦ Online **Help** Guide for Microsoft Business Solutions — Navision — `NOHG.pdf`

- Dynamics NAV Rapid Implementation Methodology Users Guide 2.0
- Microsoft Dynamics™ NAV Training Manuals and Videos (various topics)
- Many whitepapers on specific NAV (Navision) application and technical topics (even the old ones are useful)

There are other documentations possibilities that you will find valuable as you move into specialized or advanced areas. But many of the preceding will be quite broadly and frequently helpful.

Last, but definitely not least, become a regular visitor to websites for more information and advice on C/AL, NAV, and many more related and unrelated topics. The following websites are especially comprehensive and well attended. Other, smaller or more specialized sites exist as well.

`dynamicsuser.net`

`www.mibuso.com`

Summary

We have covered a lot of topics with the goal of helping you to become productive in C/AL development much quicker than if you had not read this book. Your concluding assignments are to continue learning, to enjoy NAV, C/SIDE, and C/AL and to do your best in all things.

> *Imagine all the people living life in peace. You may say I'm a dreamer, but I'm not the only one. I hope someday you'll join us, and the world will be as one.*
> *— John Lennon*

Index

testing 354-356
Where Used 352
development tips
cache settings for development 441, 442
careful naming 445
simple system administration 442-445
two monitors 442
development tools
Client Monitor 447
Code Coverage 446, 447
help files, creating 448
implementation tool 448
reference material 448, 449
dialog form 139
dialog fucntion debugging
about 364
CONFIRM statements 364
DIALOG fucntion 364
ERROR fucntion 365
MESSAGE statements 364
text output 365
documentation
about 41
Documentation trigger 294
internal documentation 294
document reports 177

E

ERROR function 266
external interfaces
Dataports 394
interface tools 419
MenuSuites 385
XMLports 406

F

FieldClass
filter type 116
Flowfield 114
Flowfield type 115
Flowfilter 117, 118
normal 114
field numbering
about 94
data type, changing 96, 97
renumbering 95, 96

field properties
about 87
accessing 88
data type properties 88
Option data type 92, 93
related to numeric content 90
text field properties 89
fields
about 16, 87
data structures 99
numbering 94-98
properties 87-93
triggers 98
field triggers 98
filtering
about 12, 118
CLEARMARKS function 318
COPYFILTER function 317
COPYFILTERS function 317
experimenting with 123-131
filter syntax, defining 119, 123
filter values, defining 119, 123
functions 315
GETFILTER function 317
MARKEDONLY function 318
MARK function 318
RESET function 318
SETFILTER function 316
SETRANGE function 316
FIND-NEXT function 272
Flow control
BREAK function 311
CASE - ELSE statement 307
EXIT function 311
QUIT function 310
REPEAT - UNTIL control structure 306
SHOWOUTPUT function 311
SKIP function 311
WHILE - DO control structure 307
WITH - DO statement 309
FlowField functions
CALCFIELDS 305
CALCSUMS 305
form
about 133
bound 134
components 141

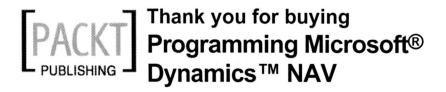

Thank you for buying
Programming Microsoft®
Dynamics™ NAV

About Packt Publishing

Packt, pronounced 'packed', published its first book "*Mastering phpMyAdmin for Effective MySQL Management*" in April 2004 and subsequently continued to specialize in publishing highly focused books on specific technologies and solutions.

Our books and publications share the experiences of your fellow IT professionals in adapting and customizing today's systems, applications, and frameworks. Our solution based books give you the knowledge and power to customize the software and technologies you're using to get the job done. Packt books are more specific and less general than the IT books you have seen in the past. Our unique business model allows us to bring you more focused information, giving you more of what you need to know, and less of what you don't.

Packt is a modern, yet unique publishing company, which focuses on producing quality, cutting-edge books for communities of developers, administrators, and newbies alike. For more information, please visit our website: www.packtpub.com.

Writing for Packt

We welcome all inquiries from people who are interested in authoring. Book proposals should be sent to authors@packtpub.com. If your book idea is still at an early stage and you would like to discuss it first before writing a formal book proposal, contact us; one of our commissioning editors will get in touch with you.

We're not just looking for published authors; if you have strong technical skills but no writing experience, our experienced editors can help you develop a writing career, or simply get some additional reward for your expertise.

Business Process Execution Language for Web Services 2nd Edition

ISBN: 1-904811-81-7   Paperback: 350 pages

An Architects and Developers Guide to BPEL and BPEL4WS

1. Architecture, syntax, development and composition of Business Processes and Services using BPEL

2. Advanced BPEL features such as compensation, concurrency, links, scopes, events, dynamic partner links, and correlations

3. Oracle BPEL Process Manager and BPEL Designer Microsoft BizTalk Server as a BPEL server

BPEL Cookbook

ISBN: 1-904811-33-7   Paperback: 188 pages

Ten practical real-world case studies combining business process management and web services orchestration

1. Real-world BPEL recipes for SOA integration and Composite Application development

2. Combining business process management and web services orchestration

3. Techniques and best practices with downloadable code samples from ten real-world case studies

Please visit **www.PacktPub.com** for information on our titles

Printed in the United States
95171LV00001B/201/A